PREPARATORY COURSE FOR THE
ASWB BACHELORS LEVEL EXAM

Interventions with Clients / Client Systems

**Association for Advanced Training
in the Behavioral Sciences**
212 W. Ironwood Drive, Suite D #168 Coeur d'Alene, ID 83814
(800) 472-1931

© Association for Advanced Training in the Behavioral Sciences. All rights reserved. No part of these materials may be reproduced in any form, or by any means, mechanical or electronic, including photocopying, without the written permission of the publisher. To reproduce or adapt, in whole or in part, any portion of these materials is not only a violation of copyright law, but is unethical and unprofessional. As a condition of your acceptance of these materials, you agree not to reproduce or adapt them in any manner or license others to do so. The unauthorized resale of these materials is prohibited. The Association for Advanced Training in the Behavioral Sciences accepts the responsibility of protecting not only its own interests, but to protect the interests of its authors and to maintain and vigorously enforce all copyrights on its material. Your cooperation in complying with the copyright law is appreciated.

BACHELORS LEVEL

INTERVENTIONS WITH CLIENTS/CLIENT SYSTEMS

Table of Contents

Intervention Processes and Techniques for Use Across Systems 1

I. Overview of Interventions for Use Across Systems 1
    A. The Intervention Process 1
    B. Guidelines for Successful Intervention 3
    C. Interdisciplinary Teaming and Collaboration 5

II. Intake and Engagement 6
    A. Intake Procedures at Social Agencies 6
    B. The First Telephone Contact With a Client 7
    C. The First Face-to-Face Meeting With a Client 7
    D. Engaging Clients 10

III. Intervention Planning, Goal Setting, and Contracting 17
    A. Intervention Planning Steps 17
    B. Tailoring the Treatment Plan 17
    C. Establishing Goals and Objectives 18
    D. Selecting Intervention Strategies 20
    E. Choosing the Therapeutic Configuration (Modality) 24
    F. The Frequency and Duration of Treatment 28
    G. Formulating the Treatment/Service Contract 29
    H. Treatment Planning for Inpatients 31

IV. Verbal and Nonverbal Communication Techniques 32
    A. Guidelines for Effective Communication With Clients 32
    B. Gauging the Effectiveness of Your Communications 33
    C. Verbal Communication Skills (Verbal Messages) 33
    D. Nonverbal Communication 42
    E. Communication With Culturally Diverse Clients 43
    F. Telephone and Written Communications 44

V. Intervention Techniques 46
    A. Information Giving and Advice Giving 46
    B. Encouragement, Reassurance, and Universalization 48
    C. Reframing 49

D. Reflective Discussion 49
　　E. Confrontation 51
　　F. Cognitive Restructuring Techniques 52
　　G. Behavioral Techniques 53
　　H. Role-Playing, Empty Chair, Role-Reversal, Psychodrama, and Sculpting 54
　　I. Homework Assignments 55

VI. Referral, Case Management, and Case Advocacy 57
　　A. Resource Systems 57
　　B. Social Networks 59
　　C. Referral and the Referral Process 60
　　D. Case Management 65
　　E. Case Advocacy 71

VII. Monitoring the Change Process and Maintaining Progress 74
　　A. Monitoring the Change Process 74
　　B. Maintaining Progress Throughout the Change Process 75

VIII. Practice Evaluation 79
　　A. Evaluation Activities 79
　　B. Techniques for Measuring Client Change 80

IX. Termination 86
　　A. Making the Decision to Terminate 86
　　B. Unplanned Terminations 87
　　C. Facilitating Terminations and Transfers 89
　　D. Identifying and Addressing Clients' Reactions to Termination 90

X. Crisis and Change 93
　　A. Stress and Coping 93
　　B. Crisis 94
　　C. Suicide 105
　　D. Danger to Others 109
　　E. Trauma 113
　　F. Children Exposed to Disaster 115
　　G. Out-of-Home Displacement 116
　　H. Rape 116
　　I. Grief 118
　　J. Caregiving: Middle-Aged Adults and Aging Parents **122**

XI. Practice Perspectives, Theories, and Models **125**
　　A. Traditional Social Casework Models 125
　　B. Generalist Perspective 132
　　C. General Systems Perspective 133
　　D. Ecosystems Perspective and Life Model Approach 133
　　E. The Task-Centered Model 135

F. Brief Therapy Model 137
G. Problem-Solving and Decision Theory 137
H. Psychodynamic Theories and Models 138
I. Humanistic Theories and Models 142
J. Postmodern Approaches 149
K. Behavioral Therapies 152
L. Cognitive-Behavioral Therapies 158
M. Motivational Interviewing 161
N. Dialectical Behavior Therapy 163
O. Play Therapy 164
P. Evidence-Based Practice 166

XII. Family Therapy Models 167
A. Communication/Interaction Model 167
B. Extended Family Systems Therapy 168
C. Structural Family Therapy 170
D. Strategic Family Therapy 171
E. Milan Systemic Family Therapy 172
F. Behavioral Family Therapy 173

XIII. Group Psychotherapy and Counseling 175
A. Types and Purposes of Work With Small Groups 175
B. Forming a Group 176
C. Programming – Selecting and Arranging Group Activities 178
D. The Stages of Group Development 179
E. Intervening in Social Work Groups 182

XIV. Intervention With Diverse Populations 190
A. Culturally Diverse Clients 190
B. Older Adults 196
C. Clients Who Are Gay 201
D. Clients Who are Physically Disabled 203
E. Adult Female Clients 206
F. Adolescent Clients 209
G. Clients of Lower Socioeconomic Status 211
H. Immigrant and Refugee Groups 212

XV. Intervention for Specific Problems and Disorders 213
A. Decision-Making Difficulties 213
B. Mediation and Interpersonal Conflict 213
C. Difficulties Understanding or Expressing Feelings 214
D. Stress Management 216
E. Anger Management 217
F. Powerlessness and the Empowerment Approach 220

  G. Child Abuse and Neglect 221
  H. Spousal/Partner Abuse 224
  I. Social Skills Training for Children and Adolescents 228
  J. Parenting and Parent-Training Programs 230
  K. Budgeting and Personal Debt 232
  L. Clients Who Are HIV Positive 233
  M. Working With People Near Death 236
  N. Substance Use Disorders 237
  O. Treatment for Various DSM-5 Disorders 247

XVI. Case Recording and Managed Care, and E-Therapy **257**
  A. Case Recording 257
  B. Managed Care and Service Provision 260
  C. Online Therapy (E-, Internet, Cyber Therapy, Internet Counseling) 263

XVII. Child Welfare Work, School Social Work, and Health Social Work **266**
  A. Child Welfare Work 266
  B. School Social Work 271
  C. Health Social Work: Interventions in Health Care Settings 278

Intervention Processes and Techniques for Use with Larger Client Systems **284**

Introduction to Macro Level Intervention **284**

XVIII. Policy Practice **289**

XIX. Planning, Implementing, and Evaluating Macro Change **292**
  A. Build Support and Plan the Intervention 292
  B. Implement, Monitor, and Evaluate the Intervention 300

XX. Organizations and Organizational Theory **302**
  A. Organizational (Agency) Structure 303
  B. Management Theories 305
  C. Organizational Behavior and Decision-Making 309

XXI. Administration in Social Work **311**
  A. Social Agencies 311
  B. Overview of Administration in Social Agencies 312
  C. Management of Policies and Programs 314
  D. Create and Maintain the Agency's Formal Structure 315
  E. Resource Development and Budgeting 316
  F. Program Evaluation 318
  G. Staff Development 322
  H. Interorganizational Relations 323
  I. Public Relations 326
  J. Management 327

XXII. Community Practice Models and Activities **332**

A. Community Organization 332
   B. Community Development 335
   C. Macro-Level Advocacy 337
   D. Community Mental Health Intervention 338

Appendix: Research Design and Statistics 340
   A. "Research" and "Statistics" Defined 340
   B. Variables 340
   C. Samples and Sampling 342
   D. Control Groups 343
   E. Research Strategies: Descriptive vs. Experimental Research 343
   F. Methods of Control in Experimental Research 345
   G. Internal and External Validity 347
   H. Experimental Research Designs 349
   I. Scales of Measurement 352
   J. Descriptive Statistics 353
   K. Introduction to Inferential Statistics 356
   L. Inferential Statistical Tests 360
   M. Correlational Techniques 362

BACHELORS LEVEL

INTERVENTIONS WITH CLIENTS/CLIENT SYSTEMS

NOTE: The use of pronouns is extensive in our study material. To avoid cumbersome phrasing and simplify your reading, we use primarily masculine pronouns in some chapters and primarily feminine pronouns in others.

This chapter has two major divisions. The first major division, comprised of Sections I through XVII covers topics related to Intervention Processes and Techniques for Use Across Systems; the second major division, comprised of Sections XVIII through XXII, covers topics related to Intervention Processes and Techniques for Use with Larger Systems.

Intervention Processes and Techniques for Use Across Systems

I. Overview of Interventions for Use Across Systems

Intervention processes and techniques for use across systems refers to social work activities involving frequent face-to-face interaction with clients. Examples of direct service activities include individual, couples, and family counseling and psychotherapy, group therapy and other social work with small groups, referral work, case management, and case advocacy. All of these activities are reviewed in this chapter.

Psychotherapy is defined as "a specialized, formal interaction between a social worker ... and a client (individual, couple, family, or group) in which a therapeutic relationship is established to help resolve the symptoms of a mental disorder, psychosocial stress, relationship problems, and difficulties in coping in the social environment" (Barker, 2003, p. 349). Counseling is a less formal procedure in which a social worker guides an individual, couple, family, group, or community by, for example, giving advice, helping to articulate goals, defining alternatives, and providing needed information (Barker, 2003).

A. The Intervention Process

The term "planned change process" refers to a deliberate series of actions directed toward improving a client's social functioning or well-being. The term "intervention" means essentially the same thing – i.e., an intervention is a planned effort designed to bring about a specific change in a condition, behavioral pattern, or set of circumstances affecting a client's social functioning. Some authors refer to the planned change process as the "helping process." In these materials, we use the terms "planned change process," "change process," and "helping process" interchangeably, and they all refer to the same thing.

1. Systems Involved in the Planned Change Process: Four systems are critical to a successful planned change process: the change agent system, client system, target system, and action system.

- The *change agent system* is you (i.e., the social worker) and, if you work at an agency, your agency.

- The *client system* is the person (or group) who has requested your/your agency's services and expects to benefit from what you do. Planned change usually begins when you/your agency (a change agent system) and a client system come together and contract to address a client concern.

- The *target system* is the person, group, or organization that needs to change and is targeted for change so that the client will benefit from the intervention. In practice, the client system and the target system are often the same.

- The *action system* is all of the people, groups, and organizations that you (i.e., the change agent system) work with or through in order to influence the target system and help the client system achieve the desired outcome.

2. The Phases of Intervention: The intervention process consists of several phases that build on each other. These phases occur in a specific sequence, but, during intervention, you may return to an earlier phase if necessary (e.g., to reformulate the problem, to select new tasks).

Phase 1 – Intake and engagement: Begin the relationship, identify and define the client's concern or problem, and determine the client's eligibility for service.

Phase 2 – Data collection and assessment: Gather information and "study" the problem or situation and decide what needs to change, what can be changed, and how it can be changed. (Data collection and assessment are reviewed in the Assessment chapter.)

Phase 3 – Planning and contracting: With the client, formulate goals and objectives, evaluate possible strategies, agree on a treatment plan, and determine who will do what and when it will be done.

Phase 4 – Intervention and monitoring: Carry out the plan, monitor progress, and modify the plan if it is not achieving the desired results. This phase is sometimes called the "action phase" because it is when you, the client, and others take the steps and complete the tasks defined in the treatment plan. Another name for this phase is the "change-oriented phase."

Phase 5 – Final evaluation and termination: Evaluate the client's overall progress, bring the helping relationship to an end, and, if relevant, provide feedback to your agency about how its services and programs might be improved. (Note that "monitoring" occurs *during* an intervention, while "evaluation" takes place at the end of a change process when you look back to assess what took place.)

B. Guidelines for Successful Intervention

1. General Guidelines: The following guidelines are important for facilitating successful intervention:

- Keep in mind that a positive helping relationship is the foundation of an effective change process.

- Always remember that your role is to enhance the clients current level of functioning and facilitate problem-solving by the client.

- Allow the client to participate as much as possible in all professional decisions that affect his life.

- Be aware that even dysfunctional behavior serves a purpose for the client by meeting a need, mitigating a conflict, or relieving some other problem.

- Because change usually brings on intense feelings, remember to reach for and explore the client's feelings.

- Have a tentative plan for each contact with the client. The word "tentative" is used because your plan must be flexible so that you can respond to unexpected client needs or concerns.

- Do your best to make good decisions concerning the client (see also below).

- Never defend an unfair or unreasonable procedure or policy. Instead, acknowledge to the client that the procedure or policy needs to be changed, but that it can't be changed immediately and, therefore, has to be followed.

- Be aware of and recognize your limitations. Be sure to seek consultation when faced with a situation you don't know how to handle. Refer a client to another professional when he has needs that are beyond your scope of competence (or your agency's program).

- Engage in regular self-assessment of your professional strengths and weaknesses so that you can draw on your skills and correct your deficiencies and identify when you need to seek supervision or consultation.

2. Decision-Making Guidelines: As noted above, effective helping requires you to make good decisions concerning your clients. The following guidelines are useful for maximizing the quality of your decisions (Hepworth et al., 2006; Sheafor & Horejsi, 2003):

- Consider all available options before making a decision. Avoid approaching a decision as if there were only two alternatives (e.g., yes or no).

- To the extent possible, base your decisions on solid evidence (e.g., unbiased observations, relevant and reliable facts, logical arguments). Never rely on opinions or hearsay (unconfirmed information). When weighing information from other people (including your client), consider whether these people may have reasons to persuade you to choose one decision or reject another. Never base a decision solely on what's been done in the past, on tradition, or on precedent. Never make a decision as a way of justifying a past decision or action.

- Avoid tendencies that can result in poor decisions. For example, don't give excessive weight to information that supports a decision you've already committed to, that you heard first or most recently, or that you find interesting, easiest to understand, or easier to obtain. Similarly, don't devalue information that supports decisions you've already rejected, that would be difficult to obtain, or that conflicts with your personal values, beliefs, feelings, or preconceived ideas. Also avoid the effects of groupthink – in other words, don't either accept or reject an alternative simply because of how others in your group, agency, or profession think about the issue.

- Don't allow time constraints to pressure you into making a premature decision. If you can, you should delay a decision when the available alternatives are still unclear or uncertain or when you lack sufficient information. If delaying a decision is impossible, then choose the most cautious alternative. "Erring on the side of caution" usually helps to minimize the negative effects of a wrong decision.

- Never allow your own needs to influence your decision-making concerning a client. Meet your own emotional needs and handle your own problems outside your professional relationships. Never allow your own convenience or that of another professional or agency to override the needs and rights of your client.

3. Guidelines for Workload Management: At agencies administrators and supervisors have the authority to assign tasks to workers, and workers may be given additional tasks even when they already have a full workload. Depending on the agency, workers may be required to accept all assigned tasks or they may have discretion to either accept or refuse additional tasks. Workers given this latitude can better manage their workload by screening work assignments before they accept them. Workload and stress management is important for avoiding "burnout," a term used to describe workers who feel apathy or anger as a result of on-the-job stress and frustration. Burnout is typical among workers who have more responsibility than control, and a common source of burnout is heavy caseloads. Burnout is associated with physical, emotional, and behavioral symptoms, most of which have negative effects on not only the worker but also her clients. (The topics of delegating tasks to workers and burnout are reviewed in more depth in Section IV of Professional Relationships, Values, and Ethics.)

Important questions to consider when deciding whether to accept a task include the following (Sheafor & Horejsi, 2003): Is the request for your time reasonable given your current workload? Does the assignment make sense given your job description? Are you responsible for the task or is someone else? Is the task a matter of high priority? Will you feel angry, resentful, or overburdened if you accept the task? If the task seems unreasonable, are you tempted to accept it anyway to avoid a conflict or be seen by others as uniquely helpful?

If you are uncertain as to whether the request is reasonable, get more information about it before deciding what to do. If you are still unsure after getting this information, ask for some time to consider the request and set a deadline for making and reporting your decision (for example, tell your supervisor that you'll get back to her in 20 minutes). If you refuse the task, do so firmly and professionally. You may explain your reasons in a straightforward way but should avoid apologizing or making excuses.

C. Interdisciplinary Teaming and Collaboration

1. Interdisciplinary Teaming: Interdisciplinary teaming is a form of intervention in which the members of different professions or disciplines (e.g., social work, medical, psychiatric) work together on behalf of a client. Other labels used to describe interdisciplinary teams include "interprofessional teams" and "multidisciplinary teams." Teams are central to direct social work practice in many settings, including hospitals, mental health clinics, schools, and child welfare agencies.

The term "interdisciplinary team" implies the following (Abramson, 2002):

- There is a group of professionals from different disciplines.
- The professionals have a common purpose.
- The professionals integrate their various professional perspectives in decision-making.
- The professionals coordinate their work.
- The professionals interact and communicate frequently.
- There is a division of roles based on expertise.

For team practice to be effective, team members from different professions must be able to reach an agreement regarding approaches to care. Team members must be willing to move beyond their own expertise to address the needs of the "whole" client. Social workers bring several unique skills and perspectives to interdisciplinary teams including the following: a group work knowledge base; communication skills (such as active listening and reaching for feelings); a respect for differences in values, knowledge, and problem-solving approaches; and, perhaps most important, attention to psychosocial issues during all phases of intervention.

2. Collaboration: While teaming is a collaborative approach to service delivery, some forms of collaboration in social work don't involve a team approach. Collaboration occurs whenever you work with one or more other professionals to serve a client. In some cases of collaboration, you and the other professionals work together as part of a single helping team. In other cases of collaboration, however, you and the other professionals work relatively independently of one another while making sure to communicate and coordinate your respective efforts in order to prevent a duplication of services (Barker, 2003).

II. Intake and Engagement

A. Intake Procedures at Social Agencies

Intake procedures are used by social agencies to make initial contacts with clients productive and helpful (Barker, 2003). During intake, a social worker's primary goal is to obtain preliminary information from a client in order to determine whether she can work with him or should refer him to a more suitable agency or professional.

1. Basic Intake Procedures: Basic intake procedures include the following:

- informing the client about the services offered by the agency;
- providing the client with information about the conditions of service (fees, appointment times, etc.);
- collecting relevant demographic data from the client;
- interviewing the client to get a preliminary sense of the nature of his problem, concern, or request;
- determining the client's eligibility for service;
- reaching an agreement with the client about his willingness to be served by the agency; and
- assigning the client to the social worker(s) best suited to providing the services he needs.

The term **fact-gathering interview** has been used to describe the initial interview conducted with a prospective client when he contacts an agency. A fact-gathering interview involves collecting predetermined, specific data from a client and is largely nontherapeutic: The social worker asks the client specific questions and records his answers on a **face-sheet** or other form. The fact-gathering interview doesn't offer the client an opportunity to ventilate his feelings or work through his problem.

If a client is in crisis, a social worker should postpone the intake dialogue and focus initially on providing immediate assistance designed to relieve the client's distress and protect him from harming himself or others.

2. Intake (Screening) Decisions: During intake, a social worker needs to quickly determine if there is a match between her agency's eligibility criteria requirements and the client's problem, concern, or request. If no, then she must refer the client to another agency or professional that is better suited to address his problem, concern, or request. If yes, then she must decide whether she can provide the services or should transfer the client to another worker at her agency. Factors that influence this decision include the division of labor at the agency and the social worker's own competence to address the client's needs.

B. The First Telephone Contact With a Client

If your first contact with a prospective client is by telephone, you will usually use the phone call to obtain a basic understanding of what he expects from you or your agency and reduce any fears he expresses about seeking help. Avoid sharing too much information over the phone because you lack access to the caller's nonverbal behavior. If it is appropriate for you to meet with the caller, schedule a face-to-face meeting. The specific guidelines described below are also important during this phone call (Sheafor & Horejsi, 2003).

1. Phone Call With a Voluntary Client: With a voluntary client, briefly explore the presenting concern or request so that you can determine whether it will be appropriate for the caller to come to your office or agency for help. (If not, you should attempt to provide the caller with relevant referrals.) Detailed information about the caller's concern or request should not be collected over the phone. If the caller is misinformed or uncertain about what you or your agency can do for him, provide only basic information about your practice or agency and relevant procedures and services at this time.

If the caller lives with family members or others with whom he has close relationships, ask him if these people know about his request for help. If secrecy is not required to protect the caller from physical harm, encourage him to think about involving significant others in the intervention process. For instance, explain that the assessment will be more accurate if you are able to speak with family members who are also affected by the problem. However, if the caller insists on attending the first meeting alone, you should agree to see the caller by himself. You can try again later to involve significant others in the process, if you determine that doing so would be appropriate.

2. Phone Call With an Involuntary Client: An involuntary client is one who is required or mandated to seek professional help. The requirement, mandate, or other pressure may come from a legal authority (e.g., a probation officer, judge, child protection agency), an employer, or a family member. With a caller who is an involuntary client, try to limit the phone conversation to scheduling a face-to-face meeting. Provide encouragement or explanations only if doing so is necessary to persuade the caller to come in. His negative feelings about being required to seek help will be easier to detect and address during a face-to-face meeting.

3. Choosing a Time and Location for the First Face-to-Face Meeting: Try to choose a time and a location that are convenient for the client. The location may be your agency or private practice office, the client's home, a hospital, a group home, etc. When selecting the location, consider issues of comfort, privacy, freedom from distractions, and accommodation to any special needs the client has (e.g., wheelchair access, arrangements for an interpreter). If the meeting will take place at your office or agency, verify that the client has accurate information about its location and, if relevant, knows how to use public transportation to travel there.

C. The First Face-to-Face Meeting With a Client

1. Planning the First Face-to-Face Meeting: Planning carefully before the first face-to-face meeting can help set a positive tone for the helping relationship. Preparation activities include reviewing available information on the history of the client's situation, considering factors that may affect the client's view of the helping process and willingness to invest in it, and trying to anticipate what the client may be feeling or thinking. For example, has the client had negative experiences with other service providers or resources in the past? If so, he may be feeling discouraged or reluctant to begin a professional relationship with you. An involuntary client may be feeling resentful, angry, or hostile.

2. Opening the First Face-to-Face Meeting:

a. General Guidelines: Be sure to anticipate what a client may be thinking and feeling as he meets you for the first time and begin to develop empathy for him, address his feelings, and identify ways of making him more at ease with the helping process. Shulman (1999) calls this the **tuning-in phase** of intervention.

You will usually open the first face-to-face meeting by introducing yourself and, ideally, greeting the client by name. Make sure to find out how the client prefers to be addressed. Experts agree that the use of last names is appropriate in the introductory stage of helping with African-American clients, Asian-American clients, Mexican-American clients, and older adults. If a client prefers to be addressed in this way, you should use his last name (e.g., Mr. Garcia) until he invites you to do otherwise.

After you've introduced yourself, provide the client with a brief explanation of the purpose of the first meeting (i.e., to explore the problem, concern, or request and how you can be helpful to him). If you have very limited time to spend with the client that day, explain this in order to ensure that high priority issues receive adequate attention.

b. Opening the Interview With a Voluntary Client: With most voluntary clients, you will begin the interview process by allowing the client to tell you why he has come in. If the client doesn't begin describing his concerns, you may make a short statement to help him get started (e.g., "You've come in to see me about something today"). With some clients, you'll need to begin with a brief **warm-up period** (i.e., an "ice-breaker" or small talk, such as comments about the day's weather). This can help the client feel more comfortable with you and the assessment process before he begins sharing his reason for coming in. You should use small talk only when you truly believe it will be helpful. In addition, you should proceed quickly to eliciting the concerns that led the client to come in. An overly long warm-up period may make a client uncomfortable or cause him to misunderstand the purpose of the interview. Warm-up periods are most appropriate to use when a client appears resistant or defensive. Warm-up periods can also be useful with adolescent clients.

c. Opening the Interview With an Involuntary Client: If you initiated the contact with an involuntary client, begin by explaining who you are, who you represent, and why you need to speak to him (i.e., state the purpose of the interview). If a client has been mandated by a court or other authority to meet with you, it is recommended that you do the following:

- Begin by sharing the factual information you have about why the client has been referred to your practice or agency and mandated to seek professional help. Then allow the client to tell his version of the story. If the client alleges any misunderstandings or discrepancies, tell him you will seek clarification from the referring source.

- Inform the client about the consequences that may follow if he doesn't cooperate (but also respect his right to choose the consequences rather than your services). This discussion should occur *after* you reveal the factual information you have about the client's referral because opening the meeting by discussing the consequences of not cooperating would set a negative tone.

- Provide the client with a clear and honest explanation of your role and responsibility and what you or your agency expect of the client. This includes explaining the limits to confidentiality that apply – for example, if you are required to prepare a report for the court, you must inform the client that what he tells you may end up in this report and be discussed in open court.

3. Exploring Expectations: In the initial meeting with a client, you should explore his expectations concerning you or your agency and the type of help you can offer. A client's expectations may be influenced by many different factors, including his socioeconomic status, cultural background, level of psychological sophistication, and past experiences with helping professionals.

Knowing a client's expectations usually allows you to better tailor the treatment plan to his primary needs and goals. On the other hand, a client may have inappropriate expectations. For instance, his expectations may differ from what you or your agency can realistically provide or he may anticipate that you will "fix" the problem for him or that the problem can be resolved more quickly than is realistic. Inappropriate expectations should be addressed openly with a client. One effective way of overcoming a client's inappropriate expectations is to clarify for him that social work is a mutual problem-solving process.

4. Other First-Meeting Activities: Whether you have a private practice or work at an agency, you should also undertake the following activities during the first face-to-face meeting with a client:

- Explain your own and client's roles and responsibilities in the helping process. This includes, among other things, letting the client know that he will need to provide personal information so that his problem and situation can be accurately assessed.

- Explain confidentiality and its limitations to the client. Obtain signed releases of confidential information as needed.

- Explain what fees the client will need to pay. If approval for your services is required from a managed care company, initiate the process of getting this approval. Also identify and discuss with the client any restrictions on your services imposed by the client's insurance plan.

- Reach an agreement with the client on the time, place, and frequency of future meetings and a tentative agreement about the number of sessions that will be required.

- Obtain an informed consent to treatment.

Additional information on role clarification, consent to treatment, and releases of confidential information can be found in your Professional Relationships, Values, and Ethics chapter.

Finally, if exploration of the problem reveals that a client needs resources or services that you or your agency cannot provide, your initial contact with him must also include making appropriate referrals. A client with multiple unmet needs usually requires referrals to other resources or service providers.

5. Taking Notes: You may take notes while interviewing the client if you wish to. If the client objects, explain why the notes are needed and, if appropriate, show him your notes. If the client continues to object, it is best to stop taking notes. If you are filling out an agency form during the meeting, you may give the client a copy of the form that he can refer to during the interview.

D. Engaging Clients

Engaging a client requires establishing rapport and may also involve enhancing his motivation. Most clients approach the first interview with some uncertainty or fear. They may be uncomfortable sharing personal information with a stranger, may fear that you'll make negative judgments about them or their problems, or might worry about being misunderstood or mistreated. The latter is especially common among clients who are members of an ethnic, racial, or sexual minority.

Clarifying Your Role and the Client's

At the start of the relationship, you should engage in a **role clarification** procedure so that you and the client will have congruent expectations about your work together:

- Establish **mutuality**. This entails adopting a posture of confidence and professional competence and communicating to the client that you and he are equal partners in the relationship and both responsible for what happens in treatment.

- Be aware that a client may expect that you will do more for him than you actually can or should do. You should identify, acknowledge, and resolve conflicts between your own expectations and those of your client. Be realistic and honest about what you can and cannot do for the client. Do not do things for the client that he can do for himself or that he can be taught to do for himself.

Establishing Rapport

Rapport is characterized by a sense of trust, a comfortable atmosphere, and a mutual understanding of the purpose of the interview. Many experts believe that rapport must begin to develop in the first face-to-face meeting because a client's sense of trust and comfort are vital for facilitating a productive assessment. Because most clients will sense right away whether you view them as unique, worthy, and capable of change, all of your verbal and nonverbal behaviors must support these beliefs from the first moment you meet with a client.

1. Guidelines for Establishing Rapport: From the very first moment you meet with a client, you must begin both exploring his problem and establishing rapport, as these two tasks reinforce each other.

a. Communicate in a Way That Puts the Client at Ease:

- Adapt your vocabulary to the client's capacity to understand.

- Allow the client to answer your questions without frequent interruption.

- Avoid asking questions that the client is probably unwilling to answer. Asking such questions may force the client to lie and interfere with the development of rapport.

- Use verbal and nonverbal messages to convey understanding and acceptance of the client's feelings, perceptions, needs, concerns, attitudes, etc., including his attitude about seeking professional help.

b. *Demonstrate Genuine Interest in the Client and Concern About the Problems and Needs He Expresses:*

- "Start where the client is" (i.e., focus on the client's priorities, including his emotional state and here-and-now concerns). This shows the client that you are interested, perceptive, and understanding.

- Listen actively and attentively. Attend to the client's verbal and nonverbal messages and then reflect back to him what you have understood.

- Use encouragers to convey interest in and attention to what the client is saying and invite him to continue speaking. Your responses may include verbal minimal prompts (e.g., "I see"), nonverbal encouragers (e.g., nodding), or accent responses in which you repeat, in an emphatic or questioning way, words that the client has used in order to convey your understanding of his feelings.

- Display empathic understanding. In initial interviews, **reciprocal empathic responses** are used to prepare the client for deeper exploration of his feelings later on. This level of empathy promotes a climate of trust and understanding that enables the client to self-disclose and explore his feelings and problems. At the reciprocal level, your verbal and nonverbal responses convey understanding but are more or less interchangeable with the client's obvious message – they accurately reflect the factual aspects of the client's statement and his surface feelings.

c. *Convey an Attitude of Acceptance and Respect:*

- Demonstrate a commitment to the client's right to and need for self-determination (e.g., emphasize mutuality and convey respect for the client's autonomy).

- Be nonjudgmental and noncritical, especially in response to the client's personal disclosures. While still building trust, don't challenge the client or point out his mistakes. Avoid displaying surprise, shock, or disbelief in response to anything the client discloses. If you suspect that a client is deliberately trying to shock you, simply "red flag" that behavior for the future – the initial phase of helping is not the time to address that kind of behavior (unless it places the client or someone else at risk). Before trust has developed, your focus must be on conveying acceptance.

- Individualize the client – appreciate his uniqueness, never stereotype. Use this opportunity to be mindful of the client's ethinic/racial background and how possible values and perceptions may play a part in establishing rapport.

- Treat the client with consistency, fairness, and dignity and speak and behave in ways which communicate that you value him and respect his dignity and worth. For example: (a) Consistently reinforce your assumption that the client has personal control and can learn to take responsibility for his own behavior. Point out and reinforce his strengths and skills and support his efforts to cope. (b) Avoid interaction patterns that may suggest that the client is helpless (e.g., avoid giving advice, don't offer sympathy for excessive complaining) and avoid giving in to inappropriate demands made by the client. (c) Use verbal and nonverbal messages to show the client that your responses will be different from other people's. For example, demonstrate that it's possible to acknowledge another person's feelings, beliefs, and values with respect and acceptance even if your own are different; and let the client know that you will gently challenge communication or behavior that is ungenuine.

d. *Be Authentic and Genuine:* Be sincere, open, straightforward, and nondefensive.

- Your own verbal and nonverbal messages must be consistent (**congruent**). When there is inconsistency between verbal and nonverbal messages, the latter tend to be given more weight (Cormier & Cormier, 1991).

- Being "open" in the first meeting usually includes telling the client about your background and approaches to helping so that he will be comfortable working with you. Briefly describing your qualifications can contribute to the development of rapport because, when the client knows you are well qualified, he will usually have more confidence in your ability to understand him and offer meaningful assistance.

e. *Additional Guidelines:*

- Demonstrate your commitment to confidentiality. Explain any legal or ethical obligations you may have regarding the confidentiality of information shared by the client.

- Address any **ambivalence** the client has about receiving services – for instance, most clients initially feel some conflict over whether their felt need for change outweighs the discomfort that change may cause.

- Explore the client's expectations of you and/or your agency and identify any fears or misunderstandings the client has about you, your agency, or the services. Explain relevant eligibility requirements that may affect service provision. If you don't know the answer to a client's service-related question, explain this and offer to find the answer. Avoid making any promises that you may not be able to keep.

- Whenever possible, provide early relief through concrete assistance that addresses one or more of the client's needs (e.g., offer direct assistance with obtaining a needed resource).

2. Establishing Rapport With Culturally Dissimilar Clients: Establishing rapport can be more difficult when you and the client come from different cultural or socioeconomic backgrounds. This is partly because your respective views of self, others, and the world will have been shaped by different life experiences. Some guidelines for building rapport with a culturally different client include the following:

- Openly acknowledge your awareness of the differences between you and the client and actively and supportively explore whether the client has any concerns about the differences.

- Use Sue's (1981) concepts of "credibility" and "giving" to establish your trustworthiness early. **Credibility** refers to the client's perception of your ability to be a trustworthy and effectual helper. With a culturally dissimilar client, you often need to *achieve* credibility. This can be done by acknowledging your differences to the client and demonstrating that you can conceptualize his problems within a culturally understanding and understandable framework. **Giving** refers to the client's perception that he has gained something from meeting with you. Attempt to be of concrete assistance in the very first meeting with the client.

- Be aware that self-disclosure may be difficult for a client who is a member of a minority group when the social worker belongs to the dominant (majority) culture because it requires a level of trust that may not exist initially. This is particularly true when the client is a member of an oppressed minority group or one that is discriminated against. Such a client often has had negative experiences with members of the dominant culture and/or with governmental agencies and institutions. If a client's level of **cultural mistrust** is so high that it prevents the development of rapport, referral to a culturally similar therapist is usually indicated.

Enhancing Motivation

If a new client appears to lack sufficient motivation to change or engage in the helping process, you can do one or more of the following things to enhance his motivation:

- Encourage the client to express his feelings by using empathic responding and providing a soothing, nonthreatening environment. Encourage all feelings, including negative feelings about the helping process and toward you or your agency.

- Identify relevant incentives for the client (e.g., a better relationship with his spouse, greater success at work).

- Offer hope that therapy will improve the client's situation. For example, outline a relevant treatment plan, tell the client about past successes you've had with cases like his, or explain that his problem is not uncommon and can be resolved.

- **Normalize** or **reframe** the client's problem (cast it in a different light) to make him more receptive to change. For example, you might suggest to parents that their teenager's mild misconduct is part of his developmentally expectable effort to form a personal identity and gain more independence rather than a sign of psychopathology. Or, with a family, you can briefly educate the identified patient and his family about systems theory and emphasize that the "patient" will be the family system, not one individual.

- Convey a willingness to help the client in active, concrete, and meaningful ways. A client's commitment to change can be enhanced by providing him with choices and framing change in a way that makes it personally meaningful and rewarding to him. When possible, try to be of concrete assistance to the client in the first meeting (e.g., provide information to help the client locate a resource he needs).

- As appropriate, either decrease or increase the client's level of concern or anxiety about his problem. A client who is very anxious about his situation or the prospect of change may have difficulty participating in treatment in a meaningful way, while a client who seems indifferent to or unconcerned about the problem may not be sufficiently motivated to work toward change: (a) The most effective tool for reducing anxiety is catharsis, in which you help the client to acknowledge and ventilate his feelings. It's important to strike a balance here: to reduce anxiety to a point where the client is not too anxious to participate but is still sufficiently anxious to continue. (b) Increasing anxiety is necessary if the client displays a lack of concern about his problem, and you firmly believe that his problem requires professional attention. In this case, you can, if appropriate, point out the consequences of not changing or refusing to engage in the helping process.

Engaging Clients – Special Situations

1. Involuntary Clients: The following guidelines can help you engage an involuntary client (Hepworth et al., 2006; Sheafor & Horejsi, 2003):

- Assume that the client has negative feelings (e.g., hostility, anger, shame, embarrassment, defensive reactions) about being forced into contact with you and be prepared to deal with them. Address the client's negative feelings directly. Use basic interviewing skills to help the client express these feelings. Avoid simply defending the benefits of your services.

- If the client is visibly upset or angry, you may say something like, "I know you're here today because you were sent to me for help. I guess that might be why you look [upset, angry]." After this, stop speaking and allow the client an opportunity to respond. Most clients will start talking when they begin feeling uncomfortable with the silence.

- Let the client know that you understand he may be tempted to lie, but that you don't want him to lie and that lying may make him feel guilty or worried about being caught in a lie and will waste time. Tell the client that, rather than lying, he should tell you when he doesn't want to answer a question, and then seek his agreement to this arrangement. Don't ask questions that the client could perceive as an effort to catch him in a lie.

- Discuss the client's previous experiences with mental health professionals and other social services. Identify any assumptions he has about social workers or other professional helpers.

- There may be legal and other constraints limiting the client's choices. To the extent possible, however, you should allow the client to make choices so that he feels like he has some control over the helping process. Allowing the client control over even minor matters (such as appointment times) can serve to reduce his resistance.

- If your initial efforts to engage the client fail, you can try using the "**let's make a deal**" tactic in which you agree to do something that will make the client more comfortable or help him get something he wants in exchange for his cooperation. Of course, whatever you agree to do or get for the client must be legal, ethical, and legitimate. Do not ever bend or break your agency's rules to engage a client.

- With an involuntary client, the goals of treatment may be identified by a third party such as the legal system. Still, you can identify the client's needs and wants and then attempt to establish additional treatment goals that are at least partly consistent with these. This tactic is called "**moving with the motive**."

2. Clients Who Are Resistant or Defensive: When it's critically important to engage a defensive or resistant client – for example, you are meeting with a client accused of abusing his child – you should be assertive and deal directly with the client's resistant or defensive behavior. Sheafor and Horejsi (2003) recommend that you make the following responses to specific client behaviors:

- If the client is silent, say something like, "I can see you don't want to talk to me about [the purpose of the interview], but I'm going to stay here until we have discussed it."

- If the client seems overly agreeable, say something like, "I hope you will take the actions you have promised, but how will I know you've followed through on those plans?"

- If the client tries to divert attention away from the purpose of the interview, say something like, "I can sense you don't want to focus on [the purpose of the interview], but that's why I'm here and we have to get back to it."

- If the client becomes upset and tries to make you feel responsible, say something like, "I know you're upset but it's my job to talk to you about [the purpose of the interview]; take a few minutes to collect yourself and then we'll need to return to [the purpose of the interview]."

3. "Hard-to-Reach" Clients: A "hard-to-reach" client is one who is especially distrustful and reluctant to become involved in the helping process. Many hard-to-reach clients are socially isolated, have a mental illness, and/or are acutely uncomfortable in interpersonal relationships. Guidelines for building trust with a hard-to-reach client include the following (Sheafor & Horejsi, 2003; Hepworth et al., 2006):

- Because the client may form judgments quickly and interpret situations in negative ways, you should be warm, giving, and dependable from the start and willing to self-disclose at a higher rate than usual so that the client will see you as a real person. Similarly, because the client may be very sensitive to signs of rejection, you must avoid any statements and behaviors that he could interpret as criticism. If you accidentally say or do something that hurts the client, discuss it with him immediately in an effort to restore the relationship.

- While it's critical to show the client that you are caring and fair, you must also show him that you are firm. You should gently set limits on what is and is not acceptable behavior in your relationship.

- Encourage frequent contact. Supplement face-to-face meetings with phone calls or letters to demonstrate your concern and interest in the client.

- You may need to do things *for* the client before you can do things *with* him. Early in the relationship, demonstrate your good will and usefulness in concrete ways (e.g., home visits, tangible expressions of concern). Initially giving-in to some of the client's dependency needs can show him that you are "safe." Don't worry about creating overdependency at this time; that problem can be dealt with after rapport is established.

- If the client doesn't want to talk about certain topics, let him know that this is acceptable and avoid asking him about these topics for now. Then try to engage him in a discussion of why some topics are hard for people to talk about (e.g., shame, embarrassment, fear of being judged). Having a general discussion about these fears can help convince the client that you are trustworthy, and once trust has developed, he may be more willing to talk about topics he initially wanted to avoid.

- Tolerate the client's testing behavior and be patient if progress is slow. He may feel hopeless about change and fearful or distrustful because he has been mistreated by others in the past. Acknowledge that change can be difficult and, once the client begins to trust you, introduce the idea that, if he wants to change his situation, he'll need to do some things differently.

4. Clients Who Passively Resist Efforts to Engage Them: The following guidelines can help you engage a client who passively resists becoming invested in the helping process:

- Explore and openly discuss the client's negative feelings or uncertainty about accepting help.

- Clarify the client's perceptions and expectations of treatment.

- Explain what the helping process will entail in relation to the client's needs.

- Inform the client about his right to refuse treatment, if this is appropriate. Or, if you believe that the client would receive substantial benefit from treatment, encourage him to accept it on a trial basis.

- Consider the cultural context when interpreting the meaning of the client's behavior because it may have a different meaning in his culture (e.g., an Arab American or Native American client may verbally agree to perform a task yet not complete it because it's considered impolite in his culture to disagree with a request).

5. Adolescent Clients: To engage an adolescent, you can do the following:

- If the client seems resistant, attempt to neutralize his negative feelings about the helping process and toward you. Useful approaches include (a) relating as a sensitive, accepting, and understanding ally rather than as an "enemy"; (b) "starting where the client is" by using empathic responding to elicit his negative feelings; and (c) responding to him in ways that are opposite to his negative expectations.

- Listen nonjudgmentally and look for the underlying meaning of what the client says and how he feels. Encourage him to talk about his situation as he experiences it and from his perspective. Because many adolescents are preoccupied with the here-and-now, however, you might need to gently encourage the client to examine his current behaviors and decisions in light of his goals for the future. If his thinking is clearly unrealistic or may be dangerous, you can tell him so in a firm but respectful way.

- Avoid questions and other interventions that may come off to the client as an effort to control him as such interventions are likely to invite resistance.

III. Intervention Planning, Goal Setting, and Contracting

After you and the client have reached an agreement about the nature of his difficulties and the systems involved and identified the problem(s) to be worked on, you move on to formulating the intervention plan (or "treatment plan" or "action plan") and entering into a formal or informal contract for implementing the plan.

A. Intervention Planning Steps

During intervention planning, you and the client mutually identify what needs to be changed and what actions need to be taken to resolve or improve the client's problematic situation. Intervention planning includes the following steps:

- Step 1 – specify the goals in a concrete and specific manner the client hopes to achieve.
- Step 2 – identify what changes need to be made to achieve the goals.
- Step 3 – select from among alternative change strategies the ones that are most likely to achieve the goals. You should evaluate each alternative in light of helpful and harmful impacts it may have on the client or others, the resources required, and the timeframe needed to carry it out; and identify the people and organizations with whom you and the client will need to work to achieve the goals.
- Step 4 – determine which actions will be taken by the client and by you.
- Step 5 – establish timelines for completing those actions.

B. Tailoring the Treatment Plan

A treatment plan (intervention plan) must be tailored to the identified problem, the client, and your professional knowledge and skills. In addition, developing an appropriate treatment plan requires you to clarify the client's expectations of treatment, including both outcome and methods, and to take note of how he formulates the problem.

The interventions you and the client select must match the following:

- The target systems, or systems targeted for change. Your interventions must be directed to the systems implicated in the client's problems and be appropriate for those systems.
- The identified problems. When attempting to match interventions to problems, you should consider empirical evidence that has demonstrated that a certain intervention is an effective treatment for a particular problem. This is discussed in more detail below.
- The client's developmental phase. Your interventions must be appropriate for the client's cognitive, social, and psychological development and stage of life.

- Stressful transitions and events in the client's life. Have the client's problems arisen in conjunction with a major life transition or situational event? Prolonged stress or dramatic events can diminish coping capacity and affect physical and emotional health.

- The client's cultural, ethnic, racial, and/or religious values and preferences.

C. Establishing Goals and Objectives

Assessment should result in the identification of one or more treatment goals. These goals may be identified by the client in collaboration with you and/or by third parties (parents, the legal system, an employer, etc.).

1. Definitions of "Goals," "Objectives," and "Tasks": In working to reach a single goal, a client may need to achieve several objectives, and in order to achieve these objectives, the client (and you) may need to complete several tasks.

Generally speaking, a **goal** is a desired end toward which an activity is directed. Therefore, each goal of intervention is an outcome sought by you and the client. A treatment goal (or "intervention goal") is generally phrased as a broad and fairly global statement that describes a desired outcome. A treatment goal can take many forms depending on the identified problem. Generic examples include learn a skill, gather information needed to make a decision, change a behavior, change an attitude about oneself or someone else, rebuild a relationship, change the way a life event is perceived, achieve a more satisfactory adjustment to an unchangeable situation, or become linked to a program or service provided by an agency or professional.

An **objective** is a discrete step that the client will take to achieve a desired outcome (a goal). In other words, objectives define a series of behavioral changes that must take place in order to reach a treatment goal. In this way, objectives are effective for giving greater direction and structure to the helping process. An objective is more specific than a goal and is always written in a manner that facilitates measurement and evaluation. For example, if a couple has a goal to reduce marital conflict, this goal could be divided, or partialized, into objectives such as the following: to recognize sources of anger, to express verbally feelings underlying the anger, to practice conflict resolution skills, and to express positive messages to each other.

A **task** (or activity) is a problem-solving action or decision undertaken by you or the client to reach a desired outcome. Often a task represents one step in a series of steps that must be completed to achieve an objective; and, usually, a single task is something that can be accomplished in a matter of days or, at most, a few weeks. While a task may be general or specific, it is always an activity that can be evaluated in terms of whether or not it was completed.

2. Guidelines for Establishing Treatment Goals:

a. The Client Must Participate: To the extent possible, the client (as well as the parents or legal guardian of a minor client) should participate in establishing the treatment goals, and you must get an agreement from the client on what the goals of intervention will be. Goals, as well as objectives, must be worth achieving from the client's point of view.

A **goal checklist** can be a useful tool when a client has difficulty articulating his concerns and identifying his goals for change. A goal checklist is a list of possible treatment goals from which a client can select ones that are relevant to his situation. Social workers familiar with the problems and concerns of particular client groups can construct goal checklists and tailor them to their particular practice setting or the services that are available in their community.

Sometimes you and a client will disagree about the treatment goals or objectives or some other aspect of treatment planning. With regard to this issue, Persons, Davidson, and Tompkins (2001) suggest the following as a useful principle for determining whether or not a disagreement is manageable: "If the disagreement is not likely in [your] judgment or as determined empirically to prevent the patient from reaching his or her goals or to lead to a catastrophe (e.g., financial insolvency), then disagreement is acceptable" (p. 44). When this is not the case, consultation or referral is often the best course of action.

b. Goals Must Match the Formulated Problem: A goal should flow in a logical way from an assessment that has examined not only the client's problems and needs but also his strengths and resources. Each goal should be directed toward resolution of the formulated problem. As relevant to the client's problem and situation, goals should be set in biophysical, psychological, and social arenas.

c. Goals Should Be Explicit: A goal should clearly define the desired outcome so that both you and the client can easily see when the goal has been reached. To increase the specificity of a goal, it is useful to divide it into two or more parts or steps (objectives). This is discussed further below, under "dividing goals into objectives." Sometimes, explicitly defining the goals also entails clearly specifying the behavioral changes expected of all individuals in the target system (e.g., a family) with regard to shared or reciprocal goals.

d. Goals Should Specify Overt and Covert Changes: An appropriately stated goal can be measured and defines both overt and covert changes. Overt behavioral changes can be observed by you and significant others in the client's life. Covert changes (e.g., ceasing negative self-talk) must be reported by the client and are, therefore, more subject to measurement error.

e. Goals Should Be Prioritized: You should help the client prioritize his goals (i.e., assist him to determine which outcome he wants to achieve first). By doing this, your initial work will be directed toward addressing the most urgent or oppressive aspect of his problem or situation. Distinguishing problems that need immediate attention from those that can be dealt with later and prioritizing the client's goals are part of the process known as **partialization**. (For more information on setting priorities for attention, see Section XI of Assessment.)

f. Goals Must Be Realistic: Goals and objectives must be realistic and achievable within a reasonable period of time given the client's characteristics, circumstances, and resources (e.g., his motivation, capacity, and opportunity; his financial resources; the severity and chronicity of his symptoms) and the services you can provide.

Finally, you and the client must also specify a timeframe during which the goals are to be achieved. This is discussed in more detail in the discussion of treatment contracts, below. Finally, treatment goals (as well objectives and intervention strategies) must be consistent with your own/your agency's policies and the NASW Code of Ethics.

3. Dividing Goals into Objectives: Even when treatment goals are specified clearly, they can seem overwhelming to a client. Therefore, an important task when planning treatment is to divide the goals into more manageable parts, known as objectives. Guidelines for formulating **behavioral objectives** include the following:

- An objective should specify one result or outcome to be accomplished.

- An objective (like a goal) must be agreed to by both you and the client. The client must never be pressured or coerced to agree.

- Whenever possible, objectives should be stated in specific and quantitative terms (i.e., behaviorally measurable terms) that give direction and purpose to the helping process, serve as indicators of the client's progress, and provide standards for evaluating the outcome.

- An objective should include a verb that describes an action to be taken (e.g., contact, demonstrate, list, decide, discuss, plan, select, obtain, bring, practice, arrange, utilize, apply, display, recognize, join). An objective usually starts with the word "to," followed by the action verb.

- Positive language should be used whenever possible (i.e., the words used to define an objective should describe what the client will do, not what the client won't do).

- As with a goal, an objective should include a timeframe for completion. Generally, an objective should not take more than a few weeks to achieve. An objective that may take months to accomplish should be broken down into several smaller objectives so that the client will be able to see that he is making progress. When a client can perceive concrete gains (i.e., reaching an objective), even if the gain is small, he will feel more motivated to continue.

- For intervention to be effective, you and the client must be willing to revise the objectives to meet changing circumstances that occur during the course of your work together.

One system for organizing objectives is to divide them into short-term (initial or early stage), intermediate (middle stage), and, if appropriate based on the client's needs, motivation, resources, etc., long-term (later stage) objectives. Ordinarily, the organization of the objectives mirrors the priorities of the problems in a problem list.

D. Selecting Intervention Strategies

Planning intervention strategies (a.k.a. change strategies) requires you to determine the most appropriate practice framework (perspectives, theories, models) for guiding the intervention process. (Available practice frameworks are reviewed in Section XI of this chapter.) As a social worker, you will generally use a systematic approach when determining what intervention strategies are most appropriate for a client and his problem, and using **systematic eclecticism** can help you do this: This approach entails choosing interventions from different practice perspectives, theories, and models based on how well they match a client's problem and the empirical research showing the interventions to be effective.

1. General Selection Principles: General principles to follow when selecting intervention strategies include the following:

- Your selection of intervention strategies must be based on an accurate and comprehensive assessment of the problem. To the greatest extent possible, all planning decisions should be based on facts and objective evidence collected and evaluated during the assessment.

- You must consider the client's understanding of the problem and his ideas about what might be helpful for resolving it. If your intervention strategies or modalities don't make sense to the client, he is unlikely to cooperate.

- The client should assist in selecting the intervention strategies. This respects his right to self-determination and increases the likelihood that he will cooperate with the change effort.

- Using the process known as **partialization** can be effective for maximizing a client's ability to participate effectively in the planning process. Partialization involves temporarily considering a client's interconnected problems as separate issues so that planning (and doing) the work toward resolving them can be more manageable. After a client's problems have been partialized, you and the client will ordinarily first deal with those that need immediate attention.

- While the principle of self-determination dictates that the client has the right to have input and make decisions during intervention planning and contracting, as his social worker you can (and usually should) offer your point of view. The final decisions should be left to the client, but it is appropriate for you to offer your own recommendations regarding the problem to be worked on and treatment goals, objectives, and approaches and to explain them to the client. Your recommendations should be based primarily on objective information collected during the assessment phase, and you should refer to this information when explaining your point of view to the client.

- Pay attention to the client's strengths and capabilities. Don't propose to do something for the client if he can do it himself or could learn to do it himself. Instead, encourage or teach the client to carry out the action himself.

- The intervention strategies must be consistent with social work ethical standards – you must avoid interventions that expose the client to emotional harm, violate his confidentiality, or otherwise oppose the ethical standards of the social work profession. Additionally, some methods of bringing about change may be effective but unethical.

- You must have the required knowledge and skill to apply an intervention strategy (e.g., you must know the rationale for the strategy, the indications and contraindications for using it, what cautions you should observe, and the specific procedures for implementing it).

- You should consider how you might utilize the **informal resources** available in your client's social support network, such as his extended family, friends, neighbors, etc. Informal resources can offer emotional support, material assistance, physical care, information, and mediation in situations involving interpersonal conflict.

2. Client Factors Affecting the Choice of Intervention Strategies:

a. Motivation, Capacity, and Opportunity: A client's **motivation** to change, **capacity** for change, and **opportunity** to change have a significant impact on the intervention process and its outcome. Your role as the facilitator of planned change is important, too, however: Your job is to take action and apply knowledge and skills designed to increase your client's motivation, expand his capacity, and identify or create opportunities for him to change.

Motivation: Motivation refers to a state of readiness to take action. Motivation requires both "the pull of hope" (the belief that change is possible) and "the push of discomfort" (dissatisfaction or distress with how things currently are). Any meaningful assessment of motivation must be tied to a specific goal or action (i.e., motivation is not a personality trait): A client can be very motivated toward one action but have little or no motivation toward another, and his level of motivation will tend to vary over time and from one context to another.

Capacity: In order for change to happen, a client must have the capacity for change. Capacity, in this context, refers to the abilities and resources that the client or people in his environment bring to the change process (e.g., time, energy, knowledge, experience, self-discipline, optimism, self-confidence, communication skills, problem-solving skills). Different kinds of change require different types and combinations of capacity.

Opportunity: Change also requires opportunity. In this context, opportunity refers to conditions and circumstances within the client's immediate environment that support positive change. Some environmental factors encourage change, while others are barriers to change.

b. *"Readiness for Change":* Another consideration when choosing intervention strategies is the client's readiness for change, which can be evaluated in terms of the change stages identified by Prochaska and DiClemente's (1992) transtheoretical model: These authors suggest that regardless of the nature of the problem, people pass through a series of six stages when changing a behavior. The six **stages of change** are as follows:

Stage 1 – Precontemplation: A person in the precontemplation stage is unaware of his problem or unwilling to change it. People in this stage rarely come to see a helping professional on their own; they are likely to be in your office at someone else's request (e.g., a spouse, a court).

Because a precontemplating client is not yet thinking about the possibility of change, your job is to raise doubt in his mind. You provide information and feedback to increase his awareness of having a problem, the difficulties and risks associated with his problem, and the possibility of change. Giving prescriptive advice at this time is not recommended because it can elicit resistance.

Stage 2 – Contemplation: A person enters the contemplation stage when he becomes aware of his problem. A person in this stage is considering the possibility of change but this stage is marked by **ambivalence** (i.e., the person is both contemplating making a change and also discarding the idea).

When discussing the problem, a client in the contemplation stage is likely to move back and forth between reasons for changing and justifications for why change is unnecessary. Your goal is to "tip" the decisional balance in favor of change. You elicit reasons to change and the risks of not changing and strengthen the client's self-efficacy for change. **Self-efficacy**, or the client's belief in his own ability to perform and succeed with a task, is thought to be a key element in the motivation for change.

Stage 3 – Determination: At some point, a person's decisional balance begins to lean in favor of change, and he begins to make statements that reflect motivation to change his problem. This marks the beginning of the determination stage, when a person becomes ready and determined to change.

Miller and Rollnick (1991) describe the determination stage as a "window of opportunity," which stays open for a limited period of time. Your job is to help the client find an appropriate and effective change strategy during the period while this window is open.

Stage 4 – Action: In the action stage, a person takes action to make the desired change. If a person enters the action stage during the "window of opportunity" (see above), then the change process continues. Otherwise, the "window of opportunity" re-closes for a period of time and the person returns to the contemplation stage.

The goal in the action stage is to produce change in the problem area. With your assistance, the client selects and performs specific actions designed to change the problem area.

Stage 5 – Maintenance: For a client in the maintenance stage, the goals are to sustain the change accomplished through "action" and to prevent relapse. To maintain change, a client is likely to need different skills and strategies than were used to make the change in the first place.

Stage 6 – Relapse: A relapse or slip may occur before the person achieves stable change (Marlatt & Gordon, 1985). Relapses are considered a normal part of the change process, especially when a person is attempting to change a longstanding behavior or pattern.

When relapse occurs, the client's job is to begin the change process again and avoid becoming stuck in the relapse. Your job is to help the client avoid discouragement, continue contemplating change, regain his determination, and persist with action and maintenance efforts.

c. Other Client Factors: Other client factors that impact your choice of intervention strategies include (a) various other personal characteristics of the client (e.g., psychological mindedness, intellectual capacity); (b) the client's medical history and, when applicable, psychiatric history; (c) diversity considerations (e.g., age, developmental level, race, culture, gender, social class, ability level); and (d) practical issues (e.g., is the client available for weekly appointments, what is his ability to pay, are there limitations imposed by his insurance coverage?).

3. Using Practice Guidelines, ESTs, and Treatment Manuals: When they are available, you should consider current research findings regarding the most effective intervention strategies for a given problem or mental disorder. Overall, cognitive, behavioral, and cognitive-behavioral therapies can apply to almost every problem or disorder and seem to have slightly more scientific support than other approaches.

a. Practice Guidelines: **Practice guidelines** are systematically developed statements to facilitate practitioner and patient decisions about appropriate health care for specific clinical circumstances. Practice guidelines are based on empirical (observed) evidence of efficacy and serve several purposes including standardizing and improving the quality of client care, helping clinicians identify the most effective treatment approaches for specific disorders, and reducing the costs of health care (Maruish, 2002).

b. Empirically Supported Treatments: **Empirically supported treatments** (ESTs) are specific psychological treatments that have been shown to be efficacious in controlled clinical trials. The research indicates that ESTs, in general, have the following characteristics: (a)

Most ESTs include homework as a component; (b) ESTs generally focus on skill building, not insight or catharsis; (c) ESTs are problem-focused; (d) ESTs incorporate continuous assessment of client progress; and (e) ESTs involve brief treatment contact, requiring 20 or fewer sessions.

One criticism of ESTs is that they are evaluated on the basis of their efficacy (effects in well-controlled conditions) rather than effectiveness (effects in actual clinical conditions). Consequently, when making decisions about the use of an EST, the best approach is to consider "the empirical evidence in light of its relevance to a particular patient for a particular purpose under particular circumstances" (Maruish, 2002, p. 150).

c. Treatment Manuals: Treatment manuals were originally developed to assist in research and training but are now considered a means of delivering ESTs to clients with specific disorders. Manuals have several advantages: They provide a theoretical framework for understanding a client's symptoms/disorder, offer concrete descriptions of therapy techniques, and present case examples that illustrate the appropriate application of the techniques. However, like practice guidelines, treatment manuals do not take into account a client's unique characteristics or the nonspecific factors that have been linked to positive treatment outcomes (Lambert et al., 1998).

4. Other Guidelines for Selecting Intervention Strategies: The following guidelines are also useful when selecting intervention strategies, particularly in a clinical setting:

- When two different intervention strategies for a problem have been demonstrated as equally effective, select the most efficient one (i.e., the one that produces the desired outcome with the least expenditure of time, money, and effort).

- Whenever possible, select a well-defined approach. This is important because, when a practice theory is abstract, it typically provides inadequate guidance on interventions. For example, the procedures of behavior modification are well defined, whereas those associated with psychodynamic theory are not as clear-cut. Using this criterion, therefore, you might select behavior modification over psychodynamic therapy.

- Apply intervention strategies prescriptively. In other words, select those strategies that are most relevant to achieving the treatment goals and that have the highest likelihood of helping the client achieve the goals.

- An intervention strategy should result in major rather than minor effects (i.e., it should address major concerns).

- An intervention strategy should produce lasting effects.

E. Choosing the Therapeutic Configuration (Modality)

The choice of modality(ies) for a client – individual therapy, couples (marital) therapy, family therapy, or group therapy – depends on a number of variables including the nature of the problem, the treatment goals, the age of the client, the availability of family members, court mandate, etc. And, for some clients, you will determine that it's appropriate to use more than one modality, either concurrently (at the same time) or sequentially (one after the other). **Combined therapy**, for example, is an intervention model in which the client participates concurrently in both individual therapy and group therapy.

In addition, several different treatment formats be may used to provide family therapy or couples therapy to clients. In **conjoint therapy**, the therapist treats a family or couple by meeting with the family members or partners together for regular sessions. Sometimes, conjoint therapy is provided by a team of therapists rather than only a single therapist. **Concurrent therapy**, by contrast, involves seeing different members of a family or client system separately in individual sessions. This intervention model is used most commonly for couples therapy to encourage the clients to reveal thoughts, feelings, and behaviors that they might not feel able to disclose in the presence of their spouses. Finally, **collaborative therapy** is a treatment format in which two or more therapists each treat a single member of a family and coordinate their efforts (Barker, 2003).

1. Individual Therapy: Below is a list of some of the issues that are commonly addressed in individual therapy (Dorfman, 1996):

Adjustment reactions: A new situation or condition (whether negative or positive) has overwhelmed a client's usual coping capacities. Examples include the diagnosis of a chronic disease, being a victim of a violent crime, becoming homeless, marriage, divorce, relocation, age-related physical changes, or a promotion at work.

Developmental issues: The stress of a developmental task or transition has precipitated an emotional or psychological crisis requiring mental health intervention. Examples include sexual identity issues or a young adult in the process of psychologically individuating and physically separating from his family.

Life span issues: A client needs help in clarifying his goals and values, resolving an internal conflict, and/or reducing stress that emerges during points in life that require decision-making and action (e.g., what career to pursue, when to make a relationship commitment).

Personality features: A client suffers from shyness, lack of assertiveness, distrust of others, low self-worth, or poor self-image, and needs to work individually before he can feel comfortable in a treatment group.

Mental disorders: A client has a mental disorder that responds well to individual treatment such as depression, a phobic disorder, obsessive-compulsive disorder, or PTSD. (Meeting with the client's family members may be indicated as well, to address effects of the disorder on family functioning and vice versa.)

Mourning: Both individual and group modalities are effective with grief work.

Additionally, there may be times when you elect to provide individual therapy simply because you have no other choice (e.g., the client has no family, his family members live too far away).

2. Family Therapy: Even a client who comes in by himself might benefit from family therapy (or couples therapy) in addition to or instead of individual therapy.

a. Issues Commonly Addressed in Family Therapy: Below is a list of issues commonly addressed in family therapy (Dorfman, 1996):

- Family life-cycle issues (e.g., the birth of a new child, rivalry between siblings).

- There is one symptomatic family member, or identified patient (IP) (i.e., the family is actively making one member a scapegoat for their shared problems). The IP is usually a child in the family.

- The entire family unit is disturbed and the symptoms of one member are manifesting this disturbance.

- Divorce, remarriage, step-families.

- Incest.

- Disability or illness of a family member.

- Caregiving obligations.

- Parenting (parent-child discord or parents in conflict over child rearing).

- Environmental stress (unemployment, poor housing conditions, poor health care, discrimination, dangerous neighborhood).

- Family violence (although, in many cases, the partners in an abusive relationship should be treated individually, at least initially).

- A family member has been institutionalized and is returning home to his family.

In addition, family therapy may be preferred over individual therapy when individual therapy for the problem has been ineffective or when improvement in one family member has caused, or is likely to cause, symptoms or distress in another member (this outcome can be addressed in family therapy).

b. Contraindications for Family Therapy: Family therapy is generally contraindicated (not appropriate) when one or more of the following conditions are present: (a) key family members are unavailable or unwilling to participate; (b) one family member is so severely disturbed that his behavior makes family treatment impossible; (c) one family member's disturbance, while affecting the family, is the result of issues outside the home; or (d) an adolescent in the family is trying to separate psychologically from his family.

c. Conditional Contraindications for Family Therapy: Conditional contraindications for family therapy include the following: (a) When the spouses are committed to dissolving the marriage, family therapy may not be indicated or may be indicated only for specific goals such as helping the couple learn to put the needs of their children first. (b) Family therapy is not considered appropriate for all psychological disturbances. However, in cases involving serious disorders, such as a psychotic disorder or bipolar disorder, family therapy may be used after the individual's symptoms have been controlled through medication and/or a period of hospitalization. (c) Family therapy should not be used in cases of severe domestic violence before the violence is brought under control. (d) Family therapy may be contraindicated, at least initially, when a client's problem involves a significant secret, such as infidelity, homosexuality, criminal behavior, or a history of sexual abuse.

3. Couples Therapy: Issues commonly addressed in couples therapy (for both opposite-sex and same-sex couples) include the following (Dorfman, 1996):

Communication difficulties: A couple has difficulties with communication and mutual problem solving (e.g., one or both partners feel misunderstood, ignored, or put down by the other; there is frequent conflict that results in hurt feelings and anger rather than resolution or renewed intimacy). The clients need to be made aware of the impact of their communications on each other and should be taught to send clear messages to each other and encouraged to practice giving and asking for feedback to prevent misinterpretations and misconceptions.

Couple and marital life-cycle changes: The couple is undergoing a predictable life-cycle change, but the change has brought about conflict, emotional upset, confusion, and/or discomfort. Examples of common life-cycle changes for couples include adjustment to marriage (or another form of committed relationship); family planning; adjusting to parenting; the last child leaving home (the "empty nest syndrome"); caring for aging parents; age-related changes in health, stamina, and appearance; and disability or functional impairment of one or both partners.

Cultural, racial, or religious differences: Conflicts arising from having differing cultural, racial, or religious backgrounds often are overcome fairly easily in the initial stages of a relationship but then tend to surface and resurface at various points along the life-cycle of the couple. Partners unable to resolve these conflicts on their own often seek help first from sources such as family, friends, or religious leaders from their faith. A social worker usually doesn't encounter the couple until one of the partners has become symptomatic or the relationship has deteriorated so much that the couple is ready to separate.

Infidelity: The couple is dealing with actual or suspected infidelity in the relationship. In this situation, the clients may have differing goals: One partner may want to work on re-establishing the health of the relationship, while the other may want to leave the relationship and expect you to address his or her partner's emotional distress. Infidelity occurs for many different reasons – it may reflect a troubled relationship, be an expression of anger or an effort to restore self-esteem or overcome boredom, or be part of a sexual addiction.

One partner is symptomatic: Woods and Hollis (1990) distinguish between "acting-in" and "acting-out" symptoms of couples and how the symptoms affect the choice of therapeutic configuration: (a) Partners with acting-in symptoms turn their emotion and other energy inwards. They tend to develop depression and anxiety and are likely to seek individual therapy for their difficulties. When invited, their partners will often agree to participate in conjoint sessions. (b) Partners with acting-out symptoms express strong anger and may engage in destructive or abusive behavior toward others. They rarely seek treatment on their own, and are more likely to be coerced into treatment by their spouses/partners, employers, or outside social agencies.

Premarital (prenuptial) counseling: This counseling may address such issues as clarifying marital roles and expectations or mediating cultural, racial, religious, or value differences that impact the relationship. Premarital counseling is preventive rather than curative.

Separation and divorce counseling or mediation: Partners who have agreed to separate or divorce and are starting (or in the midst of) the formal "divorcing process" may need help with finalizing decisions and negotiations concerning child custody, property settlement, child visitation, etc. A qualified social worker may conduct mediation for the couple; such mediation is intended to keep the relationship amiable, keep the negotiations fair, and reduce the potential for costly legal fees.

Sexual dysfunction: Sexual dysfunction may involve medical factors, psychological factors, and/or relationship issues, and assessment and intervention are likely to include collaboration with a physician. Couples therapy is indicated for sexual dysfunction unless the disorder is purely functional (due solely to a physiological cause). (A "functional disorder" is a medical condition that impairs the normal function of a bodily process.)

4. Group Therapy: Group therapy can be an important adjunct to individual therapy services, and, for some clients, it may be more effective than individual work. Many clients (including most adolescents), for example, are more receptive to ideas and confrontations offered by peers (other clients) than by professionals. It's important to assess the readiness of the client to benefit from group therapy.

a. Indications for Group Therapy: Groups are considered essential in work with individuals who tend to be defensive and manipulative, including clients whose problems involve substance use disorders, sexual offenses and related crimes, and domestic abuse. Group sessions, especially with peers, are also useful and are often indicated for people who have been subjected to incest and other forms of sexual abuse.

Other indications for group therapy include the following: (a) the primary problem involves an interpersonal issue (e.g., shyness, difficulties with intimacy, argumentativeness); (b) the client is motivated to change; (c) the client finds peer support and feedback beneficial; and (d) the client has a positive view of group therapy. Note, however, that, for some clients, it's important to delay referral for group therapy until the client has had an opportunity to work on his problems in individual therapy.

b. Contraindications for Group Therapy: Contraindications for group therapy include the following: (a) an incompatibility with group norms for acceptable behaviors (e.g., significant deviancy from other group members); (b) an inability to tolerate the group setting; (c) certain diagnoses, symptoms, or problems including severe depression and social withdrawal, paranoia, acute psychosis, brain damage, a high level of denial, high somatization, low self-esteem, low psychological sophistication, and low IQ; (d) low motivation to change; and (e) unrealistic and/or unfavorable expectations about group therapy (Yalom, 1985). Additionally, group therapy (including support groups) is generally contraindicated for clients in **acute crisis**. For clients in acute crisis, individual crisis-oriented therapy is recommended initially.

c. Concurrent Group and Individual Therapy: A potential problem with concurrent group and individual therapies is that clients may rely on individual therapy "to drain off affect from the group" (Yalom, 1985, p. 416) rather than work on issues with group members. Concurrent group and individual therapies are least likely to have detrimental effects when the group and individual therapists communicate regularly (or are the same therapist) and when individual therapy complements the group's here-and-now focus.

F. The Frequency and Duration of Treatment

To promote mutuality, you should elicit your client's preferences regarding the frequency of sessions and duration of treatment. Additionally, you must take into account any restrictions imposed by the client's insurance plan. Under managed care, most clients are limited to a specific number of sessions.

1. The Frequency of Sessions: In clinical work, holding sessions once or twice per week tends to be optimally effective, and, in social work, the norm is once per week. When a client requires greater support and monitoring (for example, because he is suicidal at the beginning of treatment), more frequent contact may be indicated at least initially; daily contact may be required when clients need intensive support and monitoring, such as in cases involving child welfare, outpatient drug treatment, homeless youth, or services for frail elderly individuals.

If a client requests more or less frequent sessions than you feel are justified, you should share your point of view with the client. While eliciting and respecting the client's input is important, the ultimate decision regarding the frequency of sessions should be made by you when possible, using your clinical judgment.

2. The Duration of Treatment: With voluntary clients, pre-setting the duration of treatment (often six to 12 sessions conducted over a time span of two to four months) during contracting is appropriate for many common problems of living and also is associated with several important advantages. For example, when you and the client preset the duration, you promote optimism by suggesting that the client can improve in a relatively short period of time, encourage him to become involved in change-oriented tasks at an early stage, and clearly separate the change process into beginning, middle, and ending phases.

You sometimes need to develop other standards for casework with involuntary clients. For instance, service duration may be affected by events over which you and the client have no control (e.g., the client is discharged from a hospital) or you may be obligated to follow a mandated function (e.g., the court may impose a time limit on treatment). Even in these cases, however, you might be able to use time-limits selectively to help the client achieve circumscribed goals.

G. Formulating the Treatment/Service Contract

The formulation of a treatment contract or service contract takes place right after you and the client have finished selecting the treatment goals and interventions. (Some practitioners and agencies use the terms "service agreement," "treatment plan," "intervention plan," "case plan," or "individual or family support plan" rather than the terms treatment contract or service contract; often these terms are used interchangeably.)

All terms of the treatment/service contract you formulate with a client should be consistent with the client's capacities, your skill, and, if you work at an agency, the agency's mission. The contract reflects an explicit commitment by you and the client to pursue a mutually agreed-on course of action, but, unless it is written into a court order, the contract is not considered to be legally binding. In the fields of child protection and probation, it is common for a service contract to be incorporated into a court order.

Note that developing a single time-limited contract may not be practical in case management when you have ongoing responsibility for a client, unless you and the client have defined circumscribed problems of living or concrete needs as goals. In this situation, however, you and the client might develop multiple short-term contracts, with each contract related to specific problems and episodes of treatment.

1. Elements Included in a Treatment/Service Contract: The language and format of contracts vary, but the content is essentially the same whether you are working with an individual, couple, family, or group. You and the client should agree on all elements specified in the contract. At a minimum, a contract should describe the following:

- The problems or concerns to be addressed.

- The goals and objectives of the intervention – i.e., the desired outcome of your (and/or your agency's) service to the client.

- Tasks or activities the client will undertake – i.e., what is to be done by the client? By when?

- Tasks or activities that you will perform – i.e., what is to be done by you and, as relevant, other agency staff? By when?

- Expected duration of the intervention (in weeks or months).

- A schedule of the time and place for interviews or meetings.

- Other people, agencies, and/or organizations who are expected to participate in the intervention and a description of what they will be expected to contribute to it. What services are to be obtained from other agencies? By when? What is to be done by the client's significant others (family, friends, neighbors, etc.)? By when?

Some contracts also cover the following elements: (a) a description of your role and the client's role in the change process (i.e., clarification of the client's expectations and the mutual problem-solving nature of the change process); (b) specific interventions, techniques, and modalities to be used; (c) the means by which progress will be monitored and evaluated; (d) the conditions for renegotiating the contract; (e) the consequences, if any, for not adhering to the plan; and (f) management and office/agency policy items such as the start date, cancellation policies, rescheduling procedures, and fee-related issues.

2. The Fluidity of Contracts: While it's important to close the initial phases of intervention with a clear contract, you should view contracting as a dynamic process. In other words, all of a contract's elements, including goals, timeframes, etc., are fluid and subject to change as the client's situation and needs change.

3. Written Contracts vs. Verbal Contracts: With most clients and in many agencies, a written treatment/service contract is not required. Instead, a less formal, verbal contract or agreement between the worker and client is considered sufficient. Social workers who are likely to use written contracts include those working in public agencies and in the fields of child welfare, developmental disabilities, and probation and parole. Additionally, some social workers who provide psychotherapy use written contracts because they reduce the possibility of misunderstanding and malpractice suits. Other benefits associated with using a written contract include the following: It clarifies points of agreement and disagreement between you and the client, it serves as a basis for demonstrating accountability to the client and your agency, and it can facilitate transfer of the case to another social worker, agency, or program if that becomes necessary.

If you prepare a written contract, you should phrase it in simple, clear language so that the client will understand its terms accurately, and ideally, if a client has a poor understanding of English, you should compose the contract in the client's native language. If a client can't read, you should consider making an audio recording of the contract in addition to preparing a written version. Finally, a written contract should be signed by both you and the client.

4. Recontracting: Once you and a client have agreed on a definition of the problem and established a focus for the intervention, adhering to this focus is necessary for the intervention to be effective. There are instances when you may recontract with a client for additional services, however. For example, if information emerges indicating that the client has another area of concern, you can encourage the client to return for another episode of service to focus on that problem area. Or, if a client doesn't achieve the treatment goals within the established timeframe, you can do one of the following, depending on the reason for not reaching the goals: (a) recontract for a specific number of additional sessions; (b) refer the client to a different agency or practitioner for services; or (c) refer the client for more intensive, long-term treatment in a residential group home or other setting.

H. Treatment Planning for Inpatients

When a client is in a psychiatric facility (or other inpatient setting), a social worker may be a member of his **treatment team**. In this situation, the social worker and other members of the treatment team will play a significant role in selecting the problems to be worked on, but they must also include the patient in this process to the greatest extent possible. In particular, the members of the treatment team must consider the patient's expressed priorities when selecting the targets of treatment. No matter the setting, an individual's motivation to participate in and cooperate with the treatment process depends, in part, on the extent to which treatment addresses his primary needs. The treatment plan developed by the team should define not only the treatment objectives and interventions (e.g., pharmacologic, individual therapy, group therapy), but also who will implement them.

IV. Verbal and Nonverbal Communication Techniques

A. Guidelines for Effective Communication With Clients

The following guidelines are helpful for maximizing the effectiveness of your communications with clients (Sheafor & Horejsi, 2003):

- The verbal messages you convey to clients should be ones you believe will have a beneficial effect on their thinking, feelings, or behavior. Do not criticize or argue with clients because doing so is likely to create a barrier to further communication.

- When making decisions about what verbal messages to convey, consider what you know about the client and his situation, the phase of intervention, the purpose of the interview, and the phase of the interview (i.e., beginning, when you are getting started; middle, when you are doing the main work of the session; or ending, when you are bringing the session to a close).

- Always use clear, simple language that is appropriate to the client (e.g., a child, teenager, college graduate). Do not use professional jargon.

- Think about the client's capacity to receive verbal communications. Sometimes, a client's capacity to receive, as well as send, verbal messages accurately will be diminished by his emotional state or his expectations (e.g., a client may distort a message to meet his emotional needs or avoid discomfort). A client whose sight or hearing is impaired or who has brain damage also may have difficulties with receiving and sending messages accurately.

- Never overwhelm a client with information. Break up a long or complicated message into parts so it will be easier for the client to follow and understand. And, because the middle portion of a message is the part most likely to be distorted by a listener, place the most important points at the beginning and end of a message.

- After conveying a long or complex verbal message, invite the client to ask you questions and give you feedback about you said (e.g., "What I just explained may be confusing. I want to make sure you understand. Would you please repeat to me what you heard me say?").

- Pay attention to a client's nonverbal behavior. Sometimes a client's facial expressions or body language will communicate that he is confused by or disagrees with your verbal message. This can happen following any message, even one that is fairly simple. If so, follow up on your message by saying something like, "I noticed you looked puzzled when I was explaining ...".

- Remember that the client (the person receiving the message) is the one who will assign meaning to your words and nonverbal behavior. Keep in mind that a word may have a different meaning to a client depending on his belief system, life experiences, capacity for abstract thinking, and familiarity with the language being used. Also, pay attention to your body language – make sure that it is congruent with your verbal message.

- When a client communicates a verbal message that is long or seems unclear for any other reason, take steps to verify that you've understood accurately what he meant to say – e.g., "I want to make sure I understand what you've said. Let me repeat what I heard you say. If it sounds as if I've misunderstood, please let know."

B. Gauging the Effectiveness of Your Communications

Continually monitoring and evaluating your communications to a client allows you to eliminate barriers to effective communication. A good way to measure the effectiveness of your messages is to notice a client's verbal and nonverbal responses immediately after you send a message.

According to Hepworth et al. (2006), certain verbal and nonverbal cues are useful for gauging the effectiveness of your messages to clients. A message is probably helpful if clients respond in one of the following ways: they continue to explore the problem and stay on topic; they express pent-up emotions related to the problematic situation; they engage in deeper self-exploration and self-experiencing; they volunteer more personally relevant material spontaneously; they affirm the validity of your message either verbally or nonverbally.

By contrast, a message may be ineffective (too confrontational, poorly timed, or off target) if clients respond in one or more of the following ways: they reject your message either verbally or nonverbally; they change the subject; they ignore the message; they seem confused; they become more superficial, more impersonal, more emotionally detached, or more defensive; they argue or express anger rather than examine the relevance of the feelings involved.

C. Verbal Communication Skills (Verbal Messages)

Verbal messages are helping skills used to assist and encourage clients during every phase of intervention. Examples include asking questions, paraphrasing, reflecting, and empathic responding.

Communication Skills Used to Start a Session

1. Explaining Purpose: At the start of every session, take a few moments to clarify the purpose of the interview and remind the client of your respective roles in the helping process. Then encourage the client to respond to your explanation of the purpose so that he has a chance to ask for clarification or express disagreement. This skill is effective for maintaining structure and direction in the helping process. It can also serve to reduce a client's anxiety or confusion about the change process as a whole or that day's interview.

2. Sessional Contracting: Planning in advance what you intend to address in an interview is important, but you must always remain flexible because changes in the client's situation may cause his priorities to change. Sessional contacting (Shulman, 1981) is a way of "starting where the client is" in which you "reach for between-session data" by asking the client to bring you up-to-date on his situation. This allows you to identify when you should alter the day's interview plan to address new or unexpected issues in the client's life that require attention that day.

Asking Questions

In psychotherapy and other forms of direct practice, social workers use various types of questions to gather needed information and to assist clients in expressing their thoughts and feelings.

1. Types of Questions:

a. Open-Ended and Closed-Ended Questions: Generally, social workers use mostly open-ended questions during therapy sessions. Your questions may become progressively more structured as an interview moves forward, however. Typically, you will ask **open-ended questions** early in an interview (and when introducing a new topic) to allow a client a broad range of responses (e.g., "Tell me about your wife"). As discussion of a topic proceeds, you may begin asking **closed-ended questions** (e.g., "When did your wife file for divorce?"). Generally, closed-ended questions are appropriate whenever you need specific data from a client. They are also useful when a client is confused or overwhelmed and you need to provide additional structure to maintain focus and direction.

b. Narrowing the Focus: A skill called **narrowing the focus** (or **funneling**) involves asking a series of questions designed to help a client describe his concerns or situation with more specificity. For example:

Client: "Everything is falling apart at home."

Social worker: "I'm not sure what you mean by 'falling apart.' What happened?"

Client: "My wife came home from work the other night and threatened to leave me."

Social worker: "What were your feelings and thoughts right after your wife threatened to leave you?"

2. Potential Errors in Questioning Technique: Asking poorly timed or ill-constructed questions usually has a counterproductive effect on the helping process and relationship. Ineffective questioning styles include the following:

Asking too many closed-ended questions: Asking too many closed-ended questions in succession tends to inhibit the free flow of an interview and may make a client feel as though he is being interrogated. Moreover, you may find yourself talking a lot more than the client does.

Stacking questions: This refers to the practice of asking several questions all at once. Stacked questions are confusing and distracting to clients and tend to elicit superficial responses.

Asking leading questions: Leading questions push or pull a client toward a certain response (e.g., "I assume you explained to your wife why you ...?" or "Isn't it true that you were hoping he would lose his temper?"). Clients tend to feel insulted or intimidated by leading questions. In responding to leading questions, some clients feel prompted to lie in order to avoid openly disagreeing with you.

Asking questions with hidden agendas: These are similar to leading questions, but, in this case, you have a deliberate agenda in mind (e.g., "Aren't you too young to move out on your own?"). Such questions can result in resistance, feeble agreement, or diversion to another topic on the part of clients.

Asking "why" questions: "Why" questions (e.g., "Why did you get so upset when …") should be avoided because they basically require clients to justify their behavior, which tends to produce defensiveness. Also, a client may not know or may not be able to explain the "why" of his behavior and may simply guess or offer what he thinks is a socially acceptable answer. Rather than asking "why" questions, you should use questions that focus on the what, where, when, and how of a client's behavior and situation.

Active Listening

Active listening requires you to, first, attend to a client's verbal and nonverbal messages and, then, reflect back what you've heard and observed so that the client will know that his message has been understood accurately. Active listening skills are described below.

1. Using Encouragers: An encourager (also called a **prompt** or **furthering response**) is a single word, short phrase, or nonverbal gesture on your part that encourages a client to continue talking. Encouragers convey your interest in and attention to what the client is saying. Examples include the following:

- Verbal encouragers (or "minimal prompts") are single words or short phrases such as "I see" or "Please go on."

- Nonverbal encouragers include appropriate hand gestures, facial expressions, and nodding your head.

- Accent responses entail repeating in a questioning or emphatic way a phrase or word a client has just used. These responses can be used to convey that you've understood a client's feelings about a topic.

2. Using Clarification: Clarification is used in response to vague or unclear client messages. Using this skill is appropriate whenever you don't understand a client's message, would like a client to become more explicit, or wish to check your understanding of a client's message. Clarification can also help a client to better understand what he has said.

Sometimes, client messages are unclear because they include inclusive terms ("they," "we"), ambiguous phrases, or words with a double meaning ("stoned," "trip"). For example:

Client: "Sometimes, I just want to get away from everything."

Social worker: "Describe for me what you mean by 'getting away from everything'."

The social worker's message in the exchange above is also an example of **seeking concreteness**, a skill used to determine the specific meaning of vague words or phrases that a client has used. Asking a client to define a term he has used ("What do you mean by 'controlling behavior'?") can help you better understand his message and prevent you from having to make assumptions. Seeking concreteness may also be used to elicit specific information from a client that might not otherwise be revealed.

NOTE: As a therapeutic technique, clarification is rooted in psychoanalytic theory – in that context, you would, for example, paraphrase or reflect a client's statements to help him separate his distortions of external events from objective reality. Clarification is also an educational technique. For example, values clarification involves helping clients examine their personal beliefs and ideals and the relationships of those values to their behavior.

3. Paraphrasing: A **paraphrase** is a selective restatement of the main idea of a client's message that resembles his message but is not identical to it. A paraphrase emphasizes the literal meaning of a client's message (the content, rather than affect) and is expressed in fewer words than the client has used. For example:

Client: "I don't want to get so wrapped up in my relationship with my girlfriend that I lose my ability to make my own choices and decisions."

Social Worker: "Your independence is important to you."

Particularly when used in conjunction with responses that highlight a client's feelings, such as empathic responses, paraphrases are effective for encouraging a client to continue expressing himself. They can also be useful for bringing focus to an idea or situation that you would like the client to consider.

4. Using Reflection: The skill of reflection involves repeating or restating something a client has just said with an emphasis on the part of the message that is most helpful. Here are two examples of reflection:

Client: "Everything is so static in my life these days. I need things to change. The new things I try don't work out the way I want them to. If I had a better job, I'd have some money to try more new things."

Social Worker: "You're ready for things to change in your life."

or

Social worker: "You feel frustrated in your efforts to change things."

A key purpose of reflection is to build understanding. Reflection is effective for clarifying and showing clients what their here-and-now feelings are, which encourages them to continue expressing themselves. In this way, reflection helps clients understand their own feelings. Moreover, because reflection demonstrates your understanding of the client's feelings, reflection is also a useful skill for establishing rapport.

a. Reflection of Content and Reflection of Feeling: You may reflect the content and/or feelings of a client's message. The first social worker message in the client-social worker exchange above is an example of **reflecting content**; in the second message, the social worker is **reflecting feeling**.

Reflection of content: In reflecting content, you consider what elements of a client's message are most likely to promote achievement of the interview's goals and then use that content in the reflection; a simple reflection of content will then repeat, verbatim, a key word or phrase from the client's message. (A paraphrase, by contrast, *restates* the essence of the client's message.) Reflecting content is effective for facilitating momentum in an interview because it focuses the discussion productively, demonstrates that you're listening and interested in what the client has to say, and promotes the client's continued self-disclosure and emotional exploration.

Reflection of feeling: In reflecting feeling, you express the feeling, or emotional component, of a client's message. Rather than responding to only the words a client has used, you also infer from those words and from other verbal and nonverbal cues what your client is feeling about information he's disclosing – i.e., you clarify and demonstrate for the client what his feelings are at the moment and encourage his further expression and understanding of those feelings (Barker, 2003). Reflection of feeling is used to further the depth of an interview by addressing what a client is feeling.

b. *Potential Reflection Errors:* Errors in reflecting a client's message can lead him to lose some of his trust and confidence in you. The following reflection errors have been identified by Brammer (1985):

Timing error: Beginning helpers sometimes reflect every client message or wait for a long monologue to finish and then try to capture the whole message in one reflection. For example: *Client:* "Nice weather we're having, eh?" *Social worker:* "You feel happy about the current weather conditions." It's not necessary to reflect every client message; sometimes, a nod or a statement such as "I see," is sufficient for communicating acceptance and understanding of a client's message. For long client statements, using a reflective interruption can be effective for keeping a client focused on his feelings.

Stereotyping error: Another error is to begin every response in the same monotonous way: *Client:* "How come you say 'you feel that ...' after everything I say?" *Social worker:* "You feel that my responses are repetitious ..." You must vary your style of reflecting; otherwise, you may come off as limited or insincere.

Depth error: Sometimes social workers read more, or less, into client messages than is actually there: *Client:* "I don't know if I can spend a year away from her." *Social worker:* "You feel that you can't function at all without her by your side." This type of error may cause a client to lose confidence in your abilities. It may also produce defensive or inhibited expression by the client.

Language error: This error involves using language that is inappropriate to the cultural or educational experience of a client or attempting to use "fashionable" language or slang. The latter can make you come off as phony. For example: *Client:* "I'm so confused. Should I move in with my new girlfriend or stay with the old lady?" *Social worker:* "It seems as if your id is in conflict with your superego."

Fortunately, the above errors are usually not as pronounced as they are presented here. Moreover, as long as you are sincere and interested, clients will tolerate an occasional error. Brammer offers the following guide to avoiding reflection error: (a) Read the total message (stated feelings, nonverbal feelings, and content); (b) select the best mix of content and feelings that is appropriate to the phase of intervention and fulfills the goal of understanding; (c) reflect the experience just perceived; and (d) wait for the client's confirming or denying response to your reflection as a cue about what to do next.

5. Using Summarization: Summarization (summarizing) has several purposes and is used at different times in the intervention process. In all cases, however, its primary purpose is to tie together functionally related elements that occur at different times in the helping process.

Summarization can be used to highlight and pull together elements of what you and a client have discussed during the previous few minutes of an interview, with a focus on what it is most relevant or significant. Summarization may be used in a similar way to recap a lengthy client message. Among other benefits, these uses of summarization are effective for bringing focus to an interview. For example, when a client rambles or brings up many different topics, you can identify one theme and narrow the discussion to focus on that theme.

Summarization can also be used to tie together the factual and emotional components of several client messages, which is useful for helping a client see connections among several ideas or feelings he has expressed. Usually, this entails emphasizing themes or topics a client has repeatedly referred to in the current interview and/or in prior interviews. For example:

> *Client:* "I can't get along with my boss. He's always telling me what to do. I know how to do the job better than he does. It's not fair. This happens to me all the time, with every job I've ever had."
>
> *Social worker:* "It sounds like the main problem you have in jobs is that you don't like bosses who exercise authority over you."

In this example, the social worker has summarized more than one element of a message and appears to be referring to past messages as well.

Finally, summarization may also be used to provide a smooth transition between topics, review progress made during an interview as it draws to a close, recap the highlights of a previous session, and review progress on tasks during the week between sessions. The latter applications are effective for providing focus and continuity between sessions.

6. Exploring Silences: Silence on the part of a client during an interview can mean many different things, and, sometimes, it's important for you to explore and discover that meaning. Guidelines for using the skill of exploring silences include the following:

- You should assess the meaning and function of silence in the context of the specific interview. Your response to a silence should be consistent with the goals of the interview, not based on your personal needs or sense of discomfort.

- Sometimes, no response to silence is appropriate, as when a client is thinking over what you or he just said or is recovering from an emotional moment. Generally, a brief silence is best responded to with polite quietness. If the silence becomes lengthy, you should attempt to explore it using gentle probing (Sheafor & Horejsi, 2003). Sometimes (but not always), a long silence is a sign of resistance.

- Changing the subject when a client is silent usually reflects your own discomfort rather than an objective assessment of what the client needs at that moment. Therefore, you should generally avoid responding to silences with a change of topics. You should also avoid being drawn into a pattern in which you ask questions and a client repeatedly responds with silence. Instead, use gentle probing to attempt to uncover the meaning of the silence for the client.

- If a client's repeated silences in interviews are part of a wider behavioral pattern that he also demonstrates in other interpersonal situations (e.g., passive refusal to cooperate with others), you should help the client recognize this pattern and its effects on him, his relationships, and other people.

Empathic Communication (Empathic Responding)

Empathic communication involves (a) empathic recognition of a client's feelings and (b) demonstrating, through accurate reflection of those feelings, your understanding of the client's inner experiencing. Therefore, demonstrating empathy involves more than merely recognizing a client's feelings; it also involves responding to those feelings in verbal and nonverbal ways that convey to the client your understanding of his inner experiencing. First, you perceive, understand, and experience; then, you respond.

1. Reciprocal and Additive Empathic Responses: In the early stage of helping, **reciprocal** empathic responding is used to prepare a client for a deeper exploration of feelings later in the intervention process. This form of empathy promotes a climate of trust and understanding that enables a client to self-disclose and explore his feelings and problems. At the reciprocal level, your verbal and nonverbal responses convey understanding, but are more or less interchangeable with the client's basic messages: They accurately reflect factual aspects of a client's messages and his surface feelings.

Additive empathic responses are used primarily (although not exclusively) in the action, or middle, phase of the intervention process. Additive empathic responses reach beyond a client's surface feelings – they reflect the full range of surface and underlying feelings and content that have been expressed in and implied by a client's message. Because additive empathy is more interpretive than other forms of empathic responding, it can serve to increase a client's awareness of his thoughts and feelings and new ways of resolving a problem.

2. Levels of Empathic Responding: Hepworth et al. (2006) and others have collapsed the traditional nine-level empathy scale developed by Carkhuff (1969) into five levels, which are described below.

a. Level 1 (low level): Your response communicates little to no awareness or understanding of the client's feelings. For example, with a client who expresses intense frustration with the slow progress of therapy (e.g., "I've done everything, but nothing has changed; this always happens to me"), a Level 1 response might involve giving advice (e.g., "Keep at it, and you're likely to succeed"); offering simplistic or untimely reassurance (e.g., "Don't worry, things will change eventually"); judging or blaming (e.g., "You don't seem to have a positive attitude about the work we're doing"); or changing the subject. Level 1 responses usually impede communication because they come from your frame of reference and are not appropriate to the content or mood of the client's message. Level 1 responses often cause clients to become defensive or confused and discourage clients from exploring or working on their problems.

b. Level 2 (moderately low level): You respond to a client's surface message but omit some of the factual content or feelings it contains; give an overly vague label to a client's feelings (e.g., "I can see that you're upset"); inappropriately qualify a client's feelings (e.g., "You seem kind of frustrated"); or interpret a client's feelings in an inaccurate way (e.g., you respond that a client seems "angry" when he is actually feeling hurt); or your response, while diagnostically on target, is not attuned to what the client has expressed. Although not fully accurate, Level 2 responses demonstrate an effort on your part to understand; therefore, they create less of a barrier to continued exploration and problem-solving work than Level 1 responses do.

c. Level 3 (interchangeable or reciprocal level): Your verbal (and nonverbal) response conveys understanding, but it is more or less interchangeable with the client's obvious message – e.g., "You're very frustrated about the slow progress of change and worried that your efforts may not succeed." Your response accurately reflects the factual content of your client's message, as well as his surface (immediately apparent) feelings. A Level 3 response encourages continued exploratory and problem-focused responses from the client.

d. Level 4 (moderately high level): Your response is somewhat additive – it accurately identifies the client's implicit, underlying feelings and/or subtle aspects of his problem – e.g., "I can see that you're very frustrated with the slow progress of change and worried that your efforts may not succeed, especially since you've been frustrated in the past, as well." By shedding light on the more subtle aspects of a client's message, a Level 4 response helps a client get in touch with somewhat deeper feelings and unexplored meanings and purposes of his behavior. In this way, a Level 4 response can improve a client's self-awareness.

e. Level 5 (high level of empathic responding): Level 5 responses are highly additive. They reflect the full range of surface and underlying feelings and content expressed in and implied by a client's message – i.e., they are highly attuned to a client's moment-by-moment experiencing. In making a Level 5 response, you may connect a client's current feelings and experiencing to previously expressed feelings and experiences or accurately identify implicit themes, patterns, purposes, and/or goals contained in a client's message. For example, "I can see that you're very frustrated with the slow progress of change and worried that your efforts may not succeed, especially since you've been frustrated in the past, as well. You want to be able to trust that your efforts will pay off this time ... " (in this example, the social worker's final remark identifies a goal that was implied in the client's message). Such responses can serve to greatly increase a client's awareness of his thoughts and feelings and of new ways of resolving his problem.

3. Uses of Empathic Responding: Uses of empathic responding with clients include the following:

Establishing a relationship in the first sessions: When you communicate accurate understanding, a client is more willing to self-disclose and explore his thoughts and feelings. He is also more likely to return for further treatment.

Staying in tune with the client: Empathic responding allows you to "start where the client is" and remain in synch with his immediate feelings.

Accurately assessing problems: Additive empathic responding encourages a client's exploration of himself and his problems, which increases your ability to gather information for an accurate assessment.

Responding to nonverbal messages: Empathic responding is effective for conveying your understanding of the feelings expressed by a client's nonverbal communication. By using a reflective response to verbalize those feelings, you encourage the client to explore his feelings and thoughts.

Making a client more receptive to confrontation: Immediately following confrontation, you respond empathically to the client's reaction to your challenge.

Managing obstacles to change: For example, you might monitor a client's verbal and nonverbal messages of resistance and use empathic responding to reflect those messages and encourage discussion about them. Or, if a client rambles or his messages are unproductive, you might use empathic responding to promote structure, direction, and depth in the interview.

Helping a client manage strong feelings: Empathic responses encourage a client to continue expressing intense feelings, and, as a result, he has an opportunity to ventilate his feelings, clarify them, let go of them, and experience different ones. Empathic responses are also effective for moderating a client's intense emotions in the moment and enabling him to attain a more rational and thoughtful state of mind.

Other Verbal Communication Skills

1. Putting Clients' Feelings into Words: Using the skill of putting feelings into words involves articulating what a client is apparently feeling but has stopped just short of expressing in words. Its purpose is to give the client a supportive invitation to verbalize what he is feeling but is reluctant to say out loud.

2. Using and Teaching I-Statements: I-statements (a.k.a. I-messages) are used to send clear and direct messages, thereby reducing the likelihood that the person receiving the message will be put on the defensive. An **I-statement** consists of three elements: (a) a brief, clear description of a behavior engaged in by another person that one is bothered by; (b) the feeling one has experienced as a result of that behavior; and (c) a description of the tangible impact that the behavior has had on oneself or others. An I-statement does not accuse or blame the other person, and it states implicitly that the person making the I-statement trusts the other person to determine what change in his behavior is necessary.

During intervention, I-statements delivered by you to a client are useful for managing situations of confrontation or conflict with a client and turning them into opportunities for the client to grow.

The I-statement can also be taught to clients as a method for helping them deal with interpersonal conflicts, such as those that occur between a parent and child, a husband and wife, etc.

3. Neurolinguistic Programming: Neurolinguistic programming (NLP) is concerned with how people perceive and understand the world. Its advocates examine the "programming" (patterns) created by the interactions among the brain (neuro), language (linguistic), and the body that produce effective and ineffective behavior. NLP includes many techniques and strategies for interpersonal communication that are based, in part, on identifying a person's preferred sensory representations for self-expression and learning.

Practitioners of NLP believe that a therapist's ability to communicate effectively and build rapport with her clients is influenced by her ability to ascertain and then work with a client's dominant, or preferred, sensory mode (i.e., the representational system the client uses the most to think consciously and organize his experience). A client reveals his dominant sensory mode by frequently using certain predicates in his statements, such as, "I see what you mean" (visual), "I hear what you're saying" (auditory), or "That goal is way beyond my reach" (kinesthetic). If you can identify a client's dominant sensory mode, you can then try to match your messages to his mode. For example, "Do you have a clear picture of our plan?" (visual), "Does this plan sound okay to you?" (auditory), or "I think that plan is one we can both get hold of," or "I feel like that plan will work well for you" (kinesthetic).

NOTE: **Kinesthetic** means relating to body sensations, and, in NLP, the term is used to encompass all kinds of feelings, including tactile, visceral, and emotional. Kinesthetics organize their perceptions primarily around feelings and sensations. In their communications, they use words associated with feeling, touch, and "gut" instinct; in their learning, they prefer concrete, multi-sensory experiences.

4. Communicating in Metaphors: The skill of communicating in metaphors – anecdotes, puns, analogies, stories – is associated primarily with Milton Erikson and practitioners of NLP and is particularly useful with clients who tend to resist direct suggestions.

One way of communicating in metaphors is by using **analogies** – you identify an everyday aspect of a client's life that is analogous to his problem and then change the everyday aspect as a way of changing the problem. For instance, in work with a couple that has trouble discussing openly a conflict in their sexual relationship, you could select the topic of dining together at a restaurant as something analogous to sexual relations, and then draw the couple into a discussion about their differing preferences in that area (e.g., where to eat, what to order from the menu, how much money to spend) (Hepworth et al., 2006).

Communication at the End of a Session

1. Setting Time Limits/10-Minute Warnings: The skills of setting time limits and giving 10-minute warnings are useful for encouraging clients to stay focused on high-priority topics during sessions and reminding clients to bring up important or difficult topics before the last few minutes of an interview so that you'll have time to discuss them that day. This also allows you to provide a summary structure which cues the client to move forward with their discussion in a manageable manner.

Using these skills entails saying something like the following to a client: "I see we have to end the session in 10 minutes. Is there anything else you wanted to talk about today?" You may also remind a client of "time limits" at the start of an interview: "Before we start, I want to remind you that we can talk until 1:00 p.m.; I mention this because I want to make sure that we use our time today to talk about the issues that are most important to you" (Sheafor & Horejsi, 2003).

If a client brings up a significant topic just as an interview is about to end, you should remind him that the interview is ending and reassure him that the topic can be discussed the next time you meet. If the topic is one that the client finds difficult to talk about, you may also praise him for raising the topic in order to reinforce his willingness to broach it with you. Of course, if the topic reflects a true emergency that places the client or someone else in immediate danger, then you must address it as a crisis that day.

2. Doorknob Communication: Lawrence Shulman coined the phrase "doorknob communication" to describe any client disclosure of important or difficult information just as a session is about to end. Some experts believe that this behavior reflects an unconscious effort by a client to prolong an interview or set up the therapist for an accusation of indifference (Barker, 2003). Schulman, however, believes that a doorknob communication reflects one of the following: (a) information important to the client that the client has been uncomfortable addressing earlier in the session (e.g., the client wants to inform you about something but doesn't really want to discuss it), or (b) important information that the client did raise earlier in the session, but that you overlooked.

D. Nonverbal Communication

Nonverbal communication includes messages conveyed by means of facial expression, eye movements (including eye contact), gestures, and voice qualities (e.g., tone, pitch, resonance).

1. Observation of Your Clients' Nonverbal Communication: During every phase of intervention, your observations of a client's nonverbal behavior can provide valuable information about his emotions, attitudes, behavior, and mental status. A client's nonverbal behavior can express feelings that he is unwilling or unable to put into words. Nonverbal behavior may also tell you if what a client is saying in words truly reflects what he is thinking and feeling – in some cases, a client's nonverbal behavior will contradict or deny his verbal messages. As noted in Part B of this section, observing a client's nonverbal behavior can also provide information about how the client is receiving or responding to your messages.

2. Monitoring Your Own Nonverbal Communication: Your nonverbal messages, when they are appropriate, can serve many useful purposes in the helping process, including helping clients feel more at ease and assured that you're listening to them and reinforcing desired behaviors. The following guidelines (Sheafor & Horejsi, 2003) can assist you in using nonverbal communication effectively with your clients:

Body positioning: Leaning slightly toward a client communicates interest and acceptance. Ideally, you will face a client at a 90-degree angle since this suggests safety and openness (facing a client directly may communicate aggressiveness). A desk separating you from a client tends to inhibit openness and suggests that you're in a superior position to the client.

Facial expressions: Because facial expressions convey thoughts and emotions (and may reveal that you're saying one thing but thinking another), you should remain aware of your facial expressions at all times when communicating with clients. For example, your facial expression may reveal disapproval of a client even when you're trying hard to convey acceptance.

Arm and hand movements: Arm and hand movements can reveal emotions: (a) Arms and hands at your body's side or in an outreached position suggest openness; crossed legs, arms folded across the chest, and a rigid body suggest defensiveness. (b) Fidgety movements (finger tapping, leg bouncing) suggest impatience, nervousness, or preoccupation. (c) Clenched fists indicate anger or anxiety.

Tone of voice: Tone of voice also reveals feelings: (a) A loud, forceful tone suggests aggressiveness, control, and strength; (b) a meek, barely audible tone suggests withdrawal, fear, and weakness; and (c) a monotonous or flat voice suggests a lack of interest. On the whole, clients tend to prefer a voice tone that is warm, supportive, authentic, and calm, but also firm and serious.

E. Communication With Culturally Diverse Clients

To be able to communicate effectively with all of your clients, you must be familiar with variations in verbal and nonverbal communication patterns when there are cultural differences between you and your client. The following guidelines are also important:

- Proceed slowly and with sensitivity to differences in communication patterns and preferences when reaching for feelings or putting a client's feelings into words. In addition, when you and the client have dissimilar cultural backgrounds, certain words you use may mean something different to the client than they do to you.

- While many social workers consider verbal, emotional, and behavioral expressiveness to be important goals of therapy, these goals may be inappropriate for clients from some cultural groups. For instance, many traditional Asian cultures highly value the restraint of strong emotions and discourage disclosures of intimate personal problems especially to an "outsider." Similarly, some commonly used helping skills, such as reflection, reaching for feelings, or asking for insights, may appear inappropriate to the client.

- If a client lacks fluency with English, but must use English when interacting with you, this will influence how well he is able to articulate his problems, concerns, and needs: (a) When one is needed, you should (with the client's permission) bring in a **professional interpreter**. Don't use a translator who has a dual role with the client – for example, one who is a member of the client's family – because this could jeopardize the effectiveness of the assessment and intervention. (b) If a professional interpreter is not available, simplify your language, proceed slowly, and continuously check to verify that the client has understood you and you have understood the client. (c) If these suggestions are inadequate for facilitating understanding, provide an appropriate referral.

- Be alert to cultural differences in the meaning of nonverbal behaviors and avoid misinterpreting culturally appropriate nonverbal behaviors as indicators of pathology, hostility, rudeness, or lack of attention. For example: (a) For most white Americans, a firm handshake is an appropriate gesture of greeting among both males and females, but, for many Asian/Asian-Americans and Arab/Arab-Americans, a firm handshake suggests aggression. (b) White Americans typically prefer to be about an arm's length from one another during conversations, while people from Asian cultures usually prefer a greater distance, and many people from Hispanic or Arab cultures are accustomed to less distance. (c) Among white Americans, making **eye contact** generally indicates openness and a willingness to communicate, whereas avoiding eye contact is associated with anxiety, an unwillingness to communicate, and, sometimes, dishonesty. In contrast, for many other groups, including Native Americans, Asians/Asian-Americans, and Arabs/Arab-Americans, making direct eye contact is often considered intimidating or disrespectful.

F. Telephone and Written Communications

1. Communication by Telephone: Although communications by telephone tend to be less effective than in-person interactions, as a social worker, you will sometimes need to use the telephone as a tool in your work with clients. Following are some guidelines for telephone communications with your clients.

- Sheafor and Horejsi (2003) recommend that you limit your use of the telephone to situations in which you need a quick response from a client and the matter to be discussed is uncomplicated. If the matter is not critical and/or if the matter is complicated or involves many details, it's better to communicate about it in person or, if need be, in writing.

- If you leave voicemail messages for a client, never reveal information in a message that would violate the client's confidentiality, as the message may be heard by someone other than the client. Ideally, you should discuss this matter with a client beforehand, so that you know whether and how the client would like you communicate with him via telephone.

2. Written Communications: All of your written letters and e-mails to clients (and others) should be clear, concise, and professional looking. Letters should usually be typed, although short handwritten notes may be appropriate when writing to clients whom you know well. Other guidelines for written communications include the following:

- Use proper titles (Mr., Ms., Mrs., Miss, Dr., etc.). Use first names only when writing to children or individuals with whom you have a close relationship. Ask adult clients how they would prefer to be addressed. Don't use first names unless you have their permission to do so.

- Don't include information that would violate a client's confidentiality if the letter or e-mail may be read by someone other than the person to whom you are writing. Be aware that letterhead information or information on an envelope (such as the name of your agency) may reveal to others a client's involvement with you or your agency.

V. Intervention Techniques

This section focuses on techniques used in practice to achieve the established goals and objectives of intervention. Most of these techniques are used in the action phase of intervention when you, the client, and others complete the tasks defined in the treatment plan in order to bring about the desired outcome.

Broad categories of intervention used in practice include the following (Woods and Hollis 1990):

Sustainment interventions: These are relationship-building activities used primarily in the initial phases of the change process to reduce a client's feelings of anxiety or guilt, increase his self-esteem, and instill a sense of hope. Examples include acceptance, reassurance, and encouragement.

Direct influence interventions: Direct influence interventions are used to encourage a specific behavior in a client. Examples include providing advice or information, assigning homework, and using behavioral techniques.

Ventilation procedures: Ventilation procedures, such as techniques that encourage verbalization, are used to assist clients to identify and appropriately express their feelings. They are effective for establishing a foundation for self-exploration and rational discussion in your work with a client (i.e., once verbalized, a client's emotions become more accessible to support and reassurance from you).

Social interventions: These interventions involve a client's significant others and are useful for reducing environmental stressors and exposing the client to new social supports and resources. Examples include teaching communication skills, offering family therapy, and providing peer support or peer confrontation. Whenever you work with a client's significant others, your goal should be to find solutions that are of mutual advantage to the client and his significant others.

Social resource provision: Social resource provision involves linking clients with the community resources, services, and opportunities they need, want, and can use. This form of intervention is important for addressing discrepancies between a client's needs and the resources and opportunities available to him. Such discrepancies (i.e., client-environment mismatches) frequently play a role in a client's difficulties.

This section focuses on the first three categories of intervention. Social interventions and social resource provision are reviewed later in this chapter.

A. Information Giving and Advice Giving

Information giving and advice giving are used to enhance a client's problem-solving capacity by providing him with needed information and guidance.

1. Information Giving:

a. Definition of Information Giving: Information giving involves providing a client with information he needs in order to formulate alternatives, make a decision, or carry out a task. With information giving, a client feels free to choose whether and how he will use the information.

b. Examples of Information Giving: Examples of information giving include the following:

- You may **normalize** a client's symptoms or responses to events. Normalizing is used to place a client's problem in a new context by defining it as expectable or predictable rather than pathological. With the parents of a defiant toddler, for example, you could explain the behaviors that are expected during this developmental stage.

- You may provide a client with information about his problem. This may take the form of **psychoeducation**, in which you teach a client and his family about the nature of the client's mental illness, including its etiology, progression, consequences, prognosis, treatment, and alternatives.

- You may provide a client instruction and training about appropriate behavior (e.g., skills training related to parenting, problem-solving, anger management, assertiveness, or communication). Instruction and training can help a client learn about behavior that is appropriate in a specific situation and is typically used when a client is unable to respond adaptively or in a manner that enables him to achieve a desired goal. Role-playing or some other rehearsal strategy is often involved.

c. Guidelines for Information Giving: Guidelines for using the technique of information giving include the following:

- Information giving is most appropriate when the information you share addresses a need that the client has expressed. Information giving should not be used as a strategy for persuading a client to engage in a specific behavior.

- When giving information, adapt what you say to the client's educational background, intelligence, and fluency with the language you are using. If you think it likely that a client will misunderstand the information, seek his permission to also give the information to his family or others who can help him use it effectively.

- Consider a client's state of mind before giving him information (e.g., a client who is feeling anxious or overwhelmed may not understand or remember the information or instructions you provide).

- Provide information or instructions in an organized and step-by-step manner. If you provide complicated instructions, consider writing them down for the client.

- Don't assume that a client understands the information you share. Watch for signs of misunderstanding, invite him to ask questions, and ask him to repeat back what he heard you say.

2. Advice Giving:

a. Definition of Advice Giving: Advice giving involves offering statements that recommend what a client should do – i.e., with advice giving, the client clearly senses your preference.

b. Guidelines for Advice Giving: Guidelines for using the technique of advice giving include the following:

- When giving advice (a) phrase the advice in a manner that conveys the message, "this is what I would do" or "this is what others have done"; (b) explain your reasoning; and (c) always leave it up to the client to decide what to.

- Whether advice giving is appropriate or not depends primarily on the purpose of your interaction with the client: (a) Advice giving is often appropriate and necessary when the purpose of your interaction relates to referral, brokering, or advocacy. (b) Advice giving is rarely appropriate in psychotherapy unless the client is in crisis. (c) Advice giving *may* be appropriate, and necessary, when a client is too overwhelmed or confused to choose his own direction. This may happen when a client is in a state of acute crisis. When a client is so anxious that he can't think clearly or make decisions, you may assume a more active role than you might otherwise take by recommending specific behaviors or ways of thinking.

- Don't give advice until you know that a client genuinely wants your opinion or recommendations. Sometimes, you'll know that the time is right because a client asks you directly for advice. If not, you can test a client's openness to advice by asking a question such as, "May I tell you what other people often do in this situation?"

- Avoid giving advice in response to direct client questions, such as, "Should I quit my job?", "Should I leave my girlfriend?" You don't want to promote dependency in clients who need to take responsibility for their own decision making. Moreover, when a client is struggling with a decision, your role is to help him weigh his alternatives, not to persuade him toward one decision or the other. In addition, clients who are manipulative are likely to hold you responsible if they follow your advice and things don't turn out well. It's even possible that you could face legal consequences if a client suffers harm as a result of following your advice.

- Never give advice on a topic outside your scope of competence or practice. For example, while you might be qualified to provide very basic information to clients about certain legal or medical issues, you should *never* advise clients on these matters: Clients wanting advice about legal issues (e.g., how to write a will, how to regain custody of their children) or medical decisions (e.g., whether to stop taking a medication) should be referred to appropriate professionals or clinics.

B. Encouragement, Reassurance, and Universalization

The techniques of encouragement, reassurance, and universalization can improve a client's problem-solving capacity by helping him overcome self-doubt or uncertainty.

When providing **encouragement**, you make statements that express your confidence in a client's ability to overcome an obstacle. Any encouragement you provide a client must be both genuine and individualized to the client's situation.

Using **reassurance** is appropriate when a client is uncertain about his decisions or actions and his decisions or actions are, in fact, reasonable and realistic. Your statements of reassurance must be based in reality (if not, a client may conclude that you don't fully understand the situation or why he is distressed by it); and you should connect your statements of reassurance to facts (e.g., "You've successfully run two meetings at work over the past month so, even though you're feeling anxious right now, I'm confident that you can manage tomorrow's meeting, as well."). When clients are highly anxious or distressed, it can be tempting to say something like, "Don't worry; I'm sure everything will be okay." Simplistic statements of reassurance must be avoided, however, because they tend to make clients feel judged, criticized, and/or patronized.

When applying the technique of **universalization** (a form of reassurance), you make statements that explain to a client that his thoughts, feelings, or behavior are similar to those of other people in similar circumstances. The purpose is to counteract a client's perception that his feelings or behaviors are strange or abnormal.

C. Reframing

Reframing (a.k.a. relabeling or redefining) is used to help a client change the meaning he gives to an event, behavior, or life experience by gently persuading him that it can be viewed in a different and more positive light. When a client is able to perceive something in a new way, he usually begins to also feel and behave differently. Specific ways of using reframing include the following:

- Offer a client a new perspective on an event, behavior, or experience that he views in a negative way.

- Encourage a client to come up with alternative interpretations on his own. This approach helps a client see for himself that there are several ways of interpreting an event, behavior, or experience.

- Redefine a problem behavior as a positive behavior that has been taken to an extreme. For instance, overprotectiveness on the part of a parent can be reframed as valid concern (a strength) that has gone too far. This form of reframing can be effective for mitigating a client's defensiveness as well as for giving him hope that he can change a target behavior (i.e., a client may feel less overwhelmed if he perceives that he needs to moderate a behavior rather than eliminate it).

Reframing is particularly useful in work with clients dealing with interpersonal conflicts and is used frequently in work with families.

D. Reflective Discussion

Reflective discussion is used to help a client gain, or regain, a sense of control through achieving a better cognitive grasp on reality. This goal supports a number of ego functions that can facilitate better problem solving and coping by a client (e.g., judgment, reality testing). For example, the increased understanding that results from reflective discussion makes it easier for a client to prioritize his problems and identify and weigh alternatives for resolving them.

Some of the techniques used in reflective discussion include paraphrasing, clarification, reflection of feelings, and summarizing – these were described earlier in this chapter. Other skills and techniques used in reflective discussion are described below.

1. Exploratory Interviewing: Exploratory interviewing involves asking questions intended to direct a client's attention to specific aspects of his person-situation complex. Examples of questions include open-ended questions and closed-ended questions, which were described earlier in this chapter. Questions may also take the form of "leads," which are used to invite or encourage a client to talk about a specific aspect of himself or his experience. Leads may be direct or indirect. An **indirect lead** helps a client express himself within broad parameters:

Client: "For the first time in months, I'm feeling good today."

Social worker: "Please go on."

A **direct lead**, on the other hand, specifies the nature of the topic, thought, or feeling you would like a client to talk about:

Client: "My wife told me she thinks I hide behind drugs so that I won't have to share my true feelings with her."

Social worker: "Tell me more about your wife."

or

Social worker: "How did this make you feel?"

Indirect leads are typically used to open interviews and invite clients to engage in general exploration, while direct leads are used when a specific client response or reaction is desired.

2. Explanation: Using the technique of explanation involves presenting a client with meanings, motives, or reasons underlying a problem or event. Explanation involves less inference than interpretation (interpretation is described below).

3. Suggestion: Suggestion entails encouraging a client to look at a problem or event in a specific, new way. This technique is used, for example, in reframing or when helping a client learn to attribute a new meaning to a situation or experience.

4. Interpretation (Interpretive Responses): An interpretive response is one that encompasses not only what a client has actually verbalized but also an inference you've derived from the implicit parts of his message. It offers a client an explanatory statement that responds to something about his thinking or behavior that he is not aware of, with the goal of increasing his self-understanding and understanding of the problem, fostering his insight, and/or helping him make connections that he hasn't seen on his own. This assists a client to view a problem from a different perspective, thereby opening the door to new solutions.

Note that while helping skills such as paraphrasing, reflecting, and clarifying all remain within the client's frame of reference, interpretation goes a step further by providing a new frame of reference for the client to consider. For instance, interpretation may involve presenting an hypothesis about a cause-effect relationship or other significant meanings in a client's actions, thoughts, or feelings:

Client: "My life is so boring right now. Some good drugs and a few bucks would sure set me right."

Social worker: "It seems as if you believe you need money and drugs to feel good about yourself."

A client may be defensive at first when you offer an interpretive response; however, a relevant and responsive attempt to point out the source of a client's difficulties often turns out to be therapeutic. In particular, offering relevant and timely interpretations is an important way of facilitating a client's **insight**.

Guidelines for using the technique of interpretation include the following:

- Until you have a good working relationship with the client, use interpretive responses sparingly.

- You should use interpretive responses only when a client is engaged in self-exploration or is ready to do so (although you may also use them before that, to identify a client's strengths and goals). A client must be ready to receive an interpretation and accept the insight it provides. Do not share an interpretation if the related material is still far removed from a client's awareness. When an interpretive statement is offered too early, clients usually reject it as meaningless and inaccurate.

- Avoid making several interpretive statements in a row because a client needs time to assimilate what you have said.

- Phrase interpretive responses in hypothetical terms.

- Observe a client's reaction after offering an interpretive response in order to determine the accuracy of your response; respond empathically to the client's response if it is negative.

Many of the guidelines for using interpretation also apply to using additive empathy, since an additive empathic response is also interpretive. (Additive empathy was described earlier in this chapter, in the section on Communication Techniques.)

5. Facilitating Connections: This technique involves asking questions, making comments, and using metaphors to help a client make connections between past and current events and relationships and between the therapeutic relationship and his other interpersonal relationships.

E. Confrontation

1. Definition of Confrontation: When using the technique of confrontation (also called **challenge**), you engage in respectful and directed efforts to help a client recognize that he is using distortions, deceptions, denials, avoidance, or manipulations that are getting in the way of desired change (Sheafor & Horejsi, 2003). You challenge and invite the client to examine a thought or behavior that is self-defeating or harmful to others and to take action to change it. Here's an example:

Client: "He goes out every weekend and gets drunk. When he's home, he's hung-over. I really don't mind, he deserves some fun, but I feel that our relationship should mean more to him than it does."

Social worker: "First you said you don't mind his behavior, then you said you feel your relationship is not as important to him as it is to you."

Confrontation may be used in a similar manner to help a client see his role in a problem or to point out patterns in a client's behavior. Behavioral patterns often emerge gradually during the course of your work with a client (e.g., patterns of impulsive or fearful behavior). If you notice a pattern, you should call it to a client's attention if it is interfering with his problem-solving ability.

2. Guidelines for Using Confrontation Effectively: Guidelines for using confrontation include the following:

- Use confrontation in an atmosphere of warmth, caring, and concern: (a) Do not use confrontation until you and the client have a good working relationship. Confrontation will be effective only if a client feels respected by you and has similar feelings toward you. (b) Do not confront or challenge a client when you are feeling angry. Confrontation must come from a place of genuine concern for a client; it should never be an expression of anger or frustration.

- For confrontation to be effective, it must be used at a time when a client seems ready to hear and consider your message. Avoid using confrontation when a client is emotionally upset. For example, if you challenge a client who is feeling depressed, he may feel criticized and withdraw from the relationship.

- Pair a challenging message with a positive observation about the client (e.g., one that recognizes his strengths) and follow it with empathic responsiveness.

- A challenging message should be descriptive and nonjudgmental. When confronting a client, include a detailed description of his self-defeating or negative behavior and concrete examples of how it creates problems for him.

F. Cognitive Restructuring Techniques

Cognitive restructuring techniques help clients manage their emotional reactions and behave more effectively through modifying their distorted cognitions, or errors in logic, particularly their distorted interpretations of reality. The use of these techniques is based on theories underlying the cognitive therapies which assume that how people interpret and think about an event or experience (their self-talk) gives rise to an emotional reaction, which, in turn, gives rise to behavior. **Self-talk** refers to the messages that a person gives himself. These messages always reflect a person's unique interpretation of events and experiences.

Helping a client modify his cognitive distortions usually involves, first, helping him become aware of his self-talk, and then, encouraging him to use cognitive restructuring techniques. Two examples of cognitive restructuring techniques are self-instruction and visualization. With **self-instruction**, you ask a client to repeat to himself several times a day and whenever he feels upset statements that are incompatible with his negative self-talk. These statements should be realistic given the client's situation and capacities, should be specific, and should be tied directly to his concerns. With **visualization**, you have a client repeatedly imagine an event he is worried about and mentally rehearse the steps necessary to handle the event successfully. The images a client visualizes should involve action and be as detailed as possible.

G. Behavioral Techniques

Behavioral techniques which are based in behavior theory are effective for modifying the frequency, intensity, or duration of a behavior. They are used when the goal is to either strengthen (increase) or weaken (decrease) a particular target behavior.

Sometimes, you will use behavioral techniques in sessions as direct interventions to eliminate target symptoms (e.g., exposure techniques, relaxation training) or modify target behaviors (e.g., behavioral rehearsal). During sessions, you may also use subtle or direct reinforcers or punishers to set and maintain appropriate limits or influence a client's behavior with you. Examples include providing or withholding attention, smiling, and providing information when a client requests it. Setting appropriate limits in a client's relationship with you can be effective for helping the client learn to set better interpersonal boundaries in the real world.

In other cases, you and a client will target specific behaviors for change (increase or decrease) and develop, implement, and monitor a behavior modification plan. This often includes training the client and, where relevant, parents, teachers, and others, to implement the plan in the client's natural contexts.

In this section, we review three behavioral techniques commonly used in direct social work practice – modeling, behavioral rehearsal, and behavioral contracting. For information on other behavioral techniques based on classical or operant conditioning principles (e.g., assertiveness training, Premack principle), see Section XI in this chapter.

1. Modeling: In modeling (vicarious learning), clients learn through imitation and observation of others. In sessions with clients, you may demonstrate behaviors and skills that a client (an individual, couple, or family) needs to learn, such as communication skills, assertiveness, parenting skills, or self-disclosure. You may also arrange for a client to be exposed to other models by, for example, referring him to group therapy, a self-help group, or an activity group.

2. Behavioral Rehearsal: Behavioral rehearsal (a.k.a. behavior rehearsal) is used to help a client learn a new behavior so that he can better cope with a specific interpersonal situation, such as a job interview. The technique relies on modeling, role-playing, and coaching to provide a client with opportunities to practice the new behavior in a protected environment before trying it out in the real world: (a) First, the client describes or demonstrates how he would usually behave in the problem situation, and you make suggestions about how he could handle the situation more effectively; (b) you and the client then use role-playing to demonstrate the suggested behavioral changes (you often take the role of the client at this time, but a client may enact the behavior if he feels ready to do so and understands the changes); and (c) last, you provide feedback about the role-play performance (e.g., identify positive aspects, make suggestions for improvement). As necessary, the role-play is repeated, incorporating the feedback, and the client practices the behavior until he is satisfied with his performance. You may assign homework to further the client's learning of the behavior.

Behavioral rehearsal is effective for reducing a client's anxiety and building his confidence so that he can handle a situation effectively. Its limitation is that, sometimes, a client has trouble generalizing the new behavior, often because the real-life situation presents problems that could not be anticipated during the role-plays. Behavioral rehearsal may be used with individual clients, as well as in a group format.

3. Behavioral Contracting: A behavioral contract is an agreement between two or more people designed to bring about a change in a person's behavior through the reciprocal exchange of rewards or positive reinforcements. There are two forms of behavioral contracting: With a **contingency contract**, you arrange for a positive consequence to follow performance of a particular behavior by a client; and with a **reciprocal behavioral contract**, you arrange for the members of a dyad (e.g., husband-wife) to each agree to reward the other for the performance of a desired behavior.

Any behavior that can be described clearly can become the target of a behavioral contract. The contract should describe what a client(s) will do rather than what he won't do, and the target behavior should be easy to observe so that you and the client(s) will be able to agree about whether the behavior was completed. Ideally, it should be possible to observe even partial success or a client's genuine effort to complete the behavior.

H. Role-Playing, Empty Chair, Role-Reversal, Psychodrama, and Sculpting

1. Role-Playing: In role-playing, a client rehearses behaviors that will be useful in a particular situation so that he can meet a goal or fulfill an expectation. He practices the behavior in your presence and then receives feedback from you. When used in this way, as a part of behavioral rehearsal, role-playing is effective for increasing a client's sense of self-efficacy.

Modeling through role-playing is an effective means of helping a client learn a new behavior vicariously and reducing his anxiety about performing the behavior. When you model a behavior, you often ask the client to play the role of the other person involved in the problem situation, which helps the client learn to anticipate the other person's behavior.

2. The Empty Chair Technique: The purpose of the empty chair technique (a.k.a. double-chair technique) is to help a client understand his feelings toward himself or a significant other. In particular, the technique is useful for exploring unfinished buisness and clarifying the issues involved in an interpersonal conflict – by gaining this clarity, a client is able to view the conflict in a different light and has insight into why he is feeling and behaving the way he is. You may use this technique whenever you recognize a specific conflict that needs to be explored with the client.

Using the empty chair technique involves the following procedures: (a) Place an empty chair opposite the client. (b) Ask the client to speak to the chair, explaining to it (the other person or the situation) his perceptions and/or feelings. (c) Ask the client to sit on the chair himself (to assume the role of the other person or the situation) and respond to what was just said to the chair. The client may switch back and forth several times during this dialogue. (d) Use interview skills to explore the dialogue as it develops.

3. Role Reversal: Role-reversal is used to help clients understand the perceptions and feelings of significant others. It involves having one person (e.g., a spouse, a parent) take on the perspective of another person (e.g., the other spouse, the child) in an effort to better understand him or her.

Role-reversal is particularly useful in couples and family therapy and is indicated whenever one or both parties in a relationship have little or no awareness of how the other one feels. In a conjoint session, you will usually introduce role-reversal by focusing the clients' attention on a discussion or argument they repeatedly have without resolution. Using role-reversal then involves the following steps: (a) First, have the clients role-play the discussion or argument taking the other person's role (often, you'll ask the clients to physically change seats or chairs, so that they are seated in the other person's chair). (b) As the role-play develops, use interview skills that encourage the clients to express their thoughts and feelings. (c) After a few minutes, have each client return to his or her own perspective (his or her own chair). (d) Discuss the content of the role-reversal with the clients, with a focus on helping each party understand how the other one thinks and feels about the conflict and why.

You may also assign role-reversal as homework (e.g., have a couple reverse roles for 30 minutes at home before their next session with you).

4. Psychodrama: Psychodrama, a technique used primarily in group therapy, involves the use of dramatic techniques (such as role-reversal) through which clients are asked to act out past, present, or anticipated life situations (usually socially stressful situations) and roles in order to gain new and deeper understanding and achieve catharsis. A client sometimes plays the part of himself and sometimes takes on the role his antagonist, allowing him to act out his inner feelings and relieve his anxiety, practice handing the situation more effectively, and experience the situation from another person's perspective. Group members also play roles, so that all members have the chance to relate to one another from different perspectives.

5. Family Sculpting: In family sculpting (or family sculpture), family members position themselves (or objects that represent them) in physical space in a way that reflects their relations and roles within the family system. The process usually involves having each family member, one at a time, create his or her own "sculpture."

Sculpting can be useful for revealing family members' differing perceptions and feelings, in particular each member's view of the emotional closeness or distance between family members. Although sculpting is a highly subjective technique, it often provides important insight into how family members perceive their own and one another's roles and positions within the family.

Sculpting differs from psychodrama in that the emphasis in the former is on the interactive dimensions within the system, rather than on emotional release or discharge.

I. Homework Assignments

Homework refers to activities that you ask a client to perform between sessions. Typically, you will assign a client to complete specific tasks or activities designed to help him learn a new behavior or skill, particularly one that needs to be practiced in his natural environment.

You should provide clear and precise instructions, often in writing, when giving a homework assignment to a client.

VI. Referral, Case Management, and Case Advocacy

Any form of social/environmental resource provision – be it referral, the development of resources, case management, or case advocacy – can reduce stress in a client's life and provide him with opportunities for personal growth and more adaptive social functioning.

Specific ways of improving a client's environment through social resource provision include the following:

- Enhance resources in a client's home (e.g., day care, homemaker services) and help a client obtain needed material items (e.g., contact agencies that provide concrete goods).

- Develop and enhance a client's support systems (e.g., mobilize natural helping networks); refer a client to formal or societal resource systems (e.g., a self-help group, a social agency, community resources such as recreation centers or growth groups); and involve volunteers to extend available social work services.

- Move a client to a new environment. This may be justified in cases involving child maltreatment, elder abuse, spousal abuse, an unmanageable child or teenager (e.g., one who poses a threat to others), an unusual need that requires special care (e.g., severe emotional disturbance, physical illness or disability), or the loss of housing.

- Improve the responsiveness of organizations to a client's needs – e.g., help make services more accessible, promote a more humane delivery of services, or confirm that there is equal access to services.

- Improve interactions between organizations and institutions involved in a client's case. For example, maintain ongoing linkages directed at more effectively meeting a client's needs, mediate between two resources that a client needs, or help a client move from one environment to another (e.g., from a hospital to the community).

- Develop a new resource if a resource a client needs is unavailable. You should work with the client to develop the resource when a needed resource does not exist.

- Use advocacy and social action.

A. Resource Systems

Barker (2003) defines resource systems as, "the biopsychosocial and environmental sources of the material, emotional, and spiritual needs required for a person to survive, to realize aspirations, and to cope with life tasks" (p. 370). There are three basic types of resource systems: informal, formal, and societal.

1. Informal Resource Systems: Informal resource systems (a.k.a. "natural" resource systems) include family members, friends, coworkers, neighbors, and others who provide emotional, social, and more tangible kinds of support. Informal resource systems are not publicly incorporated as legal entities to deliver services, but they perform a wide range of mutual support activities within communities.

2. Formal Resource Systems: Formal resource systems are those in which people hold memberships. Examples include social or fraternal organizations (e.g., Rotary Club, League of Women Voters), professional associations, labor unions, and congregations. These organizations (sometimes called "voluntary associations") are largely autonomous and are composed of local people who come together voluntarily to promote a shared interest or achieve a social purpose. The organization may function, in part, to enhance the well-being of its members by providing support; if the association is strong, it may also influence non-members in positive or negative ways. Voluntary membership organizations often serve as a bridge between a community's informal and societal resource systems. Because voluntary organizations are membership groups that may require members to pay dues, their boundaries are more clearly defined than those of informal groups.

3. Societal Resource Systems: Societal resource systems are institutionalized organizations or services such as private and public social service agencies, family service agencies, governmental units (e.g., a housing authority, probation and parole divisions, health clinics), and educational organizations (e.g., public library, public schools). These resource systems are established to provide specific kinds of assistance to community members.

Social security programs are important societal resources in the United States. The original Social Security Act and the current version of the act, as amended, encompass many social welfare and social insurance programs, such as those listed below:

- **TANF** (Temporary Assistance to Needy Families) provides assistance and work opportunities to needy families by granting states federal funds and flexibility to develop and implement their own welfare programs.

- **Medicaid** is a federal- and state-government funded program that provides payment for medical and hospital services to families and individuals who can't afford them. Federal law requires states to cover certain groups (mandatory eligibility groups) and gives them the flexibility to cover other groups (optional eligibility groups). States must cover categorically needy individuals which usually includes recipients of Supplemental Security Income (SSI) and families with dependent children receiving cash assistance, as well as other mandatory low-income groups such as pregnant women, infants, and children with incomes less than a specified percent of the federal poverty level. (See also the review of the Affordable Care Act in Section VIII of Human Development, Diversity, and Behavior.) States must also cover certain low-income Medicare beneficiaries. Last, the Children's Health Insurance Program (**CHIP**) provides health coverage to eligible children through both Medicaid and separate CHIP programs. CHIP is administered by states, according to federal requirements, and funded jointly by states and the federal government.

- **Medicare** (Health Insurance for the Aged and Disabled) is a federal entitlement program that guarantees health care benefits (health insurance coverage) to most people over age 64, to some people with disabilities under age 65, and to people of all ages with end-stage renal disease (permanent kidney failure treated with dialysis or a transplant). Eligibility for Medicare for a person without a disability is based on reaching age 65 rather than on the person's need. Part A Medicare (compulsory Hospital Insurance or "HI") is the inpatient portion of benefits under the Medicare program, covering beneficiaries for inpatient hospital, home health, hospice, and limited skilled nursing facility services. Part B Medicare (a voluntary program of Supplementary Medical

Insurance or "SMI") is the outpatient portion of benefits under the Medicare program, covering beneficiaries for physician services, medical supplies, and other outpatient treatment. Part D Medicare refers to stand-alone plans that add prescription drug coverage to the Original Medicare Plan and to some Medicare Cost Plans and Medicare Private Fee-for-Service Plans.

- Supplemental Security Income (**SSI**) is a federal income supplement program funded by general tax revenues (not by social security, or FICA, taxes). It is designed to help aged, blind, and disabled people who have little or no income. It provides cash to meet basic needs for food, clothing, and shelter. Basic requirements for SSI eligibility involve citizenship, income, financial resources, age, and disability.

- Disability Insurance (**DI**) provides for the economic needs of individuals who can no longer earn an income because of chronic disability (lasting at least one year or expected to result in death) or incapacity. Others who may qualify for DI include people with HIV infection and disabled children. DI pays benefits to individuals and certain members of their family if they are insured, meaning that they've worked long enough and paid social security taxes. DI is also known as SSDI, which stands for Social Security Disability Insurance.

Examples of other social security programs include Old-Age (Retirement), Survivors, and Disability Insurance (OASDI, which is commonly known by the name "Social Security"); Unemployment Insurance; Workers' Compensation; the Food Stamp Program; the WIC program; General Assistance; Public Housing; Section 8 Programs; the Earned Income Tax Credit (EITC) for low-income workers; and veteran's benefits. If you are unfamiliar with any of these programs, you can find details about them in the Glossary provided with these materials.

NOTE: The terms "formal" and "informal" are sometimes used in different ways when discussing "resource systems" versus "resources." The term "formal resources" describes resources available from societal resource systems (for example, social security programs), while "informal resources" refer to family, friends, neighbors, fellow congregation members, self-help groups, etc. Don't worry about this distinction for the exam. No matter what terminology is used in questions, the context of the question will enable you to understand what the examiners are asking about.

B. Social Networks

1. Key Definitions: In social work, **networking** refers to efforts to develop and enhance the social linkages between people by (a) strengthening the quality of existing networks, (b) establishing new networks, (c) creating linkages among various networks to engender more competent support, and (d) mobilizing networks.

The term **network** describes any informal or formal linkage of people or organizations that share resources, skills, knowledge, and contacts with one another. **Social networks**, in particular, are made up of "individuals or groups linked by a common bond, shared social status, similar or shared functions, or geographic or cultural connection" (Barker, 2003, p. 405). Social networks develop and discontinue on an ad hoc basis depending on specific needs and interests.

2. Types of Social Networks:

a. Natural Social Networks: Natural social networks consist of family, friends, neighbors, and coworkers who exchange emotional support and other resources in times of need. When effective, they make it unnecessary for an individual to turn to institutionalized services offered by social agencies. Because geographically dispersed social networks depend on linkages such as transportation, they may be vulnerable in times of crisis.

Some authors distinguish among the following types of natural social networks:

- Close-knit networks are intimate primary groups. They consist of mutual friendships and kinship connections and provide important social support to individuals.

- Helping social networks allow individuals in a community to give and receive reciprocal help for specific problems and they exist whether a person uses them or not. They differ from close-knit networks because their concerns are specialized (i.e., they are problem-anchored), their membership is heterogeneous, and their members may lack other common values. A similar term, **natural helping network**, is used to describe the informal linkages and relationships between (a) individuals who voluntarily provide services to people in need and (b) those to whom they provide the services.

- Loose-knit (radial) social networks are temporary, heterogeneous (their members have different social statuses and don't feel as though they have a common bond), and nonintimate (their members interact only in superficial ways). These networks operate primarily in work settings and neighborhoods. Because they are flexible (i.e., they can change according to the demands of social and geographic mobility), they are important in urban settings.

b. Self-Help Groups: Self-help groups consist of nonprofessional people who come together voluntarily to help one another with a shared personal or social problem or need. These groups usually meet without the direction of a professional. The importance of self-help groups varies – generally, community members who struggle to have their needs recognized or who lack adequate access to societal resource systems are more likely to turn to these groups for support of their coping efforts. Note that the less formal self-help groups described here differ from self-help *organizations* such as Alcoholics Anonymous (AA), Batterers Anonymous, Parents Without Partners (PWP), Overeaters Anonymous (OA), etc. The latter groups are more formally structured and often have chapters throughout the United States.

c. Groups of Formal Organizations: Most social agencies are part of an interorganizational network of agencies that provide similar services to similar population groups. When relations among these organizations are managed effectively, this situation can be the basis for growth and professional and social development. Without effective management, however, this situation can result in competition and conflict among organizations over task and domain. (Ways for agencies to link with other organizations are described in later in this chapter, in Section XXI.)

C. Referral and the Referral Process

1. Why Social Workers Make Referrals: A referral is a type of intervention intended to help a client better address or deal with a specific problem, concern, or request. There are a variety of situations in which a social worker would ordinarily make a referral, including the following:

- One or all aspects of a client's case fall outside your scope of practice (license) or scope of competence (training, experience, etc.). For example, (a) you are not competent to work with a client due to a lack of experience with his problem, a difference in race, sexual orientation, or SES, or the nature of the client's diagnosis; or (b) the client needs a particular service that is outside the scope of your practice as a social worker or that you are not qualified by training or experience to provide. Examples of services outside the scope of social work practice include physical evaluations and medical treatments, psychiatric medication evaluation or advice about a medication, certain kinds of psychological testing, and legal assistance or advice.

- Your agency cannot provide a service or resource needed and/or wanted by a client.

- You have reason to believe that your values, attitudes, religious beliefs, or language will be a barrier to developing an effective helping relationship with the client. For example, the client has molested children, and you are so overcome with distaste for this behavior that you cannot be objective. Note, however, that trying to pass off responsibility for dealing with a difficult client is not an acceptable reason for referral. "Dumping" such a client on another practitioner or agency is unprofessional and unethical.

- You anticipate a conflict of interest. For example, a prospective client is a friend, relative, or employee; you determine that one member of a couple you have been treating for a while needs ongoing individual psychotherapy; or you determine that an individual client with whom you have developed a therapeutic relationship needs ongoing couples therapy.

- The client asks for a referral (e.g., for another source of assistance, for an alternative therapist).

- At termination, you determine that it would be appropriate to refer a client for continuing services from another agency or practitioner.

2. Guidelines for Making Referrals: In order to make effective referrals, you must understand the resources available in your community and keep up with changes in your community's resource system. In particular, you should know enough about the resources in your community that you can determine which one will best match a client's needs. Ideally, you will have on hand information about the resources and services available in your community so that when a referral is indicated, you can readily recommend an appropriate resource and provide the client with the information he needs to make an informed choice about whether to use it and is able to use it with relative ease if he chooses to do so.

An **information and referral service (I&R)** is a helpful tool for locating appropriate resources and other sources of help. An I&R is either an agency or an office within an agency that maintains information about existing benefits and programs and the procedures for obtaining or using them. In addition, your community may have a computerized database or clearing-house to help you identify local health and social service agencies, programs, and providers.

a. Planning and Choosing Referrals: Guidelines for planning and choosing referrals include the following:

- You should view a client as the expert on his situation and what types of resources and services will or will not be useful for him. Any referral for help with a problem that the client doesn't consider important will probably fail.

- Think about how you will discuss the referral with a client. For example, if the client didn't request the service or resource, how will you raise the issue of referral?

- Consider practical problems that may pose a barrier to a client's ability to use a service (e.g., lack of transportation, no phone, inability to read, lack of child-care during appointments, fearfulness associated with going to a high-crime area, inability to take time away from his job).

- If you work at an agency, consider all sources of assistance available within your agency before concluding that referral to a different agency is necessary. Also, make sure that you're aware of all the agencies and professionals that a client is already involved with and, whenever possible, that you use the resources of an agency to which a client is already linked. Get a client's permission to consult with the other agencies and professionals he's involved with before making a final decision about a referral.

- For services that require a fee, you need to consider your client's ability to pay. Additionally, you may need to help a client obtain relevant information from his insurance company, managed care organization (MCO), or public insurance program, such as Medicaid. For instance, will the MCO or public insurance program cover a needed medical procedure or service? Is a particular professional on the list of providers acceptable to the client's MCO? If a referral is to a health care provider, you may need to help a client get proper preauthorization from his MCO.

- When planning to refer a client to an agency, think about whether that agency will need to determine his **eligibility** for a service or benefit. Never tell a client that he is eligible for a service or benefit unless you have the authority to make the eligibility decision. You may need to help a client gather information and documents related to citizenship, income, marriage, parent-child relationships, household composition, medical conditions, etc. Private practitioners to whom you refer a client may also have their own procedures, policies, and eligibility criteria.

- If you will continue working with a client, consider how the referral might enhance or otherwise affect your work with him. What are your professional obligations to other providers in this situation? (See also Follow-Up, below.)

- Be sure to consider a client's friends, relatives, and other informal resources as possible sources of assistance for a client. (See also Using Informal Resources, below.)

b. *The Referral Process – General Guidelines:* Guidelines for making appropriate and effective referrals include the following (Sheafor & Horejsi, 2003; Hepworth et al., 2006):

- Whenever necessary, obtain releases of information signed by the client prior to engaging in the referral process.

- When telling a client about services available through another agency or professional, explain both the advantages and limitations of the services. If a client is confused, afraid, or highly dysfunctional, don't focus on the limitations, however, as this could create another barrier and prevent the client from using a service he needs.

- If possible, provide a client with several options from which he can choose the agency or professional he wants to use: (a) You can recommend the one or two out of those options that you think will best meet the client's needs. (b) If a client asks you for advice on whether to use a certain resource, you should give your honest assessment of its appropriateness and quality. (c) When referring a client for psychotherapy or counseling, you should recommend only professionals whom you know to be competent and ethical.

- Explore and address a client's feelings and concerns about the referral. This is important because if a client, for any reason, is not ready for a referral, he is unlikely to follow through on it. The following considerations and approaches are usually helpful: (a) Be aware that most clients are ambivalent about referrals. Even if they understand the benefits they stand to gain from using another agency's or professional's services, they may still be fearful or uncertain. You should explore the client's ambivalence and help him express his fears or other concerns about using the resource. (b) Encourage the client to tell you about the agencies and resources he has used in the past. How did he contact and interact with them? Has he had negative experiences? Having this information will help you know what needs to be done to facilitate the current referral. (c) A client may be reluctant to join a support group or self-help group because he doesn't want to admit that he has a problem. If so, it can be effective to discuss with the client the ways in which he may be able to draw on his own experiences to help others in the group. A client may be more willing to join the group if he sees himself as someone who can help others rather than as someone needing help. (d) Finally, if the referral means that you and a client will terminate your work together, consider how the client may be feeling about this. As necessary, address his feelings about separating from you (and, as relevant, your agency).

- If it won't jeopardize the success of a referral, allow a client to make his own arrangements for the services he wants. On the other hand, when a client is frightened, overwhelmed, or immature, you should help him to set up the appointment, arrange transportation, etc. If a referral is extremely important, do whatever is required to establish the linkage (see Connection Techniques, below).

- When appropriate, involve a client's family and other significant people in decision making related to a referral. Although this may hold up the referral process if these people disagree with you, the client, or each other about what the client needs, it has the benefit of reducing the chances that they will later behave in ways that threaten a referral's success simply because they feel left out.

- Because the referral process can be stressful and frustrating (e.g., red tape, waiting lists), a client may need emotional support throughout the process. He may also need to be coached on how to approach an agency and apply for services. Often, instruction, support, and modeling are needed to prepare a client to ask the right questions and be assertive when calling an agency and during appointments.

c. *Connection Techniques:* Weissman (1976) suggests that social workers use the following **connection techniques** when referring their clients. Using these techniques helps ensure that a client will successfully connect with the resource (professional, agency, or program) to which you are referring him.

- Write out all the information the client needs about the referral including name and address, how to make an appointment, how to contact the resource, and what the client can expect when he contacts the resource. If necessary, provide the client with detailed instructions on how to get there (e.g., print out a map or plot the bus route to take).

- Provide the client with the name of the person he is to contact. Since this person may not be available, however, it is wise to provide the client with several contact people.

- Compose a brief letter addressed to the resource that the client will deliver to the resource. This statement should briefly describe the client's concern or request, and the client should be involved in composing this letter.

- You can, if you choose, contact the resource by phone when the client is with you. After speaking to the resource and briefly explaining the intended referral, hand the phone to the client so that he will experience some conversation with the resource.

- If the client is anxious or fearful about attending the first appointment at the resource, you may arrange to have a friend or family member accompany him. If the client is extremely apprehensive, you may accompany him yourself. In addition, behavioral rehearsal can be used to allay the client's fears and self-doubt.

d. *Follow-Up:* The referral process does not end when a client has had his first appointment with the referral resource. Instead, you must **follow-up** to see what the client's experience was like. Doing so allows you to discover problems or misunderstandings that a client is having with the resource. When these issues are detected early, they can be resolved before they result in the client withdrawing from the resource.

If you are continuing to work with a client following the referral, you should obtain a progress report. You may ask a client to report back, or alternatively, you may contact the resource yourself. Follow-up tasks usually include processing with the client his experience and feelings about the resource; with the client's signed permission, contacting the referral provider to obtain reports and information about the client's progress; and acting as a coordinator to ensure that all professionals are working toward congruent goals.

If you are no longer working with the client, you should take steps to encourage his new connection with the resource in order to increase the chance that he will continue using it. With the client's agreement, you can call him after the first scheduled meeting with the resource, or you can ask the client to call you after he has had the first contact. Have the client describe what happened and what he is thinking and feeling about the resource. Listen for problems that the client may be having with the new resource. It is also appropriate to schedule a few interviews with the client while he is using the resource.

e. *Using Informal Resources:* You should always consider a client's existing social support network as a potential source of assistance. In many cases, a client's relatives, friends, neighbors, members of his church, synagogue, mosque, or other religious body, etc., can offer relevant assistance in addressing his needs or problems.

The following guidelines are useful when deciding to use **informal resources** as a source of help for a client:

- Discuss with a client both the advantages and disadvantages of using informal resources, and, as with any other kind of resource, allow the client to make the final decision about what resources he will use.

- Be prepared to provide a client with guidance on how to reach out to an informal resource, establish a relationship, and handle any expectation of reciprocity that arises.

- Usually, a client will initiate contact with an informal resource and decide for himself what he wants to reveal to the resource. In some cases, however, you may need to talk with an informal resource yourself. Regarding confidentiality, the requirement is the same as it is when you need to communicate with a professional or agency involved with the client: If you need to speak with an informal resource, you must first get the client's permission to do so.

D. Case Management

Overview of Case Management

1. The Purpose of Case Management: Case management is a "procedure to plan, seek, and monitor services from different social agencies and staff on behalf of a client. Usually, one agency has primary responsibility for the client and assigns a case manager [to his case] ..." (Barker, 2003, p. 58).

For certain clients, case management can have a positive impact on their quality of life, service outcomes, and/or the cost of service or care. Most clients needing case management services have multiple problems that require assistance from more than one provider and that need to be addressed at the same time, or around the same time, as well as special difficulties in seeking and using help effectively. These difficulties usually stem from one or more of the following factors (Ballew & Mink, 1996):

External barriers: These are barriers in a client's environment – i.e., resources are absent, unavailable to the client, or inadequate for meeting his needs. In some cases, a primary resource exists, but a client can't use it because he lacks a secondary resource such as transportation or child care.

Inherent incapacities: These are factors outside of a client's control that interfere with his ability to communicate effectively with helpers or participate actively in helping himself (e.g., intellectual disability, chronic medical condition, severe mental illness, certain physical conditions such as dementia or stroke, incapacitating alcohol or other drug abuse).

Internal barriers: These are attitudes, values, or beliefs of a client that produce patterns of behavior that interfere with his ability to seek, accept, or use help when he needs it. Examples include feeling helpless and overwhelmed, blaming others, feeling that life is chaotic and unpredictable, a tendency to act impulsively, and a pattern of denying problems.

Integrative (or **integrated**) **case management** (ICM), in particular, focuses on helping clients with chronic medical conditions and concurrent mental health needs to receive coordinated care and assistance that will stabilize their medical and mental health symptoms, while also addressing social and health care system factors that contribute to unfavorable outcomes. Case managers using ICM promote the development of an alliance with a client using motivational interviewing skills and are trained to identify physical, psychological, social, and health system barriers to a client's improvement and to develop and carry out comprehensive and coordinated physical and mental health care plans. The ICM model focuses on bringing together **interdisciplinary teams** to work with a client.

2. The Focus of Case Management: The overall focus of case management is on a client's relationship to his environment. As a case manager, you adopt an **ecological perspective**, and, therefore, you assume the following: (a) An individual has needs that are met by resources in the environment, and the environment makes demands that are responded to by capacities within the individual; and (b) for an individual to function in an adaptive way, there must be a balance of resources to needs and of capacities to environmental demands.

When assessing a client, a case manager evaluates which needs and demands must be balanced by which resources and capacities, and, ultimately, her goal to is develop the client's capacity to achieve and maintain this balance in his own. To facilitate this goal, a case manager emphasizes a strengths perspective and empowerment.

3. Case Management Roles: Case management roles include the following:

Counselor: A case manager establishes a trusting relationship with a client; provides the client with encouragement and emotional support in coping with day-to-day living situations and obstacles he encounters while using resources and services; identifies dysfunctional patterns of behavior that are preventing a client from getting and using help effectively and helps him develop more functional patterns; and provides information and skills to teach the client how to develop and maintain a resource network on his own.

As a case manager, you may provide supportive and directed treatment, along with information, advice, and linkage, to help a client cope better and gain awareness of elements of his functioning that are preventing him from getting and using help effectively. If a client requires longer-term therapy, however, you will usually refer him to another provider for that service (e.g., you will refer a client elsewhere for help in developing insight into the issues underlying his problems).

Broker/coordinator: A case manager connects a client with appropriate resources (broker) and then facilitates continuing interaction between a client and service providers (coordinator).

Advocate: As an advocate, the case manager ensures that needed resources are available to a client and that a client receives the services he is entitled to.

4. Case Management Functions: Case management functions include the following:

Assessment: A case manager gathers information and formulates an assessment of a client's needs, situation, and resources. A case manager may also reach out to clients who have not requested case management services.

Service planning: A case manager develops an overall service (or case) plan with help from the client and other relevant parties (relevant professionals and program personnel, members of the client's family, etc.). This involves identifying services that can be accessed to meet the client's needs.

Linkage and service coordination: A case manager connects a client with appropriate resources (linkage) and remains an active participant in the delivery of services to the client. She coordinates a client's use of resources by being a point person for all communications between and among the involved agencies. The client and service providers know they can contact the case manager whenever they have questions or when problems arise.

Follow-up and monitoring service delivery: A case manager makes regular and frequent follow-up contacts with a client and each service provider to make sure that the client has received the services and is using them properly. The case manager also completes the paperwork necessary to document the progress and success of the service plan.

Client support: A case manager provides assistance to a client (and his family) when they encounter difficulties in obtaining services. This function may include giving information, providing counseling, offering emotional support, resolving personality conflicts, and/or acting as an advocate on behalf of the client.

5. The Stages of Case Management: The stages of case management are engagement/assessment (problem identification), planning (plan development), implementation (problem resolution), and disengagement (termination of case management services).

a. Stage 1 – Engagement/assessment: As a case manager, your key tasks during engagement are to verify the client's eligibility for case management services (i.e., does the client have multiple unmet service needs?) and develop an effective working relationship with the client. You use interviewing skills and techniques to introduce yourself and your role, elicit information about the client's problems, and address negative feelings the client may have about getting help.

During assessment, you seek to identify the client's unmet needs, the barriers the client has encountered in obtaining and using help effectively, and what resources the client is currently using and what resources he needs. Of particular interest to you is identifying which client needs and environmental demands must be balanced by which environmental resources and client capacities.

b. Stage 2 – Planning: During planning, you organize information compiled during assessment into a sequence of activities (a plan of action) that will result in the client receiving the help he needs, including both services and assistance in developing the ability to meet future needs and environmental demands on his own. The result of planning is a document called a service plan (a.k.a. case plan, treatment plan, or care plan), which is the basis for your case management activities. The service plan is flexible and subject to change as new information emerges and/or the client's situation changes.

The planning process has five steps (Ballew & Mink, 1996): (a) You and the client formulate the goals by making specific, practical goal statements to which you and the client can both be committed; (b) you and the client set priorities among the goals so that critical, or high-priority, problems are addressed first, problems are tackled in sequence, and neither you nor the client becomes overwhelmed; (c) you and the client identify the services and other strategies that will be used to achieve the goals, including specific actions that will be taken by you and by the client to bring about desired changes; (d) you arrange for the services the client needs; and (e) you identify times and procedures for evaluating progress.

Contemporary case managers usually try to establish **wrap-around services** for their clients. This term refers to a highly individualized package of services selected or developed to address a client's unique needs and make use of his strengths to the greatest extent possible. Usually, the services are paid for with funds from several different sources which allows for greater flexibility and creativity than is available when funding is drawn from just one category.

c. Stage 3 – Implementation: The implementation stage is the period when the service plan is carried out and evaluated: (a) You connect the client with needed resources and coordinate his use of resources; (b) you monitor the services as they are delivered to ensure that they remain available, are humane, and are used effectively, and, when necessary, you use strategies, such as mediation or advocacy, to address problems in service delivery affecting the client; (c) you provide direct services to develop the client's internal resources and help him overcome barriers to seeking and using help; and (d) you revise the service plan as needed.

d. Stage 4 – Disengagement: During the disengagement phase, your activities include evaluating the results of the intervention (e.g., resolution of problems, increased ability to get and use help effectively); identifying signs of disengagement; and determining your ongoing responsibility, if any, to the client following disengagement. The latter is usually determined by agency policy. Generally, however, you should be willing to respond to the client by telephone and to meet with him at least one time if doing so would be helpful to him.

Generally, disengagement is appropriate when the goals of the service plan have been achieved, the client is able to help himself more effectively (he has demonstrated an increased capacity to meet his own needs and increased independence), and the client is making appropriate use of assistance from a helping network.

Case Management Guidelines

Important guidelines for providing effective case management services include the following (Sheafor & Horejsi, 2003; Ballew & Mink, 1996):

1. Engagement and Assessment Phase Guidelines:

- Bear in mind that a client may have had negative experiences with helpers in the past or developed attitudes and beliefs that make it difficult for him to work successfully with you and other helping professionals.

- "Start where the client is." If a client describes only a superficial need at first, acknowledge this need and convey acceptance of him and how he describes his problem. Don't correct him, even if you believe his problems involve something different.

- Acknowledge and address all negative feelings expressed by the client as they emerge. Use active listening skills and convey empathy. You don't need to probe to uncover other feelings at this time – simply encourage and legitimize the client's feelings as they emerge and demonstrate that you understand and accept them. Accept the client's feelings as reasonable for a person in his circumstances.

- Engage in a **role clarification** procedure so that you and the client will have congruent expectations about your work together. Be aware that a client may deny responsibility, be passive, feel victimized, be pessimistic because he has had ineffective help in the past, or expect that you can do more for him than you can or should. Acknowledge conflicts in expectations. Don't force a client to accept your perspective, but be realistic when telling him what you can and cannot do.

- Rely primarily on the client's report to gather information about his needs. Other sources, such as family members, records and other documents concerning the client, past employers, etc., can be used as secondary (collateral) sources who may be contacted or consulted with permission from the client to verify or supplement information he has provided. Seeking information from collateral sources can be critical when the client is particularly vulnerable and has a wide range of needs. Even with such a client, however, you should encourage him to participate in the assessment to his maximum capacity because an important goal of case management is client empowerment.

- Evaluate the client's strengths (skills, capacities, positive attitudes, personal resources, environmental resources), as well as his deficiencies. Part of assessment in case management includes providing direct counseling to the client for the purpose of identifying strengths that can be mobilized to facilitate his coping.

- Consider using an **ecomap** to uncover environmental problems. An ecomap identifies specific elements in the environment that are either supporting or detracting from a client's functioning. This, in turn, can sometimes lead a client to talk about personal and interpersonal problems (e.g., a client who sees that he has few friends may admit to feeling lonely).

- Create a **problem inventory** (a.k.a. inventory of needs and demands) from which you and the client can select target problems. Such a list helps organize assessment data and makes it easier to communicate with the client and others about what you've identified.

- Help the client in a practical, tangible, and immediate way. An effective way of building trust with a client in need of case management services is through a concrete demonstration of your ability and willingness to help. Even before the service plan is developed, you can try to identify an early opportunity to help the client in a concrete way. This can be meaningful to the client, even if the help you offer is minor or related only indirectly to his most significant problems.

2. Planning Phase Guidelines:

- The goals of the service plan must be realistic and practical. On the other hand, you shouldn't immediately reject a client's unrealistic goals. Instead, you should try to address them by breaking them down into manageable and measurable steps. This is consistent with a strengths perspective, which, in this context, involves having a client identify goals that are important to him and then developing interventions to address them. This approach provides the client with a model for addressing problems in a proactive and organized way. Some clients require goals to be broken down into very discrete steps – e.g., rather than just, "the client will have a physical exam by his doctor," you'd also include, "the client will make the appointment ... arrange transportation to the doctor's office," etc.

- Help the client list the goals in order of importance, from those he wants to work on immediately to those he is least concerned about. Then give *top priority* to goals the client wants to achieve first. (The exception to this would be when a client or another person is in danger, in which case you, yourself, may have to prioritize certain goals in order to protect the client or others.) Also give *high priority* to goals that can be achieved relatively quickly and with a reasonable amount of effort because this can enhance a client's motivation to work on subsequent goals as he begins to see that his problems can be resolved. And, at this time, give *low priority* to goals associated with problems that are difficult to resolve and goals that will require a lot of time, energy, and resources to achieve, unless these goals reflect the client's highest priorities or involve risk to the client or others.

- A **needs list** may be used during planning, particularly with clients who are very dependent on services provided by health care and social agencies (e.g., frail elderly individuals, children in foster care, people who have serious developmental disabilities or mental illness). Needs lists are also useful when case planning is being performed by a multidisciplinary team or multiagency team. In this case, the list clarifies responsibilities, facilitates interagency coordination, and reduces conflict and misunderstanding within the team.

3. Implementation Phase Guidelines:

- Your efforts to help a client overcome internal barriers to seeking and using help should generally emphasize a counseling approach that helps the client use his own strengths to get and use help effectively. As barriers are gradually overcome, you then begin connecting the client to other resources at his pace. In making decisions about this, you consider the client's capacity for forming helping relationships, his progress in overcoming internal barriers, and what sequence of resources will be most helpful.

- Depending on a client's needs, a variety of techniques can be used to connect him to resources, with each having a different level of involvement on your part. From least to most involvement by you, these techniques include the following: (a) Inform the client about the resource; (b) have the client report back to you about his experience with the resource and check with him to ensure his continued contact with the provider; (c) help the client understand what to expect when he contacts the provider (e.g., the procedures that may be necessary to obtain the help, what documents and others materials he will need to have); (d) call the other provider yourself to schedule the appointment or notify the provider that the client will be calling; (e) coach the client beforehand (e.g., role-play the first interview with the provider or talk through what the appointment will be like and anticipate possible problems); and (f) accompany the client to his first contact with the provider if he is too anxious to go on his own (Ballew & Mink, 1996).

- A case manager's **coordination** function should change over the course of her work with the client: During the initial connection period, you will tend to adopt an active leadership role so that you can establish early success for the client. As the client develops the ability to get what he needs from his helping network, you should become less active and focus more on being a supporter and consultant to the client. The same tends to be true for your interaction with the helping network – initially, you may need to put more effort into gaining cooperation from the helpers involved with your client.

- Case conferences can be effective for increasing cooperation among the members of a client's network. A **case conference** is a face-to-face meeting with either all or some members of a client's helping network (e.g., some meetings may involve only people concerned with a specific set of problems). Because case conferences tend to be time consuming, they are generally scheduled only when there is a compelling reason to meet (e.g., when members of a client's network have made conflicting demands of him, a crisis has diminished a client's ability to participate actively, or major revisions are being made to the service plan).

E. Case Advocacy

Advocacy in social work is defined as, "championing the rights of individuals or communities through direct intervention or empowerment" (Barker, 2003, p. 11). **Case advocacy** (a.k.a. client advocacy) is a form of advocacy that involves working with and on behalf of a client to ensure that he receives the services and benefits to which he is entitled and that the services are delivered in a way that protects his dignity.

1. Choosing to Assume the Case Advocate Role: Advocacy, as a form of confrontation, is associated with some risks. Therefore, you should not use advocacy until you have tried approaches with less potential for damaging the relationship with another agency or professional. On the other hand, as a social worker, you must be willing to assume the role of advocate on behalf of a client when certain conditions are met and when doing so will be of benefit to your client. Specifically, you should consider using case advocacy when a client (a) has been unable to obtain services to which he is entitled and/or has been treated unfairly or discriminated against by a professional, agency, or business, *and* (b) has been unable to respond effectively to these situations.

2. Guidelines for Using Case Advocacy: All direct social work practice, including case advocacy, requires you to "start where the client is." Before using case advocacy, you must verify that a client actually wants you to serve as his advocate and understands the potential benefits and risks. This is consistent with the principle of client **self-determination**. In addition, case advocacy can only take place after you and the client have undertaken a complete exploration and assessment of the problem and developed a contract that establishes your goals.

a. Guidelines for Assessment:

- Make sure you have all the relevant facts before deciding how to proceed (e.g., is the client truly eligible for the service or resource he has been denied?). In particular, (a) keep in mind that clients sometimes misunderstand or misinterpret explanations given to them by professionals and agency representatives; (b) never base your decision to proceed on a one-sided description of what happened and why or on hearsay (unconfirmed information); and (c) don't assume that you understand another agency's policies, procedures, or eligibility criteria – get the facts.

- Determine the extent to which the client can be empowered to deal with problems in his environment. This will influence the nature of your advocacy effort. Even when a client can't be empowered, however, you should still use advocacy when doing so is indicated.

b. Guidelines for Planning:

- Your efforts must address a client's interests and needs as he defines them. As much as possible, you should involve the client in all decisions made about the actions you will take and you should do no more than the client wishes you to.

- To the greatest extent possible, you want to **empower** the client through your efforts (i.e., you want to enhance his ability to improve his own situation).

- When selecting a design for the intervention, you should consider the specific nature of the problem, your own skills and resources as the change agent, characteristics of the target system, and the goal and authorization for the intervention. The result of the intervention will be influenced primarily by your own resources and the openness and responsiveness of the target system. (The **change agent** is the individual who initiates the process, meaning you as the advocate; and the **target system** is the target of the intervention, meaning the individual, group, structure, policy, or practice that needs to be changed.)

c. Guidelines for Intervention: The most productive advocates use a variety of resources and strategies but they usually emphasize communication and mediation rather than power. General guidelines for engaging in case advocacy include the following (e.g., Sheafor & Horejsi, 2003):

- Once you've decided to serve as an advocate for a client, arrange a meeting with the appropriate agency or program representative. Face-to-face meetings are generally more effective than phone calls or letters. Make sure to respect an agency's chain of command – for example, don't ask to speak with a supervisor before you've spoken to the line worker who's had contact with your client; don't ask to speak with an administrator before you've spoken with the worker's supervisor. Focus on facts when presenting your concerns. Don't be abrasive, but do use a tone that conveys how strongly you feel about the situation. Finally, keep a written record of whom you talk to, when and where you talk to them, and their responses.

- Make a decision on how to proceed based on what you learn from your communication with the agency or program representative: (a) If you discover that the agency or program wanted to provide the service to your client, but was prevented from doing so by an unreasonable policy or procedural requirement, ask how you might appeal the decision and who else you and your client should speak to. (b) If you discover that the agency or program has treated your client in an unfair and discriminatory way, let them know that, if the situation isn't corrected, you will take your concern to those higher in the chain of command or make a formal complaint. To pursue an appeal or formal complaint, you need to have detailed documentation of the process up to that point. You may also need legal advice before proceeding.

Sometimes an **ombudsperson** at an agency or other organization will be an available resource for you and your client. An ombudsperson is an advocate or spokesperson for the people who are served by an organization who ensures that the organization's obligations, ethical duties, and rules are being followed; or an individual employed by an organization who investigates potential illegal and/or unethical activities or unintended harmful consequences stemming from the organization's activities and facilitates fair negotiations or actions toward satisfactory solutions (Barker, 2003).

3. Levels of Case Advocacy: Ballew and Mink (1996) similarly describe six escalating levels of case advocacy, listed here from least to most adversarial:

- Level 1 involves making a direct appeal ("assertive request") for the denied resource. You offer a clear and objective description of the help that is needed, your client's attempts to get that help, the results of his efforts, and the effects that not receiving the help have had on the client's situation.

- Level 2 involves efforts to influence the situation by using your knowledge of the organization's policies and procedures (e.g., showing that you know that the client is entitled to the help he isn't receiving).

- Level 3 involves appealing to someone with greater authority in the target organization.

- Level 4 entails using the target organization's grievance procedure.
- Level 5 involves appealing to an outside authority (e.g., a licensing or regulatory agency). This becomes necessary only if you are unable to resolve the problem through the target organization's hierarchy or grievance procedure.
- Level 6 (a last resort strategy) involves taking legal action.

VII. Monitoring the Change Process and Maintaining Progress

A. Monitoring the Change Process

Monitoring the change process includes observing a client's responses to the intervention on an ongoing basis and evaluating signs of progress in accordance with the contract you and the client negotiated. Typically, a client's progress is evaluated every two to three sessions. If you collect empirical data about changes that occur during intervention, you may share that data with the client. It's also appropriate to share results in an informal way, as part of the client's regular sessions.

1. Benefits of Monitoring the Change Process: Important benefits associated with monitoring the change process include the following:

- Regular monitoring helps maintain continuity in the change process and a focus on treatment goals.

- Regular monitoring allows you to determine when to shift the focus to a different goal or initiate termination.

- Regular monitoring allows you to keep track of the extent to which the intervention is successful. If a client fails to make progress toward the agreed-on objectives within a reasonable period (as specified in the contract), you and the client may need to modify the treatment plan or renegotiate the treatment contract. In some cases, you and the client will need to return to the beginning phases to re-evaluate and clarify the issues being addressed and look for other solutions.

- Sharing the results of monitoring with a client allows the client to keep track of where he stands in relation to his goals. The client's ability to identify changes occurring during intervention is an important factor in sustaining his effort to complete intervention activities. Additionally, your acknowledging a client's progress can serve to maintain or increase his motivation.

- Asking a client for his opinions and feelings about his progress allows you to identify issues that may be impeding his progress (e.g., discouragement) or that could lead him to discontinue treatment. Sometimes, you'll discover that you need to re-engage a client in the change process.

2. Means of Evaluating Progress: You should establish and use a reliable means of evaluating a client's progress and the effectiveness of the intervention. Typically the means used to evaluate progress are specified in the treatment contract. Examples include the following: (a) You may use a scale to measure a client's behavior at the beginning of the change process and then use the same scale at various points during the process to assess changes. For instance, you might administer a structured symptom checklist at the beginning of the intervention to get baseline data, during the intermediate phase to assess progress, and then at the end of treatment to assess outcome. (b) If you don't collect explicit baseline data, you can ask a client to self-report on his progress. This might involve obtaining a self-rating from the client based on a 1 to 10 scale, where "1" indicates no progress and "10" indicates that a goal has been reached. You can plot this data on a graph so that the client is able to visualize his progress.

Ideally, each phase of intervention will include methods of evaluating progress that are relevant to the objectives for that phase. When identifying appropriate measures for each phase for a client in psychotherapy, it can be useful to consider the results of research conducted by Howard and his colleagues (1996, 1986), which found that the outcomes of therapy vary in a predictable way over time: (a) During the first few sessions, the client's feelings of hopelessness and desperation decline; (b) in the next phase, the client experiences a reduction in symptoms; and, (c) during the final phase, the client "unlearns troublesome maladaptive, habitual behaviors and ... [establishes] new ways of dealing with various aspects of life" (1986, p. 1061). Howard et al. refer to these three phases as remoralization, remediation, and rehabilitation, respectively. An implication of their research is that different treatment goals and methods of assessment may be appropriate at different times during the course of psychotherapy.

Finally, change (even desirable change) by a client tends to disrupt others in his social network, particularly his family members, and this can create difficulties that interfere with the client's continued progress. Therefore, following a change, you should monitor a client's situation for a while to determine whether the change becomes firmly established as part of the client's ongoing functioning and that of relevant others in his life.

B. Maintaining Progress Throughout the Change Process

Fear, ambivalence, and resistance are normal when people make changes in their lives, and, therefore, part of your job when involved in the change process with a client is to make "a consistent demand for work" (Shulman, 1981). You should let a client know that you believe in his strength and are willing to deal with all the difficult problems and feelings he faces. Your "demands for work" should be realistic and you should accompany them with empathic skills so that the client doesn't feel rejected or criticized. It may be necessary to revisit goals/contract and adjust accordingly.

Other general skills for facilitating a client's ongoing progress include the following: (a) Focus the intervention on one goal (or objective) at a time and encourage the client to concentrate on one goal or objective until he has made sufficient progress to warrant moving on to the next one. (b) Use summarization. In this context, summarization involves beginning each session (after the first one) with a discussion of what the client has accomplished, such as reviewing the negative and positive features of his experience with making changes or his efforts to change. (c) Reinforce the client when he engages in new, desired behaviors.

1. Skills for Maintaining Momentum: Skills you may use to maintain momentum in the change process with a client are described below (Sheafor & Horejsi, 2003):

Partialization: When a client feels overwhelmed or helpless facing a large or complex problem, break the problem down into smaller, more manageable parts. When you do this, the client is better able to focus his attention and energy.

Help the client stay on track: Make statements intended to keep the client's attention focused on a specific issue or objective. This is particularly useful when a client rambles or tries to avoid a relevant issue.

Challenge avoidance of change: This is a type of confrontation used to directly point out a client's resistance. You simply point out to the client that he seems to be avoiding discussion of the issue for which he sought help or the issue that you and he agreed to work on in the intervention.

Check for acquiescence: A client may verbally agree to take an action but, in reality, have no commitment to it, or may agree to take an action without fully knowing the difficulties he will face. Therefore, it's important to ask questions intended uncover any ambivalence or resistance a client may have toward a decision or action (e.g., perhaps a client is worried about obstacles he will face or uncertain about his own abilities). It's also important to explore whether the client is ignoring, overlooking, or underestimating likely obstacles to his success.

Address emotional blocks: When a client's unwillingness to face painful feelings (guilt, anger, etc.) is impeding his progress toward change, make statements intended to increase his awareness of how these feelings are blocking his progress and encourage him to discuss them with you.

Support the client in sensitive areas: When a client's reluctance to talk about an embarrassing topic is impeding his progress, make a statement intended to help him feel more at ease discussing the topic. For example, "You're not alone; a lot of us have been raised to believe that we shouldn't talk about money or debt ..."

Address authority issues: A client who has had difficulties with authority figures in the past (e.g., parents, police, etc.) may see you as just another person trying to control his life. If so, invite the client to talk openly about this concern, including any complaints he has about you or the helping process.

Build a communication link: Establish a connection between a client and a person or agency with whom he needs to communicate. For instance, if a client is having trouble getting needed information from his doctor, get the client's permission to contact the doctor on his behalf to encourage the doctor to communicate with the client.

2. Skills for Sustaining Client Motivation: It is common for a client's motivation to diminish during the middle, or change-oriented, phase of helping. This often happens because a client feels less anxious as a result of support from you, resistance emerges, and/or a client begins to believe he is "cured" since he feels better than he did at the outset of treatment. Skills you can use to increase or sustain a client's motivation for change are described below (Sheafor & Horejsi, 2003; Shulman 1981):

Convey a belief in the potential of work: Make statements intended to convey your belief that the intervention can be helpful. The statements you make should offer the client realistic hope.

Acknowledge the client's strengths: Express your confidence in the client's ability to complete a specific task or to cope with a difficult situation. Here, too, your statements should be genuine ones that reflect actual client strengths you have observed.

Point out negative consequences: Remind the client that change is necessary if he is to avoid undesirable consequences. Your statements in this regard should be truthful (reflect actual consequences that a client may face) and objective (don't make statements out of anger or frustration with a client).

Use persuasion: **Persuasion** is useful when a client is afraid or reluctant to take an important action. Using persuasion for this purpose may involve: (a) Explaining the action using words and examples that are easy for the client to understand; (b) pointing out how the action is compatible with the client's values and customary ways of doing things; (c) pointing out how not taking the action would be incompatible with the client's goals, values, and belief system; (d) describing the advantages of taking the action and the negative consequences of not taking it; (e) describing how the action has helped others in similar circumstances; (f) suggesting an approach that allows the client to take the action in small, gradual steps; and/or (g) asking people whom the client trusts and respects to encourage the client to take the action.

3. Skills and Techniques for Addressing Resistance: Resistance to change is common because people tend toward preserving the status quo, and, therefore, you should be prepared to deal with resistance, even with a client who has demonstrated a strong desire to change. Resistance can take many forms, including long silences, inattention, intellectualizing, changing the subject, tardiness, canceling appointments, minimizing problems, not paying for sessions, or not applying newly learned skills to life circumstances. These behaviors don't always reflect resistance, but, if a client has stopped making progress, then it's usually safe to conclude that resistance is involved. You should then focus on exploring the factors underlying the resistance.

Skills and techniques for addressing resistance include the following:

- Openly bring up the resistance and discuss the here-and-now feelings underlying it. Be empathic and accepting.

- Redefine the client's problem as an opportunity to grow.

- Positively reinterpret the resistance; in other words, ascribe a positive motivation to it.

- Help the client understand the source of his resistant behavior and encourage him to express problematic feelings more directly.

- Use additive empathy to increase the client's awareness of his negative feelings and ability to manage them.

- Use the technique of **joining the resistance**. For example, say something like, "After such a long wait, you deserve to be angry. I'd be angry, too." Aligning with a client's feelings in this way can serve to reduce resistance by removing the client's need to keep his defenses up and giving him permission to ventilate his feelings.

- If there is an ongoing pattern of resistance, you may use **confrontation**. Challenging the client can be particularly useful for facilitating his awareness of and motivation to resolve interpersonal barriers to change, including those found in his relationship with you.

- Place the client in a **therapeutic double-bind**. The therapeutic double-bind refers to a set of paradoxical techniques that are used to modify entrenched behavioral patterns: You direct a client *not* to change in a situation where he expects you to help him change; in effect, your directive is to change by remaining the same. The client is then in a bind, or trap: If he defies your directive to do nothing and begins working toward change, he learns to acquire some control over his symptom or problem, and this constitutes desired change. If he complies with your directive and does not attempt to change, then he acknowledges a voluntary exercise of control over his symptoms. Either way, the client gains control over the symptom; the symptom no longer controls him. The symptom is now under therapeutic control (Goldenberg & Goldenberg, 2004).

VIII. Practice Evaluation

Practice evaluation involves assessing your interventions and their impact on a specific client, be it an individual, a family, or a small group. The evaluation can serve two purposes: (a) **Formative evaluation** is used to guide ongoing practice decisions. It involves monitoring a planned intervention and allows you to identify when you need to modify the intervention. (b) **Summative evaluation** is used to assess the final outcome of intervention. It identifies the factors that contributed to the relative success or failure of an intervention.

At the end of the planned change process, you perform a summative evaluation of the extent to which your intervention was effective in improving a client's functioning or situation. Such evaluation is an important tool for satisfying ethical and professional demands for accountability because it provides concrete evidence of the effects of social work intervention. In addition, empirical evaluations of practice outcomes as reflected by standardized measurement tools, such as standardized rating scales, are increasingly requested by managed care companies.

A. Evaluation Activities

Often, the means by which an intervention will be monitored and evaluated are specified in the treatment or service contract. Key evaluation activities include the following:

- First, clearly define the intervention goals.

- Second, select the criteria that will be used to measure the variables (e.g., client behaviors, actions, or emotions) that are expected to change during intervention. The client's functioning is considered the **dependent variable**, and the intervention used is the **independent variable**. (For any kind of experimental research, you can usually identify the independent and dependent variables by framing the research question as: What effect does the independent variable have on the dependent variable?)

- Third, decide what procedure will be used to measure changes in client functioning.

The procedure you select must be (a) valid (it should measure what it is assumed or believed to measure); (b) reliable (it should yield similar results when the measurement is repeated under similar circumstances); (c) sensitive (it should be capable of detecting relatively small levels of change and degrees of difference); and (d) nonreactive (it should be capable of detecting differences without modifying or influencing the phenomena being measured). In addition, the evaluation design you choose should be subject to change if the anticipated treatment/service plan for the client changes.

The forms of measurement that are typically used in practice evaluation include the following:

- Developing a tool specifically tailored to the issues experienced by the client (an individualized scale).

- Using an existing scale that will accurately measure the client on the factors being considered (a standardized scale).

- Counting and recording factual information (e.g., school attendance, number of family arguments).

Finally, you must inform the client about how the data will be collected and used and get his informed consent for participation in the evaluation process. The client may worry that others, such as family members, employers, or a court, will have access to the evaluation data and could use them against him. The client should be told that he has the right to refuse permission to release the data to such parties. Or if a court or other party will have access to any of the data, you must inform the client of this fact when seeking his informed consent.

B. Techniques for Measuring Client Change

The measurement techniques described in this section can be used for both monitoring an intervention (formative evaluation) and making a final evaluation of the intervention outcome (summative evaluation).

1. Individualized Rating Scales: An individualized rating scale (IRS) may be used to assess the extent of a client's problem during assessment, follow his progress over the course of intervention, determine when intervention can be terminated, and, finally, perform a summative evaluation of the extent to which intervention was effective in improving the client's functioning.

An IRS measures the frequency, duration, or intensity of an action, event, behavior, emotion, or attitude, and is always designed specifically for the individual client (i.e., it allows you to measure change from the client's perspective). An advantage of an IRS is that some client issues, such as motivation, are difficult to describe and measure using available standardized scales.

Constructing an IRS involves first identifying what will be measured. Each IRS should measure only one dimension of client functioning. If you will be measuring more than one dimension, you should create one scale for each dimension. The next step is to develop a scale on which you can indicate the client's status along a continuum from negative to positive functioning. A general guideline is to have only as many points as the client can clearly distinguish (usually 3 to 7 points). Then, you and the client select anchoring statements that describe each point on the scale. You can use anchor points that have been used in other scales (e.g., for measures of frequency, never, rarely, sometimes, often, very often, always). On a self-anchored scale, by contrast, the anchor points are defined using the client's own words. The next step is to decide how the data will be collected. For instance, who will do the ratings (e.g., you, the client, a family member, a teacher)? When will the ratings be made? Where will the ratings be made? Ideally, you want to achieve consistency regarding the conditions under which the ratings will be made. Last, you select a way of recording and presenting the data that makes the data easy to understand and interpret, particularly for the client.

2. Goal Attainment Scaling: As suggested by its name, goal attainment scaling (GAS) is used to measure the extent to which a client has reached his goals. The basic format for GAS is the same for all clients, but you can make adjustments to accommodate the number of goals you and a client select.

Using GAS starts during the planning and contracting phase. At that time, you and the client select from two to five goals and create a five-point scale for each goal. Each scale represents a set of possible outcomes related to the particular goal. These outcomes define different levels of goal attainment. For example, using a 0-4 scale: 0 = the most unfavorable outcome (a step backward); 1 = no change (the client's status before intervention) or less than expected success; 2 = some favorable change or expected level of success; 3 = substantial change or more than expected success; and 4 = the most favorable outcome that can reasonably be expected.

You then display the scales on a table, with one row for each level of goal attainment and one column for each scale (goal). The next step is to assign a weight to each goal to indicate its importance in relation to the other goals. For example, say you and the client decide to divide 100 points among the selected goals: If the client has five equally important goals, then you would assign each goal a weight of 20 (100 divided by 5 = 20). Goals may also have unequal weights.

Then, you and the client place a checkmark in the score cell (level) on the table that best describes the client's condition or status on each goal when intervention begins. This serves as the baseline for measuring change. When intervention is terminated, you then place an "X" in the score cell on the table that best describes the client's condition for each goal at that time.

The rest of the process is mathematical (don't worry about memorizing these formulae for the exam): First you determine the weighted change score for each goal by subtracting the beginning score (checkmark) from the ending score ("X") and multiplying by the assigned weight. Then, you calculate the percentage of possible change for each scale; this involves determining the highest score a client could generate and dividing that into the actual weighted change score. Last, you calculate an overall goal attainment score. This combined score from the several scales is the most valuable information available from GAS. It gives a comprehensive measure of the client's level of goal attainment. To derive this score, you find the sum of the possible scores for all of the goals and divide that score into the sum of the actual weighted change scores.

Notice that GAS is designed to reflect before-and-after measurements of the client's condition. In long-term service cases, however, you can make measurements at intermediate points during intervention as a way of monitoring the change process.

3. Task Achievement Scaling: Task achievement scaling (TAS) was developed for use in task-centered practice, in which work toward treatment goals and objectives is broken down into many small tasks that are then worked on one after the other. It is useful as a means of evaluation whenever the service is relatively brief and the activities are concrete. As suggested by its name, TAS is used to identify the extent to which a client has completed agreed-on tasks: In each session, you measure progress on each task and calculate an overall measure of the actual level of task achievement between sessions (what the client actually achieved, not what he intended to do).

Using TAS involves defining five points on a scale for each task – i.e., 4 = task completely achieved, 3 = task substantially achieved, 2 = task partially achieved, 1 = task minimally achieved, and 0 = no progress. For each point (4, 3, 2, 1, 0), you and the client develop a very precise behavioral description of what that level of achievement for a task would consist of.

One advantage of TAS is that a client can see increments of success in task achievement, which can make an overwhelming task easier to work on and complete. And when the change process requires a client to work on several interrelated tasks at the same time, TAS allows you to calculate a global achievement score – i.e., the percent of overall achievement – for combined tasks.

4. Service Plan Outcome Checklist: The Service Plan Outcome Checklist (SPOC) is a list of outcome goals that a particular agency typically helps its clients address. The SPOC format can be used in any agency, but the list of outcome goals is unique to each agency or service unit.

To use an SPOC, you ask your client at the beginning of service to look over the list of outcome goals and place a checkmark beside each goal he wants to achieve and is willing to work toward. If any outcomes are mandated by a court, school, or other referring agency, you note these as well, in a separate column from those selected by you and the client. To help with prioritizing services, you and the client also identify the two or three most important service goals. Then, at the termination of service, you rate the selected outcomes on a scale ranging from 1 (no progress) to 7 (fully achieved). If you use an SPOC with a client over an extended period, you can also rate his achievement at various points during the change process to assess the progress of intervention.

The SPOC can also be used to accumulate outcome scores for multiple clients in a service unit. If you use an SPOC with either all or a sample of your clients, for example, you can derive compilations of ratings that allow you to identify those service categories in which your clients tend to achieve (or not achieve) their goals.

5. Client Self-Rating Scale: The client self-rating scale (CSRS) a simple evaluation format that provides a client with a visual representation of his progress and change over time. It entails plotting a client's progress on line charts. The visual nature of this technique is useful for giving clients a sense of achievement as they make progress; it also makes it easy to spot when barriers are interfering in some way with a client's progress.

Each chart you create (one per goal) has scores ranging from -10 to +10 along the left axis (y-axis). Along the bottom of the chart (x-axis), you record the date of each session you have with the client.

Using a CSRS begins with you and the client defining, in positive terms, each goal you've identified as a target for change (e.g., "I want to increase the number of conflict-free interactions with my son"). You then create one chart for each goal (if any goals are interrelated, you can record progress toward more than one goal on the same chart). Next, you and the client establish descriptors (or anchor points) that reflect the criteria for assigning each score (from -10 to +10) for each goal. Then, in each session, you and the client discuss his improvement (or deterioration) in progressing toward each goal. The client then determines a self-rating for each goal, and you record each score on the relevant chart (you place a data point or dot on each chart where the score and that session's date intersect). Over time, you and the client will usually discuss trends reflected on the line charts and try to identify factors that have influenced his scores.

6. Standardized Rating Scales: If you use a standardized rating scale during assessment, you can then use the scale again periodically during intervention to identify changes as they occur (formative evaluation). Examining these scores can help guide your decisions about continuing or changing the treatment plan. You can also use a standardized rating scale to summarize the results of intervention with a client (summative evaluation) – here, you'd compare a client's score on the scale before intervention begins and to his score at the end of service.

7. Single-Subject Designs: Single-subject designs (SSDs) are frequently used in practice evaluation to evaluate changes in client behaviors, attitudes, or beliefs over a specified period of time. Unlike other forms of research that accrue data from multiple subjects either before and after intervention or with experimental and control groups, single-subject designs involve obtaining repeated measurements from only one subject (e.g., a single individual, couple, family, or group) over time. A single-subject design can also be used to examine a single intervention with multiple applications (e.g., multiple targets of change or in multiple settings).

Below we describe different types of single-subject designs. With the exception of case studies, each type includes at least one baseline (no treatment) phase and one treatment phase. As a result, when a single-subject design is used, subjects act as their own no-treatment "controls." In most of these designs, the dependent variable is measured repeatedly at regular intervals throughout the baseline and treatment phases. (Recall from earlier in this section that, in practice evaluation research, a client's functioning is the **dependent variable**, and the intervention is the **independent variable**.) If status on the dependent variable is stable within each phase and changes only at the same time the independent variable is applied or removed, then it's likely that any observed change in the dependent variable is due to the effects of the independent variable, rather than to an extraneous factor. So, the basic theory underlying the use of single-subject designs in practice evaluation is that, if you clearly describe a client behavior, attitude, or belief (dependent variable) before you introduce the intervention (independent variable) – in other words, if you obtain a baseline measurement – then, barring any evidence to the contrary, you can attribute to the intervention any change that occurs during the period of intervention.

a. Types of Single-Subject Design:

Case study: The most basic design is the B design or a **case study** in which there are no baseline or follow-up data: You simply keep track of what happens in regard to a target behavior, attitude, or belief while intervention is occurring. This approach (called an exploratory approach) allows you to record what goes on during intervention so that you can adjust the intervention if necessary. The data you record can also be used to guide future practice decisions.

AB design: The next simplest single-subject design is the **AB design**, which includes a single baseline (A) phase and a single treatment (B) phase. As in all single-subject designs, the dependent variable is measured at regular intervals during both phases. In this approach (called a **descriptive study**), you and the client can examine differences between the baseline period and the treatment phase. Extensions of the AB design, which we describe below, are also descriptive studies.

Extensions of the AB design (ABA, ABAB, etc.): The AB design can be expanded to include more than one baseline (A) phase and more than one treatment (B) phase. When an ABA design is used, for example, if status on the dependent variable returns to the initial baseline (no treatment) level during the second baseline phase, you can be more certain that an observed change in the dependent variable during the treatment phase was actually due to the independent variable (the intervention), rather than to an extraneous factor. Because any expansion requires the withdrawal of treatment during the second and subsequent baseline phases, the extensions of the AB design are called "reversal" or "withdrawal" designs. **Reversal designs** are considered inappropriate when withdrawal of treatment would be unethical – e.g., when treatment has successfully eliminated a self-injurious behavior.

Multiple baseline design: If a reversal design is inappropriate for ethical or practical reasons, you might use a **multiple baseline design**. The multiple baseline design doesn't require withdrawal of treatment but, instead, involves sequentially applying a treatment either to (a) different behaviors of the same client (multiple baseline across behaviors) or (b) the same client in different settings (multiple baseline across settings). (In other contexts, it may involve applying treatment to the same behavior of different clients, which is called multiple baseline across subjects.) Once treatment has been applied to a "baseline" (a behavior or setting), it isn't withdrawn from that baseline during your work with the client. Sequentially applying an intervention to different settings helps you determine if the intervention is actually responsible for any observed changes in the target behavior: If the behavior changes in a particular setting only after intervention has been applied in that setting, you can be more certain that the change is attributable to the intervention rather than to an extraneous factor.

b. Conducting a Single-Subject Evaluation: The characteristic way of organizing data collected from a single-subject design is on a graph (or chart) that depicts the target behavior, attitude, or belief on the left axis (y-axis) and a timeline in days, weeks, etc., along the bottom (x-axis).

To conduct a single-subject evaluation in direct practice, you need to select a case situation that allows you to take several measurements over time. These measurements usually occur before the intervention is introduced, during intervention, and after intervention is completed – the frequency of measurement, however, depends on the case situation (e.g., daily, weekly, monthly). When using a single-subject design, the three most common methods of taking measurements are direct observation (by you, the client, a teacher, a spouse, a parent, etc.); standardized measures (e.g., questionnaires, tests, inventories, checklists); and client self-report (e.g., self-anchored rating scale).

To begin the evaluation, you and a client select the behaviors, attitudes, or beliefs that will be targeted for change. This takes place during the planning and contracting phase. Several other decisions are also made at this time: (a) You select a valid and relevant numerical measure of change which will allow you and the client to monitor change over time. This may be a frequency count (how often something happens) or a score on a standardized or individualized rating scale. (b) You and the client develop a plan for taking measurements under conditions that will be as consistent as possible each time a measurement is taken (e.g., same location, same time of the day or day of the week). (c) You choose a single-subject design and designate the phases of the process on the graph, or chart. The different phases (e.g., baseline, intervention, follow-up) of the process are identified across the top of the graph, with dashed vertical lines separating each phase.

Once these decisions are made, you're ready to begin collecting and recording data on each behavior, attitude, and/or belief targeted for change. When possible, you should collect at least three **baseline measurements** (measurements that describe the target behavior, attitude, or belief before intervention is applied). These measurements can be taken during assessment or planning (**current baseline data**) or can be based on data that's already on record (**retrospective baseline data**), such as a client's attendance records or previous scores on assessment instruments.

Over time, you will then plot on the client's chart each score or other measurement you obtain on a variable – first, at baseline, and then each time you take a measurement. Because the chart will reflect a sequence of related scores over time, a line chart is the preferred format. This format allows you to connect data points to form solid lines, which makes it easy for you and the client to see how things change over time. Once all the data points have been entered on a client's chart, you can interpret the data and compare this empirical evidence with other observations to evaluate the success of the intervention.

For a review of key terms and concepts from research and statistics, see the Appendix at the end of this chapter.

IX. Termination

Termination refers to the process of formally ending the therapeutic relationship and should be viewed as a planned component of the intervention process. Your tasks during this phase include determining when it is appropriate to terminate, resolving the client's and your own emotional responses to the process of ending your relationship, and helping the client plan how to maintain the gains he has made and achieve continued growth following termination.

Ideally, termination is a mutual decision made by you and the client that occurs because the treatment goals have been reached, but, in reality, terminations occur for many different reasons. Terminations may be either planned or unplanned. **Planned terminations** occur either when a client's treatment goals are achieved or when service is concluded because of the time-limited nature of the treatment modality or setting. **Unplanned terminations** occur when a client withdraws from services prematurely or you leave the helping relationship due to a job change or other circumstance. Service may also end at a time other than that originally planned because you determine that transfer or referral of the client is necessary.

A. Making the Decision to Terminate

As a social worker, you will usually decide to begin the process of formally ending your relationship with a client when one (or more) of the following has occurred:

- The treatment goals have been achieved. According to NASW's Code of Ethics, it is unethical for you to continue treating a client after the client has met his treatment goals and, therefore, no longer needs your services.

- An agreed-on or necessary time limit to service provision has been reached.

- The problem or situation that brought the client to you (or your agency) has been sufficiently resolved so that the client can now function at an acceptable level and not be at risk of harming himself or others.

- You and/or the client have reached a point where you and/or he do not anticipate any benefits from additional contacts. In cases when it's clear that a client is not benefiting from your services, the Code of Ethics requires you to discuss with the client the termination of your services to him and referral elsewhere. When termination is necessary before the change process is completed, you must make appropriate referral to other helping sources.

- You (and your agency) have made a reasonable investment of time, energy, and skill without adequate results.

- The client has become inappropriately dependent on you (or your agency).

- The client would benefit by being transferred to another professional or agency.

B. Unplanned Terminations

1. Premature Termination by Clients: Sometimes, clients withdraw from treatment before reaching their goals. Among the reasons for this are dissatisfaction with the social worker, discouragement with the progress they're making, or a desire to avoid the material or emotions that the intervention is uncovering (i.e., to avoid difficult material, a client may experience a "**flight into health**" in which his problems or symptoms seem to disappear without intervention). In these situations, the client more or less chooses to terminate prematurely. Other client-initiated terminations occur because clients can't continue paying the fee or an adverse life event (e.g., arrest) makes them unavailable for further treatment.

In some cases of premature termination, a client informs you ahead of time that he will be ending treatment prematurely, while, in other cases, a client simply stops showing up. Guidelines for handling client-initiated premature terminations include the following:

- Keep in mind that an adult client has the right to leave treatment when he wants to (assuming that doing so would not place him or others in danger). A child or adolescent client, by contrast, doesn't have the right to decide on his own when to terminate services – in other words, when the client is a minor, his parent or legal guardian must make the decision.

- When an adult client tells you that he wants to terminate treatment before achieving his goals, it is usually appropriate to discuss with him the pros and cons of doing so (the exception would be if a client is withdrawing from treatment because of a circumstance over which he has no control). When warranted, you may even make specific recommendations as to what you believe would be in the client's best interests. This process helps ensure that the client has thoroughly considered his decision. If the client still wants to terminate after this discussion, you must respect his decision.

- Although direct efforts to persuade a client to return to treatment are seldom effective, whenever possible you should attempt to clarify the reasons for a client's decision to terminate early (e.g., "Have I offended you?"; "Is someone or something preventing you from continuing?"). Exploring these issues in a nondefensive and accepting way can sometimes be effective in helping a client work through his obstacles to continuing treatment.

- Assist the client in the transition so that it serves his best interests and meets his needs. For example, offer relevant referrals and suggest future work that the client can do on his own.

- If a client terminates treatment without warning (is a "**no-show**"), you should attempt to make a final contact with him by phone or letter. The goal of this contact may be to acknowledge his decision to terminate, encourage him to come in for a final session so that you can bring your relationship to an appropriate closure, and/or achieve the purposes of a final session through the phone call or letter. In the phone call or letter, for example, you might review the goals the client has achieved, reaffirm your regard for the client, and inform him of other services available to meet his ongoing needs.

2. Other Unplanned Terminations:

a. A Client Needs to Be Transferred to Another Worker: Unplanned termination sometimes occurs because you need to transfer a client to another social worker at your agency or within your community if you have a private practice. Such transfers may occur under the following circumstances:

- You will no longer be available to serve the client (e.g., you are leaving the agency). Your responsibilities in this situation are described below.

- The client would be better served by another social worker at your agency or another professional in your community.

- The helping process is stalled by a problem in the relationship between you and the client. For example, you are unable to develop sufficient empathy for the client; there is a conflict between you and the client that can't be resolved and is interfering with the client's progress; or there is a significant gap in communication or understanding between you and the client as a result of differences in values, religious beliefs, language, or cultural background, and you are unable to overcome this gap.

b. You Make a Unilateral Decision to Terminate: "Unilateral" means that you make the decision without having the client participate. Reasons why you may make a unilateral decision to terminate your relationship with a client before the treatment goals are reached include the following:

- The client has filed a lawsuit or official complaint against you.

- The client has breached, without good cause, the financial agreement regarding the payment of fees for service. In this circumstance, it is ethical for you to terminate treatment if two conditions are met: (a) the client does not pose a danger to himself or others, and (b) you have discussed with him the potential consequences of nonpayment and termination of therapy.

- The client is a physical danger to you or continually harasses you.

In the case of both client transfer and unilateral termination by you, you must clearly explain to the client what is happening and why. You should notify the client of the situation in writing and, if possible, during a face-to-face meeting. In addition, you should clearly document the reasons and circumstances surrounding the transfer or termination in the client's case record.

c. You Leave Your Agency: If you leave your agency to set up an independent private practice or to begin work at another agency, you should not refer your former agency's clients to yourself unless (a) you have made a specific agreement with your former agency *and* (b) you inform the clients of the various options available to them. To refer your former agency's clients to yourself without the above considerations, it would be deemed unethical. These options can include transferring to another social worker in your former agency, transferring to another agency or a different private practitioner, terminating treatment, or continuing to see you in your independent private practice.

d. Changes at Your Agency: Unplanned terminations can occur because of administrative decisions or other changes at the agency where you work. Examples include the agency cutting back on the services it provides, changes in your status at the agency that result in changes to a client's contract, or the end of financial reimbursement from a third-party payer such as an insurance company or Medicaid. When unplanned termination occurs for reasons like these, you should advocate, as necessary, on behalf of your client to make sure he receives the services he is entitled to and needs.

Finally, if an unplanned termination occurs for any reason and your services were being provided under court order, you must make sure that all terms of the court order have been met.

C. Facilitating Terminations and Transfers

Guidelines for facilitating appropriate terminations and transfers include the following:

- Do everything you can to prevent a client's termination from being unanticipated or sudden. Begin discussing termination with the client during the planning and contracting phase. When formulating the contract, explain that intervention is goal oriented and time-limited and incorporate time-frames and ways of monitoring progress into the contract.

- As termination nears, use the skill of **looking ahead to the end**. This skill entails reminding a client of the upcoming planned ending ("We have three meetings left") and discussing with him what remains to be done so that you can make the best possible use of your remaining sessions (e.g., you can focus on high-priority issues).

- For a client in psychotherapy, you may gradually decrease the frequency of contact as termination nears. If the client seems dependent on you, pair this process with efforts to connect him with informal resources in his social network.

- Use the skill of **reviewing progress**. In other words, review with the client what you and he have done to address his concerns. Describe the client's positive changes and ask the client to describe what he has learned.

- Openly address the client's feelings about the termination (see also Part D, below).

- Plan for the maintenance of changes and continued growth after termination: (a) Review the original problems and the steps the client took to resolve them. This gives you a chance to verify that the client understands problem-solving principles and how to apply them to future problems. (b) Emphasize that, to maintain his changes, the client must use relevant strategies in his personal life, such as setting personal goals and monitoring goal attainment. (c) Review and reinforce all other coping skills and behaviors the client has learned. (d) Use **anticipatory guidance**. This entails helping a client envision future problems and negative influences and planning ways to counteract them. (e) Link the client with resources and services in the community based on his continuing needs. For example, if a client's natural support system is inadequate, explore the availability of social and recreational programs. (f) Express faith in the client's ability to cope independently, but encourage him to return if a problem becomes overwhelming. (g) According to the client's wishes, schedule a "booster" session for several weeks after termination to assess treatment effects, convey your continued interest, and evaluate the client's functioning ability.

- Anticipate how the termination might affect people in the client's family and social network. In particular, if termination may place the client or others at risk of harm, you may choose to notify relevant others of the termination. In doing so, you must follow laws and ethical standards related to confidentiality (see Section I of Professional Relationships, Values, and Ethics).

- Monitor your own reactions as termination nears. If you feel a sense of loss over ending the relationship, you must make sure that you still emphasize the client's needs over your own.

D. Identifying and Addressing Clients' Reactions to Termination

Because termination can engender a range of emotions for a client, it's very important for you to provide an opportunity for a client to express his feelings and concerns about termination, including about the ending of his relationship with you.

1. Potential Client Reactions to Termination:

a. Emotional Responses: A client may feel a sense of loss over ending the relationship with you, have uncertainty about coping independently, and/or experience feelings of anger, sadness, or rejection.

- A client who feels angry may engage in self-destructive behaviors, angry outbursts, defiant acts, etc., rather than expressing his feelings verbally.

- There may be a return of symptoms (a **flight into illness**) or new problems may emerge. This is common when a client perceives the loss of support from you as uncomfortable.

- A client who is anxious about the impending loss of his relationship with you may criticize you or express doubts about his ability to maintain his gains without your ongoing support.

- A client may experience a rekindling of feelings that stem from previous separations and losses in his life.

- A client may feel betrayed or abandoned by you.

The positive emotions that a client may experience as termination approaches include appreciation, enthusiasm about the prospect of facing future problems independently, and a sense of relief over no longer having to experience the discomfort associated with making changes.

b. Denial: Some clients deny having feelings about termination or refuse to acknowledge that it is affecting them. Some shut off their thoughts about termination and relate to you as though nothing is different. They may behave as though they are unaware that termination is coming.

c. Avoidance: A client may express his painful feelings about the ending of your relationship by failing to appear for sessions as termination approaches. He may ignore your efforts to contact him or claim that he no longer needs your help.

d. Efforts to Prolong the Relationship: A client may request additional sessions even though he has reached his goals; in the last moments of the final session, a client may share significant information about himself or his situation; a client may initiate a discussion of death or dying (this is most common in group work); or a client may offer you a dual relationship (e.g., "We can be friends now," "Let's meet for coffee once in a while," or "I'd like to go into business with you").

The NASW Code of Ethics states that social workers should not engage in **dual relationships** with clients or former clients when there is a risk of exploitation or potential harm to the client. If a client offers you a dual relationship as treatment is coming to an end, you should politely decline the offer, briefly explain why, and help the client identify and express the feelings underlying his request, such as a sense of loss. (For more information on dual relationships, see Section I of Professional Relationships, Values, and Ethics.)

2. Addressing Clients' Reactions to Termination: In order for termination to be a positive experience for a client, you must be sensitive to his emotional reactions to it and skilled at helping him express his feelings:

- Bring up your feelings about the ending of the relationship, even if a client doesn't mention his. This skill is called **sharing ending feelings** (Shulman, 1981).

- Use the skill of **reaching for ending feelings** (Shulman, 1981) to encourage a client to articulate his feelings about termination (positive and/or negative feelings). Clients who experience negative emotions, such as anger, toward you, while simultaneously dealing with sadness or anxiety about the impending loss of your relationship may have great difficulty expressing their negative emotions to you. It's important to encourage expression of these feelings and respond empathically to them.

- If a client is denying his feelings about termination or behaving as though he is unaware that termination is coming, you can assist him in getting in touch with his emotions by (a) reintroducing the topic of termination and expressing your desire to help him formulate a plan to continue working on his goals following termination; and (b) as you bring up this topic, observing the client for nonverbal cues to his emotional reaction. Then, you can use empathic communication to convey understanding of and elicit his feelings.

- If a client expresses his feelings about termination by failing to show up for sessions as termination approaches, it's critical for you to reach out to him by telephone, letter, or a home visit. Otherwise, the client may conclude that you never cared about him. Contacting the client gives you an opportunity to reaffirm your concern for him and convey empathy and understanding of his emotional reaction to the termination.

- If a client reports that his problems are resurfacing or that he has new problems as termination approaches, your response will depend on the nature and severity of the problems he reports, what you know about the client's progress to date, and the client's degree of dependency: (a) In all cases, you should acknowledge to the client the anxiety and apprehension that normally accompany termination. (b) In some cases, you will determine that there are legitimate reasons to recontract for additional sessions. An example of this would be when the problem the client describes is one that would be important to work on or one that was set aside in favor of working on more pressing problems. (c) In other cases, you may determine that the problem the client reports is worthy of attention but continued work with you may promote unhealthy dependency on the part of the client; in this situation, you might consider referring the client to another therapist or continuing to work with the client in a less intensive format (e.g., less frequent sessions). Note, too, that some experts recommend that you have a preemptive discussion with clients about this issue as a termination approaches. That is, you may say to a client something like, "Sometimes people worry that their problems will return when they leave treatment, but I'm confident about how much you've accomplished; I trust that even if there are setbacks, it won't affect our ending" (Hepworth et al., 2006).

- If a client fears separation from you, you may schedule a follow-up interview or telephone contact for several weeks after termination. Also, inform the client that he can return to you or the agency if the need arises in the future.

- Consider using some kind of ritual to mark the ending of the relationship (e.g., culturally appropriate good-byes such as hugging and shaking hands; in group work, a pot-luck or other small celebration).

Finally, when a client's negative reactions to termination are not dealt with properly, they will often resurface in the future, including in his relationships with new providers. Some clients develop a cluster of symptoms called the **transfer syndrome** (Keith, 1966). In adults, this is manifested by such things as somatic symptoms, a loss of interest in the content of sessions, and/or repeated requests for changes in medications or appointment times. Other clients may ventilate their anger by criticizing you to a new provider, usually as a way of defending against their painful feelings over the loss of their relationship with you.

X. Crisis and Change

A. Stress and Coping

A person experiences "stress" when an internal conflict and/or environmental demand challenges or exceeds his adaptive resources. A "stressor" is "a stimulus that leads to anxiety or other mental disorders unless the individual's coping skills are used effectively" (Barker, 2003, p. 420).

1. Coping Skill, Coping Mechanism, and Coping Strategy: *Coping skills* are effective behaviors used to avoid or respond to sources of stress, and *coping mechanisms* are behavioral and personality patterns used to adapt to environmental pressures without giving up one's own goals. Some authors use the terms "coping strategy" and "ego defense mechanism" interchangeably. Others (e.g., Sheafor & Horejsi, 2003) distinguish between them based on the degree to which a person's response is under his conscious and voluntary control and whether reality distortion and self-deception are involved: They define a *coping strategy* as a deliberate and conscious effort to solve a problem or manage distressing feelings, and an *ego defense mechanism* as an habitual or unconscious maneuver that allows a person to avoid a problem.

2. Responses to Stress: Stress, by definition, interferes with normal functioning and creates internal anxiety. Responses to stress may include physiological reactions (e.g., ulcers, high blood pressure); psychological reactions (e.g., anxiety, depression, anger, concentration problems, sleeplessness, self-doubt, self-blame, avoidance of the stressful event in the future); and more serious mental conditions (e.g., learned helplessness, anxiety disorders, dissociative disorders).

People under stress face two primary challenges: They need to (a) manage their emotional and cognitive responses to the stress and (b) determine how to address the stressor itself. The first challenge requires **emotion-focused coping**, which is used to decrease one's anxiety and other emotional responses to the stress; and the second challenge requires **problem-focused coping** (a.k.a. task-focused coping), which involves using strategies to deal directly with the source of the stress. Usually a person must manage his psychological reactions before moving on to problem-solving, but emotion-focused coping and task-focused coping can occur simultaneously.

People's responses to stress are typically determined by certain moderating factors, including their social resources and personal characteristics. Adequate social support, for example, can serve to lessen a person's vulnerability to stress and risk of developing mental or physical illness in response to stress. Research on the **buffering hypothesis** shows that the subjective perception of social support is actually more critical than actual support, not only for alleviating feelings of loneliness but also for reducing the effects of stress and the risk for coronary heart disease (Seeman, 1985). Other critical determinants of a person's response to stress are his perception of control and beliefs about his ability to cope. When a person believes that he has no control over a situation or that he doesn't have the necessary coping skills or mechanisms, stress will have a more negative effect. This is consistent with Bandura's **self-efficacy theory**, which proposes that a person's belief about his own self-efficacy is the most significant mediator of his adjustment. Additionally, individuals are better able to tolerate and cope with stress when they have an **internal locus of control** (i.e., when they believe they have a degree of control over the causes or consequences of stress).

Note that the term "**eustress**" is sometimes used to refer to what can be considered "good" stress. Rather than being associated with discomfort or emotional distress, eustress motivates people to continue participating in and enjoying activities and events that require effort, but ultimately promote their physical and emotional well-being. Examples of eustress include engaging in physical exercise, completing coursework to graduate from school, having a baby, and pursuing and landing a desirable job.

B. Crisis

Crisis Theory

1. What is "Crisis?": "Crisis" is a state of acute emotional upset that includes a temporary inability to cope by means of one's usual problem-solving methods. A typical crisis lasts for no more than six to eight weeks because a person cannot remain for too long in a state of acute emotional upset. At the end of a crisis, the person's subjective discomfort diminishes.

Events alone do not activate crisis. Instead crisis occurs when a person's interpretation of the event and available coping methods and social resources produce tension so severe that the person cannot find relief. Key determining factors include the person's cultural values related to the event, previous problem-solving ability, previous level of functioning and coping skills, and current levels of social, material, and other support.

The **stages of crisis** (or components of crisis) include the following (Golan, 1978):

Stage 1 – Hazardous event: The **hazardous event** is an initial shock that disrupts a person's equilibrium and initiates a series of reactions that may culminate in a crisis. The hazardous event may be anticipated (e.g., marriage, retirement) or unanticipated (e.g., the unexpected death of a family member).

Stage 2 – Vulnerable state: The vulnerable state is a person's subjective response to stressful events in his life. It is marked by an increase in anxiety which the person attempts to relieve by using his customary coping strategies. If these are unsuccessful, the person's tension continues to rise and, eventually, he is unable to function effectively.

Stage 3 – Precipitating factor: The **precipitating factor** is the final stressful event in a series of events that moves a person from a state of acute vulnerability into crisis. The precipitating factor often is a minor event, but it can assume catastrophic proportions in the context of other stressful events and the person's inability to use his usual problem-solving strategies. The precipitating factor can produce a range of responses, from a strong desire to seek help to a suicide attempt.

Stage 4 – Active crisis state: The active crisis state always includes disequilibrium, or disorganization, and normally involves three stages: (a) physical and psychological agitation (e.g., disturbed appetite, disturbed sleep, impaired problem-solving ability, anxiety, depression); (b) preoccupation with the events that led to the crisis; and (c) a gradual return to a state of equilibrium. During the active state, a person usually recognizes that his customary coping mechanisms are inadequate and, therefore, may be highly motivated to seek and accept help.

Stage 5 – Restoration of equilibrium: Successful reintegration following a crisis depends on several factors, including the person's ability to objectively evaluate the crisis situation and the development and use of adaptive coping strategies.

2. Crisis Origins:

a. Situational Crises: In a **situational crisis**, the crisis origin is a sudden, random, shocking, and often catastrophic event that cannot be anticipated or controlled. The event threatens the person's sense of biological, psychological, and/or social well-being and, therefore, produces some disequilibrium and a possible crisis. Factors that determine whether a person will experience such an event as a crisis include his perception or interpretation of the event and available coping mechanisms and social supports. A situational crisis leads to emotional and psychological trauma when the stressful event shatters the person's sense of security and makes him feel helpless and vulnerable.

Sources of situational crises include physical illness and injury (e.g., diagnosis of a serious illness, physical disability, surgery); unexpected or untimely death of a loved one (e.g., fatal accident or illness, suicide, homicide); crime, including the experiences of victims and offenders (e.g., assault, rape, domestic violence, incarceration or release of an offender); natural and man-made disasters (e.g., flood, fire, earthquake, airline crash, car accident); war and related acts (e.g., terrorist attack); other unexpected social or interpersonal events (e.g., separation or divorce); and other material or environmental losses or events (e.g., the loss of one's job, a disease epidemic, severe economic depression) (Slaikeu, 1984).

b. Maturational (Developmental) Crises (Transition States): With a **maturational crisis**, the crisis origin is embedded in maturational processes – that is, the person struggles with a transition from one life stage (or role) to another. Because these transitions are part of normal development, they can be anticipated. Most transition states are universal in that they consist of normal life-cycle passages from one developmental stage to the next. Other transition states are nonuniversal in that not all people experience them during the course of normal development. These include changes in social status, such as a shift from student to worker or from worker to retiree. Like universal developmental transitions, nonuniversal transitions are usually anticipated and can be prepared for.

During each stage of development, a person undergoes significant psychological, social, and/or physical change and is challenged by certain developmental tasks. Transition issues, tasks, and possible crisis events associated with each developmental stage include the following (Slaikeu, 1984):

Childhood: Tasks center on socialization, relationship with parents, friendships, and success/failure in school. Potential crisis events include peer conflict, loss of friends through moving, conflict with parents, school difficulties, and, in early childhood, entering school.

Adolescence: Identity issues dominate. Potential crisis events include success/failure in academics or athletics, graduation from high school, going to college, conflict with parents over personal habits and lifestyle, breakup with boy/girlfriend, unwanted pregnancy, career indecision, and difficulty on the first job.

Young adulthood (ages 18-34): The person is preoccupied with intimacy, parenthood, and getting started in a career or occupation. Potential crisis events include rejection by a boy/girlfriend, an extramarital affair, separation/divorce, unwanted pregnancy, birth of a child, inability to have children, illness in a child, discipline problems with children, inability to manage the demands of parenthood, academic difficulties, job dissatisfaction, poor performance in a chosen career, financial difficulties, and conflict between career and family goals.

Middle adulthood (ages 35-50): Preoccupations include reworking previous developmental issues and confronting new issues and challenges – the person evaluates what he has accomplished personally and professionally. Potential crisis events include an awareness of physical decline, chronic illness (in self or spouse), rejection by adolescent children, decision-making about caring for an elderly parent, death or prolonged illness of parents, career setback, conflicts at work, financial concerns, moving associated with a job promotion, unemployment, sense of discrepancy between life goals and life achievements, dissatisfaction with goals achieved, regret over past decisions related to marrying/not marrying or having children/not having children, marital problems, returning to work after raising children, and death of friends.

Maturity (ages 50-65): Preoccupations include consolidating one's experience and resources and reorienting one's life toward later years. Potential crisis events include health problems, decision-making related to retirement, resistance to retirement, changes in physical living arrangements, conflict with grown children, adjusting to an "empty nest," death of a spouse, divorce, and conflict with parents.

Old age (i.e., retirement until death): The person is preoccupied with sharing wisdom from life experiences, evaluating the past, and achieving a sense of satisfaction with his life. Potential crisis events include illness and disability, death of a spouse and/or friends, financial difficulties, interpersonal conflicts with children or with peers in one's new living arrangements, neglect by adult children, difficulty in adjusting to retirement, and awareness of loneliness.

Although people generally experience an increase in anxiety during transition states, a crisis is not inevitable. Whether or not a transition state activates an emotional crisis depends on several factors, including the following:

- The probability of crisis is higher when a person does not, or cannot, prepare for one of these changes. For example, a young adult whose parents have been overprotective may find it difficult to transition from adolescence into adulthood. A stage theorist would predict that this person would have difficulty functioning fully as a young adult because he did not (could not) successfully complete the tasks associated with adolescence.

- Crisis can occur when accomplishment of the tasks associated with a developmental stage is blocked or disrupted because the person lacks needed skills or knowledge, is unable to take risks, or is socially disadvantaged. People need social, cultural, and material (e.g., money) resources to avoid acute emotional upset during transition states.

- When an unanticipated traumatic event (e.g., the sudden death of a loved one, serious physical illness, the loss of one's job) occurs while a person is attempting to negotiate a key developmental task, the probability of crisis is higher because the added pressure of this event may overwhelm the person's ability to cope.

- A person may go into crisis because he perceives a life event or situation as inconsistent with society's expectations for his age group (e.g., a person has not married by age 40).

c. Cultural/Social Crisis: A crisis may stem from various social/cultural factors operating in the larger society. Job loss, for example, may be due to discrimination rather than poor job performance.

3. Crisis Outcomes: Crisis includes not only danger but also the potential for growth.

Positive outcomes: Two positive outcomes are possible: (a) Problem-solving efforts are successful, and the person returns to his precrisis state. (b) The person not only returns to his precrisis state but also grows from the crisis experience because he discovers new ways of solving problems and new resources. Most people in crisis are open to trying new problem-solving approaches because they want to reduce their emotional discomfort as quickly as possible.

Negative outcomes: Negative outcomes of crisis can include the following: (a) The person lacks effective means of resolving problems and reducing his anxiety, his emotional upset persists, and the crisis produces severe affective, cognitive, and/or behavioral malfunctioning (e.g., the person becomes depressed, withdrawn, or suspicious; the person seeks temporary solutions by engaging in impulsive, destructive behavior or by abusing alcohol or other drugs; the person resorts to extreme behavior and attempts or commits suicide or abuses or kills others). (b) The person in crisis regains a state of equilibrium and believes that the problem is resolved, when, in fact, it has only subsided. The crisis event is buried below the person's awareness, and, when new stressors occur, it resurfaces and quickly triggers a new crisis. People in such **transcrisis states** (James & Gilliland, 2005) are usually able to function at a minimal level, but they are always at risk because any single stressor may send them back into crisis again.

The Impact of Crisis and Trauma on an Individual

1. Potential Effects of Crisis on a Person's Functioning:

a. Affective (Emotional) Functioning: In a crisis, as in other situations, a person's feelings are usually consistent with his perceptions of the situation.

- There may be abnormal or impaired affect. This is often the first sign that a person is in a state of disequilibrium.

- Most people in crisis experience a high level of anxiety and tension (e.g., a sense of dread; fear of losing control; inability to focus; physical symptoms such as sweating, tachycardia, or chest or abdominal pain).

- A person in crisis may experience a sense of loss or emptiness stemming from the actual or threatened loss of self-esteem, social relationships, or material goods, or the failure to meet a life challenge.

- Hopelessness or helplessness may be present and would indicate that the person's emotional strength is low (i.e., he may be in severe crisis and need a very directive response from the social worker or other helper).

- A person in crisis may fear losing control or be afraid because he doesn't understand why he's responding the way he is.

- A person in crisis may direct anger at himself for not being able to manage recent events, or at somebody else for leaving, dying, being abusive, etc. Guilt and embarrassment may follow anger if the person believes his anger was unjustified (e.g., he was angry at a family member who died).

b. *Cognitive Functioning:*

- Concentration may be impaired (e.g., the person may be bothered by intrusive thoughts about the crisis event or unable to concentrate on anything other than the crisis event).

- The person's problem-solving and decision-making abilities may be diminished by confusion, obsessiveness, or self-doubt. A person in crisis may not be able to make any decisions at the present time.

- Some people in crisis have irrational beliefs about the crisis situation. People vary in the extent to which they are open to changing irrational beliefs about a crisis situation and reframing them in more rational terms.

- A high level of tension may be distorting the person's perception of reality. As a result, his interpretation of the crisis event may not be consistent with the reality of the situation. It even could differ so much from reality that it constitutes a threat to the person's (or someone else's) welfare.

c. *Behavioral Functioning:* A person's behavior is generally determined by what he feels and thinks, including his interpretation of events. The following behavioral indicators are associated with crisis:

- Diminished ability to perform vocational functions (e.g., can't accomplish required household chores, concentrate on schoolwork, or perform effectively at an outside job).

- Difficulty handling responsibilities involved in activities of daily living (e.g., self-care/hygiene, cleaning, cooking, child care, management of financial resources, shopping, transportation, safety).

- Change in social behavior (e.g., withdrawal from usual social interactions, uncharacteristic efforts to avoid being alone and "clingy" or "demanding" behavior). If social connections are severely disrupted, the person may be isolated or feel detached or distant from others.

- Impulsive behavior (e.g., driving recklessly, alcohol or other drug abuse, a suicide attempt, attacking others). These reflect desperate means of solving the problem.

- Behavior inconsistent with thoughts and feelings (e.g., laughing when talking about the traumatic event).

- Rejection of help offered by family and friends. This may stem from a sense of helplessness and/or from embarrassment at not being able to cope. The person may fear that accepting help will be misinterpreted as proof of his perceived weakness.

- Atypical behavior (e.g., driving while intoxicated by a person who has no previous history of such behavior).

2. The Role of Personal, Family, and Community Resources: An individual's personal and social resources can affect both the origin and resolution of the crisis. In particular, a person's ability to cope with recent stressful events can be affected by the following:

- His family's response to and interpretation of the events. These can play a role in activating or prolonging a crisis state.

- The personal, social, and institutional strengths or supports available to him. Is his usual support system present/available, absent, or exhausted?

- His view of family and other social contacts as actual or potential assets or as liabilities.

- The existence of personal, social, financial, vocational, or other obstacles to his progress. Cultural and socioeconomic factors can contribute to crisis vulnerability as well as the ability to resolve the crisis (e.g., environmental barriers to becoming economically self-sufficient).

- His success or failure in obtaining necessary help from community resources.

3. The Impact of Culture and Socialization: Socialization processes and value systems affect how people interpret and respond to life events. For example, diverse cultural, ethnic, and religious groups attach different meanings to and have distinct patterns of response to events such as death, physical illness, divorce, pregnancy outside of marriage, etc. Different cultural, ethnic, and religious groups also have differing role expectations for males/husbands and females/wives. Thus, for example, job loss may be more traumatic for an adult male if males in his culture are expected to provide for the family's material needs.

4. The Family in Crisis: Change, whether expected or not, requires transformation in the organization of a family system and may result in disequilibrium, role confusion, and heightened conflict within the family. The development of symptoms in one or more family members is fairly common during a period of change and usually indicates that the family is having difficulty negotiating the transition.

Family events with crisis potential include the following: (a) normal transition points that require a change in roles (e.g., having a child, retirement); (b) unanticipated traumatic events including those that disrupt the expected course of the family's development (e.g., the birth of a child with a disability, serious financial losses, the death of young family member, the loss of a parent during childhood); and (c) the loss of family morale and family unity (e.g., due to imprisonment of a family member or alcoholism) (Eliot, 1955; Hill, 1965).

Whether a traumatic event leads to a family crisis or not depends on (a) the family's personal, social, and material resources for handling the situation, including their ability to engage in effective collaborative efforts to cope with difficulties, and (b) how they perceive and define the event. Whether a family regards divorce as a catastrophic event or not, for example, depends, in part, upon the family's cultural or religious values. And job loss might precipitate a crisis for a family with limited material resources, but not for a wealthy family; the latter family may experience a crisis as a result of job loss, however, if the loss lowers their social status, and the family values external respectability.

Crisis Assessment

1. General Crisis Assessment Tasks and Guidelines: The main objective of crisis assessment is to rapidly evaluate the degree of client disequilibrium and immobility (inability to take autonomous action).

a. Crisis Assessment Tasks: Most crisis assessments involve performing the following general tasks:

- Identifying the precipitating factor.

- Identifying the client's response to the crisis.

- Evaluating the client's strengths, coping strategies he has used in the past, and possible sources of external support.

- Determining what resources the social worker (or agency) has in relation to the client's assessed needs.

- Identifying specific goals and targets of crisis intervention.

b. Crisis Assessment Guidelines: General guidelines for crisis assessment include the following:

- Crisis assessment should be carried out *with* a client. The social worker needs to define and understand the problem from the client's point of view. If she doesn't view the crisis situation as the client does, her intervention strategies and procedures may fail.

- The social worker asks open-ended questions to elicit information about the client's feelings, thoughts, and behaviors, and closed-ended questions to quickly elicit specific details from the client about what's occurring in his life (e.g., "Are you thinking about harming yourself?" "When did that happen?"). The social worker also uses restatement and summary clarification to verify that she understands the client's messages. This is important because crisis clients may have great difficulty in expressing themselves clearly. Restatement is also useful for refocusing clients who are overwhelmed or whose thoughts are racing.

- Whenever possible, the social worker solicits information from the client's significant others.

- The assessment process should be tied directly to crisis resolution. The focus is on immediate, identifiable problems. Because many crisis clients have complicated problems and most have more than one problem, the social worker may need to distill multiple problems into one immediate problem that can be worked on first.

- Although there is no time to collect the type of historical material that might be relevant in a non-crisis situation, certain historical information should be collected and incorporated when possible: First, the social worker should explore the client's history of problem solving and success and failure in dealing with past stressful events or resolving past crises. This information is important for understanding and mobilizing the client's personal and social resources to resolve the crisis in a positive way. And, depending on the nature of the crisis and the client's condition, completing an assessment may also require obtaining recent medical and/or psychiatric histories.

2. Assess Threat to Life: Crisis has the potential to overwhelm a person to such an extent that severe pathology results. Therefore, every client in crisis should be assessed with regard to danger to self (e.g., self-harm/suicide) and others (e.g., assault, homicide). Note that **self-harm** also includes self-destructive/self-injurious behaviors that are not explicitly suicidal. These behaviors may occur when a client is not in an acute crisis state and can intensify during a crisis. For example, some people are chronically self-destructive – they habitually abuse alcohol and/or other drugs, refuse to follow necessary medical programs for serious illnesses, or engage in lifestyles or activities that frequently place them at high risk for serious injury or death. Other people cut their own bodies.

3. Determine the Severity of the Crisis: The degree of severity of the crisis will generally affect a client's mobility (capacity to act autonomously and to cope), which gives the social worker a basis for deciding how directive to be. A client experiencing a severe crisis is usually too confused or overwhelmed to choose his own direction.

a. General Guidelines:

- The social worker should assess the severity of the crisis immediately, from both the client's subjective viewpoint and her own objective viewpoint. An objective assessment is based on evaluation of the client's affective, cognitive, and behavioral functioning. Examining these factors helps the social worker determine whether the client requires referral for medical examination or treatment or to a specific agency. In some cases, a mental status exam is needed to clarify the client's current cognitive and behavioral functioning.

- Most people in crisis manifest emotional upset, biophysical upset, cognitive disturbance, and behavioral changes. The emotional upset is seen as a normal reaction to a hazardous event, and most people in crisis do not have a diagnosable mental disorder. Some people in crisis have pre-existing mental or emotional disturbances, however, and these may play a role in triggering or exacerbating a crisis state.

- Distress signals highly associated with crisis include difficulty managing feelings, suicidal or homicidal tendencies, alcohol or drug abuse, trouble with the law, and an inability to effectively use available help. These signals usually indicate that a client is coping ineffectively with a crisis and needs immediate assistance to prevent a negative outcome.

- When possible, the social worker should assess the client's precrisis functioning within the affective, cognitive, and behavioral domains so that she can determine the degree of change from the client's typical functioning level within these domains. This will tell the social worker the extent to which the client's current functioning is atypical and whether the client's current functioning is related to the current crisis or chronic.

b. Specific Questions: Generally, the social worker should explore the following:

- How much has the crisis disrupted the client's life and in what ways? What are the effects of this disruption on significant others?

- Is the client's coping behavior appropriate to the crisis event? To what extent is the client able to use effective coping behaviors? Does the client display coping behaviors that are ineffective or maladaptive? Does the client display coping behaviors that are likely to exacerbate the crisis situation? How does the client usually handle upsetting problems? Why did these strategies fail this time?

- Can the client perform tasks necessary for daily functioning? Does the client perform these tasks with noticeable effort? Does the client neglect some tasks necessary for daily functioning? Is the client's ability to perform these tasks noticeably compromised?

- Is the client's behavior erratic or unpredictable? Are the client's behaviors harmful toward himself or others?

- Is the client using alcohol or other drugs? Use, misuse, or abuse of alcohol or other drugs may be affecting the crisis, its severity, and the client's current functioning.

In addition, a crisis client may be feeling immobilized. The basic problem in immobility is a loss of control, and getting a client involved in taking concrete action to resolve a problem will begin to restore his sense of control. The social worker may explore the following questions: In similar situations in the past, what actions did the client take that helped him regain control? What would the client have to do now to get back in control? Is there anyone who would be supportive to the client at this time?

4. Assess Crisis Origin and Development: The objective here is to identify the specific events or situations that led to the client's current distress. Key questions to explore include: What recent stressful events have occurred in the client's life? In what developmental stage is the client? Is the client in the initial or acute phase of crisis? Identifying both the hazardous event and precipitating factor is useful for distinguishing between an acute crisis and chronic stress. The precipitating event can be difficult to identify, however, particularly when a client's problem has been present for a long time and/or when his report is long or rambling. Early in the interview, the social worker should ask, "What event brought you here today?"

5. Explore Personal and Social Resources: A client's personal and social resources can affect both the origin and resolution of a crisis. Therefore, assessing this domain can help clarify the source of the crisis and enable the social worker to determine what alternatives (choices, actions) the client has at this time that would resolve the crisis and restore him to a precrisis state of mobility.

6. Explore Cultural/Social Factors: Effective crisis intervention requires the development of goals and use of methods and strategies that are consistent with the life experiences and cultural values of the client. In particular, behavior that seems unusual to the social worker may be considered normal within the client's cultural reference group. To determine whether a crisis client's behavior is abnormal or not, a social worker must know *that* client's cultural definition of what is "normal" or "abnormal" under the circumstances. If the client is too upset to provide this information, the social worker should attempt to obtain it from family or friends of the client. If this isn't possible, she should seek consultation from someone of the client's cultural or ethnic group. The social worker should also consider cultural concepts of distress described in the DSM-5.

Crisis Intervention

Crisis theory proposes that individuals in crisis pass through a predictable response sequence and that this sequence can be interrupted or changed through education and assistance with developing more adaptive coping behaviors. Whenever possible, a desired goal of crisis intervention is to help clients learn more effective coping behaviors so that they will be able to respond more adaptively to future crisis situations.

Because, by definition, crisis is short-term and overwhelming, crisis intervention involves assessment and treatment methods that differ from those used in long-term situations. For example, in crisis intervention, a client's behavior is seen as an understandable, rather than pathological, response to a stressor or event; a here-and-now orientation is used; treatment is time-limited; and the social worker assumes a more active and directive role than she normally does.

1. Principles: The treatment plan for a crisis must be realistic (it must match the client's needs and resources), time-limited (including a clear time-frame for each action), and concrete. This provides the client with a sign that something definite will happen to change his present state of discomfort. Other important principles of crisis treatment include the following:

Intervention must be immediate: People are most amenable to treatment when they are at the peak of the crisis and ask for help. If a social worker cannot see a client who is in crisis immediately, she should refer the client to a colleague or other service provider who can.

Concentrate on limited goals: While a client is in crisis, intervention focuses only on goals that are directly related to the crisis.

Focused problem-solving: While a client is in crisis, treatment focuses on resolving the problem that underlies the crisis.

Active and directive treatment: While a client is in crisis, a social worker should participate actively and be directive in developing activities that will help the client resolve the crisis. The social worker's specific level of action and involvement, however, must be appropriate to the client's present functional level and current dependency needs. Important considerations include how the client is presently thinking, feeling, and acting: (a) A "directive mode" is appropriate when a client is too immobile to cope with the crisis (e.g., he is very depressed, anxious, or confused, in a state of shock, out of touch with reality, in need of hospitalization, and/or a danger to himself or others). In this mode, the social worker takes the lead in defining the problem, identifying alternatives, and developing a plan of action, and instructs, leads, or guides the client. (b) A "collaborative mode" is appropriate when a client has enough ego strength and mobility to participate as a partner in assessing the problem, identifying alternatives, and carrying out action steps. The social worker serves as a temporary catalyst, consultant, facilitator, and support person. (c) A "nondirective mode" focuses on helping a client use existing problem-solving capacities that have been temporarily unavailable. It is used only rarely at the beginning of crisis intervention, but can be appropriate once a client is able to initiate and perform action steps on his own.

Encourage self-reliance: While a client is in crisis, the social worker must strike a balance between providing the support and direction the client needs and encouraging him to be self-reliant and independent.

Support the client: A lack of support often contributes to a crisis, so providing support (and mobilizing a client's social support network) is crucial. If the client is feeling pent up with emotion, the intervention plan must include adequate time for the client to express his suppressed feelings.

Give the client hope: People in crisis usually feel hopeless, so a primary task during intervention is to provide the client with the expectation that the crisis will be resolved.

Enhance the client's self-esteem: A person in crisis usually feels inadequate, so the social worker should use an approach that protects and raises the client's self-esteem.

2. Goals: The goals of crisis intervention depend on the nature of the crisis, but generally involve those listed below. According to Rapoport (1970), the first four goals must be addressed in all types of crisis intervention, while the last two are feasible only in some situations.

- Alleviate the client's symptoms.
- Discover what led to the crisis.
- Identify and implement appropriate measures to remedy the crisis.
- Help the client regain his previous level of functioning.
- Help the client develop adaptive coping strategies that he can use now and in the future.
- Help the client connect the current situation to past life experiences.

3. General Techniques: The general techniques applied in crisis intervention depend on the type of crisis, the social worker's orientation to treatment, and the client's resources. Here are some examples:

Affective interventions – e.g., help the client express the feelings produced by the crisis.

Cognitive interventions – e.g., help the client understand the crisis, help the client eliminate mistaken or irrational beliefs that contributed to the crisis, help the client view the precipitating event in a different way.

Assigning behavioral tasks – e.g., provide relaxation training, require the client to spend more time with significant others.

Environmental manipulation – e.g., mobilize support, refer the client to an agency that can help alleviate his immediate problems (e.g., for income maintenance).

4. Specific Techniques: Specific crisis treatment techniques include the following (Hollis, 1972):

Sustainment: Sustainment includes engendering catharsis, providing reassurance, and empathetic listening. Sustainment is used in the first stages of crisis intervention to reduce the client's tension, anxiety, and guilt, as well as provide emotional support.

Direct influence: The social worker encourages a specific course of action and accesses the client's support systems. This often includes contacting other agencies, as well as including significant others in the intervention plan.

Person-situation reflection: The social worker helps the client understand and manage specific personal and situational aspects of the crisis. This can entail exploring questions such as the following: How objective is the client about the crisis? What is his role in the crisis; is he aware of how his emotional response to the precipitating event influenced the crisis? Can the client use other coping strategies?

Dynamic and developmental understanding: Later in the intervention, the social worker and client can explore in greater depth what the client's role in the crisis was (e.g., defense mechanisms, resistances, or communication patterns that contributed to the crisis). This should take place only when the client is cognitively and emotionally able to confront deeper issues.

Crisis Counseling Groups

The conduct and content of crisis counseling groups are determined by their primary purpose – the resolution of the members' crises by means of a group process. In crisis groups, individual historical information and any feelings not associated with the members' crises are limited in group discussions. Instead, group sessions focus on the crises identified by the group members. The leader uses techniques similar to those used in individual crisis treatment, including encouraging members to express feelings relevant to the crisis event, helping them gain an understanding of the crisis situation, exploring resources and solutions to the problem, and exploring social change strategies that might reduce the risk for crisis in the future.

C. Suicide

Suicide assessment has the following characteristics:

- The primary goal is to arrive at a reasonable estimate of the probability that the client will actually attempt suicide in the near future. Your intervention will depend on the level of risk involved.

- Suicide assessment is ongoing because the level of risk for a given client can increase or decrease over time.

- Any suicidal crisis, be it ideation, a threat, a gesture, or an actual attempt, should be dealt with as a true emergency situation. Even so-called "low-risk" situations must be taken seriously.

- Whenever possible, suicide assessment should integrate information from a variety of sources, including, for example, your interview with the client, a mental status exam, consultations with the client's physician or other help providers, and information from significant others.

- When you suspect that a client is at risk for suicide, you should address this immediately through the use of direct questions, such as "Have you ever thought about hurting yourself?" When a client responds in the affirmative, the next step is to determine his level of risk for an immediate suicide attempt.

- Assessment of suicide risk ordinarily involves indirect and direct assessment techniques, which are described below.

1. Indirect Assessment of Suicide (Suicide Risk Factors): Indirect assessment of suicide entails evaluating the client in terms of the demographic, clinical, and psychological **risk factors** that have been consistently linked with a high risk for suicide. Factors associated with a risk for suicide include the following:

Age: From 1991 to 2003, suicide rates were consistently highest for individuals ages 65 and older, but beginning in 2004, the rates for individuals ages 25 to 64 began to surpass the rates of the older age group; and, in 2010, the highest rate when males and females are considered together was for individuals ages 45 to 54. However, when the 2010 rates for females and males are considered separately, the highest rate for females was for those ages 45 to 54 and, for males, for those ages 75 and older (CDC, 2012, 2014).

Gender: Four times as many males as females commit suicide, but females attempt suicide two to three times more often than males (CDC, 2007; CDC, 2012). One reason why males are more likely to kill themselves is because they use more lethal methods: Men are more likely to attempt suicide with a gun, by hanging, or by carbon monoxide poisoning, while women are more likely to use poison or drugs (especially barbiturates).

Race/ethnicity: For most age groups, the suicide rates are highest for whites. The exception is for American Indians/Alaskan Natives ages 15 to 34 who have a suicide rate 2.5 times higher than the national average for that age group (CDC, 2012).

Marital status: Divorced, separated, and widowed people have the highest rates of suicide, followed by those who are single. The lowest rates are found among people who are married.

Suicidal thoughts and behaviors: As many as 60 to 80 percent of people who commit suicide have made at least one previous attempt, and about 80 percent give a definite warning of their intention.

Early warning signs: Early warning signs include threatening self-harm or suicide, writing or talking about death or suicide, seeking a means to commit suicide, and making preparations for dying such as preparing a will, giving away possessions, or saying goodbye to loved ones (Chehil & Kutcher, 2012).

Life stress: Failure at work or school, rejection by a loved one, living alone, and an absence of social support and social ties are associated with an increased risk for suicide.

Psychiatric disorders: Most suicide victims have a mental disorder, and major depression and bipolar disorder are most common, with individuals with a mood disorder being about 15 to 20 percent more likely than individuals in the general population to commit suicide (Jaimison, 1999). When suicide is associated with depression, it is most likely to occur within three months after depressive symptoms begin to improve.

Personality correlates: Hopelessness has been found to be more predictive of suicide than the intensity of depressive symptoms (Beck, et al., 1985). In addition, self-oriented and socially prescribed perfectionism have been linked to an elevated risk for depression and suicide, although self-oriented perfectionism may be associated with an elevated risk only when it is combined with high levels of life stress (Hewitt, Flett, & Ediger, 1996).

Biological correlates: Low levels of serotonin and 5-HIAA (a serotonin metabolite) have been linked to an increased risk for suicide and violent suicide attempts (Winchel, Stanley, & Stanley, 1990).

Risk factors specific to children and adolescents: (a) Suicidal ideation and attempts in young people are associated with interpersonal conflicts and loss, physical and sexual abuse, family discord, and psychiatric disorders, especially mood disorders, conduct disorder, and substance use disorders. Among teens who complete suicide, the most common precipitant is an interpersonal conflict, such as rejection by a boyfriend or girlfriend or an argument with a parent (Brent et al., 1988). (b) In adolescents, the risk for suicide increases dramatically when depression co-occurs with conduct disorder, a substance use disorder, or attention-deficit/hyperactivity disorder (ADHD) (Garland & Zigler, 1993). (c) The suicide attempts of adolescents are often impulsive and typically motivated by a desire to influence others, gain attention or affection, express anger, or escape an undesirable situation. Early warning signs of suicide for this age group include talking about death, talking about a reunion with a deceased person, and giving away prized possessions. (d) Exposure to suicide and suicidal behavior (e.g., through the media or the death of friends) has been linked to an increased risk for suicide among adolescents (Gould, 1990).

Finally, although suicidal thoughts and behavior are observed in children as young as preschool age, completed suicides are rare before adolescence.

Risk factors specific to older adults: For older adults, risk factors include chronic or acute physical and mental illness; failure to respond to medical treatment; elder abuse; alcoholism; prolonged stress; the stress of coping with multiple losses that may accompany growing older (e.g., death of a spouse, loss of work roles and income); and having fewer friends, living alone, being excluded or living on the periphery of social and family events, and being separated from family through children leaving home.

Generally, clients who have or may have one (or more) of the following mental disorders must be evaluated for suicide risk: major depressive disorder, a bipolar disorder, schizophrenia, a substance use disorder, posttraumatic stress disorder (PTSD) or acute stress disorder, and borderline personality disorder. A client with the latter disorder, in particular, should be monitored for suicidality and other self-injurious behavior during the entire course of treatment. Finally, people who experience recurrent panic attacks are also at risk for suicide attempts.

2. Direct Assessment of Suicide: Direct assessment of suicide entails questioning the client about his intent to commit suicide.

Any suspicion that a client is at risk for suicide should be immediately addressed through the use of direct questions. Examples are the following: Have you ever thought that life is not worth living? Have you ever thought about hurting yourself? Do you plan to hurt yourself? If you suspect that a client is suicidal (even a new client who is meeting with you for the first time), do not hesitate to ask direct questions to clarify his intent.

Direct assessment should emphasize indicators that directly suggest an elevated and more imminent risk of a suicide attempt – these indicators are **intent**, **plan**, and **means**. A communication of **intent** may be spoken or written and either direct ("I'm going to kill myself") or indirect ("I'm useless and I matter to no one"). All suicide threats should be taken seriously and examined through direct questioning in relation to the client's intention. If the client has communicated an intent, explore the following questions:

- Does the client have a suicide **plan**? If yes, find out whether the plan is specific and concrete. For example, can the client say exactly how, when, and where he plans to commit suicide? Has the client recently made preparations for death, such as writing a will or giving away his possessions?

- If the client has a concrete suicide plan, find out whether he has the **means** available to carry out his plan.

The risk to life is highest when the client has both a concrete, lethal suicide plan *and* the means available to carry it out. Past history of suicide is also high risk.

Direct assessment primarily takes place via an interview, although other information, such as reports from family members, may be used as well. You may also supplement the interview with instruments such as the Beck Hopelessness Scale or the Beck Suicide Intent Scale.

3. Preventing a Suicide: Consultation with colleagues is often an important adjunct when choosing the management strategy for a suicidal client and making treatment decisions. In particular, if you are unclear about the meaning of a client's threat or unsure what to do, consult with a colleague and keep notes of the consultation.

Both legally in many states and ethically, you must take reasonable steps to prevent a threatened suicide by a client. To determine what these "reasonable steps" should be, you consider the level of risk and the client's ability and willingness to comply with your recommendations. As we detail below, the steps you take should then be consistent with the level of risk currently posed by the client (i.e., low risk, high risk, or very high risk).

a. Prevention Steps When the Risk Appears Low: If you assess lethality to be *low*, you can talk over the problem with the client and attempt to elicit his ambivalent feelings about suicide, offer emotional support, and explore alternatives for meeting the client's needs, including his immediate needs. The latter may include providing referrals for outside help. You should also obtain an agreement from the client to contact you should there be any change in his situation, such as increased hopelessness leading to more concrete suicidal thoughts.

b. Prevention Steps When the Risk Appears High: If you assess lethality to be *high*, you need to take a more directive approach. You can abandon your therapeutic neutrality by making a statement such as, "I don't want you to harm yourself." Then, beginning with the least intrusive measure, you should take one or more of the following protective steps:

- Attempt to develop and maintain a **safety contract** (or "no-harm" contract) in which the client promises to not commit suicide for a specified period of time (e.g., the next two or three days), to not stay alone during that period of time, to remove all lethal means of suicide from his immediate environment, and to contact you or a suicide hotline if he feels worse or feels an impulse to commit suicide. Recommend that the client temporarily stay with friends or relatives. Arrange to see the client more often, at least temporarily, and to have the client touch base with you over the phone at regular intervals.

- If the client cannot, or will not, make these promises, you may notify members of his immediate support system about his condition. You should seek the client's permission to do this, but, if he refuses, you can break his confidentiality if you truly believe that enlisting the help of his support system is necessary to protect him from a suicide attempt. In addition to providing support, family members or close friends can be a source of logistical help by keeping an eye on the client and making sure that all weapons are removed from the client's immediate environment.

c. Prevention Steps When the Risk Appears Very High: If lethality is assessed to be *very high* (i.e., the client has a lethal suicide plan and previous suicide attempts and is socially isolated) or the client cannot, or will not, cooperate with any of the above methods of protection, then hospitalization is necessary. First encourage voluntary commitment to a psychiatric facility by the client, utilizing the client's support system if one is available. If the client will not enter a facility voluntarily, then arrange for an involuntary hold by contacting a person or agency designated by your county or state. Follow-up with the client until the crisis is stabilized. After the crisis is stabilized, proceed with treatment, if possible. Work to repair any damage to your therapeutic relationship arising from a breach of confidentiality.

4. Outpatient Intervention Techniques: Outpatient management is indicated when the risk for suicide is low or when a client at high risk has an adequate support system, is willing to use available resources, and agrees to a no-suicide contract and seems sincere. Outpatient management may also be indicated when a client has personality pathology characterized by a history of vague, nonlethal suicidal threats and gestures (for such individuals, however, a traumatic life stressor can sometimes precipitate a crisis, resulting in greater risk of suicide and the need for hospitalization).

Outpatient management of suicidal clients includes using general crisis intervention techniques, as well as the following specific interventions (Hoff, 1978):

- Many suicidal people are in a state of acute crisis and, therefore, experiencing a high degree of emotional upset and temporary disruption in cognitive functioning. This makes it difficult for them to clarify their intentions or make sound decisions. Reassure the client that the desire to commit suicide is a temporary state and encourage him to avoid making a decision about suicide until after the crisis state has ended and alternatives have been considered.

- Suicidal people often perceive that they have encountered a situation that is inescapable, intolerable, and permanent. An important goal of intervention is to change at least one of these three conditions. Ways of doing this include (a) quickly establishing rapport in order to provide the client with a connection to life, (b) working to establish in the client a greater sense of hope and reduced sense of helplessness by taking immediate steps to address his current pain and the situation causing it, (c) teaching the client to use existing problem-solving skills or helping him develop new ones so that he can overcome the sense that his problems are unsolvable, and (d) teaching distancing and distraction skills to facilitate toleration of painful feelings.

- When suicide is a way for the client to express anger toward someone, discuss alternative methods for dealing with that anger.

- Provide the client with opportunities for ample social contact (e.g., refer him to family or group crisis counseling or a self-help group once he is out of acute crisis).

- If the client gives you permission to do so, meet with his family members and/or friends. Teach them to recognize the warning signs of suicidality and encourage them to help the client increase his connectedness with others.

- Refer a client who is extremely anxious and/or unable to sleep to a physician or psychiatrist for medication.

- Use strategies to increase compliance with continued treatment (e.g., actively pursue "no-shows," involve family members and friends). Provide the client with 24-hour clinical back-up (e.g., emergency phone numbers).

D. Danger to Others

When a client seems potentially violent or threatens violence, your assessment goals are to identify the cause of the current crisis and determine the probability that the client will carry out a violent act in the near future. The cause of the crisis and the level of lethality will determine your intervention.

1. Factors Associated With a High Risk for Violence: Violent and assaultive behavior are difficult to predict. Factors associated with a high risk of violence include the following:

Intention: A specific plan for injuring or killing someone, possession of a weapon.

History: One or more previous acts of violence, history of homicidal threats, history of juvenile violence, history of alcohol or other drug abuse, abused as a child, recent provocation. A critical variable is a **personal history of violence** – the person has perpetrated, experienced, or witnessed violence.

Behavior: Signs of tension or agitation (e.g., pacing), loud, abusive, or bizarre speech.

Personality characteristics: Excessive aggressiveness, extreme or labile affect, poor impulse control.

Psychiatric diagnosis: Drug and alcohol intoxication or withdrawal, delirium, delusional disorder (paranoid delusions), mania, antisocial or paranoid personality disorder, dissociative disorder, or disruptive, impulse-control, or conduct disorder.

Demographic factors: Male, young age (beginning around age 15-18 and continuing up to age 30-35), lower socioeconomic class, less educated.

Other variables: Lower IQ, unstable school and/or vocational history.

2. Clarifying the Level of Danger: A client's threat to injure or kill someone else may be either spoken or written and either direct ("I'm going to kill my wife") or indirect ("I'm so angry that I may lose control and do something crazy"). All threats of harm against others should be taken seriously and examined through direct questioning in relation to the client's intention and history.

a. Key Variables for Identifying the Level of Danger: When faced with a dangerous client in your office, three variables in particular are critical for determining how dangerous the client is at the present time and how directive you should be: plan, history of violence, and willingness to use outside resources.

Plan: Ask the client directly about his present intentions (e.g., "Are you thinking about hurting someone?"). Attempt to determine how far has the client proceeded in thinking about harming someone else. Does the client have a specific and concrete plan? Can he say exactly how, when, and where he plans to commit the violent act? Does he have the means available to carry out his plan?

Previous violence: Ask the client directly about his history of violence (e.g., "Have you ever seriously harmed another person?"). Inquire about previous aggressive behavior and its outcomes, as well as previous fantasies about harming others and their outcomes. Find out what precipitated these actions or fantasies.

Willingness to use outside resources: Assess the client's support system. Determine whether family, friends, or community services are available to help the client. Clients who live alone and have no family or friends are greater risks than those who have others to whom they can turn. It is critical to distinguish between the availability of others to the client and the client's willingness to reach out to them.

Low lethality is considered to be present when the client has no specific plan for harming someone, has no history of prior violence, and is not socially isolated. The level of lethality then increases with each affirmative answer concerning a plan, history of violence, and social isolation. High lethality is judged to be present when the client has a specific, concrete plan for harming someone, has a history of violence toward others, and is socially isolated or unwilling to make use of available outside resources.

b. Other Variables for Clarifying Level of Danger: Other factors useful for determining a client's level of danger toward others include the following: (a) the extent to which the client is able to understand what he is contemplating; (b) the extent to which the client is willing and able to exercise self-control; (c) the extent to which the client is willing and able to collaborate with you; (d) the client's overall level of functioning, including alcohol or other drug use; (e) the presence of sources of stress and their levels of severity; (f) the client's available coping skills and strategies; and (g) the client's access to his proposed or potential victim(s). If there is time, you can use a mental status exam to gather information about the client's current mental functioning. Also incorporate any information you have from significant others.

In addition, consultation with colleagues is often a very important adjunct when choosing the management strategy for a dangerous client and making treatment decisions. If you are unclear about the meaning of a client's threats or unsure what to do, consult with a colleague and keep notes of the consultation.

3. Prevention and Intervention With a Dangerous Client: The cause of the crisis and the level of risk determine your management strategy. Key goals and procedures include those listed and described below.

a. Meet Legal Obligations/Ethical Responsibilities: If the client appears to pose a high risk of danger to another person(s), then you must adopt a highly directive stance and fulfill all relevant legal obligations and ethical responsibilities:

- Patiently and firmly explain your concerns to the client. Tell the client what you are doing to keep him and others safe and why. Tell the client in a supportive, but emphatic, way of your responsibility to protect him and those he has threatened and invite the client to participate in the process if possible. Ask the client to surrender any weapons he has.

- If the client has threatened a specific or identifiable person, and you determine that his threat is serious, discharge your duty to protect/warn. If the client has threatened to destroy or damage someone's property, attempt to find out whether his plan might pose a serious threat of physical harm against an identifiable person or persons (e.g., a client might threaten to cut the brake lines of a specific person's car); if the client's plan poses such a danger, then you should execute your duty to protect/warn. (See also Section I of Professional Relationships, Values, and Ethics.)

b. Help the Client Regain Control of Hostile Impulses: Don't touch an angry client or do anything else that he could interpret as a threat. If possible, sit rather than stand because sitting is a less aggressive stance. Also encourage the client to sit since sitting usually has a calming effect. Other specific ways of helping a client regain control of hostile impulses include the following:

- Allow the client to vent his feelings, provide support, and demonstrate empathy for his feelings of frustration and anger. Use **active listening skills** to acquire an accurate understanding of his feelings. Supportive feedback can mitigate the client's fears, hostility, anger, or frustration. For example, "You seem very upset and angry. Could you tell me what's wrong?" With an angry or violent client, wounded self-esteem is often an issue underlying his feelings; therefore, be sure to communicate an attitude of respect and authentic concern. If you say or do something inappropriate that causes the client to become more angry, admit your error and apologize. Use I-statements when expressing your concerns or explaining your intentions, role, and responsibilities. Do not argue, accuse, or give advice to an angry or otherwise potentially violent client.

- Make a **no-violence contract** with the client. Before a client who has expressed violent urges leaves your office, he should be calm and should have committed to not acting on these urges. Do your best to verify that the client's commitment is sincere.

- Set firm, consistent limits. Letting the client know what you need from him so that you can help may serve to lessen his anxiety by providing structure. For example, "You seem very angry. I'd like you to sit down and tell me what has happened and we'll figure out how it led to your anger." On the other hand, to the extent possible, you should also attempt to increase the client's sense of being in control himself by offering him options and choices and saying such things as, "Take a moment to think about what we've discussed and then let me know which course of action you want to follow" (Sheafor & Horejsi, 2003).

- It may be necessary to refer the client for a medication evaluation. To reduce the client's agitation and increase his cooperation, explain the purpose of the medication (e.g., "You seem very agitated; getting your prescription filled and taking the medication will help you regain control").

- Secluding the client is an alternative method for helping him regain control. The purpose of seclusion must be explained to the client (e.g., "I am going to leave you alone for about 10 minutes in order to give you a chance to calm down").

- If none of the above work, then hospitalization where the client can be physically restrained may be the only choice.

c. Hospitalization: If a dangerous client is unable to regain control over his hostile impulses and/or if the danger that the client poses seems imminent, encourage voluntary commitment in a psychiatric facility by the client, utilizing the client's support system if he has one. If the client will not enter a facility voluntarily, then arrange for an involuntary hold by contacting a person or agency designated by your county or state. Follow-up with the client until the crisis is stabilized. After the crisis is stabilized, proceed with treatment, if possible. Work to repair any damage to your therapeutic relationship arising from a breach of confidentiality.

d. Outpatient Intervention Techniques: Continued outpatient management is indicated when a client is able to regain control over his feelings and you believe he is sincere and/or when the lethality level is assessed to be low (i.e., the client has no specific plan, no history of violence, and adequate social support, or the client has made a nonspecific, apparently idle threat following a difficult life stressor). You should use the general crisis intervention techniques described earlier in this section. Other important interventions include the following:

- Explore with the client options for effectively resolving the problem (the cause of the crisis) without resorting to violence.

- Provide strategies for anger management. Teach and model how to express feelings, needs, and wants in appropriate ways; teach anger management skills (e.g., time-out, counting to 10); assign journaling to keep track of angry feelings; and/or recommend physical activity for the constructive release of anger (i.e., physical activity that requires concentration such as tennis, lifting weights, or mountain biking).

e. Protecting Yourself: When necessary, you should take steps to protect yourself and others around you from a potentially violent client:

- Some less intrusive methods of self-protection include describing the consequences of violent behavior, leaving the door open, and maintaining an adequate physical distance from the client.

- More intrusive methods may be used if the above methods fail. For example, you may leave the room, call for help, pick up a potential "weapon," and, if necessary, fight back. Calling for help, such as phoning the police, is acceptable if you determine that the client's condition permits you to breach his confidentiality. If feasible, however, you should attempt to get the client's permission before calling others for help.

Additionally, you should never enter a situation that you believe may be dangerous without first making others aware of your plan. For instance, when making a home visit that has the potential to develop into a dangerous situation, you should alert your office or agency about your concern, notify them of your itinerary, and check in by phone according to a prearranged schedule. Before entering the home or other building, assess your safety: Are you alone? Where are the escape routes? Do you hear an argument in progress? If you must enter a dangerous situation, don't hesitate to call for **police protection**. Situations that are likely to pose a high risk of danger to you include meeting with a client who has a history of violence (including violence against family members) or has firearms or other deadly weapons and meeting an unfamiliar client in a nonpublic or isolated place.

E. Trauma

1. Sources of Trauma: Emotional and psychological trauma results from highly stressful events that damage or destroy a person's sense of security and make him feel vulnerable and helpless. In crisis theory, these events are referred to as **situational crises**. Although traumatic experiences often involve a threat to one's own or others' life or safety, any event that leaves a person feeling overwhelmed and alone can be traumatic whether or not it involves actual or threatened physical harm. It is not the nature of an event that determines whether the event is traumatic, but, rather, the person's subjective emotional experience of the event.

Generally speaking, a stressful event is more likely to result in emotional and psychological trauma if it happened unexpectedly and/or repeatedly, if the person was unprepared for it, and/or if the person felt powerless to prevent it. Stressful events occurring in childhood and those resulting from the deliberate actions of another person are also more likely to be traumatic. Trauma can also arise from ongoing, unremitting stress, such as stress associated with living in a dangerous neighborhood or struggling with a life-threatening illness.

2. Responses to Trauma: Patterns of reaction to the extreme stress associated with traumatic events vary. Some people respond immediately and other have delayed reactions; and some people recover fairly quickly, while others experience adverse effects for a long time. In some cases, a person is energized initially by a traumatic event and this helps him cope for a while; afterwards, he may feel a sense of discouragement or depression.

Initial responses to traumatic events usually include a temporary state of **shock** and **denial**, which are considered to be normal protective reactions. A client who had recently experienced a traumatic event may be experiencing emotional disequilibrium; he may feel stunned, dazed, numb, and/or disconnected from life. He may not acknowledge that something traumatic has happened or may not be experiencing fully the intensity of the event. Reactions after the initial shock subsides vary from person to person. Normal reactions that you might see in a client include the following:

- The client may have *physical symptoms* such as headaches, fatigue, insomnia, racing heart, chest pain, nausea, muscle tension, and feeling on edge or "keyed up." When physical symptoms are persistent or severe or the client is upset by them, referral to a medical professional is usually indicated. In addition, pre-existing medical conditions may worsen as a consequence of the stress associated with a traumatic event.

- The client may experience intense and sometimes unpredictable *feelings*. The client may have dramatic mood shifts, be more irritable than usual, feel angry, experience feelings of guilt, shame, or self-blame, be very anxious or nervous, feel sad or hopeless, and/or become depressed.

- There may be changes in *thoughts* and *behavior patterns*. The client may have recurring and vivid memories or flashbacks of the event, which may result in physical reactions such as sweating and rapid heart beat. He may find it difficult to concentrate or make decisions, he may be more easily confused than usual, and his sleep and eating patterns may be disrupted.

- The client's *interpersonal relationships* may be disrupted or damaged. The client may be experiencing more conflict with others than usual or be withdrawn and isolated and avoiding his usual activities.

These reactions may last for days, weeks, or months after the trauma has ended. In addition, anniversaries of the traumatic event, such as at one month or one year, may trigger upsetting memories of the experience; these may be accompanied by fears that the stressful event will happen again.

Although the reactions described above are normal and some people are able to cope effectively with the emotional and physical effects of trauma by using their own support systems, others need mental health intervention in order to cope and recover. Treatment is indicated when serious symptoms or problems persist and continue interfering with the client's functioning (e.g., the client feels overwhelming nervousness or persistent sadness that adversely affects his interpersonal relationships or job performance). In addition, treatment is also indicated if the client has developed posttraumatic stress disorder (PTSD) or acute stress disorder as a result of experiencing a highly traumatic event.

3. Determinants of a Person's Trauma Response and Recovery: Factors that tend to affect a person's reaction to trauma and the length of time required for recovery after a trauma include the degree of intensity and amount of loss involved in the trauma, whether the person was experiencing other significant stressors or losses when the trauma occurred, and the person's general ability to cope with emotionally challenging events.

People are also more likely to be traumatized by a highly stressful event if they have been traumatized before, especially if the earlier trauma occurred in childhood. When childhood trauma is not resolved, a fundamental sense of fear and helplessness may carry over into adulthood, increasing the person's vulnerability to further trauma.

F. Children Exposed to Disaster

1. Children's Reactions to Disaster: Children impacted directly by a disaster (those who have a firsthand experience of personal or material loss) are at higher risk for developing long-term emotional problems than those who are impacted indirectly (e.g., those who view news coverage of a disaster on TV). The common reactions of children exposed to disaster, whether directly or indirectly, include the following (Sheafor & Horejsi, 2003):

Fear: The child may fear for his own safety and the safety of loved ones and have fantasies about the disaster or other disasters that could happen. These may be manifested in his play or artwork.

Loss of control: The child may feel overwhelmed as a result of the loss of control he experienced during or after the disaster. To maintain or regain a sense of control, he may be defiant or cling to his parents for safety.

Anger: The child is most likely to direct his anger at those to whom he feels the closest (e.g., parents, siblings, peers, teachers).

Loss of stability: The child may feel anxious and upset because of disruptions to his usual routine.

Confusion: The unpredictability of certain disasters (terrorist attacks, war) can cause a child to feel confused. The child may have trouble differentiating between a disaster that takes place in real life and the violence he sees on TV or in movies.

Isolation: A sense of isolation is particularly likely when a child has family members serving in the military. If the child doesn't have friends in the same situation, he may feel lonely. He may also develop jealousy toward children whose family members are not serving in the military.

Posttraumatic stress disorder (PTSD): Some children develop PTSD following exposure to a disaster. PTSD symptoms in children can include difficulty sleeping, nightmares, increased aggression, increased clinging, crying or sadness, appetite changes, social withdrawal, obsessive play, hyperactivity, and increased physical complaints (e.g., stomachaches, headaches).

2. Intervention With Children Exposed to Disaster: Important tasks when working with children who have been exposed to disaster include assessing for behavioral changes in the child, encouraging the parents to monitor the child for changes (behavioral changes may reflect emotional and psychological problems), informing the parents about relevant services and professionals who can provide support and assistance, and providing the parents with strategies for responding to the child's emotional needs during the crisis. The parents should be advised to do the following: (a) Also take care of their own needs because the child will be affected by their emotional state; (b) talk with the child about the event so that he knows it's okay to discuss it; (c) extend multiple invitations to the child to talk about the event without forcing him to do so; and (d) spend extra time with the child and provide him with ample emotional support.

When the child is ready to talk about the event, parents should be advised to do the following: (a) explain the event using simple and direct language; (b) take cues from the child regarding how much information to share; (c) ask the child what he has heard about the event and listen for misinformation, misconceptions, and underlying fears or concerns; and (d) encourage the child to ask questions and answer his questions directly (the child will tend to cope better with the event if he understands it). If the disaster receives media coverage, the parents should be advised in the following way: If the child is young, they should limit his television or Internet viewing of the event; if the child is older, the parents should watch coverage of the event with him, discuss what they see, and encourage him to share his feelings (Ashford et al., 2006).

G. Out-of-Home Displacement

With the emerging environmental crises, millions of people have become environmentally displaced. Lambert (2002) discusses five factors that have contributed to environmentally displaced persons (EDP): (a) natural disasters (e.g., flooding, fire, earthquakes), (b) eco-system degradation (e.g., pollution, soil erosion), (c) development projects (increased urban development, infrastructure projects), (d) industrial accidents; and (e) conflict and warfare.

Environmentally displaced persons call into practice three core values of social work:

- Obligation to social justice
- Commitment to understanding the human condition in context of the environment
- Dedication to social and political reform

While the study of the impact of environmentally displaced persons on service delivery is ongoing, social workers should focus their education on international and global cultural competence. Emerging curriculum to better under these individuals and groups focus on anti-oppressive practice. From this perspective, a social worker would not only seek to understand a client's immediate and social environment, but also their institutional, global, and natural environments. The main viewpoint of anti-oppressive perspective is to not only meet the immediate needs of the EDP, but to work to change the issues that created the problem. Adjustment and coping strategies are the heart of working with EDP at the micro level, while advocating in the political spectrum at the macro level.

H. Rape

Those who are raped are predominantly women, but men may be raped as well. Men who are raped by men may suffer traumatic and long-term consequences, particularly because they never thought of themselves as potential rape victims.

1. Acquaintance Rape and Date Rape: Only about 20 percent of all rapes are committed by strangers. *Acquaintance rape* occurs when a woman is raped by someone she knows; *date rape* occurs when she is raped by someone she is dating. In date rape, a woman is forced into having sexual intercourse with her date without her consent, and this includes cases in which a woman is too intoxicated to give her consent. Even men who admit to forcing a woman to have intercourse on a date may not perceive this act as "rape."

2. The Survivor's Response to Rape: Women who are raped experience many intense emotions and reactions. During the attack, the woman is rendered helpless, is the target of her attacker's rage, and may believe that her life is in danger. In other words, she experiences a loss of control that can result in overwhelming feelings of fear and stress. Common fears following rape include a fear of being alone, a fear of men, and an inability to trust a dating partner. Common feelings include depression, anger, guilt, shame, and anxiety.

Regardless of the type of rape women experience, a common reaction is the **rape trauma syndrome**, which may include the following phases:

Disorganization phase: This phase consists of the immediate expressed or controlled physical and emotional reactions to the trauma. Typical feelings are fright, anger, and disbelief. A common reaction is "second guessing" – for example, asking, "What could I have done to avoid this?" Such questioning can lead to intense feelings of guilt and self-blame.

While many women react to rape by crying, shaking, etc., others do not. Even when a woman reacts to the rape in a controlled way, she is still experiencing emotional pain and other trauma effects.

Reorganization phase: This phase reflects the adjustment and adaptation that are necessary following the rape. Reorganization takes place as the survivor works to regain equilibrium in physical, psychological, social, and sexual areas. The recovery process follows a pattern similar to that of people who must adjust to grief. Matsakis (2003) has identified four issues that are important to the rape survivor during the reorganization process: (a) regaining a feeling of physical well-being and safety, (b) working through fears and phobias, (c) coming to terms with losses such as the loss of trust, and (d) redefining a new sense of self.

3. Crisis Intervention with Rape Survivors: The following procedures are usually important with a client who was recently raped:

- You should emphasize *listening* and providing *emotional support*. Medical and legal procedures may still need to be carried out (e.g., medical care, gathering of evidence), but, as a therapist, you should emphasize these procedures at the expense of addressing the client's emotional needs.

- You should participate actively and be directive in establishing activities that will help the client manage the crisis and its aftermath. For individuals who have been raped or otherwise physically assaulted, it can be very useful to have a specific plan for the days immediately following the attack so that they can begin to move from victimization toward empowerment.

- Once the client is out of acute crisis, referral to a peer support group may be indicated. In the group, the client can "tell her story" and begin the process of accepting what has happened to her and learn how to assimilate her experience into her sense of self.

Finally, support from family members can critically affect a rape survivor's ability to recover from the trauma, yet the partners of rape survivors frequently have conflicting feelings. Participating in a support group with others facing a similar situation can help the partners understand that their feelings are normal and reduce their sense of isolation.

I. Grief

Types of loss that may precipitate a grief reaction include not only the death of a loved one, but also the separation or divorce of one's parents, receiving a terminal diagnosis, having a planned or spontaneous abortion, delivering a stillborn child, placement of one's child in foster care, voluntarily relinquishing one's parental rights, experiencing a decline in one's physical or mental functioning, retiring or losing a job, losing a pet, and facing the loss or destruction of one's personal belongings in a robbery, house fire, or natural disaster.

How Grief is Expressed

Grief refers to the intense emotional suffering brought on by the loss of or separation from someone or something that is deeply loved. Grief may be expressed both emotionally and physiologically. Emotional expressions include sadness, anger, self-reproach, anxiety, loneliness, helplessness, numbness, and, sometimes, relief or a sense of freedom. Physiological expressions include emptiness in the pit of the stomach, shortness of breath, tightness in the throat, muscle weakness and fatigue, sensitivity to noise, and dry mouth (Worden, 2002). Grief is considered to be a normal reaction in response to a significant loss. When using the DSM-5, the condition **uncomplicated bereavement** is recorded when an individual is having a normal reaction to the death of a loved one.

Other terms associated with grief and loss include the following:

Acute grief: Acute grief refers to the reaction that occurs at the time of the loss, such as a parent's immediate reaction to his child being killed in an accident. Acute grief typically occurs in response to a sudden and unexpected loss.

Anticipatory grief: Anticipatory grief is triggered by the realization that a significant loss will occur in the near future. The diagnosis of a terminal illness may precipitate anticipatory grief.

Anniversary reaction: An anniversary reaction (or anniversary grief) occurs when grief returns as a result of remembering a previous loss (e.g., a person feels sad each year during the month when his spouse died).

Secondary losses: Secondary losses are additional losses that stem from a primary, or initial, loss, and can be a significant source of grief. For example, following his parents' divorce, a child may lose not only his two-parent family, but also have to move to a new neighborhood and change schools.

1. Phases of Grief (Death of a Loved One): Expressions of grief are affected by the person's relationship to the lost person or object; the person's age, gender, developmental stage, cultural background, and coping patterns; and the suddenness or type of loss or death the person has experienced. For example, diverse cultures and religious groups have different beliefs and rituals surrounding death, grieving, and the acceptance of loss. Typically, however, a grief reaction to the death of a loved one and the mourning that follows includes the following phases:

Phase 1 – Numbness: The person is shocked, confused, and overwhelmed. Physical symptoms may include nausea, tightness in the chest and throat, shortness of breath, disturbed sleep, loss of appetite, headaches, etc. This phase lasts from several days to several weeks.

Phase 2 – Longing (yearning): The person may seek in some way to recover the person who died. He may become preoccupied and withdrawn, may wander around as though he is searching for the deceased person, and may report seeing or being with the deceased person. Intense crying and feelings of anger, guilt, anxiety, and frustration are common.

Phase 3 – Despair and disorganization: As the reality of the loss sinks in, the person experiences feelings of helplessness, despair, depression, and extreme fatigue.

Phase 4 – Recovery and reorganization: Over a period of months, the person gradually resumes his usual routines at home and elsewhere. He feels less depressed, sleeps better, and has more energy. Certain events and memories may bring on periods of crying and sadness, but these become less frequent and less intense.

For many people, intense grief diminishes in six months to a year, but the process of grieving can take from three to five years or even longer.

2. Dual Process Model of Coping with Grief: The dual process model of coping with grief (Stroebe & Schut, 1999) suggests that grieving takes place on two levels: *Loss-oriented coping* focuses on the negative feelings associated with grieving and is most common early in the bereavement process; while *restoration-oriented coping* focuses on distractions from grief, such as finding new roles and relationships, and predominates later in the bereavement process.

These two levels of coping occur both simultaneously and successively. In other words, a person may take breaks from loss-oriented coping in which he begins to seek new relationships. These breaks are beneficial because focusing exclusively on negative feelings and negative events surrounding the loss is associated with lower levels of well-being in bereaved individuals (Richardson, 2003).

3. Children and Grief Over the Loss of a Parent: Children's reactions to and understanding of the death of a parent differ depending on their age. Following are the typical reactions and needs of children in different age groups (Sheafor & Horejsi, 2003).

a. Up to Age 2 Years:

- The child doesn't understand what death is but does sense the feelings of the adults around him. He won't remember the deceased parent.
- Common symptoms/reactions include general distress, sleeplessness, shock, despair, and protest. Other symptoms/reactions can include nervousness, frequent sickness, rebellious behavior, hyperactivity, nightmares, depression, compulsive behavior, excessive anger, and excessive dependency (usually on the remaining parent).
- The child needs affection and reassurance from adults. If he has lost his mother, he needs a consistent nurturing figure to take her place. The child should be included in funeral rituals.

b. Age 2 to 5 Years:

- The child's understanding of death is limited (he believes it is temporary or reversible), but he will probably understand that something significant has happened. He may not remember the deceased parent later.

- Symptoms/reactions may include confusion, behavioral and/or emotional regression, frightening dreams, and a short period of sadness. Some children in this age group, however, appear unaffected by the loss.

- The child may ask many questions, attach quickly to "substitute" people, experience the loss as a punishment, escape from the loss through play, fear that no one will take care of him, and/or fear losing his remaining parent and become very clingy.

- The child needs adults to communicate with him in a simple and honest way. He also needs adults to provide him with reassurance, a secure and loving environment, and a daily routine and structure. The child should be included in funeral rituals.

c. *Age 5 to 8 Years:*

- The child is beginning to understand the finality of death and may fear that someone else will die.

- The child may ask many questions, feel angry, blame himself for the death, have difficulty expressing his feelings in words and express them through behavior instead (compulsive "good" or "bad" behavior as a response against feeling helpless), and/or identify with the deceased parent a way of hanging on to him or her. Other symptoms/reactions may include denial, sorrow, general distress, disorientation, and confusion. Some children in this age group, however, behave as though nothing has happened.

- The child needs adults to communicate with him in a simple and honest way and provide him with reassurance about the future. The child may benefit from physical activity as an outlet for his feelings. He should be included in funeral rituals.

d. *Ages 8 to 12 Years:*

- The child understands the finality of death and may worry about his own death.

- The child may experience anxiety (including phobic behavior and an intense fear of the future), have physical complaints, feel angry, develop a strong interest in the morbid, and/or question his religious beliefs.

- The child may exhibit denial (e.g., he may not want to talk about what happened). A child who hides his feelings and tries to appear as though he is coping well may become depressed.

- The child is likely to ask many questions about the death (e.g., what happened to the body?).

- The child needs adults to communicate with him directly and honestly and encourage him to talk about his feelings. He also needs adults to provide him with reassurance about the future. He may need physical activity on a regular basis as an outlet for his feelings. He should be included in both funeral plans and funeral rituals.

e. *Adolescence:*

- An adolescent may react in ways that are similar to how adults react, but he has fewer coping mechanisms available than most adults.

- The adolescent understands the finality of death and may worry about his own death.

- The adolescent may exhibit denial (e.g., he may not want to talk about what happened), develop an intense fear of the future, hide his feelings from others, repress feelings of anger or sadness and become depressed, have physical complaints, question his religious beliefs, and/or exhibit aggression or withdrawal.

- The adolescent may feel very vulnerable. If so, he may want to talk about what happened and his feelings about it. He should be allowed and encouraged to express all of his feelings. Peer support (including in a support group) is usually important. An adolescent may also benefit from reading about grief.

- The adolescent needs supportive adults and a consistent environment and should be included in both funeral plans and funeral rituals.

Working with Clients Who Are Grieving

1. Supportive Counseling: A common form of intervention for clients who are grieving is basic supportive counseling, which provides reassurance, guidance, explanation, encouragement, support, and the opportunity to express emotions and reinforces clients' healthy and adaptive patterns of thought and behavior. A client is encouraged to grieve, identify the scope of his loss, talk about the events of the loss, and learn about and understand the process of grieving. As a client begins to accept the loss, he is encouraged to recall and talk about positive memories from before the loss occurred. A client may also require help in moving forward with his life (e.g., developing new roles and relationships) or resolving problems arising from his loss (e.g., insurance claims, learning how to take on new day-to-day tasks that were handled before by the person who died).

2. Grief Counseling: Another approach to helping clients cope with grief over the death of a loved one is grief counseling, which is designed to help individuals work through the feelings, thoughts, and memories associated with their loss. Grief counseling may also be used with clients facing major life changes that elicit feelings of grief, such as getting divorced.

The basic tasks of grief counseling are the following:

- Help the client express and work through the feelings associated with the loss.
- Help the client cope with the pain associated with the loss.
- Support the client through the anxiety surrounding life changes that follow the loss.
- Help the client develop strategies for seeking support and self-care.
- Help the client accept the loss.

The client is also provided with information about the normal grieving process to help him understand that many of the feelings, symptoms, and changes he is experiencing are a normal, temporary reaction to loss.

As these counseling tasks are achieved, the client is encouraged to resume his normal activities and social relationships in the absence of the person who died. For some clients, however, engaging in day-to-day activities may feel overwhelming, and, in these cases, grief counseling may also focus on specific coping skills or behavioral strategies to help the client resume some normalcy in his daily routine. If a client is having difficulty falling or staying asleep, for example, grief counseling may include consultation with his physician to assist with temporary strategies to regulate sleep. Eventually, a client may also need help with establishing new patterns of social interaction in the absence of the person who died, but this goal should be encouraged only after the client has had a chance to work through the intense feelings associated with his loss.

Additional work in grief counseling may involve identifying ways for the client to let go of or say good-bye to the person he lost. Therapeutic letters can be a helpful way for a client to share thoughts or feelings that he did not express to the person before he or she died. If, like many survivors, the client has dreams about the lost loved one, these dreams also may be a focus in grief counseling. Dreams can often be an effective way of consolidating memories about a loved one who died.

Following counseling, aftercare is usually provided through informal support systems which may include family and friends, as well as a support group. Ideally, the client can be referred to a group whose members have experienced a form of loss that is similar to his.

Grief counseling is indicated for clients experiencing uncomplicated bereavement or normal grief. For clients experiencing traumatic or complicated grief reactions (e.g., grief reactions that are prolonged or manifested through behavioral symptoms), **grief therapy** may be more appropriate. The goal of grief therapy is to identify and resolve the psychological and emotional problems that have appeared as a consequence of the loss.

J. Caregiving: Middle-Aged Adults and Aging Parents

An increasing number of middle-aged adults are providing care for their elderly parents. This role often emerges at a time when caregivers are also raising teenagers, working at demanding jobs, or nearing retirement age. The term **sandwich generation** is used to describe a generation of people who care for their aging parents while also supporting their own children. Caring for elderly parents is most commonly left to a female member of the family, usually a daughter or daughter-in-law. And, as might be expected, caring for an older parent tends to be more difficult and more stressful for low-income families and single adults.

1. Caregiver Functions: As caregivers for their elderly parents, adult children may provide direct assistance with activities of daily living, hire and monitor professional caregivers, make decisions about placement, or monitor the care their parent receives in a nursing home or other location. Specific kinds of support typically given by adult children to their elderly parents include emotional support ("checking in" by phone or in person, affection, listening, etc.); instrumental support (transportation, help with chores, etc.); and management of medical conditions (help with medications, etc.) (Spitze & Gallant, 2004).

2. Adjusting to the Caregiver Role: Being a caregiver to one's parent(s) can be a fulfilling experience but also tends be stressful and can lead to emotional and physical consequences for the caregiver. Even aging parents and adult children who feel a sense of responsibility to care for each other may feel ambivalent about giving and receiving this kind of help (Connidis & McMullin, 2002); often the role reversal that takes place when aging parents become dependent on their children can be distressing for both parties. Sibling relationships may become strained if the children disagree on the best way to meet their parent(s)' needs or if the caregiving responsibilities are unequally or unfairly divided among them. Some caregivers end up feeling abandoned by friends and other family members and are at risk of developing feelings of depression, anxiety, and/or self-blame (Peak & Toseland, 1999).

Factors that increase the **resilience** of caregivers include having emotional support, spending reasonable periods of time away from the caregiving situation, engaging in regular physical exercise, maintaining personal hobbies, having personal religious beliefs, and having a philosophy of duty toward their parents (Ross et al., 2003).

3. Placement Decisions: At some time, adult children (or other family members) may face the need to make a placement decision for their elderly parent; this situation is particularly common when the parent has dementia (e.g., major neurocognitive disorder due to Alzheimer's disease). In making placement decisions, the goal is always to preserve the greatest autonomy for the older person, while also ensuring that he receives appropriate care and services. An older parent in need of placement may want to remain at home in familiar surroundings despite the deterioration in his cognitive and/or physical functioning. However, if an older parent requires ongoing supervision, is incontinent, or is bedridden, he should generally be placed in a nursing home.

4. Intervention With Caregivers: Guidelines for working with adult children who are providing care to their elderly parents include the following:

- Offer support and validation as the caregivers and other family members cope with their feelings (e.g., stress, anxiety, depression, self-blame, loss, ambivalence).

- Help the adult children accept their limitations and the limitations of what can be done for their parents.

- Help the adult children figure out how to prioritize their parent(s)' needs while also continuing to take good care of themselves and their own children.

- Identify the family's resource needs and help connect them to appropriate programs and services (e.g., support group, adult day care, respite care).

- Provide the family with the information they need to make informed choices concerning care for the elderly parent. If requested, help them identify and weigh their alternatives, including options for long-term care. (Options for long-term care are described in Section XIV of this chapter.)

- Be aware that decisions regarding placement tend to be very difficult for family members – it can be important to elicit and address their feelings about the decision and its consequences (e.g., sadness, guilt, ambivalence).

In addition, an important resource for caregivers is a social support group (**caregiver support group**). The group can provide needed emotional support, validate feelings and thoughts about the caregiving situation, reduce isolation and loneliness, provide a respite from caregiving duties, reduce anxiety and stress, educate caregivers about chronic illnesses and disabilities and community resources, and encourage caregivers to use systematic problem-solving procedures and coping strategies to reduce the stress they are experiencing (Toseland & Rossiter, 1989). Social workers leading such groups should provide supportive interventions that emphasize ventilation of stressful experiences in a supportive environment, validation of shared caregiving experiences, affirmation of caregivers' ability to cope with their situations, praise for providing the care, and support and understanding of caregivers' struggles with difficult situations (Peak & Toseland, 1999). Another important resource may be **respite care** which provides caregivers with temporary relief from continuous support and care of their elderly parent; because it reduces stress on the caregivers, respite care is useful for preventing individual and family breakdown, institutionalization, and elder abuse/neglect.

Finally, geriatric care managers (who may be social workers or registered nurses) can work with older adults and their families to assess living arrangements and service needs and arrange for needed care. This may include helping a family decide whether it is practical and safe for the older person to remain in his home or whether a move to another kind of housing or long-term care is needed.

XI. Practice Perspectives, Theories, and Models

This section focuses primarily on work with individual clients; family therapy models are reviewed in the section following this one.

A dual focus on person and environment is a defining characteristic of social work practice, and the psychosocial model has long been the mainstream approach. On the other hand, because clients present a broad range of problems, no single practice framework is sufficiently comprehensive to adequately address them all. Thus, rather than limiting themselves to one approach when selecting interventions for a case, social workers typically choose from among a range of practice perspectives, theories, and models. They choose interventions based on approaches that match a client's problem and the extent to which empirical research has found the interventions to be effective. This approach to selecting intervention strategies is termed systematic eclecticism. In addition, a key perspective guiding social work practice is the strengths perspective, which reminds you to pay close attention to a client's strengths during both assessment and intervention.

A. Traditional Social Casework Models

Psychosocial Model

The primary theorists associated with the psychosocial model are Florence Hollis, Gordon Hamilton, Charlotte Towle, and Helen Northen, among others. For many years, the psychosocial model has been the mainstream approach to practice in social work. Its theoretical underpinnings are broad, and include, to name a few, Freudian personality theory, ego psychology, systems theory, role theory, communications theory, learning theory, Rankian personality theory, existential psychology, and socialization theory.

The psychosocial model is mainly a set of principles used to guide social work intervention. When using this approach, a social worker applies certain principles but can use just about any intervention technique that applies well to the client's problems (i.e., a social worker selects strategies and techniques to fit the problem at hand).

1. Principles: The psychosocial model assumes that human beings are not only acted on by the environment but also are capable of controlling their lives by adapting to or changing their external situation. The major principles emphasized in the psychosocial model are described below.

a. Emphasis on the Person-in-Situation System: The psychosocial model emphasizes both the internal (psychological) and external (social) causes of dysfunction. It is a systems approach and the primary system of interest is the **person-in-situation** – the individual in interaction with his environment or social situation (e.g., family, friends, employment setting, medical facilities, governmental organizations).

b. Adoption of an Organismic Perspective: The psychosocial model adopts an organismic perspective on the person-in-situation system. This perspective suggests that change in one part of a system will bring about changes in other parts – in other words, because a client and his situation interact, it is believed that changes in the client will affect the functioning of aspects in his environment and that changes in the environment will affect the client's functioning.

c. Emphasis on the Therapeutic Relationship: The therapeutic relationship is an important component of treatment and is thought to develop from the verbal and nonverbal communication between a social worker and client. Obtaining the client's trust in the competence and good will of the social worker is viewed as critical to the success of treatment. The social worker attends to both transference reactions (she provides feedback and interpretation, and the transference relationship serves as a means of engendering insight); and reality-based aspects of the relationship (her empathy, warmth, and acceptance are thought to have direct beneficial effects on building the client's self-esteem and self-acceptance and reducing his defensiveness and anxiety). Thus, the relationship is consciously used as a means of providing the corrective relationship, motivation, and energy that a client needs in order to change.

Indeed, because the quality of the therapeutic relationship is viewed as a critical element in determining the extent to which the social worker can help a client, it is guided by several core values and characteristics:

Acceptance of the client: The social worker must accept the client, which means being nonjudgmental. This posture is reflected in a social worker's unconditional respect for the client and commitment to his welfare. The assumption is that the client will be more open and honest in expressing himself when he recognizes that the social worker has accepted him.

Person-centered approach: The social worker uses a person-centered approach that emphasizes a client's needs. This entails attending to the client's view of his problem, demonstrating sensitivity to his attitudes and preconceptions, and conveying empathy, warmth, and acceptance. These, in turn, build the client's self-esteem and self-acceptance and reduce his anxiety and defensiveness. The ultimate goal is to use the relationship to create conditions within which a client's innate problem-solving abilities (ego strengths) and tendency to grow will be stimulated.

Respect for self-determination: The social worker respects the client's need and right to make his own decisions and encourages his self-determination and self-direction. The social worker, however, also recognizes when a client's self-determination should be limited in order to protect the client or others.

Scientific objectivity: The social worker is committed to understanding a client's problems "with scientific objectivity" (i.e., without personal bias) (Hollis, 1970).

d. Use of an Eclectic Approach: The psychosocial model is an eclectic approach in which a social worker develops solutions that will fit the problem at hand, the client's preferences, and the functions of the agency where she is employed. With a single client, for example, a social worker may incorporate behavior therapy, client-centered therapy, and elements of psychoanalytic therapy (e.g., interpretation of transferences).

2. Data Collection and Assessment: The goal of data collection in psychosocial casework is to "understand clients, their potential and limitations, the sources of [their] strengths and stress, [their] resources for change and the barriers to desired change" (Turner, 1978). Therefore, the smallest unit of attention is the client in interaction with his situation. The social worker seeks to identify the most relevant interacting determinants underlying a client's problem; these determinants can include deficiencies in a client's personal functioning, a harmful or deficient social situation, or both. This understanding allows the social worker to determine what kind of help a client needs.

3. Treatment: The psychosocial model assumes that treatment can produce personality change and growth and that environmental changes brought about by treatment can also promote a client's adaptation. Change is believed to occur as the result of the following: (a) a client acquiring greater insight and resolving conflicts; (b) a client modifying his affective, cognitive, and behavioral patterns, which in turn evoke changes in his interpersonal relationships; and (c) changes that are made to a client's environment. Thus, treatment attempts to modify the individual, the individual's social environment, the exchanges between them, or all three.

Interventions generally include communication with a client or a client and significant others (direct treatment) and the provision of concrete services (indirect treatment). The following are emphasized in treatment:

- A client's ever-increasing understanding of his situation, others, and himself.
- A client's adaptive potentialities.
- The benefit (e.g., reduced distress) a client acquires from expressing his emotions in therapy.
- The support a client receives in an accepting therapeutic relationship.
- The effects of a client's relationship with the social worker.

The social worker continuously seeks the client's active involvement during treatment in achieving these goals.

Psychosocial treatment also emphasizes the importance of differentiating treatment on the basis of a client's need – the social worker attempts to understand that need and then respond to it in an individualized way according to her understanding. A "need" is conceptualized as a social dilemma or discrepancy between a person and others with whom he is associated. It is assumed that this discrepancy is what motivates a client to change because it produces a sense of disequilibrium (i.e., a client feels a sense of discomfort because he has conscious and/or unconscious needs that are not being met).

Problem-Solving Model

The problem-solving model was developed by Helen Harris Perlman and is based on concepts associated with ego psychology, role theory, and John Dewey's theories of cognition and problem-solving. It is essentially a combination of the functional and diagnostic social casework approaches. The latter is an early form of psychosocial casework that was based primarily on Freud's personality and practice theory.

1. Principles: The focus of the problem-solving model is on the person who cannot resolve a particular problem related to either relationships or the performance of role tasks. The person is not viewed as mentally or emotionally ill but, rather, as needing help to resolve a specific problem. Because the felt need for help produces a sense of disequilibrium, the person is motivated to come to a social agency to receive assistance in coping with the problem. Problem-solving social work, therefore, focuses on providing material and social resources to help clients resolve a specific problem. The primary assumptions underlying this model are summarized below.

a. Human Living is an Ongoing Problem-Solving Process: Growth and change occur as individuals face and resolve problems associated with normal developmental crises. Moreover, individuals form interpersonal relationships as a means of dealing with shared problems, and these relationships, in turn, present some of the most significant problems in a person's life.

b. The Problem is Emphasized: When a client comes in for help, the assumption is that he is motivated to solve a specific problem (which may or may not be the presenting problem) and this problem should be the focus of treatment. Even though this problem might be an expression of the client's overall personality pattern or psychosocial situation, it is believed that a social worker can be optimally effective by working to change the specific problem rather than by directly working to change the overall context – i.e., personality and situations are thought to change one problem at a time.

c. Problem-Solving Relies on the Use of Ego Functions (e.g., perception, cognition, memory, impulse control, and judgment): Reliance on the use of ego functions is related to the ego psychology concept of **competence motivation** – i.e., that people derive pleasure not just from the release of primitive impulses but also from experiences that challenge, develop, and reward their competence. The innate tendency to overcome problems is associated with the concept of a **conflict-free ego sphere**.

d. The Role of Motivation, Capacity, and Opportunity is Emphasized: Deficiencies in problem-solving ability are believed to be caused by a lack of motivation, capacity, and/or opportunity to resolve problems in an appropriate way. Therefore, problem-solving casework attempts to correct deficits in a client's problem-solving abilities by:

- releasing, energizing, and giving direction to his **motivation** (e.g., minimizing anxiety and fears and freeing a client's ego functions for use in resolving the problem);

- releasing and exercising a client's mental, emotional, and action **capacities** for coping with the problem, which, in turn, releases and exercises the ego functions required by the problem; and

- finding and making available to a client environmental **opportunities** and material and social resources needed to solve the problem.

2. The "Fours P's": Techniques for providing help using the problem-solving model vary according to the client, the problem, the social worker's style, and other factors. In general, however, the content of social casework includes "4 P's" (Perlman, 1971): "A Person [with] a Problem seeks ... solution from a Place ... and is offered help by a social worker whose professional Process simultaneously engages and enhances his problem-solving powers and/or supplements his problem-solving resources." The 4 P's can be understood as follows:

Person: A person is an open-ended system that reacts to and interacts with situations in and feedback from his environment. He is not viewed solely in terms of his problem but as someone who is both acting and being acted upon. The therapeutic encounter is used to bring about changes that will promote the person's motivation and capacity to engage in appropriate problem-solving.

Problem: A problem is a situation that is causing discomfort. It is not just an effect of a sequence of events – it is also a cause that shapes a person's current and future life. Learning to cope with a problem is expected to interfere with the cause-effect-cause cycle. An important element of treating a problem is **partialization** – a reduced version of a larger problem is thought to provide the person with a less threatening model for learning to cope.

Place: The problem-solving model emphasizes the specific agency (place) that uses casework as a means of resolving the problem. The agency's purpose defines its function, service, and area of social concern. Thus, in regard to place, the problem-solving approach resembles other models of social casework.

Process: A primary goal of the problem-solving process is to stimulate and support the person's use of his **ego functions**. This is accomplished through the proper use of the therapeutic relationship – the social worker responds to, questions, and guides the person's feelings and perceptions about the problem, its solutions, and decisions about what to do next. By encouraging the person's active participation, the social worker helps him recognize his innate problem-solving potential.

3. Assessment and Treatment: In casework using a problem-solving model, engagement, diagnostic assessment, and intervention include the following activities (Perlman, 1971).

a. Engagement: To engage, motivate, and support a client, a social worker focuses on the problem (starts where the client is by emphasizing why he came in) and provides empathy, warmth, and a genuine presence. She also clarifies the purpose of helping and explores the client's expectations of the social work process.

b. Diagnosis: In working to recognize and define the problem, a social worker uses the relationship to elicit a client's thoughts and feelings. In formulating the problem, the social worker acknowledges, but does not emphasize, the role played by a client's inner life (e.g., unconscious motivations, intrapsychic conflicts). That is, diagnostic assessment entails evaluating the following, with an emphasis on the client's immediate situation rather than his personality:

- How and why a client's motivation (sense of purpose), capacity (ego functions), and/or opportunities (availability of needed material and social resources) are inadequate to support or promote his functioning.
- The variety and quality of a client's social roles and role functioning. A client is viewed as belonging to a role system, and his problems are conceptualized in terms of his ability to carry out his roles.

Diagnosis continues throughout the intervention process. However, by emphasizing a specific problem focus, the social worker sets the stage for the development of short-term, achievable goals directed at resolving the target problem.

c. Intervention: The social worker and client set time-limited goals and objectives and plan the action. The action is then carried out, followed by evaluation and termination. Two major types of help are offered: The social worker stimulates a client's ability to use his own faculties for dealing with the feelings, perceptions, and behaviors that are causing the problem or can be used to resolve it; and the social worker makes needed social and material resources available to a client and facilitates use of these resources by interceding with those who control them. Intervention can also be viewed in terms of working with the content of the problem and the relationship process:

- In working with the content of the problem, a social worker and client apply problem-solving and decision theory (which are described later in this section). The social worker is viewed as an expert in problem-solving and teaches or guides a client through the problem-solving steps.

- In terms of the relationship process, all contacts with the client are expected to be therapeutic; an empathic, warm, and accepting relationship is used to energize a client's motivation, increase his awareness, and facilitate his ability to use his own natural problem-solving capacities. In order to help a client deal with problems of daily social functioning, casework may include the client's significant others.

d. Termination: Termination occurs when a client has achieved his goals. However, while the primary purpose of helping is to enable clients to resolve a current problem, an important secondary objective is to have them develop problem-solving skills to apply themselves to future problems.

Functional Model

The functional model evolved in the mid-twentieth century as a response against social work's emphasis on Freud's psychoanalytic personality and practice theory which stressed "diagnostic understanding" of one's clients. The functional approach de-emphasizes diagnosis and focuses, instead, on a client's inherent capacity for growth, change, and problem solving. It is assumed that these qualities can be facilitated by means of the therapeutic relationship, regardless of the social worker's diagnostic understanding.

1. Principles: Smalley's (1970) five principles of functional casework – diagnosis, time phases, function, structure, and relationship – emphasize the importance of recognizing the realistic limits, both in life and social work practice, that underlie all primary and secondary social work processes.

- *Diagnosis* (understanding the problem) is most effective when it is related to the use of a service; developed in the course of providing service to a client and with a client's participation; recognized as being subject to change; and given to a client to use in the course of service.

- The effectiveness of any social work process is improved by a social worker's knowledgeable use of *time phases* (beginnings, middles, ends) so that the characteristics and techniques of each phase are used fully in helping a client.

- The use of *agency function* and a social worker's professional role provide focus and content for the social work process, assure accountability in terms of society's and the agency's interests, and provide a client with the "difference" required to achieve his purpose.

- The knowledgeable use of *structure* – time, place, policy, procedures, and agency function – provides form that improves the effectiveness of social work processes. Too much form, however, can limit creativity, while too little form can produce wasted effort and confusion.

- All effective social work processes use the *client-social worker relationship* to engage a client. In turn, this helps a client achieve his own social purpose.

These five principles, in turn, are founded on three bases for practice:

Psychological base: Human growth "expresses purpose and constitutes a process" – a drive toward fulfillment is a primary aspect of human nature (purpose), and individuals are capable throughout their lives of changing themselves and their environment to fulfill their purposes (process). The functional model doesn't outright deny the influence of unconscious and environmental factors but it emphasizes the potential for growth.

Social base: The social agency is "the place where the interests of society and the individual are joined" (Marcus, 1937). Thus, agency function is emphasized – i.e., the social work process is accomplished via the social agency. The social work process provides a client with "something ... to come to grips with, so that he can ... use the agency ... in his own interests, when this interest coincides with that of society" (Smalley, 1971).

Process base: All phenomena (individuals, communities) are processes (they are not static). The functional model is process based, and the helping relationship is a means for helping a client achieve his ever-changing goals and purposes.

2. Assessment and Treatment: Functional treatment can be understood in terms of Smalley's five principles (which were introduced above).

a. Diagnosis: The social worker has general knowledge and understanding of people and specific knowledge of the client (e.g., through records), but she does not develop a diagnosis on the basis of this information alone. Instead, she helps the client "reveal himself in the immediacy of the beginning relationship as a highly individual person who will be discovering and understanding himself as he is and as he becomes" (Smalley, 1970). The understanding a social worker obtains at this stage is shared with the client so that the client can make optimal use of the services that are offered.

b. Use of Time Phases:

- In the *initial phase*, the social worker attempts to reduce a client's fears and resistances. To do so, she uses a variety of techniques to make the "unknown known" (e.g., clarifies the agency's services and her own and the client's roles). An important goal in this phase is to find "a common base for the social worker and client to work together toward a common purpose" (Smalley, 1970).

- During the *middle phase*, a client begins to assume more responsibility for his role in the process and the relationships that are part of the social work process deepen. The social worker's role is to determine how she can use the helping relationship to assist the client in moving toward greater independent functioning.

- Some *endings* are resisted and others are welcomed. The social worker is sensitive to the significance of endings for the client so that the ending phase can be used effectively.

c. Agency Function: The social worker helps a client use the specific agency services that are offered (e.g., she shares agency services with the client to work with him in establishing the focus of the social work process).

d. The Use of Structure: The social worker uses the structure of helping in ways that maximize the effectiveness of the services provided. She determines the length of the social work process, the interval between and length of sessions, the number of people to be involved in the process, etc.

e. The Client-Social Worker Relationship: An important goal of the initial phase of treatment is to identify a client's purpose, determine how the agency can respond to his purpose, and determine whether the client wants to or can use the services. Therefore, attention in the beginning is on questions such as "Where do you want to go?" and "Can we work together?" Eliciting answers to these questions requires a social worker to use the client-social worker relationship effectively (i.e., to engage the client in active participation in answering these questions).

B. Generalist Perspective

A generalist perspective reminds social workers to approach every client and situation in a way that is open to using a wide range of theories, models, and techniques and that considers all available levels of intervention, from micro to macro.

1. Key Beliefs and Assumptions: A generalist perspective underlies much of social work practice. Its key characteristics include the following:

- Social workers using a generalist approach (i.e., generalists) adopt a multidimensional perspective in which they emphasize the interrelatedness of human problems, life situations, and social conditions.

- Generalists adapt their practice activities to fit each case. The type and level of intervention selected fit the client's unique situation and concerns and the community's characteristics. Generalists never expect a client to conform to their own or their agency's usual way of responding.

- Generalists draw ideas and techniques from many different practice theories and models (i.e., they adopt an **eclectic** approach).

- Generalists are willing to work with a variety of client systems and to assume a variety of professional roles (e.g., advocate, case manager, counselor or therapist, group facilitator, broker of service, program planner, policy analyst, researcher, etc.).

2. Application: For all social workers (whether generalists or specialists), a generalist perspective is particularly relevant in the initial phases of intervention when they are assessing and defining the problem and making decisions about what needs to change and what approaches would be most effective for bringing about that change.

A social worker using a generalist perspective does the following:

- During assessment, she focuses on identifying what specific intrapersonal, interpersonal, and/or environmental factors are contributing to the client's problems in social functioning. These factors may be a lack of knowledge and information, distortions of thinking, conflicts among values and beliefs, damaged relationships, destructive individual and family patterns, alienation and loneliness, oppression, injustice, and racism, poverty, misuse of power by those in authority, and/or misguided programs and policies.

- She chooses a type and level of intervention only after completing an assessment of the client that emphasizes the interrelatedness of his problem and situation and the social conditions: (a) She selects intervention strategies and roles based primarily on the client's problem, goals, situation, and the size of the systems targeted for change; (b) she considers several levels of intervention, ranging from micro to macro, and selects the one (or ones) that are most appropriate and feasible for the case; and (c) she may end up working directly with the client, working with key people in the client's immediate environment, and/or working to change agency and community factors that affect the client or the services.

- She recognizes that she is not an expert in the application of all theories and models and, when necessary, refers her clients elsewhere for specialized interventions.

C. General Systems Perspective

Key concepts associated with systems theory are reviewed in Section I of Human Development, Diversity, and Behavior.

General systems theory concepts can be integrated into any casework approach as a way of helping a client establish and maintain a steady state, or **homeostasis**. Social workers adopting a systems approach to intervention assume the following:

- Human beings are active and purposeful and have the potential to grow, adapt, and solve problems throughout their lives.

- Individuals are **open systems** that continuously interact with other systems in their environment. Because all of these systems are interdependent, change in one will bring about changes in the others.

- The presenting problem does not belong to just the individual client but, rather, arises from interactions among behaviors or social conditions that have produced a state of disequilibrium.

- Improvement in treatment occurs as a result of changes in a client, the environment, the interaction between the two, or all three. Therefore, in seeking to help a client, a social worker may intervene with specific individuals, the social support network, and/or the larger environment, and her role may be primarily supportive, facilitative, collaborative, etc., or any combination of roles, depending on a client's problem and the target of change. The specific intervention strategies a social worker selects depend on the target of change (individual, group, institution, community).

D. Ecosystems Perspective and Life Model Approach

Key concepts underlying the ecosystems perspective are reviewed in Section I of Development, Diversity, and Behavior.

The **ecosystems perspective** (ecological systems perspective) contributes to social workers' understanding of how clients may adapt to ever-changing environments in order to cope, survive, and compete for resources, and reminds social workers to focus on the interplay between a client (person) and his environment (Sheafor & Horejsi, 2003). For these reasons, it is particularly useful during the data collection/assessment and planning/contracting phases of intervention.

From an ecosystems perspective, intervention attempts to enhance a client's growth, development, and adaptive capacities; remove environmental barriers to a client's effective functioning; and expand the availability of limited resources. A key goal of intervention is to restore an adaptive balance between a client and his environment by helping the client adapt, by changing his environment, or both.

Principles of the ecosystems perspective underlie the **life model approach** to intervention. This approach views individuals as active and purposeful and as having the potential for growth and development throughout life and emphasizes the transactional nature of the person-environment relationship (i.e., the idea that problems stem from stressful person-environment relationships). When using this model, a social worker attempts to eliminate obstacles and mobilize forces that will promote a client's growth.

1. Underlying Concepts: The life model approach is based on two primary concepts:

Life space: An individual's life space consists of three interdependent realms: (a) life transitions (developmental changes, status and role changes, loss, other crises); (b) interpersonal processes (relationships, communication patterns in dyads, families, groups, social networks, and communities); and (c) environmental properties (aspects of social and physical settings that affect individuals and groups). Growth and social functioning take place in all three of these realms, so all three are important for social work.

Problems in living: Individuals and groups may encounter stress in any or all of these realms. Thus, a second concept of this model is "problems in living," or problems in which stressful demands in one or more life space realms have led to maladaptive person-environment transactions.

2. Assessment: Most people who come for professional help are experiencing stressful demands that they can't resolve with their current internal and environmental resources. Assessment using the life model approach seeks to identify the stressors that have caused the problem and to locate the realm(s) in which they exist (e.g., job stress may be wrongly assessed as a family problem if a social worker doesn't give proper attention to environmental forces). Therefore, a social worker explores, engages, and assesses both elements of the person-environment transaction before making a diagnosis.

3. Treatment: Based on the assessment, intervention using the life model approach seeks to change maladaptive person-environment transactions so that a client's potential for growth, health, and adaptive social functioning is released and his environment becomes more responsive to his needs.

When designing the intervention, a social worker considers the full range of available practice theories and interventions. To be optimally effective, she directs the interventions to all systems that play a role in affecting a client's problem. The interventions seek to (a) mobilize and improve personal and environmental resources required to help a client cope with life stress, raise his self-esteem, and regulate negative feelings caused by life stress; and (b) engage the support of formal and informal helping systems.

E. The Task-Centered Model

The task-centered model is based on learning theory and cognitive and behavioral practice theories. Task-centered treatment is highly structured. The social worker and client determine the duration of treatment in the first session, and treatment is usually brief (8 to 12 sessions).

1. Principles: The task-centered approach emphasizes the following principles:

- Human beings are influenced by internal and unconscious drives, as well as by environmental forces.

- Problems stem from unfulfilled desires and are an inherent part of human life. They are not a sign of pathology.

- Human beings can learn to cope with problems and usually find strategies to resolve their own problems. Therefore, those who seek treatment are resourceful problem-solvers whose usual coping strategies have failed because of specific obstacles or a lack of resources.

- The helping process focuses on a client's view of the problem.

- A client is a consumer of services and primary agent of change. A social worker's role is to help a client bring about the changes he (the client) wants and is willing to work on.

- A social worker provides leadership in response to a client's needs. However, a client is a collaborator in the helping process and encouraged to be active in setting and changing goals and strategies and accepting the treatment plan.

- A social worker uses whatever practice theories fit the case but adopts a systems view of the problem.

2. Assessment and Planning: Assessment is problem-centered:

- The social worker and client mutually select the problem to be worked upon. The social worker emphasizes the client's view of the problem but also uses her expertise to suggest difficulties of which a client might not be aware and the consequences of these difficulties. The selected problem, therefore, often reflects a combination of the client's and social worker's views.

- To gain a full understanding of the problem and how to resolve it, the social worker and client explore its psychological and situational aspects and what resources the client will need if he is to change. This includes aspects of a client's beliefs, behaviors, and environment that can be influenced. The problem is always viewed in a multisystems framework (e.g., physical, cognitive, family, community) and these systems are explored in relation to the problem, including identifying what has caused the problem and how best to resolve it.

- The focus is on the present. The past is only studied to the extent that it currently affects the client.

By the end of the first or second session, the social worker and client develop an explicit, concrete agreement concerning the problem to be worked on. The problem is then divided into subgoals, and tasks are designed to achieve these subgoals. An explicit contract (which delineates the problem, goals, and duration of treatment) is formulated by the social worker and client. The contract is used to define the remainder of the helping process and address any hidden agendas between the parties. The contract may, however, be renegotiated if new needs arise, and the client must also agree to the new contract.

3. Treatment: The social worker provides respect, acceptance, and understanding, conveys an expectation that the client will work on tasks to resolve his problem, and seeks the client's input at all stages of treatment. The worker is viewed as an authority with expertise who can be trusted to work on the client's behalf, and the therapeutic relationship is viewed as a means of enhancing and supporting the client's problem-solving actions. However, compared to most other models, the role of the relationship is minimized in task-centered treatment; for example, transference and countertransference aspects of the relationship are never emphasized.

Treatment procedures are eclectic but drawn most heavily from behavioral techniques. For example, while traditional therapeutic techniques (empathy, role-playing, advice giving) are important, they are not seen as sufficient for bringing about change. Instead, change is thought to occur because a social worker and client perform a series of well-defined tasks during and between sessions. "General tasks" are those which give a client direction for action but don't specify the behaviors to be performed. "Operational tasks" assign specific behaviors to a client and are usually preferred.

The intervention consists of the following processes:

- The social worker and client develop **problem-solving tasks**. To support and stimulate the client's problem-solving abilities, the social worker encourages him to help develop the tasks and seeks his agreement to perform them. All tasks are developed based on an evaluation of obstacles to the client's problem-solving ability, such as missing resources that need to be mobilized to resolve the problem.

- When a problem doesn't immediately suggest a task, the social worker and client explore alternative ways to resolve the problem (alternative tasks). The social worker has specialized knowledge and the client has come in for help because he can't resolve a problem alone – thus, the social worker usually provides most of the suggestions. However, the client's suggestions are also important, and a social worker rarely "assigns" tasks without discussion.

- The social worker and client discuss task implementation until a well-defined plan has been developed. The plan defines a specific task and must be clear to the client; therefore, sessions usually end with a review of the task.

- The social worker prepares the client to perform the task. She uses simulation and guided practice to model behaviors and asks the client to rehearse or role-play these behaviors in the session. If the rationale for a task is not apparent, the social worker and client discuss its objective, particularly its benefits.

- At the start of each session, progress is reviewed: (a) If a task has been accomplished, the social worker and client formulate a new task aimed at either the same or a different problem. (b) If a task was not accomplished, the social worker and client develop a new plan for carrying it out, redesign or replace the task, or redefine the problem. (c) Sometimes, the social worker and client need to reassess obstacles (internal and external) to achieving the task and develop a plan for minimizing their interference. (d) When obstacles can't be overcome, the social worker may use a process called contextual analysis (focused exploration and interpretation) to help the client understand the obstacles and mobilize and use appropriate resources (including external resources and resources within the client). For example, the social worker may encourage the client to re-evaluate unrealistic expectations or modify behaviors that interfere with problem-solving.

4. Termination: Termination begins in the first session, when the social worker and client preset the duration of treatment. After the specified number of sessions has elapsed, the social worker and client review their progress, particularly in terms of what the client has achieved. The social worker also helps the client plan how he will continue to work on and plan relevant tasks to achieve.

F. Brief Therapy Model

Social workers using a brief therapy model adopt a strengths perspective. The brief therapy models relies on the following assumptions:

- Both the social worker and client have resources that can be used during treatment to facilitate change.
- A client has resiliency, knowledge, abilities, coping skills, and problem-solving skills, but he is temporarily stuck or overwhelmed and unable to use fully his own strengths. The social worker's role is to help the client access and use his own resources so that he can move forward and find solutions. This assumption has been described by the term **utilization**, which refers to conducting the work with what a client brings.
- The social worker believes firmly that change is possible and conveys this expectation to the client. This assumption is termed **expectancy**, and is a key part of a brief therapist's stance. The objective is to set a client up for a self-fulfilling prophecy.

Other key features of the brief therapy model include the following:

- The focus is on measurable goals. Goals should be small steps toward an end and must be meaningful to the client; and measures should be used before, during, and at the end of treatment to document progress.
- The relationship is collaborative and avoids hierarchy.
- The social worker's role is to be an active and engaged participant.
- The overall goal is to empower the client.
- Relies on a time-limited perspective.

G. Problem-Solving and Decision Theory

Problem-solving and decision theory is based on social psychology and cognitive learning theory. Application of the **problem-solving process** is similar to the scientific method:

Step 1. The problem is acknowledged and analyzed. The goal is to identify a client's specific needs.

Step 2. The social worker and client negotiate explicit goals.

Step 3. The social worker and client identify all possible alternative actions for achieving the goals.

Step 4. The social worker and client determine the pros and cons of pursuing each alternative action.

Step 5. The social worker and client evaluate the pros and cons according to a set of predefined criteria in terms of how close they are to the client's needs and goals. They then select the most promising alternative.

Step 6. The social worker and client implement the selected option.

Step 7. The social worker and client evaluate the outcome.

H. Psychodynamic Theories and Models

For additional information on the personality theories underlying psychodynamic therapies, see Section I of Human Development, Diversity, and Behavior.

As a general rule, the practice frameworks based on psychodynamic concepts give more attention to a client's thoughts and feelings than to social and environmental factors. They seek to improve clients' social functioning by helping them understand their conflicting thoughts and feelings.

The therapies categorized as psychodynamic – i.e., classical psychoanalysis, the therapeutic approaches of the ego-analysts, the object-relations theorists, and the neo-Freudians, Adler's individual psychology, and Jung's analytical psychotherapy – share several assumptions: (a) They view human behavior as being motivated largely by unconscious processes; (b) they regard early development as having a profound effect on adult functioning; (c) they propose that there are general (universal) principles that explain personality development and behavior; and (d) they consider insight into unconscious processes to be a key component of psychotherapy.

Classical (Freudian) Psychoanalysis

1. View of Maladaptive Behavior: For Freud, psychopathology stems from an unconscious, unresolved conflict that occurred during childhood. He believed, for example, that hysteria arises from a conflict related to childhood sexual experiences and that a phobia is the result of anxiety which has been displaced onto an object or event different from (but symbolic of) the original object or event involved in an unresolved conflict.

2. Therapy Goals: The goal of psychoanalytic psychotherapy is to reduce or eliminate pathological symptoms by bringing the unconscious into conscious awareness and integrating previously repressed material into the personality.

3. Therapy Techniques: Analytic **neutrality** is a key component of psychoanalysis. The therapist remains objective at all times and doesn't take sides in the client's conflicts.

a. The Targets of Analysis: The primary technique of psychoanalytic psychotherapy is analysis. The main targets of analysis are the client's free associations, dreams, resistances, and transferences. Underlying the analysis of these events is the assumption of **psychic determinism** or the belief that all behaviors are meaningful and serve some psychological function. Freud believed, for instance, that slips of the tongue (parapraxes) are not meaningless accidents but expressions of unconscious motives.

> *Free association:* Free association requires the client to say whatever comes to mind without censure. The use of free association is based on the premise that "associating" without censure allows unconscious material to surface into consciousness.
>
> *Dream analysis:* Freud considered dreams to be "the royal road to the unconscious" and used dream analysis to help uncover unconscious conflicts and motives. In dream analysis, the client relates a dream's manifest content (the events that occurred in the dream) and then free associates to the elements of the dream to identify its latent (unconscious) content.
>
> *Resistance:* As a client begins to become aware of previously unconscious material, he may resist further confrontation with that material in order to avoid anxiety. Resistance can be manifested in many ways including missed appointments, tardiness, avoidance of certain topics, and periods of silence during free association.
>
> *Transference:* The therapist's neutrality allows the client to project onto the therapist feelings he originally had for a parent or other significant person in the past. Such transference can involve positive or negative feelings and can take many forms including direct comments about the therapist or the effectiveness of therapy, sexual advances toward the therapist, extreme dependency on the therapist, and competitiveness with the therapist or her other clients. "Positive transference" often underlies what appears to be a quick improvement in symptoms during the early stages of therapy. Later, however, positive transference and improvements are likely to be replaced by "negative transference."
>
> Transference is viewed as a form of resistance and is considered a crucial aspect of therapy since its analysis helps the client understand how he misperceives, misinterprets, and misresponds to the present due to the influences of past events. When transference is at its most intense level, the client actually confuses the therapist with another person. This is referred to as a "transference neurosis."

The term "countertransference" is used to describe a therapist's inappropriate emotional reactions to a client. Freud considered countertransference to be detrimental to psychoanalysis and believed that a therapist must always be aware of any countertransference feelings to ensure that they do not interfere with the progress of treatment. Current forms of psychotherapy, however, view countertransference as a helpful tool in gaining understanding of a client's process.

b. The Process of Analysis: The analysis of free associations, dreams, resistances, and transferences consists of a combination of clarification, confrontation, interpretation, and working through.

> *Clarification and confrontation:* Clarification involves restating the client's remarks and feelings in clearer terms, while confrontation entails making statements that help the client see his behavior in a new way. "You seem to feel that people judge you negatively because you didn't go to college" is an example of clarification; "I wonder if the reason you

missed your last appointment has anything to do with what we were talking about during the last few sessions?" is an illustration of confrontation.

Interpretation: Interpretation goes a step further than confrontation by more explicitly connecting current behavior to unconscious processes. "Is it possible that your workaholism is a way to make sure that you don't have to face being rejected by women?" is an example of an interpretative statement. Interpretations are less likely to elicit anxiety and resistance and, therefore, tend to be more effective when they address motives and conflicts close to a client's consciousness than when they relate to material buried deep in the unconscious.

Working through: Finally, improvement in psychoanalysis is attributed to a combination of catharsis, insight, and working through. Catharsis is the emotional release resulting from the recall of unconscious material; it paves the way for the client's insight into the relationship between his unconscious processes and current behaviors. Working through, the final and longest stage in psychoanalysis, allows the client to gradually assimilate new insights into his personality.

The Ego Analysts

The ego analysts include Anna Freud, Heinz Hartmann, Ernest Kris, David Rapaport, and Erik Erikson. Although the specific theories of these individuals differ, they share in common the following: (a) They believe that personality development continues throughout the lifespan. (Freud, by contrast, considered personality to be more or less fixed during childhood.) (b) They emphasize the effects of the ego on personality development. (In contrast, Freud emphasized the id.) (c) They describe two types of ego function: **Ego defensive functions**, which are used to resolve conflicts and are similar to Freud's conceptualization of ego functions; and **ego autonomous functions**, which encompass the "conflict-free ego sphere" and consist of adaptive, conflict-free functions, such as speech, memory, learning, and perception.

1. View of Maladaptive Behavior: For the ego analysts, healthy behavior is under the conscious control of the ego. When the "ego loses its autonomy from the id or from reality, behavior is no longer under conscious control and pathology may ensue" (Wolberg, 1988, p. 253).

2. Therapy Goals and Techniques: Ego analytic psychotherapy does not differ significantly from classical psychoanalysis in terms of therapy goals and techniques. However, ego analysts place greater emphasis on the present than the past, they focus on both the neurotic and adaptive (non-neurotic) aspects of a client's personality, and they attempt to increase a client's awareness of and conscious control over the events underlying current problems. The ego analysts also rely less on transference and more on providing a client with opportunities for "reparenting."

Of all the psychodynamic theories, ego psychology has probably had the most influence on social work practice. As noted above, ego psychology emphasizes not only childhood development but also adulthood development and the capacity to resolve problems and deal with social realities. And, although based on psychoanalytic theory, ego psychology emphasizes the growth and development of reality-oriented ego functions (such as memory, language, judgment, and decision making) and processes rather than unconscious drives.

Therefore, for social workers, ego psychology is useful because it (a) provides a framework for understanding the specific tasks individuals must master during each developmental stage; (b) emphasizes the role of the social environment in either helping a person master developmental tasks necessary for healthy functioning or preventing him from doing so; (c) emphasizes the development of adaptive coping mechanisms including identifying ego functions that are associated with effective social and occupational functioning and a subjective sense of personal comfort; and (d) integrates both the psychological and social realms.

Adler's Individual Psychology

1. View of Maladaptive Behavior: For Adler, mental disorders represent a mistaken style of life, which is characterized by maladaptive attempts to compensate for feelings of inferiority, a preoccupation with achieving personal power, and a lack of social interest.

2. Therapy Goals and Techniques: Adlerian psychotherapy entails establishing a collaborative relationship with the client, helping the client identify and understand his style of life and its consequences, and reorienting the client's beliefs and goals so that they support a more adaptive lifestyle.

Specific techniques used by Adlerians include the following:

Lifestyle investigation: To identify the nature of a client's style of life, Adlerians obtain information about the client's family constellation, fictional (hidden) goals, "basic mistakes" (distorted beliefs and attitudes), and earliest memories. With regard to the latter, Adler believed that a person's lifestyle is relatively fixed by age 6 and, consequently, that early recollections can provide important information. He found, for instance, that the earliest memories of physicians are often related to an illness or death in the family.

Study of dreams: Adlerians regard dreams as rehearsals of future courses of action and consider dreams to be a source of information about a client's lifestyle and progress in therapy.

Interpretation of resistance and transference: Resistances and transferences are viewed as reflections of the client's style of life, and an interpretation of these phenomena helps the client understand the purpose of his feelings and behaviors.

Acting "as if": When a client says "If only I could ...," an Adlerian is likely to ask the client to role-play the behavior described in his statement.

Paradoxical intention: Adlerians make use of a client's resistance by asking the client to pay closer attention to or exaggerate his undesirable thoughts and behaviors.

Giving encouragement and advice: Adler viewed clients as "discouraged" rather than sick and felt that a therapist's primary task is to provide a client with encouragement. He also believed that therapists should offer advice by suggesting alternative courses of action from which the client can then choose.

Jung's Analytical Psychotherapy

Like Adler, Carl Jung adopted a broader view of personality development than Freud and defined libido as general psychic energy. Jung also believed that behavior is determined not only by past events but also by future goals and aspirations.

1. View of Maladaptive Behavior: From the Jungian perspective, symptoms are "unconscious messages to the individual that something is awry ... [and that present] him with a task that demands to be fulfilled" (Kaufmann, 1979, p. 109).

2. Therapy Goals and Techniques: The primary goal of Jung's analytical psychotherapy is to rebridge the gap between the conscious and the personal and collective unconscious. To achieve this goal, Jungians rely primarily on interpretations that are designed to help a client become aware of his inner world. Because material in the collective unconscious is often expressed symbolically, Jungians are particularly interested in dreams, and the interpretation of dreams (dreamwork) is a key component of therapy.

Jungians consider a client's transferences to be projections of the personal and collective unconscious. Although Jung wavered during his career about the importance of transference, he ultimately concluded, like Freud, that the analysis of transference plays a crucial role in therapy. In contrast to Freud, Jung considered a therapist's countertransference to be a useful therapeutic tool that can provide the therapist with information about what is actually occurring during the course of therapy.

I. Humanistic Theories and Models

The humanistic ("third force") psychotherapies are a diverse collection of therapeutic techniques that share a number of characteristics, many of which are consistent with core social work values. These characteristics include the following:

- Adoption of a phenomenological approach, which assumes that, to understand a person, one must understand his subjective experience ("phenomenal field").

- An emphasis on the uniqueness and "wholeness" of the individual.

- A focus on current behaviors.

- A belief in the individual's inherent potential for self-determination and self-actualization.

- A view of therapy as involving an authentic, collaborative, and egalitarian relationship between therapist and client.

- A rejection of traditional assessment techniques and diagnostic labels.

Existential Therapy

Logotherapy (Frankl, 1959) and other existential therapies are derived from existential philosophy. These therapies share an emphasis on the human conditions of depersonalization, loneliness, and isolation and the assumption that people are not static but, instead, are in a constant state of "becoming."

1. Assumptions: For existential therapists, maladaptive behavior is a natural part of the human condition. Anxiety, for example, is considered a normal response to the constant threat of nonbeing (death).

2. Therapy Goals and Techniques: The goal of existential therapy is to help clients overcome their troublesome feelings (e.g., feelings of meaninglessness) so that they can live in a more committed, self-aware, authentic, and meaningful way. Key techniques of existential therapy include the following:

- Clients are helped to recognize their freedom and to accept responsibility for changing themselves.

- An existential therapist temporarily puts aside her technical expertise and focuses on the client's accounts of his experience. (Existential therapy is a "phenomenological approach" – **phenomenology** emphasizes examining a person's immediate subjective experience and attempting to describe it with as little interpretation or bias as possible.)

- The therapist pays close attention to factors that move clients toward an authentic mode of existence. There are two states of existence for a human being: a "forgetfulness of being" in which the person is absorbed in only the way things are, and a "mindfulness of being" in which the person lives authentically, embraces possibilities and limits, and is aware of his responsibility for his life.

- The therapist-client relationship is considered the most important therapeutic tool. Other interventions are sometimes used, as well, however. For example, paradoxical intention, which is used to reduce a client's fear, requires the client to focus in an exaggerated and humorous way on the feared situation.

The existential therapy known as **logotherapy** uses a flexible approach centered around confrontation. Clients encounter a unique, intense, and here-and-now human interaction between themselves and the therapist, and are challenged to examine the quality of their existence and choices (Coon, 1995). Successful therapy results in a reappraisal of what is important in life, and the client regaining a strong sense of meaning in life (Dyck, 1987).

Person-Centered Therapy (Rogers)

1. Assumptions: Carl Rogers's person-centered therapy (a.k.a. client-centered therapy) is based on his assumption that all people have an innate "self-actualizing tendency" that serves as their major source of motivation and that guides them toward positive, healthy growth. For Rogers, **self-actualization** is "the directional trend which is evident in all organic and human life – the urge to expand, extend, develop, mature – the tendency to express and activate all the capacities of the organism" (1961, p. 351).

The central concept in Rogers's personality theory is the notion of the self, or the "organized, consistent conceptual gestalt composed of perceptions of the characteristics of the 'I' or 'me' and the perceptions of the relationships of the 'I' or 'me' to others and to various aspects of life, together with the values attached to these perceptions" (Rogers, 1959, p. 200). To grow toward self-actualization, the self must remain unified, organized, and whole. The self becomes disorganized when there is **incongruence** between the self and experience:

- Incongruence results when a person encounters conditions of worth. This occurs, for example, when a child finds out that positive regard from his parents is conditional rather than unconditional; that is, when the child learns that he will receive affection and attention from his parents only when he behaves in certain ways. In this situation, the child will feel incongruence between his sense of self (how he acts) and his experience in the world (how his parents want him to act).

- Incongruence between self and experience produces unpleasant visceral sensations that are subjectively experienced as anxiety and serve as a signal that the unified self is being threatened. A person may attempt to alleviate anxiety through the defensive maneuvers of perceptual distortion and denial. Although these maneuvers may be temporarily effective, they are counter to self-actualization: If a person learns as a child that his parents approve of him only when he acts unemotionally, he may deny his emotions and, as a consequence, will not develop his capacities to their fullest.

2. Therapy Goals: The primary goal of person-centered therapy is to help the client achieve congruence between self and experience so that he can become a more fully functioning, self-actualizing person.

3. Therapy Techniques: Rogerian therapy is based on the premise that, if the right environment is provided by the therapist, then the client will achieve congruence between self and experience and be carried by his own inherent tendency toward self-actualization. In therapy, the "right environment" involves providing three **facilitative conditions**:

Unconditional positive regard: The therapist must genuinely care about the client, affirm the client's worth as a person, and accept the client without evaluation. The provision of unconditional positive regard does not mean that a therapist must feel positively about all of a client's actions, but, instead, that she must accept those actions and avoid any overt or covert judgment of them. Because an evaluation of any kind represents a condition of worth, positive and negative judgments are both considered non-therapeutic.

Accurate empathic understanding: Accurate empathy refers to the therapist's ability to see the world as the client does and to convey that understanding to the client. Person-centered therapists use a number of techniques to express empathy such as nodding, maintaining eye contact, and reflection of feeling.

Genuineness (congruence): The therapist must be genuine and authentic in therapy since any lack of genuineness (as manifested, for instance, by incongruence between the therapist's words and behaviors) will undermine the client's trust. The requirement for genuineness does not mean that a therapist must always self-disclose, but that the therapist must honestly communicate her feelings to a client whenever it is appropriate to do so.

Rogerian therapy is considered to be "nondirective" because it deliberately avoids the use of such directive techniques as interpretation, manipulation, probing questions, advice giving, and the assignment of diagnostic labels. Indeed, assessment and diagnosis are viewed as detrimental since they put the therapist in a role of authority, which can interfere with the client's movement toward self-actualization. Rogerian therapy is "client-centered" because it considers the client to be the expert of his own inner processes and encourages clients to arrive at their own insights and decisions. Because of the latter assumption, Rogerians rely primarily on clients' self-reports to obtain information about them.

Gestalt Therapy

Gestalt therapy was founded by Fritz Perls. Like other forms of humanistic psychotherapy, Gestalt therapy incorporates principles drawn from psychoanalysis, phenomenology, and existentialism. It also makes use of concepts from Gestalt psychology, a branch of psychology that addresses issues related to perception. These concepts include the following: (a) People tend to seek closure; (b) a person's "gestalts" (see below) reflect his current needs; (c) a person's behavior represents a whole that is greater than the sum of its parts; (d) behavior can be fully understood only in its context; and (e) a person experiences the world in accord with the principle of figure/ground (Passons, 1975).

A gestalt (pattern) is organized according to the relationship between figure and ground. "Figure" refers to what stands out in an individual's experience and it is regulated by the person's needs and the nature and demands of the situation; "ground" is the entire context of phenomenologically relevant variables from which a figure emerges. Gestalt formation is continuous: Ideally, a figure remains prominent for as long as it is of primary interest. During that time, a person's energy is directed toward clarifying the figure and taking action to meet the need it represents. If the figure produces successful action to meet the need of the moment, the person's attention is released from it, and his energy is then free to focus on the next figure. If the need is not met, the gestalt remains unfinished and maintains a hold on the person's attention. Unfinished gestalts can operate at different levels of awareness. One that is kept out of awareness is called "unfinished business" and can have a lasting effect on a person's self-esteem, cohesive identity, and relationships with others.

1. Assumptions: Gestalt therapy is based on the premise that each individual is capable of assuming personal responsibility for his own thoughts, feelings, and actions and living as an integrated "whole."

According to Perls, the personality consists of the self and the self-image. The self is the creative aspect of the personality that promotes the individual's inherent tendency for self-actualization or the ability to live as a fully integrated person. The self-image, the "darker side" of the personality, hinders growth and self-actualization by imposing external standards. Which aspect of the personality dominates depends, in large part, on the person's early interactions with the environment. During childhood, for instance, an individual's parents must provide him with support and opportunities to overcome frustration in order for the self to develop. If the child is given support only in the form of approval and/or is shielded from all frustration, this will curtail development of the self and distort development of the self-image.

Neurotic (maladaptive) behavior is considered a "growth disorder" that involves an abandonment of the self for the self-image and a resulting lack of integration. Neurotic behavior often stems from a disturbance in the boundary between the self and the external environment, which interferes with the person's ability to satisfy his needs and to maintain homeostasis. There are four major boundary disturbances (Perls, 1973): (a) Introjection occurs when a person psychologically swallows whole concepts (i.e., when he accepts concepts, facts, and standards from the environment without actually understanding or fully assimilating them). Introjectors have trouble distinguishing between "me" and "not me," and in therapy, are often overly compliant. (b) Projection involves disowning aspects of the self by assigning them to other people. Extreme projection can result in paranoia. (c) Retroflection entails doing to oneself what one wants to do to others. A retroflector may, for instance, turn his anger toward another person inward. (d) Confluence refers to the absence of a boundary between the self and the environment. Confluence causes intolerance of any differences between oneself and others and often underlies feelings of guilt and resentment.

2. Therapy Goals: The major goal of Gestalt therapy is to help a client achieve integration of the various aspects of the self in order to become a unified whole.

3. Therapy Techniques: Gestalt therapy has been described as "a noninterpretive, ahistoric, existentially based system of psychotherapy ... [that focuses on the] immediate present awareness of one's experiences ... [and that rejects] cognitive explanations or interpretations of 'causes' or 'purposes'" (Simkin, 1979). Gestalt therapists avoid diagnostic labels and view historical events as important only when they directly impinge on the client's current functioning. They regard transference as counterproductive and respond to it by helping the client recognize the difference between his "transference fantasy" and reality.

The main curative factors in Gestalt therapy are contact, conscious awareness, and experimentation: Contact refers to being in touch with what is happening in the here-and-now; awareness refers to focused attention in situations requiring it (i.e., full understanding of one's thoughts, feelings, and actions in the here-and-now); and experimentation is the act of trying something new in order to increase understanding. Among these, Gestaltians consider **awareness** to be the primary curative factor in therapy. Techniques used to foster awareness include the following:

Directed awareness: Gestalt therapists use simple, direct questions to encourage clients to stay in the here-and-now (e.g., "What are your hands doing now?").

No questions: Because questions tend to foster intellectualizing and mask true feelings, clients are discouraged from asking questions, especially those beginning with "why."

Using "I" language: Clients are encouraged to begin sentences with "I" in order to help them assume responsibility for their actions.

Assuming responsibility: Clients are asked to add the phrase "and I take responsibility for it" to the statements they make in order to increase their sense of responsibility for their own thoughts, feelings, and actions.

Games of dialogue (enactment): The empty-chair technique and other games of dialogue are used to help clients become aware of and integrate aspects of the personality that have been disowned or denied. A client may be asked, for example, to role-play an interaction between opposing aspects of his personality such as Top Dog/Underdog or aggressive self/passive self or to alternately play himself and someone with whom he has unfinished business. Games of dialogue are also used to help a client "externalize the introject."

Dreamwork: Gestaltians view the elements of recurring dreams as representations of parts of the self that have not been fully accepted and use dreamwork to help clients recover disowned parts of their personalities.

As a therapeutic technique, Gestalt therapy is considered most effective for intelligent, educated clients and neurotic clients who have trouble expressing their feelings freely. Because the confrontative techniques of Gestalt therapy tend to evoke strong feelings, it is contraindicated for clients with borderline personality disorder or psychosis and others who tend to act out impulses rather than inhibit them (Korchin, 1976).

Transactional Analysis

Eric Berne's transactional analysis (TA) incorporates elements of psychoanalysis, Gestalt psychology, rational emotive therapy, psychodrama, and behavioral therapy. It has been described as "a rational approach to understanding behavior ... [that is] based on the assumption that all individuals can learn to trust themselves, think for themselves, make their own decisions, and express their feelings" (James & Jongeward, 1971, p. 12). Some authors classify TA as a type of group therapy since it is commonly used in group settings, but others include TA as a humanistic therapy because of its positive view of human nature.

1. Assumptions: Ego states, life position, and life scripts are key elements of the personality theory underlying TA. All three are affected by early environmental conditions, especially the child-rearing practices of one's parents. Adequate parenting involves the consistent provision of unconditional positive strokes, or units of attention and affection that are given for "being" rather than for "doing," while inadequate parenting is characterized by conditional negative strokes and injunctions (harsh "don't" messages).

Ego states: Everyone possesses three ego states – Adult, Parent, and Child – which loosely correspond to Freud's ego, superego, and id. Positive parenting leads to an appropriate balance of the three ego states.

Life position: All children begin life with a healthy "I'm OK-You're OK" life position. The child-rearing practices of their parents determine whether that life position is maintained or, instead, an unhealthy position is eventually adopted. There are three unhealthy life positions: "I'm OK-You're not OK"; "I'm not OK-You're OK"; and "I'm not OK-You're not OK."

Life script: A script is a person's life plan, which develops out of decisions made during childhood and forms the core of the person's identity and destiny (Corey, 1991). The choice of a life script is affected largely by early experiences that indicate a person's worth and place in life.

TA practitioners assume that maladaptive behavior reflects the adoption of an unhealthy life script.

2. Therapy Goals: Although TA recognizes the role of early experiences and decisions on personality and behavior, it also proposes that people are not entirely bound by the past: Decisions made early in life are reversible. Consequently, the primary goal of TA is to help clients make new decisions about their lives that reflect integration of the three ego states, an "I'm OK-You're OK" life position, and flexible, autonomous ("scriptless") behavior.

3. Therapy Techniques: TA is an intellectual, insight- and action-oriented therapy. It begins by establishing an egalitarian relationship between the therapist and client and having the therapist and client agree on a contract that clearly defines the client's goals for therapy. To achieve these goals, transactional analysts make use of several techniques, including the following:

Transactional analysis: For transactional analysts, whatever happens between people always involves a transaction between ego states: A complementary transaction occurs when a message sent from a particular ego state of one person evokes a response from the appropriate ego state of the other person, while a crossed transaction occurs when a communication is received by or receives a response from an inappropriate ego state. Ulterior transactions involve two ego states in the initiator and/or responder and an ulterior (disguised) message.

Game analysis: "Games" are repetitive ulterior transactions that may initially appear to generate intimacy and provide strokes but that actually help people avoid getting close to each other and serve to advance their scripts. Common games include "RAPO" (in which the individual is first seductive but then blames the other for making advances); "If It Weren't For You" (a favorite game of angry couples); and "Why Don't You/Yes But" (a game in which the therapist and client alternate roles as Victim, Rescuer, and Persecutor). Several techniques are used to identify a client's games including the "drama triangle" and a "symbiosis diagram."

Script analysis: The client's current script is identified, often with the aid of a "script checklist," which contains items related to life position, games, and rackets (unpleasant feelings that the client uses to justify his decisions).

Reality Therapy

William Glasser, the founder of reality therapy, was influenced by control theory, which proposes that "human behavior is purposeful and originates from within the individual rather than from external forces" (Corey, 1991, p. 372). Consequently, reality therapy is based on the premise that people can take control of their own lives, also now known as "**Choice Theory.**"

1. Assumptions: According to Glasser, people have several basic innate needs – four psychological needs (belonging, power, freedom, and fun) and one physical need (survival). Individuals choose different ways to satisfy these needs. When a person fulfills his needs in a responsible way – that is, in a conscious and realistic manner that does not infringe on the rights of others to fulfill their needs – the person has adopted a success identity. In contrast, when a person gratifies his needs in irresponsible ways, the person has assumed a failure identity.

Most forms of mental and emotional disturbance are viewed as the result of the decision not to fulfill one's psychological and physical needs in a responsible way, which then produces a failure identity. From the perspective of reality therapy, people are not depressed or angry but, instead, are "depressing" or "angering" themselves through the conscious decisions they make about how to fulfill their needs.

2. Therapy Goals: The primary goal of reality therapy is to help clients identify responsible and effective ways to satisfy their needs and thereby to develop a success identity.

3. Therapy Techniques: Reality therapy is verbally active, intellectual, and confrontative. In contrast to more traditional psychotherapies, it (a) rejects the medical model and the concept of mental illness; (b) focuses on current behaviors and beliefs rather than past behaviors, feelings, attitudes, and experiences; (c) views transference as detrimental to therapy progress; (d) stresses conscious rather than unconscious processes; (e) emphasizes value judgments, especially the client's ability to judge what is right and wrong in his daily life; and (f) seeks to teach clients specific behaviors that will enable them to fulfill their needs (Glasser & Zunin, 1979).

The therapist-client relationship is considered a crucial aspect of therapy, and, to be effective, reality therapists must exhibit the qualities of warmth, respect, caring, and interpersonal openness. Reality therapists model responsible behaviors for their clients and make use of techniques that are designed to help clients learn to live more intentionally and responsibly (e.g., role-playing, systematic planning, exploring wants, needs, and perceptions). Reality therapists also use a questioning framework called the **WDEP system**, in which W = explore the client's Wants and perceptions; D = Direction, or what the client is doing (acting, thinking, feeling, etc.) to get what he wants; E = Evaluate whether what the client is doing is getting him closer to or farther from a goal; and P = Planning, or creating and implementing a workable plan to make positive changes.

J. Postmodern Approaches

Postmodernism emerged as a challenge to "modernism," a worldview which maintained that truth could be learned through objective scientific measurement and observation. Modernists attempted to discover broad theories to explain human behavior and assumed that, if such universal laws were discovered, we would be able to control our environment. Postmodernism, in contrast, rejects the idea of objective reality and challenges the notion that absolute truth can be known. Examples of postmodern approaches include narrative therapy, solution-focused therapy, constructivism, and collaborative, conversational approaches.

Narrative Therapy

1. Assumptions: Narrative therapy is concerned with understanding how experience produces expectations and how expectations influence experience through the creation of organizing stories. Key constructs underlying narrative therapy are described below.

a. Objective Reality vs. Interpretation:

- All "knowing" requires the act of interpretation.
- The meaning people attribute to events in their lives determines their behavior.
- A particular event no longer exists by the time it is responded to, but the meaning ascribed to it survives over time.
- Because people organize their lives around specific meanings, they unintentionally contribute to the maintenance and "lifestyle" of a problem.

b. Text Analogy: This describes how people organize their lives around certain problems. This organization reflects the interaction of "readers" and "writers" around particular stories, or narratives:

- To make sense of their lives and express themselves, people arrange their experiences in a sequence across time in a way that enables them to attain a coherent account of themselves and the world around them. Such "storying" determines the meaning people give to their experiences.
- People's lives and relationships unfold in terms of the reading and writing of "texts," or the performance of stories. Every new reading is a new interpretation of the text and, therefore, a new writing.
- A "problem" is constructed in terms of the performance of a **dominant story**; and a solution is constructed in terms of opening space for the authoring of an **alternative story**. The unstoried parts of experience are believed to provide the basis for the development of alternative stories.

2. Therapy Goals: The overall goal of narrative therapy to help clients identify "unique outcomes" and perform new meanings based on those outcomes.

3. Therapy Processes:

a. Explore the Problem Using Story Metaphors: The therapist listens to the client's narratives. Using a "story metaphor" rather than history-taking implies the following things: (a) What a client discloses is a reformulation of his memories not necessarily the objective truth. (b) Stories about the same thing can change over time. (c) Each client's description of the problem and its effects is "**privileged**." In other words, details about the effects of the problem and each client's experience of the problem are unique.

The client's disclosures at this time are influenced by the therapist's presence as a "participant observer" and the context in which the story is being told and heard. The therapist asks questions to expand a client's story and tries to clarify the story in ways that might be meaningful to the client.

b. Deconstruction: New meaning is given to a client's dominant dysfunctional story based on an understanding of other truths and alternative realities. A type of deconstruction called "deconstructing dominant cultural discourses" promotes externalization of the problem and gives clients the distance they need to see the problem in a new light.

c. Reauthor the Story: The therapist asks questions that focus on the client's competence in relation to the problem, and the client's answers serve as the start of new narratives. Initially, questions explore the client's past competence in relation to the problem; questions then shift to the future to help the client envision changes that will fit the new story.

4. Therapy Techniques: All intervention is in the form of questions. Examples include deconstruction questions, which invite clients to examine and undermine taken-for-granted realities; opening space questions, which facilitate the authoring of alternative stories; and preference questions, which help clients evaluate their answers to other questions. Key narrative therapy techniques include the following:

Externalization: This encourages clients to objectify the problem. In the first meeting, the therapist begins asking questions to help clients revise their relationship with the problem (e.g., when clients refuse to cooperate with the requirements of a problem, they undermine it). When clients separate from the dominant stories that are shaping their lives and relationships, they can identify overlooked parts of their experience – these are called **unique outcomes**.

Mapping the influence: To facilitate externalization and the discovery of unique outcomes, the therapist asks "relative influence questions," which map the influence of the problem and the influence of the clients and their relationships on the problem.

Ascribing meaning to unique outcomes: Questions are then used to help clients "plot" unique outcomes into an alternative story: (a) "Unique outcome questions" invite clients to notice actions and intentions that contradict their dominant story. (b) "Unique account questions" invite clients to make sense of exceptions to their dominant stories and embrace them as part of an alternative story. (c) "Unique redescription questions" invite clients to acquire meaning from the unique accounts they've identified as they redescribe themselves, others, and their relationships. (d) "Unique possibility questions" invite clients to imagine the futures that can emanate from unique accounts and redescriptions.

(e) "Unique circulation questions" include others in a client's developing alternative story; and "experience of experience" questions invite clients to see themselves in their unique accounts through the eyes of other people.

Solution-Focused Therapy

1. Assumptions: Key assumptions underlying solution-focused therapy include the following:

- There is no one right way to view things. Different views may all be valid.
- Clients (and all people) want to change, but they become "stuck" because of limited, pessimistic perspectives that generate repetitive patterns of solutions that haven't worked.
- Clients have resources and strengths, are the experts about their own lives and what their experiences mean, and are competent to co-construct treatment goals and strategies. Clients have, within themselves, the solutions to their problems.

In solution-focused therapy, the causes of problems are de-emphasized, and the focus, instead, is on helping clients become "unstuck" and focus on solutions. The therapist encourages clients to see change not just as possible but as inevitable, and one of her most important tasks is to get clients to begin the solution process.

2. Therapy Goals: The main goal of solution-focused therapy is to shift the client from a "problem-orientation" to a "solution-orientation."

3. Therapy Techniques: Treatment is short-term (often five to ten sessions). Important techniques used in solution-focused therapy include the following:

Formulation of treatment goals: The therapist moves the client to a position where the client himself is generating the treatment goals. During the first meeting, the therapist begins asking **goal formulation questions** designed to initiate goal construction. Goals are defined by the client, stated in concrete (behavioral) terms so that the client can see when he is accomplishing the goals, and focus on presence rather than absence (goals are stated in positive terms). The formulation of treatment goals is believed to produce a shift in context from "complaint narratives" to "solution narratives."

Exception questions: The therapist asks for a time when the problem did not exist. This can then lead to a self-fulfilling prophecy.

Miracle questions: The **miracle question** is often the first intervention used by a solution-focused therapist. Miracle questions are designed to stimulate a client's visualizing capacity to reach a goal. An example is, "Suppose there is a miracle one night and, while you're sleeping, the problem is solved. How would you know? What would be different?"

Skeleton keys: These are suggestions for unlocking solutions without focusing on the problem.

Narratives (stories) and language games: "Narratives" are conversations between the therapist and client that have a beginning, middle, end, and overall plot. They change as the therapist injects her own perceptions of the problem, usually in the form of a solution: (a) Narratives emerge from transactions of "shared meaning" with the client. Deeper meanings are achieved when the combination of the therapist's and the client's meanings result in "binocular vision." This is most effective when these meanings are neither too similar nor too different. (b) A "progressive" narrative reflects how the client is progressing toward a goal; a "stability" narrative reflects how the client's life is static or unchanging; and a "digressive" narrative reflects how the client is moving away from a goal. (c) Learning from "the misunderstanding" (i.e., "**creatively misunderstanding**") is used to help the client develop a more coherent reality out of the confusion he is currently experiencing.

Formula tasks: These are prescriptions for change that are developed with the client.

K. Behavioral Therapies

Behavioral therapy is not a single approach to therapy but a collection of diverse approaches that are used to decrease maladaptive behaviors and increase more adaptive ones. Although the various behavioral therapies differ in terms of both theoretical base and techniques, they all share several characteristics. Most important, perhaps, these therapies emphasize current behaviors and utilize a scientific approach to the study and treatment of maladaptive behaviors. The behavioral therapies reject the premise that a maladaptive behavior is symptomatic of underlying pathology and regard the behavior itself as the psychological disturbance – they view the elimination of the current maladaptive behavior as the primary goal of treatment and consider symptom substitution a rarity. Adoption of a scientific approach is reflected in the incorporation of multiple assessments during the course of treatment. An assessment is initially conducted to identify the behaviors that are to be the targets of treatment and then to evaluate the intervention's effectiveness. At the onset of treatment, the assessment often takes the form of a functional analysis, which involves clarifying the nature of the target behavior including the stimuli that precede the behavior and the consequences that maintain it.

Therapies Based on Classical Conditioning

Behavioral therapies based on classical (respondent) conditioning principles can be traced to the work of the Russian physiologist Ivan Pavlov (if you need to review Pavlov's research, refer to Section I of Human Development, Diversity, and Behavior). These therapies are directed primarily toward helping a client "unlearn" previously learned connections between specific stimuli and certain maladaptive behaviors. Included in this category are treatments based on counterconditioning, aversive counterconditioning, and classical extinction.

1. Treatments Based on Counterconditioning: Behavioral techniques using counterconditioning pair a maladaptive behavior with an incompatible behavior in order to eliminate the former. Counterconditioning underlies Wolpe's technique of **reciprocal inhibition**, which he believed could be used to weaken and eliminate anxiety reactions. According to Wolpe (1958), if a response antagonistic to anxiety can be made to occur in the presence of anxiety-evoking stimuli and cause a complete or partial suppression of the anxiety responses, the bond between these stimuli and the anxiety response will be weakened. Wolpe identified a number of incompatible responses that can be used to eliminate anxiety reactions, including relaxation and assertiveness. In each situation, the undesirable behavior or a stimulus associated with it (conditioned stimulus, or CS) is paired with an incompatible response or stimulus that produces that response (unconditioned stimulus, or US). As a consequence, the undesirable behavior is replaced by the incompatible (and more adaptive) response.

Treatments based on counterconditioning include systematic desensitization, assertiveness training, and behavioral sex therapy.

a. Systematic Desensitization: Systematic desensitization is commonly used to treat anxiety-related disorders and involves pairing relaxation with hierarchically arranged anxiety-evoking events. There are four stages to the systematic desensitization process:

Stage 1. Muscle relaxation: The therapist trains the client in some type of deep muscle relaxation.

Stage 2. Anxiety hierarchy: While the client is learning the relaxation technique, the client and therapist construct an anxiety hierarchy, which consists of events related to the target behavior that are ordered based on the amount of anxiety they evoke.

Stage 3. Desensitization in imagination: Relaxation is paired with presentation of items in the anxiety hierarchy beginning with the least anxiety-evoking item. The therapist instructs the client to relax using the technique the client learned during the first stage of treatment; once the client is relaxed, the therapist instructs him to imagine the appropriate anxiety hierarchy item. The client signals the therapist when he feels anxious, and the therapist then helps the client re-establish a state of relaxation. Once the client is able to imagine an item without experiencing anxiety, the next item in the hierarchy is presented. This process is repeated until the client is able to imagine the most anxiety-arousing item without experiencing anxiety.

Stage 4. In vivo desensitization: After the client has been desensitized to about 75 to 85 percent of the anxiety hierarchy items, he begins to confront anxiety-arousing situations in vivo (in real life) if it is feasible to do so. In vivo desensitization is highly structured and involves facing "real life" situations that correspond to hierarchy items that have been successfully desensitized in imagination.

b. Assertiveness Training: Assertiveness training is based on the assumption that assertive behaviors are incompatible with anxiety and, therefore, can be used to eliminate maladaptive anxiety reactions. Assertiveness training incorporates a variety of methods including behavioral rehearsal, modeling, coaching, shaping, relaxation training, and in vivo practice.

c. Behavioral Sex Therapy: Counterconditioning has also been found useful for treating sexual disorders that are related to performance anxiety. Behavioral treatments for sexual disorders often use in vivo techniques that resemble systematic desensitization. Masters and Johnson's (1970) sensate focus, for example, involves pairing situations that evoke performance anxiety with pleasurable physical sensations and relaxation. When using this technique, partners are told to refrain from genital sex and are given a series of homework assignments that involve taking turns at giving and receiving pleasure through touch. Initial assignments entail non-genital touching; these are followed by increasingly more intimate encounters that eventually include non-demand genital touching.

2. Treatments Based on Aversive Counterconditioning: Aversive counterconditioning pairs a target maladaptive behavior with a stimulus that naturally evokes an unpleasant response (an unconditioned stimulus, or US). As the result of such pairing, the maladaptive behavior elicits an undesirable response (conditioned response, or CR) and is avoided. Aversive counterconditioning is also known as aversive conditioning and aversion therapy. Examples of treatments based on aversive counterconditioning include in vivo aversion therapy and convert sensitization.

a. In Vivo Aversion Therapy: In vivo aversion therapy involves pairing the target behavior with an aversive stimulus such as an electric shock, noxious odor, or nausea-inducing drug. For example, to eliminate a sexual fetish, the fetish object (CS) might be paired with electric shock (US) so that, eventually, the fetish object itself produces an unpleasant sensation (CR) and is, therefore, avoided. Due to the practical and ethical problems associated with aversion therapy, it is generally used only when the target behavior poses a greater danger than the aversive technique and/or when the behavior has not responded to other treatments.

b. Covert Sensitization: When using covert sensitization to eliminate a maladaptive behavior, the client imagines (rather than actually confronts) an aversive condition while simultaneously imagining that he is engaging in the maladaptive behavior. To reduce cigarette smoking, a therapist might instruct the client to imagine smoking a cigarette and then to visualize becoming nauseated by the cigarette, throwing up on the floor and on himself, becoming embarrassed, etc. Then, to help establish alternative behaviors, the therapist might have the client envision a "relief" scene, in which nonsmoking is accompanied by pleasant sensations.

3. Treatments Based on Classical Extinction: The two-factor theory of learning (Mowrer, 1960) proposes that the development of an anxiety response is the result of both classical and operant conditioning: A person first develops an anxiety reaction to a neutral stimulus (CS) when that stimulus is paired with a stimulus (US) that naturally elicits anxiety or other aversive responses (classical conditioning). The person then avoids the previously neutral stimulus because this enables him to avoid anxiety (negative reinforcement, which is associated with operant conditioning). Treatments based on classical extinction include flooding, implosive therapy, and graduated exposure.

a. Flooding: When using **flooding** to eliminate an anxiety response, the client is exposed to a high anxiety-arousing stimulus for a prolonged period of time (usually 30 to 60 minutes). The key is to expose the client for long enough that he comes to see that none of the consequences he fears actually take place. Flooding can be conducted in vivo or in imagination. When conducted in vivo, it is also known as in **vivo exposure with response prevention**. Imaginal flooding is useful when it is not feasible to actually expose a client to the feared stimulus. The effectiveness of flooding is increased when it is used in conjunction with other techniques such as modeling, anxiety-management training, stress inoculation, cue-controlled relaxation, cognitive restructuring, or guided mastery.

b. Implosive Therapy: Like flooding, implosive therapy is based on the assumption that certain events are consistently avoided to reduce anxiety and that prolonged exposure to those events without the feared consequence will produce extinction of the anxiety response. Implosive therapy is always conducted in imagination and involves presenting the feared stimulus vividly enough to arouse high levels of anxiety. Stampfl (1966), the developer of this technique, believed that avoidance behaviors are learned during childhood and represent conflicts related to sexual or aggressive impulses. Consequently, the images used during treatment are embellished with psychodynamic themes. A snake phobic client, for example, might be asked to imagine a scene that not only involves a personal encounter with a snake but also emphasizes the sexual symbolism of snakes.

c. Graduated Exposure: Graduated exposure involves exposing the client initially to situations that produce minimal anxiety and then gradually progressing to those that evoke strong anxiety. Graduated exposure is helpful for reducing the avoidance and fear that may be caused by initial exposure to high-anxiety arousing situations.

Therapies Based on Operant Conditioning

The principles of operant conditioning are most often attributed to the work of B.F. Skinner (if you need to review Skinner's principles of reinforcement and punishment, refer to Section I of Human Development, Diversity, and Behavior). Behavioral therapies based on operant conditioning principles focus on behaviors that operate or act on the environment with the goal of obtaining some response. They most commonly involve increasing a desirable behavior through positive reinforcement and/or decreasing an undesirable one with punishment or extinction. Immediate reinforcers and punishers are more effective for modifying behaviors than delayed ones.

1. Increasing Behavior With Reinforcement: While both positive and negative reinforcement are useful for increasing the frequency of a behavior, most behavioral treatments rely on positive reinforcement.

a. Conditions Influencing the Effectiveness of Positive Reinforcement: Generally, the establishment of a new behavior is most rapid when reinforcement is applied on a continuous schedule, while maintenance of the behavior (resistance to extinction) is maximized when the behavior is reinforced on an intermittent schedule. Consequently, the best procedure is to first use a continuous schedule of reinforcement and, when the behavior is well-established, to then change to an intermittent one. The process of reducing the proportion of reinforcements is referred to as **thinning**.

Verbal and/or physical prompts also facilitate the acquisition of a new behavior. When a prompt signals that the behavior will be reinforced, it is acting as a positive discriminative stimulus. For instance, if a father tells his child to clean her room and always praises the child after she has done so, the father's instruction is a discriminative stimulus that signals that praise will follow the behavior. The gradual removal of a prompt is referred to as **fading**.

Finally, transfer of training (**generalizability**) is maximized when (a) the person's behavior will continue to be reinforced in his natural environment (e.g., because the behavior is self-reinforcing or others in the person's environment have been trained in reinforcement techniques) and (b) reinforcement is gradually withdrawn in order to maximize resistance to extinction.

b. Techniques Based on Positive Reinforcement: Examples of behavioral techniques based on positive reinforcement include the following:

Shaping: Shaping involves reinforcing successive approximations to the desired behavior; that is, providing reinforcement only for behaviors that come closer and closer to the desired one.

Premack Principle: The **Premack Principle** (Premack, 1965) involves using a high probability behavior to reinforce a low probability behavior in order to increase the frequency of the low probability behavior. A therapist would be using the Premack Principle to increase the amount of time a student spends studying when, after learning that the student frequently watches television, she tells him to watch TV only after studying for at least one hour. In this situation, watching TV (a high probability behavior) is being used to reinforce studying (a low probability behavior) in order to increase study time.

Differential reinforcement for alternative behaviors (DRA): When using DRA, all behaviors except the target behavior are positively reinforced. Because DRA also involves withholding reinforcement following a behavior, it is actually a combination of positive reinforcement and extinction. As an example, a child who engages in stereotyped hand movements might be reinforced with pennies or tokens for each two-minute period he plays with available toys rather than engaging in the hand movements. Related techniques include differential reinforcement for incompatible behaviors (DRI), differential reinforcement for lower rates of responding (DRL), and differential reinforcement for other behaviors (DRO).

2. Decreasing Behavior With Punishment: The use of punishment involves applying or withdrawing a stimulus following a behavior in order to decrease that behavior.

a. Conditions Influencing the Effectiveness of Punishment: The effectiveness of punishment is influenced by the following factors: (a) The sooner a punishment is administered, the more successful it will be. Ideally, punishment should be applied at the onset of the behavior. When punishment is applied after a behavior occurs, the longer the interval between the behavior and the punishment, the less effective it will be. (b) To be successful, punishment must be applied on a continuous schedule (i.e., it should follow each performance of the target behavior). (c) Because punishment only teaches a person what not to do, its effectiveness increases substantially when it is combined with reinforcement for alternative behaviors. It is also important to determine if an undesirable behavior is due to inadequate skills; if so, punishment must be accompanied by training in those skills.

b. Criticisms of Punishment: Some authorities consider the use of punishment and other aversive techniques to be clearly unethical in all cases; others believe its use is justified only when other treatments have been ineffective and/or when the target behavior is more harmful than the treatment. In terms of practical considerations, it is important to keep in mind that punishment does not actually eliminate a behavior but merely suppresses it. Consequently, the effects of punishment are often short-term, inconsistent, and limited to the specific situation in which the punishment was applied. The various forms of punishment are also associated with several negative side-effects including increases in aggressiveness and negative emotions, escape and avoidance behaviors (e.g., lying, running away), and fear of the punishing agent.

c. Techniques Based on Punishment: Behavioral techniques based on punishment include the following:

Overcorrection: Overcorrection is a form of positive punishment that entails applying a penalty following an undesirable behavior in order to eliminate it. Overcorrection encompasses two procedures: (a) Restitution involves having the individual overcorrect any negative effects of his behavior; and (b) positive practice requires the person to practice more appropriate behaviors, usually in an exaggerated fashion.

Response cost: Response cost is an application of negative punishment that involves removing a specific positive reinforcer each time a negative behavior is performed. Although response cost is most commonly associated with token economies (in which token fines are imposed for undesirable behavior), it can be used whenever the control of positive reinforcers is possible. A parent, for example, could use response cost to reduce the misbehavior of her child by taking away the child's TV privileges for a specified period of time. Other examples of response cost include fines for traffic violations and late fees for not paying your credit card bill on time.

Time-out from reinforcement: **Time-out** involves removing all sources of positive reinforcement for a brief, prespecified period of time following a behavior in order to decrease the behavior. A teacher would be using time-out to eliminate a student's disruptive behaviors if she places the student in a partitioned corner of the room for five minutes each time he is disruptive. The use of time-out is ordinarily contraindicated for people whose problems are related to self-stimulatory behaviors or social withdrawal. Like other forms of punishment, time-out is most effective when combined with reinforcement for alternative behaviors.

3. Decreasing Behavior With Extinction: Operant extinction entails withholding reinforcement from a previously reinforced response in order to eliminate (or decrease) the frequency of that response. Underlying extinction is the assumption that behaviors which no longer produce reinforcement will be weakened and eventually cease.

a. Conditions Influencing the Effectiveness of Extinction: For extinction to be effective, positive reinforcement must be consistently withheld following the behavior since a single exception can re-establish the behavior and maintain it for a considerable length of time. Like punishment, extinction is most successful when it is used in conjunction with reinforcement for alternative behaviors.

b. Criticisms of Extinction: Extinction is associated with several disadvantages. For example, it often produces a temporary increase in the behavior being extinguished (i.e., "extinction burst" or "response burst"). Therefore, it is not considered the best intervention for self-injurious behaviors and other behaviors that must be eliminated quickly. In addition, extinction often causes undesirable emotional responses such as aggressiveness, agitation, frustration, and anger (Rekers & Lovaas, 1974; Skinner, 1953).

4. Modifying Behavior with Contingency Management: Operant techniques are the primary components of a number of interventions that rely on contingency management, including contingency contracts and the token economy. Contingency contracts were described in Section V of this chapter.

A **token economy** is a structured environment in which (a) desirable behaviors are increased by reinforcing them with tokens (generalized conditioned reinforcers) that can be exchanged for desired items, activities, and other back-up (unconditioned) reinforcers; and (b) undesirable behaviors are decreased by withholding or removing tokens following those behaviors. Establishment of a token economy involves defining the target behaviors, selecting the conditioned and back-up reinforcers, developing a system for monitoring and assessing the token economy, and developing a plan for fading out the reinforcers.

Social Skills Training

Social skills training (SST) is used to improve communication, assertiveness, problem-solving, and other socially adaptive skills. It is classified as a type of behavior modification and incorporates techniques derived from operant and classical conditioning as well as social learning theory. Specific techniques include modeling, coaching, behavioral rehearsal, feedback, reinforcement, and homework assignments. There is evidence that SST is useful for reducing symptoms, decreasing the risk for relapse, and improving the social adjustment of patients with schizophrenia and for improving the behavior of children with conduct problems. The benefits of SST may be enhanced when the intervention begins with identification and correction of deficits in social perception.

L. Cognitive-Behavioral Therapies

For information on theory underlying cognitive-behavioral therapies, see Section I of Human Development, Diversity, and Behavior.

The cognitive-behavioral therapies assume that, because cognitive processes influence behavior, restructuring a client's cognitions can change his behavior. In other words, these therapies rely heavily on cognitive restructuring, which involves replacing maladaptive cognitions with more adaptive ones.

Cognitive-behavioral therapies are active, structured, and time limited (usually about 15 sessions) and rely on both verbal procedures and behavior modification techniques to help the client identify, test the reality of, and then modify his distorted cognitions as well as the habitual dysfunctional beliefs that underlie his cognitions. For social workers, the cognitive-behavioral therapies provide a useful system for evaluating and resolving problems that are the result of a client's mistaken beliefs and patterns of thought. Such beliefs and patterns often mediate a person's dysfunctional emotional and behavioral patterns.

1. Beck's Cognitive Therapy: The primary goal of Beck's cognitive therapy (CT) is to modify the dysfunctional assumptions and beliefs that maintain a client's maladaptive behaviors and emotions.

CT is distinguished from other cognitive-behavioral therapies by several characteristics:

- First, CT is referred to as collaborative empiricism because it is founded on a collaborative therapist-client relationship and involves gathering evidence and testing hypotheses about the client's beliefs and assumptions.

- Second, CT is a time-limited treatment, with the average length of therapy being 15 sessions, and sessions are always structured and goal-oriented. With regard to the latter, the first session ordinarily addresses the following goals (Beck, 1995): (a) establishing rapport and trust; (b) socializing the client to cognitive therapy; (c) educating the client about his disorder, the cognitive model, and the therapy process; (d) normalizing the client's difficulties and instilling hope; (e) determining and, if necessary, correcting the client's expectations about therapy; (f) collecting additional information about the client's problems; and (g) developing a goal list.

- Third, while the focus of CT is on the client's current experiences, historical material may be addressed in order to clarify core beliefs.

- Fourth, because CT assumes that relevant cognitions become accessible and modifiable only with affect arousal, imagery and other techniques may be used to foster affect.

- Fifth, questioning is a primary therapeutic tool and often takes the form of **Socratic dialogue** (questions designed to help the client reach logical conclusions about a problem and its consequences).
- Sixth, relapse prevention is a focus throughout treatment. For instance, during the course of therapy, the therapist emphasizes the client's part in causing change in mood and behavior, and, toward the end of therapy, the therapist works with the client to develop a self-therapy plan.

CT makes use of a broad range of behavioral and cognitive techniques. Behavioral strategies include graded homework assignments, activity scheduling, behavioral rehearsal, social skills training, and relaxation; cognitive strategies include the **downward arrow** ("If so, then what?"), questioning the evidence, decatastrophizing, mental imagery (e.g., replacement imagery), and cognitive rehearsal. An early homework assignment requires the client to keep a Daily Record of Dysfunctional Thoughts, which helps the client and therapist identify the client's **automatic thoughts** – automatic thoughts reflect the client's underlying assumptions and "intercede between an event or stimulus and the individual's emotional and behavioral reactions" (Beck & Weishaar, 2000, p. 254).

2. Rational Emotive Behavior Therapy: Albert Ellis, the founder of rational emotive behavior therapy (REBT), views behavior as a chain of events (A, B, and C) where A is the external event to which a person is exposed, B is the belief the person has about A, and C is the emotion or behavior that results from B; and believes that the primary cause of neurosis is the continual repetition of certain common **irrational beliefs**. In REBT, two more events – D and E – are added to the ABC chain: D is the therapist's attempt to alter the individual's irrational beliefs, and E is the alternative thoughts and beliefs that result from D. To help clients replace irrational beliefs with more appropriate ones, rational-emotive therapists adopt an educational, confrontative, and persuasive approach and use a variety of techniques including modeling, behavioral rehearsal, problem-solving, in vivo desensitization, rational-emotive imagery, and cognitive homework assignments. Note that REBT is sometimes called rational emotive therapy, or RET.

3. Cognitive-Behavioral Couples Therapy: Practitioners of cognitive-behavioral couples therapy believe that each partner's cognitive processing (e.g., attributions, perceptions, interpretations, expectancies) influences the couple's behaviors, transactions, and emotional and behavioral reactions. As such, a couple's relationship problems are thought to reflect dysfunctional behavioral exchanges and the rigid, distorted appraisals that each partner adopts about the other.

The goal of treatment is to change both partners' cognitive processing of their own and their partner's behavior in order to increase satisfaction with the relationship. The therapist usually examines the following: (a) maladaptive affective and instrumental behaviors and environmental contingencies that maintain them; (b) how the partners' reciprocal interactions affect their relationship satisfaction; (c) each partner's beliefs about individual functioning and intimate relationships; (d) the causal attributions each partner makes about their relationship problems; and (e) the expectancies each partner has about the probability of certain behaviors occurring in particular circumstances. Cognitive techniques are used to help the partners evaluate the accuracy of their cognitions about their interactions, and the couple is then guided through a process of changing their faulty beliefs and cognitions into more realistic and adaptive ones.

4. Self-Instructional Training: Meichenbaum (Meichenbaum & Goodman, 1971) originally used self-instructional training to help impulsive and hyperactive children perform academic and other tasks more successfully. Like cognitive therapy and REBT, self-instruction is a cognitive restructuring technique that involves substituting adaptive statements. The goal is to interpolate discriminative and self-controlling thoughts between the stimulus situation and the individual's response. In addition, it is based on Vygotsky's theory that true voluntary behavior does not occur until there is a shift from external to internal language control.

Self-instruction involves five steps: (a) *Cognitive modeling:* The client observes as a model performs the task while making self-statements aloud. Self-statements include questions about the nature of the task, answers to those questions, specific instructions on how to do the task, and self-reinforcement. (b) *Cognitive participant modeling:* The client performs the task as the model verbalizes the instructions. (c) *Overt self-instruction:* The client performs the task while instructing himself aloud. (d) *Fading overt self-instruction:* The client whispers the instructions to himself while carrying out the task. (e) *Covert self-instruction:* The client performs the task while saying the instructions covertly.

5. Thought Stopping: Thought stopping entails eliminating obsessive ruminations, self-criticism, depressive or anxiety-arousing ideas, and other unwanted or unproductive thoughts by using such techniques as covertly yelling, "Stop, stop, stop!" or snapping a rubberband placed around one's wrist. Thought stopping is often combined with covert assertion, which involves making alternative assertive self-statements following thought stopping.

6. Stress Inoculation: Stress inoculation (Meichenbaum & Jaremko, 1982) was designed to help people deal with stressful events by increasing their coping skills. Treatment is divided into three phases: (a) The *cognitive phase* is primarily educational and involves helping a client understand his behavioral and cognitive responses to stressful situations. (b) During the *skills acquisition phase*, the client learns and rehearses a variety of coping skills. Specific interventions during this phase include direct-action techniques (e.g., physical relaxation, pleasant imagery, arranging "escape routes") and cognitive techniques (e.g., replacing negative self-statements with coping self-statements). (c) In the final *application phase*, the client applies the coping skills he has acquired to imagined, filmed, and in vivo stress-producing situations.

7. Problem-Solving Skills Training: As its name suggests, problem-solving skills training targets problem-solving skills, especially those related to interpersonal situations. Specific targets include alternative solution thinking, means-end thinking, consequential thinking, causal thinking, and sensitivity to interpersonal problems (Spivack et al., 1976). As in self-instructional training, individuals are taught to make self-statements related to the requirements of a particular situation, to identify alternative courses of action, and to choose an appropriate solution. Problem-solving skills training has been found useful for reducing depressive symptoms, decreasing disruptive and impulsive behaviors, increasing popularity among peers, and reducing parental neglect.

8. Self-Control Procedures: The self-control procedures encompass a variety of techniques that share the characteristic of being administered by the client himself. Self-control procedures include self-monitoring, stimulus control, and relapse prevention. In addition, several of the previously described techniques (e.g., self-instruction, thought stopping) are often included in this category.

a. Self-Monitoring: Self-monitoring, a common initial procedure in self-control programs and other cognitive-behavioral interventions, involves having the client record information about the frequency and conditions surrounding the target behavior. The results of self-monitoring provide the therapist and client with specific information about the nature and magnitude of the behavior so that an appropriate treatment strategy can be developed and the effects of the treatment can be evaluated. Interestingly, self-monitoring itself often changes the nature of the target behavior in the desired direction. Because of the reactive nature of self-monitoring, it is often used not only as an assessment tool but also to promote behavior change.

b. Stimulus Control: Behavior is said to be under stimulus control when its performance or non-performance is contingent on the presence of certain stimuli. Cigarette smoking, for example, may be controlled by a number of phenomena including coffee drinking, talking with friends, being alone, and the presence of a "no smoking" sign. The stimulus control techniques are designed to alter the associations between stimuli and the behavior and/or its consequences and include the following: (a) *Narrowing* involves restricting the target behavior to a limited set of stimuli (e.g., eating only at mealtimes). (b) *Cue strengthening* entails linking the behavior to specific environmental conditions (e.g., studying in a particular location at home). (c) *Fading* consists of changing the stimulus conditions associated with the behavior (e.g., replacing a fetish object with more appropriate sexual stimuli).

c. Biofeedback: Biofeedback can be classified as a self-control technique since it involves having a client learn to modify his own behaviors and is based, like many other self-control procedures, on the principles of operant conditioning. Biofeedback involves the use of monitoring equipment that provides feedback from the body that would otherwise not be available, such as information about heart rate, blood pressure, brain activity, stomach acidity, or muscle tension, while the client experiments with changes in posture, breathing techniques, and different thinking patterns. By receiving this feedback, the client learns to identify the processes that achieve the result he wants (e.g., relaxation, reduced heart rate and blood pressure).

M. Motivational Interviewing

Motivational interviewing (MI) is an approach designed to help clients reach a personal commitment and decision to change their behavior. The goal is to increase a client's intrinsic motivation to change so that change and the reasons for change come from him rather than being imposed by the therapist (or a spouse, an employer, etc.) (Miller & Rollnick, 1991). Both the decision to change and the selection of what to do about the problem are left to the client. Motivational interviewing is particularly useful with clients who are ambivalent about changing or reluctant to change.

Key assumptions and strategies of MI include the following:

- MI does not focus on the cause of maladaptive behavior, but, instead, on factors that impede a client's ability to change that behavior.

- MI is not confrontational in a conventional sense, but it does involve "confronting" clients with a reality that may be difficult for them to accept – the reality that they have a problem and should attempt to change it.

- "Motivation" is understood as the client's present state of readiness for change. The ultimate objective of motivational strategies is usually behavioral change (i.e., action); however, motivation is required for the client to move from one stage of change to the next for all change stages, not just the "action stage" (when the client takes action to make the desired change). Therefore, motivational considerations must be stage specific, and a client's resistance, ambivalence, and commitment must be understood within the context of these stages. (Information on the stages of change alluded to here appears in Section III of this chapter.)

- **Ambivalence** is considered a normal, acceptable, and understandable part of many psychological problems (it is usually viewed as an **approach-avoidance conflict**), and the way in which a therapist handles a client's ambivalence is believed to influence the outcome of treatment. For example: (a) An MI therapist takes a client-centered approach in which she creates a safe atmosphere where a client can explore his experiences and ambivalence openly and come up with solutions to his problem. The goal is to communicate acceptance of the client. The therapist starts where the client is, uses empathic warmth and reflective listening, and strives to understand the client's feelings and perspectives without judging, criticizing, or placing blame. (b) Instead of attacking a client's "denial" or attempting to break down his "defenses," an MI therapist emphasizes strategies that are persuasive and supportive (rather than coercive and argumentative). Strategies such as reflective listening and developing discrepancy (see below) are effective for helping a client gradually change his self-perception. (c) Because ambivalence is not entirely rational, the therapist remains aware of the client's feelings, values, and beliefs. Empathic skills are effective tools for doing this.

- A critical motivational strategy is to explore the specific elements of a client's approach-avoidance conflict in order to understand his unique motivations. These elements include the particular costs and benefits associated with his problem, the relative importance he assigns to these factors, and his expectations regarding the results of alternative courses of action. The therapist seeks to develop and intensify, in the client's mind, a **discrepancy** between his current behavior and his important personal goals (e.g., health, success, self-esteem, family well-being). In other words, the therapist tries to increase the client's awareness of the difference between where he is currently and where he would like to be. An effective way of doing this is to elicit and highlight the costs of the client's current behavior. The therapist may use a **balance sheet** to define and clarify what the client perceives as the benefits and costs associated with the problem behavior. Creating and examining this sheet usually uncovers competing motivational factors for the client and encourages him to consider the possibility of change.

- Finally, consistent with a transtheoretical model, motivational interviewing assumes that interventions are most effective when they match a client's stage of change. Therefore, an MI therapist uses different approaches with a client, depending on where the client is in the process of change. When a client seems "unmotivated" or "resistant," this is because the therapist is using strategies inappropriate for the client's present stage of change and should change strategies (Miller & Rollnick, 1991). ("Transtheoretical" refers to an eclectic, integrative approach to treatment that emerged from a comparative analysis of major systems of psychotherapy. It draws, in a methodical way, from all the major systems, incorporating their strengths and, whenever possible, avoiding their weaknesses.)

N. Dialectical Behavior Therapy

Dialectical behavior therapy (DBT; Linehan, 1987, 2006) is an approach designed for patients with borderline personality disorder (BPD) that combines cognitive-behavioral techniques with the Rogerian assumption that acceptance of the client is necessary for change to occur. In developing DBT, Linehan relied on the assumptions that the primary impairment in individuals with BPD is an inherent dysregulation of emotion and that a number of specific behavioral outcomes result from this underlying problem. DBT has four broad priorities of behavioral change, in this order from highest to lowest priority: decrease suicidal/parasuicidal behaviors and ideation; decrease behaviors that interfere with therapy; decrease behavior that interferes with quality of life; and increase coping and relational skills. DBT also includes mindfulness and dialetic principles.

DBT utilizes three basic strategies: (a) group skills training to help clients regulate their emotions and improve their social and coping skills; (b) individual outpatient therapy to strengthen clients' motivation and newly-acquired skills; and (c) telephone consultations to provide additional support and between-sessions "coaching."

The **skills training** component of DBT is usually carried out in the group setting, and its goals are to change behavioral, emotional, and thinking patterns that cause personal misery and interpersonal distress. Four groups of skills are emphasized:

Distress tolerance skills: Acceptance without pushing for change is a key element of DBT, and distress tolerance skills emphasize a client's ability to perceive his environment without having to change it. The client is helped to accept, without evaluation or judgment, both himself and the current situation so that he can tolerate and cope with crises and accept his life as it is in the moment. Four sets of crisis survival strategies are taught: distracting (e.g., through activities, opposite emotions, thought blocking); self-soothing; improving the moment (through imagery, prayer, relaxation); and thinking of pros and cons. The key is to provide the client with techniques for tolerating distressing emotional states that can't be changed for the time being.

Core mindfulness skills: Clients are taught to attend to the moment without judgment or impulsivity (the assumption is that impulsive and mood-dependent behaviors stem from a lack of awareness) and to focus on the current activity rather than splitting their attention.

Interpersonal effectiveness skills: Clients are taught effective ways of achieving their objectives with other people. Examples of skills that are taught include how to ask for what they want effectively, how to say no and have it taken seriously, how to maintain their relationships, and how to maintain their self-esteem in their interactions with other people.

Emotion modulation (regulation) skills: Clients are taught to change distressing emotional states and increase positive emotional states.

Finally, a unique aspect of DBT is that the individual therapist focuses on all suicidal behavior as a priority. In other treatments for borderline personality disorder, there is a tendency to avoid or dismiss the client's suicidal behaviors. "Chain analysis" is an example of a technique used to reduce self-injurious behavior. A chain analysis examines the personal and environmental antecedents and consequences of the behavior in detail. An important goal of this procedure is to identify points during the chain of events when the client has an opportunity to do something different, so that the client can avoid the problematic behavior in the future.

O. Play Therapy

Play therapy is not a theoretical model per se. Rather, it is a method of achieving therapeutic goals.

1. Play Therapy Goals and Techniques: The goal of play therapy is usually to address a child's feelings, primarily by helping the child become aware of his feelings and more able to express them in appropriate ways. Playtherapy can be an effective means of addressing suppressed trauma memories and interventions are used to encourage the child's self-expression. Under most circumstances, play therapists encourage clients to express themselves freely through play behavior. For instance, when a child in play therapy expresses a metaphor or other symbol in his play, the therapist simply stays with it, without forcing the child to explain the symbol or express himself in a more straightforward way. Play therapists, do, however, provide structure and set limits when doing do is necessary to ensure that clients feel safe and don't get hurt or hurt others.

2. Indications for Using Play Therapy: Most young children are not linguistically and cognitively sophisticated enough to talk about their feelings or complex human interactions, while some older children are uncomfortable discussing these matters. Thus, play techniques can be useful for both younger and older children. While play techniques are generally used with children between the ages 3 years of 12 years, there are exceptions at both ends of this range, and, to the degree that they facilitate communication, play techniques can be useful for clients of any age. For instance, play techniques may be appropriate for a 2 year old or an adult, or, conversely, they may not be useful for a particular 10 year old. Moreover, a child above age 11 might be given the option of working in the playroom or the therapist's regular office.

Play techniques are considered most appropriate for children with internal problems such as anxieties, poor self-image, feelings of being deserted, jealousy, grief, guilt, or anger, but they also may be used to modify a specific behavior or teach a child a specific skill.

3. What to Do When a Child is Upset During Play Therapy: Unless the child's distress is mild, a play therapist should acknowledge a crying child's feelings (fear, anger, sadness), both verbally and nonverbally, before introducing play activities. The therapist should not attempt to distract the child or merely reassure him that he will feel better soon; toys and games should be introduced after the child is feeling better.

In addition, the therapist must usually evaluate whether the child's distress is due to fear, sadness, anger, or illness or other physical discomfort. A child's **fear** during play therapy may be due to separation from his parent, the novelty of the situation, or an intervention the therapist has just attempted:

- If the child's fear is due to *separation from his parent*, the therapist can begin by briefly reassuring the child that his parent is nearby (e.g., "Mom is waiting for you right outside").

- If the child's fear is due to the *novelty of the play therapy situation*, the therapist can acknowledge this briefly ("You've never been here before, so you're frightened"), and then should attempt to move forward quickly ("But we've got many fun things to do together …").

- When the child's crying is due to a genuine *fear of the therapist's interventions*, the therapist should proceed more slowly; openly acknowledge the child's fear ("I see that what I did scared you. Let's make sure you feel safe"); and, if there is someone with whom the child does feel safe nearby (such as a parent in the waiting room), invite that person into the session to provide the security the child needs before he can accept the therapist's interventions.

4. Approaches to Play Therapy:

a. Client-Centered Play Therapy (CCPT): CCPT is a method of play therapy developed by Virginia Axline, an associate of Carl Rogers. It follows the principles of a person-centered approach and is nonjudgmental and emotionally supportive, with clear boundaries that provide psychological safety. CCPT has been shown through research to be an effective method for decreasing problems associated with traumatic experiences. It also can be used to develop creativity, build self-esteem, and teach socially acceptable behaviors.

Axline's eight principles of nondirective play therapy are designed to help the therapist provide an environment that promotes freedom and security: (a) As soon as possible, the therapist should develop a warm, friendly relationship with the child, in which rapport is established. (b) The therapist must accept the child exactly as he is. (c) The therapist should establish a sense of permissiveness in the relationship so that the child feels free to express his feelings completely. (d) The therapist should be alert to the feelings the child is expressing and reflect those feelings back to the child in a way that enables the child to gain insight into his own behavior. (e) The therapist must maintain respect for the child's ability to solve his own problems, if given the opportunity. (f) The therapist should not direct the child's actions or conversation in any manner. The child should lead the way, and the therapist should follow. (g) The therapist does not hurry the therapy along. Play therapy is a gradual process and should be recognized as such by the therapist. (h) The only limitations the therapist should establish are those necessary to anchor the therapy to the world of reality and to make the child aware of his responsibility to the relationship.

The playroom is the therapeutic environment and is furnished with toys and equipment that are used to create expressive scenes for the therapist to interpret. In addition, the therapist meets regularly with the parents to share her observations and give suggestions on how they can support their child.

b. Psychoanalytic Play Therapy: Psychoanalytic play therapy views play as "free association with toys." The therapist's role is to interpret free associations and analyze transferences to provide the child with insight into the working of his unconscious. Interpretation involves connecting the child's play behavior to his presenting problem. The therapist adopts a neutral role and neither encourages nor discourages any particular behaviors.

c. Cognitive-Behavioral Play Therapy (CBPT): Like other forms of play therapy, cognitive-behavioral play therapy (CBPT) involves the establishment of a positive therapeutic relationship, communication through play, and creating a safe container for the child. In other ways, however, CBPT differs from traditional forms of play therapy; in particular, the therapist plays an active role in selecting materials and activities, uses play to educate the child, and uses reinforcement to encourage specific behaviors. For example, when play is being used to teach and reinforce a desirable behavior, the child is not-so-subtly encouraged to play appropriately and is also discouraged through nonreinforcement from playing inappropriately.

Before beginning treatment, the therapist uses information from the parents, observation, and sometimes psychological testing to learn about the child's behavior, self-statements, assumptions, and beliefs. Following a thorough assessment of the child, specific goals are set and then cognitive-behavioral interventions are presented through role-playing, positive reinforcement, and modeling. For instance, a child with school phobia might role-play the experience of going to school while using new coping skills, such as positive self-statements.

The therapy is designed to promote generalization: Therapeutic play scenarios are designed to parallel the child's real-life situations, and significant adults in the child's life are encouraged to reinforce the new behavior and be involved in the treatment. Relapse prevention is also included in the treatment, in order to prepare the child and family for the possibility of future problems. The therapist and family, for example, may identify high-risk situations and the therapist may then provide training in problem-solving and coping skills to manage these situations.

P. Evidence-Based Practice

Evidence-Based practice (EBP) combines the results of research with clinical experience, professional ethics, and client's needs and preferences, helping to guide the social worker in developing effective interventions. This helps to improve the services a social worker performs in focusing on the most effective approaches. Using a multi-step process, practitioners identify the questions for which they require answers, seek empirical evidence to answer those questions, and then apply selected approaches and evaluate the outcomes (Jenson & Howard, 2008).

Some criticism against EBP states that in working in clinical settings with individuals and families, EBP does not allow the social worker's input and expertise in guiding treatment. Advocates disagree and believe that evidence-based practice encourages the use of the social workers knowledge and incorporates that into the selection and implementation of EBP interventions. As with any dispute, you must weigh the information with your own values and ethical beliefs to determine your own professional stance.

XII. Family Therapy Models

For more information on general systems theory, see Section I of Human Development, Diversity, and Behavior.

Although the various approaches to family therapy differ in terms of theoretical orientation, concepts, and strategies, all were influenced, to some degree, by general systems theory and cybernetics:

- Consistent with general systems theory, family therapists view the family as primarily an **open system**. In contrast to a closed system, an open system continuously receives input from and discharges output to the environment and is more adaptable to change. The influence of general systems theory is also evident in the family therapy concept of **homeostasis**, which is the tendency for a family to act in ways that maintain the family's equilibrium or status quo. A consequence of homeostasis is that, if the problems of one family member improve, the disturbance is likely to reappear elsewhere in the family.

- Cybernetics is the study of processes that regulate systems, especially the flow of information. It was described by a mathematician in the 1940s and was subsequently applied to family communication processes by Gregory Bateson. A key feature of cybernetics is its concept of the feedback loop through which a system receives information. A **negative feedback loop** reduces deviation and helps a system maintain its status quo, while a **positive feedback loop** amplifies deviation or change and thereby disrupts the system. Although positive feedback can lead to breakdowns, in some situations it has beneficial effects. In therapy, positive feedback promotes appropriate change in a dysfunctional family system.

Family therapists distinguish between "second order" change and "first order" change. **Second order change** involves changes in the structure and functioning of a system that alter its fundamental organization – a symptomatic family undergoes second order change when an intervention fundamentally disrupts the pattern of symptomatic interaction so that it ceases. By contrast, **first order change** involves changes in a system that are superficial and leave unaltered the fundamental organization of the system; the changes may look significant, but the system itself remains the same in terms of its processes and dynamics.

A. Communication/Interaction Model

1. Assumptions: Communication/interaction family therapy grew primarily out of research conducted at the Mental Research Institute (MRI) in Palo Alto in the 1960s by Gregory Bateson, Don Jackson, Virginia Satir, Jay Haley, and others. The results of their research on communication processes eventually led these investigators to recognize the role of communication in family and individual dysfunction, such as the role of the double-bind in the development of schizophrenia, and then to the development of a family therapy school built on the principles of communication. In a **double-bind situation**, a person (often a child) repeatedly receives contradictory messages from another person (often a parent), and the person sending the messages forbids any comment on the contradictions. Because the messages are contradictory, the person receiving them is never able to respond in the "right" way.

The communication/interaction approach is based on the following assumptions:

- Since all behavior is communicative, people are always communicating, even when they are "doing nothing."

- All communication has both a report function and a command function. The report function is the content (informational) aspect of the communication; and the command function is often conveyed nonverbally and makes a statement about the relationship between the communicators. Problems arise when report and command functions are contradictory.

- Communication patterns are either symmetrical or complementary. **Symmetrical communications** reflect equality between communicators and may become highly competitive. **Complementary communications** reflect inequality and maximize differences between communicators.

- No matter where in a system change occurs, the end result will always be the same. This assumption is referred to as the principle of equifinality.

Family therapists adopting a communication/interaction approach accept a **circular model of causality** that regards a symptom as both a cause and effect of dysfunctional communication patterns. Dysfunctional communication patterns include blaming and criticizing, mindreading, overgeneralizing, making statements that imply that things can never change, and making incomplete statements (e.g., saying "I'm very mad" without stating why or at whom) (Bandler et al., 1976).

2. Therapy Goals: Although communication/interaction therapists do not deny the role of individual intrapsychic factors in family problems, they view observable interactions between family members as the appropriate targets of therapy. Thus, the primary goal of therapy is to alter the interactional patterns that maintain the presenting symptoms.

3. Therapy Techniques: The techniques of communication/interaction family therapy can be divided into two types, direct and indirect.

- Direct techniques include (a) pointing out to family members problematic interaction patterns as they occur, (b) teaching family members the rules of clear communication, and (c) interpreting interactional patterns.

- Indirect techniques include paradoxical strategies, or therapeutic double-binds, such as **prescribing the symptom** (instructing the family to engage in the dysfunctional behavior) and relabeling (changing the label attached to a problem by the family in order to change its meaning).

B. Extended Family Systems Therapy

1. Assumptions: As its name implies, extended family systems therapy extends general systems theory beyond the nuclear family. Murray Bowen, the dominant figure in this school of family therapy, describes the functioning of the extended family and its members in terms of eight interlocking concepts, which we describe below:

Differentiation of self: **Differentiation of self** refers to a person's ability to separate his intellectual and emotional functioning from the functioning of other family members. The lower a person's level of differentiation, the more likely it is that he will become "fused" with the emotions that dominate the family. The term "undifferentiated family ego mass" is used to describe a family whose members are highly emotionally fused. According to Bowen, people tend to choose mates whose level of differentiation is similar to their own.

Emotional triangle: When a two-person system, such as a husband-wife or parent-child, experiences instability, a third person may be recruited into the system in order to increase stability and reduce tension. The lower the level of differentiation in family members, the greater the probability that an **emotional triangle** will be formed.

Nuclear family emotional system: A nuclear family can be described in terms of the mechanisms it uses to deal with tension and instability. Emotional distance between spouses, chronic, overt marital conflict, and psychological impairment in one or more family members all reflect a dysfunctional nuclear family emotional system.

Emotional cutoff: Emotional cutoff refers to the dysfunctional methods used by children to free themselves from emotional ties to their families. The avoidance of all emotional involvement is an example of emotional cutoff.

Sibling position: A child's functional position in a family is often related to his birth order and affects the child's future relationships. The oldest child, for example, is usually expected to assume responsibility for the younger children, and he is likely to choose a youngest child for a spouse.

Family projection process: The family projection process is the process by which parental conflicts and emotional immaturity are transmitted to the children. The projection process often involves only one child, typically the oldest child, the child born during a time of family stress, or the child who is perceived as "special." This child is the one who exhibits the lowest level of differentiation.

Multigenerational transmission process: Severe dysfunction is viewed as the result of the transmission and escalation of a family's dysfunctional emotional system through several generations.

Society emotional process: Bowen believes that emotional factors in a society affect the functioning of the family: As the stress level in society increases, so does the family's dysfunction.

For Bowen, behavioral disorders are the result of a multigenerational transmission process in which progressively lower levels of differentiation are transmitted from one generation to the next.

2. Therapy Goals: The primary goal of extended family systems therapy is to increase the **differentiation** of all family members.

3. Therapy Techniques: Bowen regards family relationships as involving "triangles," and Bowenian therapy typically includes only two family members (usually the spouses) so that the therapist can become the third member in a therapeutic triangle. As long as the therapist remains objective and neutral (doesn't become emotionally triangled), her presence helps family members resolve the fusion between them and achieve higher levels of differentiation. An extended family systems therapist may also work only with the family member who displays the greatest amount of maturity and differentiation since increased differentiation by this person is likely to motivate other family members to also self-differentiate.

Extended family systems therapy begins with an assessment designed to identify the history of the family's presenting problems, especially the intergenerational emotional processes underlying them, and often includes the construction of a **genogram**, which indicates the relationships between family members, the geographic location of family groups, the dates of significant life events, and other important information.

During therapy, Bowenians assume the role of an active expert or "coach" who helps each partner achieve greater differentiation. Sessions are educative, cognitive, and controlled. To avoid conflicts and reduce tension, partners are encouraged to talk to the therapist rather than to each other and to speak in a factual, calm manner. A key technique is questioning: The therapist frequently asks questions designed to defuse emotion and help the partners think clearly about their problems. Bowenians also send clients home for frequent visits with their families-of-origin, not to resolve past conflicts or reconcile long-standing differences, but to detriangle family members and increase their self-differentiation.

C. Structural Family Therapy

1. Assumptions: Structural family therapy was developed by Salvador Minuchin largely as a result of his work with disorganized, lower socioeconomic-status families, which suggested that these families respond best to interventions that use a here-and-now, directive, and concrete approach. Structural family therapy is based on the following concepts:

Family structure: All families are believed to have an implicit structure that determines how family members relate to one another. Important elements of a family's structure include its alignments and power hierarchies. **Alignments** refer to the ways in which family members join or oppose one another in carrying out family activities and have to do with the emotional or psychological connections between different family members. With **triangulation**, for example, each parent in the family demands that a child ally with him or her against the other parent; whenever the child chooses a side, the other parent feels betrayed, and, thus, the child is in a no-win situation. **Coalitions** are alliances between specific family members against a third member. A stable coalition is one that remains fixed. With a detouring coalition, the allied pair holds a third family member responsible for their problems, thus reducing stress on themselves or their relationship. **Power** in a family is concerned with both authority (who the decision-maker is) and responsibility (who carries out decisions); thus, power addresses the relative influence of different family members.

Subsystems: Family members join, on the basis of family function, to form subsystems such as husband-wife or parent-child.

Boundaries: Boundaries are the "barriers" or rules that determine the amount of contact that is allowed between family members. When boundaries are overly rigid, family members are **disengaged** (isolated) from one another; when boundaries are too diffuse or permeable, family members are **enmeshed** (overdependent and close).

Family dysfunction is viewed as the result of an inflexible family structure that prohibits the family from adapting to maturational and situational stressors in a healthy way. Anorexia in a child, for example, is often associated with enmeshment, with the child's symptoms serving to diffuse stress when parents are experiencing conflict.

2. Therapy Goals: Restructuring the family is the main long-term goal of structural family therapy. Therapy may also address one or more short-term goals (e.g., the relief of symptoms) using techniques drawn from other forms of therapy. Behavioral techniques, for example, are often used to get an anorectic child to eat.

3. Therapy Techniques: Structural family therapy is based on the premise that action precedes understanding and it is geared more toward changing behaviors and transactions than fostering insight. The process of structural therapy involves three overlapping steps:

Step 1 – Joining: The therapist's first task is to develop a therapeutic system by joining the family in a position of leadership. Joining involves blending with the family and includes **tracking** (identifying and using the family's values, life themes, and significant life events in conversations) and **mimesis** (adopting the family's affective and communication style).

Step 2 – Evaluating the family structure: Once the therapist has joined the family, she is in a position to evaluate the family's structure including its transactional patterns, power hierarchies, alignments, and boundaries. The evaluation, which may include construction of a family (structural) map, enables the therapist to make a structural diagnosis from which the specific goals of therapy can be derived (e.g., strengthening boundaries in an enmeshed family).

Step 3 – Restructuring the family: Structural therapists use a number of techniques, many of which are designed to deliberately unbalance (stress) the family's homeostasis in order to facilitate transformation of the family structure. Techniques include **enactment**, in which family members are asked to role-play their relationship patterns so that they can be identified and altered, and **reframing**, which involves relabeling behaviors so that they can be viewed in more positive ways.

D. Strategic Family Therapy

1. Assumptions: Jay Haley, who began his career at MRI, is now most associated with strategic family therapy, which combines the communication/interaction approach with structural family therapy. Haley coined the term "strategic therapy" when describing the techniques used by the psychiatrist Milton Erickson, who also influenced Haley's approach. For Erickson, "an effective therapist needs to be a strategist who approaches each new client with a specific therapeutic plan tailored to that individual" (Goldenberg & Goldenberg, 1991, p. 191).

Like communication/interaction therapists, strategic therapists emphasize the role of communication in maladaptive behavior; however, strategic therapists focus more on how communication is used to increase one's control in a relationship. For strategic therapists, a symptom is an interpersonal phenomenon rather than an intrapsychic one and is defined as "a strategy for controlling a relationship when all other strategies have failed" (Goldenberg &

Goldenberg, 1991, p. 193). Although struggles for control are inherent in any relationship, they become pathological when one or both parties denies his or her intent to control the other person and when this produces symptomatic behavior.

2. Therapy Goals: The focus in strategic family therapy is on alleviating current symptoms through altering a family's transactions and organization, especially its hierarchies and generational boundaries. Achieving insight is considered counterproductive because it tends to increase resistance.

3. Therapy Techniques: In strategic family therapy, the initial session is considered an important determinant of the entire course of therapy. The first session is highly structured and involves four stages: (a) During the *social stage*, the therapist observes the family's interactions and encourages the involvement of all family members. (b) This is followed by the *problem stage*, in which the therapist gathers information about the reasons why the family came to therapy. (c) In the *interaction stage*, family members discuss the identified problem(s), and the therapist observes their interactions in order to gather information. (d) Finally, the session ends with *goal-setting:* The therapist and family members agree on a contract that defines the goals of treatment.

Strategic family therapists assume an active, take-charge role and utilize a variety of techniques that are tailored to the family and its particular problems. During the course of therapy, the therapist often issues directives, which are assignments to be performed outside of therapy.

Directives often take the form of **paradoxical interventions** that use the client's resistance in a constructive way (i.e., by resisting the directive, a client ends up abandoning his dysfunctional behavior). For example, a husband and wife who have frequent unproductive fights might be instructed to argue for at least two hours every evening; ideally, the couple will resist the therapist's request and, thereby, stop fighting. **Ordeals**, another paradoxical intervention, are unpleasant tasks that a client must perform whenever a symptom occurs. The use of ordeals is based on the premise that "if one makes it more difficult for a person to have a symptom than to give it up, the person will give up the symptom" (Haley, 1984, p. 5). For instance, a man who dislikes his mother-in-law might be instructed to give her an expensive present each time he has an argument with her. Other paradoxical interventions used by strategic therapists include restraining (encouraging the family not to change); positioning (exaggerating the severity of a symptom); and reframing (placing the symptom in another frame of reference).

E. Milan Systemic Family Therapy

1. Assumptions: Milan systemic family therapy was developed by Mara Selvini-Palazzoli. It was influenced by work done at MRI, in particular, by Bateson's adoption of cybernetic circularity as a model for individual and family functioning (Boscolo et al., 1987).

Systemic family therapy is based on the premise that, in a family system, there are circular patterns of action and reaction. Maladaptive behavior results when a family's patterns become so fixed that family members are no longer able to act creatively or make new choices about their lives.

2. Therapy Goals: The primary goal of therapy is to "help family members see their choices and assist them in exercising their prerogative of choosing" (Gelcer et al., 1990, p. 22). To achieve this goal, systemic therapists emphasize understanding – i.e., helping family members understand their relationships and problems in alternative ways, which paves the way to seeing new solutions and making new choices.

3. Therapy Techniques: A distinguishing characteristic of systemic family therapy is its use of a therapeutic team. One or two members of the team meet with the family during sessions, while the remaining team members observe sessions behind a one-way mirror. Team conferences are frequent, and an observer may call a therapist out of a therapy session for a "strategy conference" to share her observations, make suggestions, etc. Team members and family members are viewed as parts of a single system.

Systemic family therapy involves three basic processes:

Hypothesizing: Systemic therapists use the initial contact with the family as an opportunity to collect information, which the team then uses to derive tentative hypotheses about the functioning of the family system. These hypotheses are subsequently tested by the team in conjunction with the family and revised as necessary during the course of treatment.

Circularity: The process of therapy is viewed as involving a circular pattern of action and reaction: Therapy "begins with the effect of the family on the team; they present a problem. A reciprocal process ensues whereby the therapist widens the focus of questions and family members provide clearer answers. Gradually, through the circular process, the family, in a parallel fashion to the team, begins to understand its own interactional pattern and identify its own resources and use them more effectively" (Gelcer et al., 1990, p. 62).

Neutrality: Throughout therapy, the therapist remains the ally of the entire family rather than becoming recruited into family coalitions or alliances.

Systemic family therapists make use of paradoxical strategies, such as counterparadox (therapeutic double-bind), positive connotation (reframing), and paradoxical prescription. In contrast to strategic therapists, however, systemic therapists use these techniques not to elicit an individual's resistance, but to provide the family with information that will help family members derive solutions to their own problems.

Systemic therapists also use **circular questions**, which are designed to help family members recognize differences (and similarities) in their perceptions about what is occurring. Circular questions usually address one of the following: differences in perceptions about relationships ("Who was more upset, Mom or Dad?"); differences in degree ("On a scale of 1 to 10, how serious was last night's fight?"); now/then differences ("Did his behavior change before or after your oldest daughter left home?"); or hypothetical and future differences ("If Mom and Dad divorced, what do you think would happen?").

F. Behavioral Family Therapy

Behavioral family therapy is based on the principles of operant conditioning, social learning theory, and social exchange theory. (**Social exchange theory** proposes that social behavior is the result of an exchange process. The purpose of exchange is to maximize benefits and minimize costs – people weigh the potential benefits and risks of social relationships, and when risks outweigh rewards, people end or abandon a relationship.)

Included in this category are behavioral marital therapy, behavioral parent training, and conjoint sex therapy. For behavioral family therapists, maladaptive behavior, like all behavior, is learned and maintained by its consequences.

Achievement of therapy goals involves establishing a therapeutic relationship with the family, making a behavioral assessment of the family's problems, and using reinforcement, modeling, and other behavioral strategies to foster change in family members.

As applied to marital therapy, the behavioral approach addresses the following goals (Liberman et al., 1980): (a) increasing the couple's recognition and initiation of pleasurable interactions; (b) decreasing the couple's aversive interactions (negative exchanges); (c) teaching the couple effective problem-solving and communication skills; and (d) teaching the couple to use a contingency contract to resolve persisting problems.

XIII. Group Psychotherapy and Counseling

Groups are used in direct social work for therapy or behavior change, education, recreation, socialization, and mutual support and self-help.

Therapy groups may be used for either counseling or psychotherapy. *Counseling groups* are used to prevent and remediate problems and include members who have decision-making or mild situational problems. *Psychotherapy groups*, in contrast, are more intensive and usually of longer duration, have the goals of remediation and character change, and include members with relatively serious mental or emotional disorders or social problems. A psychotherapy group differs from a support or self-help group in that it not only helps people cope with their problems, but also provides for their change and growth. *Support groups* may be led by professionals or by members who are trained in facilitating group discussions. The members of a support group share a common problem or disorder (e.g., anxiety, depression) and offer one another ideas and emotional support; the focus of the group is usually directed toward alleviating members' symptoms.

A. Types and Purposes of Work With Small Groups

Work with groups occurs in a variety of different settings for a range of different purposes (Sheafor & Horejsi, 2003).

1. Group Treatment Approach (Remedial Model): In this approach, the group is seen as a therapeutic environment that has the potential to influence members to change their behavior. Examples include psychotherapy groups and counseling groups.

- Treatment groups help members cope with serious problems or correct dysfunctional behavior.

- The social worker assumes the role of therapist, expert, and group leader.

- The focus is on the members as individuals and correcting problems that they are having outside of the group. However, members' behaviors during group sessions are often used as means of assessing, illustrating, and addressing these problems.

- In some treatment groups, such as those for sex offenders or individuals with substance use disorders, confrontation is frequently used, and the members are required to follow established rules and complete homework assignments. In such groups, there is much less emphasis on the members' self-determination.

2. Growth/Development and Training Groups: These groups are used to promote members' normal growth and development and teach ordinary skills for living. They are common in agency settings. Examples of topics addressed in these groups include parent training, learning communications skills, learning job skills, or learning about a medical condition.

- Groups used for teaching and training are goal oriented, and the social worker assumes the roles of leader and teacher. The social worker also takes on the role of planner and arranger of group activities and relies heavily on programming (reviewed later in this section).

- Some of these groups emphasize member interaction, building trust, and developing a sense of belonging to the group, while others do not. This depends on the topic being addressed and the number of times the group will meet.

3. Self-Help Groups: Self-help groups are intended to improve members' social functioning through the group experience and discussions with others who have similar problems or concerns. Examples of self-help groups include those available in many communities through self-help organizations such as Alcoholics Anonymous, Overeaters Anonymous, and Parents Without Partners.

- Self-help groups are most effective for clients who are willing and able to attend a series of meetings, share personal information and concerns, and listen to others. Some self-help groups, however, include involuntary members or court-ordered participants.

- Many self-help groups rely on leaders who are also members of the group. Some, however, are led by professionals or by members who have received training on how to conduct and lead meetings.

- Self-help groups usually rely on the following assumptions and beliefs: (a) All people have strengths that can be mobilized (e.g., everyone has a lot to teach others and can learn from others). (b) People need to tell their story and be heard by others. (c) People are especially open to suggestions from others with whom they share similar concerns and life experiences. (d) People feel more comfortable in small, informal groups. (e) People want to learn practical rules and principles that will provide them guidance on how to cope with day-to-day problems (e.g., live one day at a time, follow the 12 steps, etc.).

4. Other Small Groups Used in Social Work: (a) *Interactional model:* In a group using the interactional model (a.k.a. mediating model), a social worker assumes the role of mediator between group members and between the group and its environment (including the agency that has sanctioned the group's formation). This approach places a strong emphasis on client self-determination. (b) *Task groups:* The primary purpose of task groups is to complete the work for which the group was created (i.e., task groups are not specifically concerned with the needs of their members). Task groups are goal-oriented and tend to be structured and formal – they use written agendas and Robert's Rules of Order, and leadership roles and member responsibilities are clearly assigned. Examples of task groups include agency boards, committees, staff meetings, and community planning groups.

B. Forming a Group

1. Determining the Group's Purpose: The initial consideration when forming a group is what the group's purpose will be and how it will benefit the members. Answering these questions first is critical because other decisions made when forming the group will be impacted directly by decisions made about the group's purpose and desired outcome.

Generally, clients benefit more from groups that are relatively focused and specialized – they tend to be more comfortable and more willing to self-disclose in group sessions when they agree on the group's purpose and know that they and the other members are there for similar reasons.

2. Screening and Selecting Group Members: While it's difficult to predict precisely how a client will behave and function as a member of a group, most people behave in formed groups pretty much as they do in other situations (e.g., a client who has difficultly expressing his feelings to loved ones will probably have difficulty expressing his feelings in a group).

a. Heterogeneous vs. Homogeneous Groups: The members of **heterogeneous** groups differ in terms of their background, age, gender, problem, and other significant characteristics. In contrast, **homogeneous** groups include members who are similar in terms of significant characteristics. In general, homogeneous treatment groups tend to gel faster, become more cohesive, offer more immediate support to group members, have better attendance and less conflict, and provide more rapid symptomatic relief.

b. Member Similarities for Treatment Groups: Treatment groups are those formed to help members cope with serious problems or correct dysfunctional behavior.

- According to many experts, the members of a treatment group should share roughly the same level of intelligence (Dreikurs, 1951).

- Most authorities recommend an age span of no more than two years between the oldest and youngest child in a treatment group. Because very young children do not develop permanent peer relationships, however, group intervention is usually not appropriate for children younger than age 8.

- With adolescents, group leaders should carefully consider each adolescent's developmental level. For example, teens who have not resolved the identity issues arising in this developmental period should not be placed in a treatment group with more mature teens.

- In treatment groups for adults, age is a less important variable, unless the group is being formed for a particular population, such as older adults or young married couples.

- Same-sex treatment groups are usually recommended for children. Based on their maturity level, some adolescents are ready for co-educational treatment groups, while others are not. For adults, sexually-mixed treatment groups tend to offer more opportunity for lasting change.

- The most controversial issue in forming treatment groups is whether the clients should have the same problem. Yalom believes that it's best to have heterogeneity for conflict areas and homogeneity for ego strength. Some authors point out that when a group is "too homogeneous" in terms of undesirable characteristics (e.g., deviant behaviors), these characteristics will be reinforced.

c. Voluntary and Involuntary Group Membership: A group may be for voluntary clients, involuntary clients, or both.

- Once they are part of the group, voluntary members should be free to drop out if they feel uncomfortable or the group is not meeting their needs.

- Involuntary members can be forced by court order to attend group meetings, but they can't be forced to interact in meaningful and productive ways during group sessions. Effective group work with involuntary clients (e.g., in chemical dependency or child abuse treatment programs) usually requires a strong group leader who is skilled at confronting resistant and manipulative behavior.

- The inclusion of involuntary members in a primarily voluntary group is usually not a problem if the group has been functioning well for a while and the involuntary member is willing to cooperate to at least some extent. Problems are likely to develop, however, when the group is newly formed or has not been functioning well and/or the involuntary member is very resistant or disruptive.

d. Protecting the Safety of Group Members: Unless group meetings will take place in an institutional setting where patients can be closely supervised, individuals who exhibit bizarre or dangerous behavior should be excluded from consideration for membership in a group. This is necessary in order to protect the safety of the other group members. Clients at high risk of suicide or those who are actively using illicit drugs may also need to be excluded from consideration.

3. Group Entry – Open vs. Closed Groups: Forming a group may also involve deciding whether the group will be open or closed to additional members. This decision is sometimes made by the group's members. If so, the decision needs to be made during the first or second meeting. **Closed groups** begin and end with the same members and usually have a preset termination date. They are most effective for short-term, task-oriented work and groups conducted in inpatient settings. **Open groups** allow members to join and leave the group at different times. Some authorities also identify open groups as those without a preset number of sessions or termination date.

Before a new member joins an open therapy group, the group leader should meet individually with the new member to explore his feelings about joining the group. In this interview, the group leader should discuss with the new member the feelings he might have as he enters the group and reassure him that he will be allowed to enter and participate at his own rate.

4. Deciding on the Group's Size: The appropriate size for a group depends on such factors as the age of the clients, the concerns to be addressed by the group, and the experience of the group leader or facilitator. For children, a group of three or four is often appropriate; for adolescents, a group of six to 10 is typically recommended; and for adults, a group of about eight to 12 is usually best.

C. Programming – Selecting and Arranging Group Activities

"Programming" in group work involves selecting and planning activities (drama, art, dance, music, crafts, games and sports, parties, work tasks, etc.) that will guide the group process in desired directions and create opportunities for members to learn new behaviors and experience positive interactions with others. Structured activities and socialization games, for example, can be used to improve members' interpersonal skills, increase social awareness, and encourage prosocial behavior; and, if a group leader is properly trained, she may use art therapy and other expressive techniques to address issues related to aggressive behavior, self-esteem, body image, and awareness of emotions. In addition, the way members behave during group activities can provide the group leader with important assessment information.

The type of programming used depends on (a) the group's members (their ages, interests, social skills, physical capacities, attention spans, need for control and protection, etc.), (b) the functioning of the group as a whole, and (c) the group's purpose. Key programming guidelines include the following (Sheafor & Horejsi, 2003):

- Whether or not an activity will be useful depends, in part, on the stage of group development. For example, in a newly formed group, activities that promote positive interaction are useful, but ones that require a member to assume a leadership role are not.

- Selecting an activity requires the group leader to think about what behaviors and attitudes she wants to encourage. Generally, the leader should select activities that (a) elicit or teach behaviors she wants to promote in the group, (b) reinforce behaviors and attitudes that benefit members, (c) advance the group's development, and/or (d) help the group achieve its purpose.

- When selecting an activity, the leader also considers the members' ages and developmental levels: (a) Games are useful with all ages but are especially important for children. Games are effective for promoting creativity, reinforcing the importance of rules, challenging members to test themselves against others, and teaching a wide range of skills including self-control, problem solving, communication, cooperation, leadership, and handling feelings toward those in authority. (b) Activities such as auto repair, woodworking, cooking, etc., are often appropriate for adolescents and young adults because they combine movement and the learning of useful skills with social interaction and purposeful communication.

- The leader must also consider what existing skills or knowledge an activity requires (e.g., oral communication, cooperation, competition, movement, initiative, memory, judgment, self-control, ability to follow directions). She should avoid activities for which members don't have the required abilities. Activities should challenge members but not engender too much frustration.

- Last, the leader should think about how the rules of the activity will affect the members (e.g., does a game involve choosing teams or eliminating a "loser" from further competition?). She should consider whether the members can cope with any limits or frustrations that may result from the rules.

D. The Stages of Group Development

All groups go through expected stages of development, and understanding these stages helps a group leader anticipate and address the behaviors that characterize each stage so that the group's goals and objectives can be met. A model proposed by Garland, Jones, and Kolodny (1965) suggests that groups pass through the five stages described below.

1. Stage 1 – Preaffiliation (Approach and Avoidance Behavior): Members are tentative about becoming involved in the group and may be uncertain about the group's purpose and benefits:

- Communication among members is stereotyped, restricted, and rational rather than in-depth or revealing. Their communications are directed primarily toward the leader. Some members may demand that the leader adopt a "take charge" approach.

- Members are preoccupied with their own problems and feelings of apprehension and may be sensitive to the responses of others. They evaluate possible social threats and try to determine the kinds of behaviors the group wants and expects.

- Members may use testing behaviors to evaluate other members, test the group's limits, find out how competent the leader is, and determine whether the leader will protect them from hurt and humiliation.

- Members may move hesitantly toward the group as they attempt to find common ground with other members, search for possible roles, and seek approval, acceptance, and respect.

The leader's role is primary, and she is highly active during this stage. She initiates and directs group discussion and encourages participation.

2. Stage 2 – Power and Control (A Time of Transition): The group transitions from a non-intimate to an intimate system of relationships. As members decide that the group experience may be safe and rewarding, they shift their concerns to matters of power and control.

- Members are concerned with how they "rank" in relation to other members. Those who fail in their efforts to achieve favored status with the leader may develop feelings of hostility toward her.

- Members seek support and protection from others in the group who are like themselves and form subgroups. A status hierarchy emerges. Over time, the group process becomes stylized as relationships solidify.

- Conflicts between subgroups are common.

- Dissatisfaction or disappointment with the group may be expressed through hostility, withdrawal, or uncertainty about the group's purpose. Members may team up to express anger toward the leader.

- There may be verbal abuse or other attacks directed toward lower-status members. Lower-status members may be actively rejected.

- Isolated members may stop coming to sessions. Other attrition in membership may also occur if members find other activities more appealing than the conflicted group experience.

The leader's role in the group changes from primary to variable: Members start to take over some of what the leader has been doing; because the group's systems are not yet stabilized or functioning at full capacity, however, the leader must sometimes resume her primary role in order to keep the group operating in a functional way.

3. Stage 3 – Intimacy (Developing Familial Frame of Reference): Conflicts recede, personal involvement between members grows deeper, and members display a growing recognition of the significance of the group experience. Members begin to experience a sense of "we-ness" and a group character emerges as the group develops its own style, culture, and values.

- Members experience an increase in morale, a growing commitment to the group's purpose, and increased motivation to carry out plans and tasks that support the group's objectives. They may express genuine concern for absent members.

- Mutual trust increases as members start to recognize one another's uniqueness, spontaneously reveal feelings and problems, and seek the opinion of the group. To achieve intimacy, however, members may avoid expressing negative feelings that could produce conflict.

- Clear norms are established based on positive forces, roles develop as members find ways to contribute to the group, and leadership patterns become stable. Members now relate their group experience to their experience with their own nuclear families.

Because the group is better able to govern itself, the leader only rarely adopts a primary role during sessions; instead, she serves primarily as a facilitator, or resource, for the group.

4. Stage 4 – Differentiation (Developing Group Identity and an Internal Frame of Reference): This stage is marked by cohesion as members come to accept intimacy and choose to draw closer to others in the group. Gradually the group becomes a mutual-support system in which members spontaneously give emotional support according to the needs of each individual.

- A dynamic balance between individual and group needs emerges.

- Members feel more free to express themselves and come to feel genuinely accepted and valued as their feelings and ideas are validated by other members.

- Members begin to view the group experience as unique. Customs emerge and the group's energy is directed toward purposes and tasks that are clearly understood and accepted.

- New, more flexible and functional roles emerge to support the group's purpose, status hierarchies become less rigid, and members may assume leadership roles spontaneously as the need for particular abilities arises.

- Members bring conflict out into the open and identify obstacles to their progress; when attempting to resolve differences, members consider dissenting positions and try to achieve consensus.

Members have experience in working through problems and skill in analyzing their own feelings and the feelings of others, offering support to others, communicating their needs and opinions, etc. To the extent that the group has achieved full capacity to govern itself, the leader remains in a facilitative role.

5. Stage 5 – Separation (Breaking Away): Members begin to loosen their bonds with one another and the leader and search for new resources and relationships to meet their needs. They struggle to reconcile their positive feelings about the group with their feelings of apprehension, abandonment, or rejection about the group's ending.

- Members experience a range of feelings about the group's ending. They may be anxious, express anger toward other members or the leader, show increased dependence on the leader, and/or deny the positive meaning of the group experience. Conflicts that were resolved earlier may reappear.

- Members begin focusing on "life after the group." They may discuss their fears, hopes, and concerns about the future and about one another and talk about how to apply what they have learned in the group to other situations.

The leader resumes a more active role to support members as they prepare to leave the group.

E. Intervening in Social Work Groups

The Group Leader's Functions

The primary functions of the group leader include the following: (a) creating and maintaining the group (e.g., minimizing negative forces that threaten the group's cohesiveness); (b) creating a group culture that is maximally conducive to effective group interaction ("culture building"); and (c) activating and illuminating the here-and-now ("process illumination"). The latter function involves focusing the group's attention on the here-and-now and helping the members understand processes that have occurred in the present.

In order to maintain the group and foster a positive group culture, the leader must attend to shaping important structural elements of the group during all stages of its development. These elements include cohesion, norms, roles, subgroups, and leadership (Hepworth et al. 2006).

1. Developing Cohesion: Research on the effectiveness of group therapy suggests that high levels of group cohesion are associated with better attendance and punctuality, lower dropout rates, and greater self-disclosure, openness to influence by other members, tolerance for conflict and the expression of hostility, and adherence to group norms. Thus, cohesion plays a critical role in the success of a group.

To develop the group's cohesion, the leader does the following: (a) promotes connections among members; (b) encourages subgroup members to relate to members outside their subgroup; (c) encourages cohesive behaviors (e.g., points out who is present and who is absent, uses words such as "we" and "our," includes the group as a whole in her statements); (d) comments on and reinforces positive group-building behaviors as they occur; (e) helps members successfully achieve their goals and meet their needs; and (f) provides access to rewards and resources that individual members alone could not obtain.

In the termination phase, the leader reverses these principles in order to help members become less invested in the group and more attracted to other relationships. The exception to this is in group psychotherapy, where cohesion is usually maintained until the end.

2. Fostering Appropriate Norms: Creating a culture that is maximally conducive to effective group interaction and achievement of group and individual goals requires the leader to intervene in ways that encourage appropriate norms. To facilitate the development of constructive group norms, the leader does the following:

- She helps the group identify and articulate the behavioral norms that they want the group to follow; she records the norms, revisits them regularly in meetings, and takes an active role in helping members consistently adhere to them. Ultimately, however, the responsibility for enforcing these norms should rest with the group, rather than with the leader, and, in established groups, members may speak up to hold one another accountable to the norms.

- She observes group behavior, determines whether the behavioral patterns support or undermine the group's purposes, and, as necessary, intervenes to promote functional group behaviors and help members modify behaviors that are damaging to individuals or the group.

Especially during the power and control stage (stage 2), promoting functional norms may require the leader to intervene in situations such as the following: when distracting behavior significantly interferes with a group task; when one or several members monopolize the group's time; when members experience strong feelings of hurt, anger, or disappointment; when several members or the group as a whole begins talking about one member; when a member's behavior is incompatible with the norms set by the group; when members intellectualize about emotional material; when members scapegoat, interrogate, or gang up on one member or exhibit hostility through sarcasm or criticism; when the group offers advice without first encouraging a member to fully explore a problem; when there is silence or withdrawal by members or by the group as a whole; or when a member adopts a "co-leader" role.

When problems like these emerge, the leader focuses the group's attention on what is happening in the here-and-now: She usually shares what she sees by describing specific behaviors or events and then requests input from the group. Once the group is focused on the problem, the leader then facilitates discussion and problem-solving, rather taking decisive action on her own. Ultimately, the responsibility for resolution needs to rest with the group.

3. Shaping Roles in the Group: Whereas norms define behavior in a wide range of situations, roles define behavior in relation to a specific function or task that a member is expected to perform. Like norms, roles can help fulfill group functions or meet individual treatment goals. Counterproductive roles, however, tend to impede the creation of an effective group and achievement of individual goals, and, therefore, the leader addresses them as they emerge. For example, a member who is very anxious may talk excessively (adopt the role of "monopolist"). When addressing problematic roles, the leader encourages members to monitor their own behavior, helps members avoid becoming stuck in dysfunctional roles, and empowers other members to confront a member about his role and its impact.

4. Addressing the Impact of Subgroups: The presence of subgroups can sometimes impede group processes. Negative subgroups are ones that actively exclude others, create issues of loyalty, challenge the leader's authority, or splinter communication (i.e., the members of a subgroup talk only among themselves).

To address the impact of negative subgroups, the leader may do one or more of the following (Hepworth et al., 2006): (a) Initiate discussion of the reasons why the subgroups formed and their impact on the group as a whole. (b) Neutralize their effects through programming or structuring (e.g., challenge diverse subgroups to work toward a common goal, use a "round robin" approach to get feedback from all members, use programming activities to separate subgroup members, or change seating arrangements). (c) Help powerful subgroups or powerful members surrender power or use it sparingly in the interest of other members (e.g., encourage concern for others in the group, help the members understand how domineering behavior can be self-defeating). (d) Find ways to "connect" with negative subgroups and demonstrate concern for their wants. (e) Provide ways for subgroups to attain legitimate power by giving them useful roles and tasks. (f) Create roles for less assertive or less involved members that require little activity but still involve them in a group activity. (g) Appoint powerless members to roles that have power (e.g., arranging for group activities).

The leader may use a **sociogram** to identify alliances in the group and assess whether they are growth-oriented. A sociogram is a graphic representation of patterns showing which members of a group are drawn to one another, which ones do not interact, and which ones have a one-way attraction, mutual attraction, or aversion to each other.

5. Sharing Leadership Functions: As the group matures, the leader gradually allocates her leadership functions to members, while continuing to attend to the goals of the group and its operations. Helping members assume leadership behaviors increases the likelihood that they will become invested in the group, allows them to develop skills that they can transfer to other social groups, and promotes the development of their self-efficacy as they perform leadership activities.

The leader can facilitate the sharing of power by encouraging member-to-member (rather than member-to-leader) communications, asking for members' input into the agenda for meetings and the direction the group should take, supporting members in their first tentative efforts to exercise their own influence on the group, and encouraging efforts at mutual sharing and support among members during the first meeting.

Because challenges to her leadership are an inherent part of a group's development, a group leader should avoid interpreting them as negative or personal attacks. Instead, she should identify what they reveal about issues or roles that are important to individual members. For instance, if a member criticizes her style, the leader should respond to the challenge empathically, explore the statement, elicit feedback from other members regarding her leadership style, and ask for input.

Interventions Used by Group Leaders

A group leader must ensure that the issues and concerns worked on by the group resemble the ones that members will face outside of the group. Throughout the life of the group, she should reinforce the connection between what members are learning in the group and "real life" and help members acquire and practice skills that prepare them for situations they will face outside of the group. This includes, for example, teaching the therapeutic principles that underlie such intervention techniques as assertiveness, communication, and problem-solving skills training and assisting members to perform the requirements of roles that they want to adopt or already hold, such as parent, spouse, etc. (e.g., the leader may help members assess their own interactions, practice skills needed for their roles, and apply new ways of enacting their roles). Members can be assisted in these tasks through role-playing, giving feedback, and sharing personal experiences.

1. Intervention in the Preaffiliation Stage – Stage 1:

a. Prepare Members for the Group Experience: The leader prepares members for the group experience by providing direct instruction regarding group process (e.g., stages of development, ways to create a therapeutic working environment, behaviors and attitudes characteristic of an effective group). The leader should repeatedly review basic information in subsequent sessions to reinforce members' understanding.

b. Address Members' Initial Concerns: The leader intervenes to address the concerns that members typically have during the first stage of a group's development. For example, she may ask members to share their feelings about coming to the first group session. The leader elicits all members' feelings and reactions, validates the importance of fully disclosing feelings, and emphasizes the need for the group to be a safe place where issues can be expressed openly. She seeks an agreement from and among all members regarding each one's right to confidentiality and each one's obligation to maintain the confidentiality of information shared by the others, while also letting members know that she cannot guarantee that all members will abide by the confidentiality agreement. The leader also elicits suggestions for a group structure that will address members' concerns and uses these suggestions when formulating guidelines for the group.

c. Establish the Group's Goals: In preliminary individual interviews, members contract with the leader for goals they would like to achieve. In initial group sessions, the leader then combines these individual goals with the group's collective goals. She helps the group identify its collective goals and establishes a way of functioning as a group that allows each person's goals to be addressed.

2. Intervention in the Power and Control Stage – Stage 2: Many of the group's patterns are established in this stage, including its power structure, the ways members interact and communicate, and how the group chooses to negotiate and resolve problems. The leader's task is to intervene carefully so that she can influence these patterns in positive ways. She must successfully guide the group through this stage so that members develop the capacity to carry out leadership functions and cope with individual differences and the group remains intact. To fulfill this responsibility, the leader uses the strategies described below (Hepworth et al., 2006).

a. Facilitate Effective Communication: The leader regularly encourages basic communication and social skills that increase personal efficacy and the ability to create satisfying relationships (e.g., positive feedback, empathic listening, authentic responding), as well as communication skills that enable members to relate effectively as a group (e.g., taking turns in talking, exploring problems before offering solutions, speaking for themselves not others, speaking directly to the person for whom the message is intended). The leader can increase the chances that members will learn and use effective communication skills by modeling the skills, assuming the role of "coach," and intervening to shape communications occurring in the group.

b. Help Members Give and Receive Feedback: In this stage, negative interactions are common in which members criticize each other and the leader. To address these, the leader focuses the group's attention on the need to provide balanced feedback that incorporates attention to positives as well as negatives. In addition, the leader helps members acknowledge and accept positive feedback. If one member has difficulty accepting positive feedback, the leader may assist not only that member, but also the group as a whole, by eliciting the experience of other members and initiating a discussion of the difficulties that people sometimes have in accepting positive feedback. The leader may also help members identify dysfunctional cognitions that underlie their discomfort in accepting positive feedback.

c. Manage Conflict: Conflict is common during this stage. If conflict is handled properly, it can benefit the group and its members in the long run. According to Yalom (1985), the therapeutic use of conflict involves two steps: (a) experience (affect expression) and (b) understand the experience. Thus, the leader should allow a conflict to be expressed as long as no member is being harmed (see below), and then process it with the group by discussing the conflict and what underlies it. The primary focus of this discussion must be on the here-and-now (events occurring in the group). It's also recommended that the leader respond authentically to conflict and resistant behavior. When a leader shares her feelings and thoughts about what's happening in the group, without blaming or criticizing members, she allows members to experience an authentic and constructive interaction with her, and her modeling can encourage members to behave in a similar way.

d. Address Aggressive and Other Dysfunctional Behavior: The leader must intervene immediately to refocus the process when members criticize, label, or attack others or argue excessively among themselves. The leader's interventions should focus on group-related matters, rather than individual attitudes or behaviors, because destructive or self-defeating behavior by an individual or subgroup will almost always affect the entire group; moreover, some destructive behaviors may be fostered or reinforced by the group as a whole.

When preparing to address dysfunctional behavior, the leader examines the behavior in the context of the group process and considers how the behavior affects and is affected by group members. The leader's response should then (a) focus on *all* the members (i.e., she must avoid singling out one member or inadvertently "siding" with one group of members); (b) objectively describe the behavior that's occurring; and (c) encourage the group process (i.e., she should assume a facilitative role, rather than an authoritarian one, and avoid imposing a solution on the group).

When a significant group disruption occurs, the leader may respond decisively by using verbal or physical tactics as needed, such as speaking louder than the members, clapping her hands loudly, standing up, or putting herself between members who are arguing.

e. Reinforce Appropriate Behavioral Patterns: Finally, the leader also comments on or elicits examples of behaviors that support the group's work in accomplishing its tasks (e.g., self-disclosing, showing support to others, speaking in turn, attending to the task at hand, accepting differing values, beliefs, and opinions); and highlights the absence of counterproductive behaviors that occurred earlier in the group's life (e.g., whispering, introducing tangential topics, dominating, verbally and physically harassing other members).

3. Intervention in the Intimacy and Differentiation Stages – Stages 3 and 4: Stages 3 and 4 represent the group's "working phase."

a. Facilitate Ongoing Growth and Change:

- The leader continues to promote conditions that help members make adaptive choices in resolving issues – she encourages members to straightforwardly address and resolve conflict, openly disclose personal problems, take responsibility for their problems, and make choices that benefit the group.

- The leader enhances individual and group growth by focusing on the **universality** of underlying issues, feelings, and needs that members share.

- Because members feel comfortable at this time, the leader can heighten therapeutic conditions in the group. She may further refine feedback processes, for example, by coaching members to give specific (rather than global) feedback and give feedback in nonjudgmental ways. The leader also continues to encourage members to analyze the rationality of their thoughts and beliefs that maintain dysfunctional behaviors.

- The leader supports an emerging trend toward differentiation as members work to establish their uniqueness and separateness from others. For example, the leader acknowledges when a member reveals possession of a needed skill or offers a unique perspective.

b. Facilitate Achievement of Goals: Much of the group's work during this phase focuses on fulfilling the contracts developed in the group's initial sessions and on achieving the members' own goals.

- Because members may have lost sight of their individual goals, the leader reaffirms these goals periodically and promotes organized efforts to work on them.

- Members may participate in activities to work on individual and group goals during this stage. Depending on the nature of the goals, activities may be designed to encourage creativity, reduce stress, develop decision-making skills, facilitate communication, etc. Activities may also assist the leader in ongoing assessment by allowing her to observe members while they're engaged in the activities (see also the review of Programming in this section).

- The leader monitors the time allocated to each member to work on goals. If the group spends a lot of time helping one member achieve his goals, the leader generalizes to the other members the issues discussed in this effort so that all members benefit. The leader also encourages other members to share relevant personal experiences with the member receiving help in order to reinforce a norm for mutual aid. In addition, she checks on the progress of members who didn't receive attention during a session and encourages their participation in the next session.

Finally, a group leader usually establishes a systematic method of monitoring goals and tasks in sessions. This is important for ensuring that she doesn't overlook members who are resistant or less assertive or involved. Systematic monitoring also ensures that tasks performed by members between sessions receive the proper follow-up. Requiring weekly progress reports can motivate members to work toward goals between sessions, reduce the need to remind members of their contract agreements, and help them gain a sense of independence and accomplishment.

4. Intervention in the Termination Stage — Stage 5: The leader intervenes to help the group come to an effective close. She encourages members to evaluate the work achieved and consolidate their learning and is sensitive to the feelings provoked by termination. To fulfill these responsibilities, the leader uses the strategies described below (Hepworth et al., 2006).

a. Reinforce Members' Readiness to Apply Their New Skills to Life Outside of the Group:

- The leader facilitates discussion of how members may respond to possible setbacks and builds their confidence in their coping skills and abilities to solve problems independently.

- The leader reviews and integrates learning that took place in the group by helping members articulate what has happened between themselves and the group from the first to the last session and what they have learned about themselves and others.

The leader encourages members to identify areas for future work.

b. Address Feelings Associated With Termination:

- The leader shares her reactions to endings in order to help members identify their own feelings, including any sense of abandonment, anger, sadness, or loss.

- The leader reinforces members' positive feelings about themselves and the group – e.g., the realization that they're capable of accomplishing goals and assuming responsibility for their own lives, the sense of satisfaction that comes from helping others.

- As needed, the leader facilitates the completion of "unfinished business" between members.

c. Evaluate the Outcome: The leader uses evaluative measures to determine the effectiveness of the group and his interventions.

5. Other Aspects of the Group Leader's Intervention:

a. Opening and Closing Group Sessions: Paying attention to how each group session opens and concludes is important for promoting member productivity and satisfaction. Procedures used by the leader for opening sessions commonly include giving members a brief opportunity to say what they want to get from the day's session, inviting members to share their accomplishments since the last session, eliciting feedback about the group's last session, and sharing any reflections she has about the last session.

When bringing sessions to a close, the leader summarizes and integrates the group experience by using the following procedures: asking members what it was like for them to be in the group that day; inviting members to identify briefly what they're learning about themselves through their experience in the group; asking members whether there are any issues they would like to explore in the next session; and asking members to state what they would be willing to do outside of the session to practice new skills.

b. Leader Errors: Leader errors that tend to impede group development and process include the following: (a) doing one-on-one work in the group; (b) having such a rigid agenda that members can't pursue emerging themes or otherwise influence the group process; (c) scapegoating or attacking individual members; (d) overemphasizing content and neglecting to universalize themes (in other words, failing to help members relate to and benefit from the experiences of other members); (e) discounting some members' need to be heard; (f) lecturing the group; and (g) failing to address offensive comments or colluding with members around inappropriate statements (Hepworth et al., 2006).

c. Changes to a Group: Changes, such as the addition or loss of members, a change in the meeting time, or the introduction of a new leader, can be disruptive at any stage of a group's development, but a group is especially vulnerable to stressors occurring within or coming from outside the group during the power and control stage (stage 2). This is particularly true when the group has a closed format. In the power and control stage, members are usually reluctant to risk revealing themselves to a new member or new leader. In addition, if the leader (or agency) makes a significant change in the group structure without involving the group, members may come to believe that the leader (or agency) doesn't care about the group or about how her decisions affect the group. Although changes are sometimes unavoidable, the group leader should keep them to a minimum (especially during stage 2), prepare members in advance whenever possible, and help them work through their feelings about the change.

d. The Leader's Conceptual Framework: In group therapy, the leader's conceptual framework influences the choice of intervention strategies and the target of interventions. An action-oriented therapist, such as one using a Gestalt or cognitive-behavioral approach, will emphasize such intervention strategies as cognitive reframing, role-playing, behavioral practice, and teaching problem-solving skills, and avoid interpretation and exploration of underlying group themes. A psychodynamic therapist, in contrast, will emphasize such strategies as interpreting transference and countertransference phenomena, resistance, and latent group process. An interpersonal-interactional therapist may also use some of these strategies, but will focus on the importance of group cohesion and leader self-disclosure. With regard to the latter, Yalom considers therapist (group leader) self-disclosure ("transparency") to be beneficial as long as it done judiciously and responsibly. Interactional and Gestalt therapists also rely heavily on structured exercises, such as psychodrama.

e. Premature Termination: The premature, or unplanned, termination of a group member may occur for many different reasons, some related to the group itself (e.g., a poor fit, discomfort in the group) and some not (e.g., time conflicts, transportation problems). Generally, premature termination from group therapy has consequences for both the member who leaves prematurely and the group as a whole. The loss of a member can threaten the group's cohesion, make other members question their own achievements or appropriateness for the group, and make them reluctant to continue building trusting relationships with the remaining members (Hepworth et al., 2006).

If a member announces his desire or decision to leave the group prematurely during a group session, the leader should process this event with the entire group since the member's statement will probably be disruptive to the group as a whole. The leader should also try to encourage some form of closure for the member who is leaving and the rest of the group, even if doing so means disrupting the group's planned agenda or timeline. And, because there is often more than one factor involved in a member's decision to terminate early, the leader should attempt to schedule an individual meeting with the departing member to discuss his decision. Depending on the circumstances, the goal of this meeting may be to clarify the reasons for the termination, provide additional closure for the member, or, if appropriate, discuss the possible consequences of terminating early and/or provide referrals to other groups or services that may be better able to serve his needs.

XIV. Intervention With Diverse Populations

For an introduction to the topic of diversity, see Section VII of Human Development, Diversity, and Behavior.

A. Culturally Diverse Clients

Sue and Sue (2003) describe **cultural competence** as involving three competencies:

Awareness: Culturally competent therapists are aware of their assumptions, values, and beliefs. For example, they are aware of their own cultural heritage and of values, attitudes, and beliefs that may be detrimental to members of culturally diverse groups.

Knowledge: Culturally competent therapists attempt to understand the worldviews of culturally diverse clients. For instance, they have an understanding of the history, experiences, and values of various groups including knowledge about the impact of oppression.

Skills: Culturally competent therapists use therapeutic modalities and interventions that are appropriate for culturally different clients. For example, they do not automatically use the same techniques for all clients and recognize their limitations with regard to helping clients from diverse groups.

As defined by Wrenn (1985), therapists are exhibiting **cultural encapsulation** when they (a) define everyone's reality according to their own cultural assumptions and stereotypes, (b) disregard cultural differences, (c) ignore evidence that disconfirms their beliefs, (d) rely on technique-oriented (simple) strategies to resolve problems, and (e) disregard their own cultural biases.

Important guidelines for assessing culturally diverse clients appear in Section II of Assessment. Other guidelines for culturally sensitive practice include the following:

- Be willing seek consultation and/or do research to learn about a client's culture.

- Be aware of and understand your own biases and level of cultural or racial identification. Examine your own value system in terms of the client's.

- Do not overgeneralize cultural patterns to all members of a particular group.

- Recognize that social, economic, and political discrimination and prejudice are real problems for members of many diverse groups in the United States.

- Identify the client's stage of racial/ethnic identity development, degree of acculturation, and worldview (beliefs, values, attitudes, etc.).

- Openly acknowledge your awareness of the differences between you and the client and supportively explore whether the client has any concerns about the differences.

- If a client comes from a bilingual background or does not speak primarily in standard English, consider whether language will pose a barrier to effective treatment.

- Be aware that establishing rapport can be more difficult when you and the client come from different cultural, ethnic, or socioeconomic backgrounds. (For more information on this, see Section II of this chapter.)

- Be careful not to evaluate culturally relevant behaviors as pathology.

- Be aware that, for a client from a non-white-Anglo culture (and especially a client who is a recent immigrant/refugee), both the concept and process of counseling/psychotherapy may be unfamiliar and/or unaccepted.

- Be aware when a client's culture emphasizes the meaning of nonverbal messages; attend to the client's nonverbal communication and carefully monitor your own. Avoid misinterpreting culturally appropriate nonverbal behaviors (e.g., avoidance of eye contact) as indicators of pathology, hostility, rudeness, or lack of attention.

- Be sensitive and flexible when establishing treatment goals and selecting modalities. Investigate the client's expectations of treatment (e.g., beliefs about the nature of helping relationships, people's ability to change, and how people realize psychological, cognitive, and behavioral changes).

- Be aware that the use of appropriate therapeutic interventions for clients from culturally diverse groups may involve incorporating indigenous healing practices, which are "culture-specific ways of dealing with human problems and distress" (Sue & Sue, 2003, p. 189).

- When a client who is an immigrant or refugee seeks your services due to stressors related to acculturation, an important goal of treatment may be to teach cognitive and behavioral skills that will enable him to function well in both his culture of origin and the dominant culture.

Based on their review of 16 non-Western **indigenous healing practices**, Lee, Oh, and Mountcastle (1992) conclude that these practices share three characteristics: (a) They rely on community and family networks to care for the disturbed individual; (b) the religious and spiritual practices of the community are integrated into the healing process; and (c) the healing process is often conducted by a traditional healer or other respected member of the community. Also, as noted by Sue and Sue (2003), while treatments based on a Euro-American (Western) worldview emphasize separation, isolation, and individualism, non-Western indigenous treatments adopt a holistic perspective and stress interconnectedness and harmony.

Finally, many experts believe that a **multisystems approach** is appropriate for clients from non-white-Anglo cultures. The concept underlying this approach is familiar and acceptable to many non-dominant cultural groups (i.e., "it takes a community to raise a child"). Using a multi-systems approach entails taking full advantage of all appropriate resources available in the community. The goals are to increase the client's awareness of all available support systems and resources and empower the client to use them.

NOTE: Many of the intervention guidelines we provide below apply best to individuals who adhere to the traditional values, attitudes, beliefs, etc., of their native culture or racial group. Before developing a treatment plan with any client, you must perform an assessment that individualizes that client and identifies his particular needs and expectations. The information may be a point of reference when working with someone from the cultural or racial group, but may not be representative of the group as a whole.

African-Americans

African-Americans are the largest ethnic minority group in the United States and, in contrast to stereotypes, are diverse in terms of family structure, education, socioeconomic status, religious affiliation and spirituality, ethnic identity, reactions to racism, and other characteristics (Sue, Zane, & Young, 1994).

1. Racism, Prejudice, and Cultural Mistrust: Because of their experiences with racism and prejudice, it is not uncommon for African-American clients to mistrust white therapists.

a. Nonresponsiveness as a Protective Mechanism: Sue and Sue (1999) have suggested that aloofness and nonresponsiveness on the part of an African-American client (particularly a male client) may be a protective mechanism (i.e., the client may believe that sharing personal information will make him vulnerable to racism). Rather than reflecting resistance, this behavior may be an active way of evaluating the therapist. It is recommended that therapists respond to this behavior in a straightforward way because doing so can facilitate the development of trust.

b. Cultural vs. Functional Paranoia: Ridley (1984) places nondisclosure by African American therapy clients in the context of two types of paranoia: cultural and functional. A client is exhibiting **cultural paranoia**, or a healthy reaction to racism, when he does not disclose to a white therapist due to a fear of being hurt or misunderstood. In contrast, a client is exhibiting **functional paranoia**, "an unhealthy condition that itself is an illness" (p. 1238), when he is unwilling to disclose to *any* therapist, regardless of race or ethnicity, due to general mistrust and suspicion. Ridley notes that distrust of white mental health professionals by members of ethnic minority groups is related to the fact that professionals often misinterpret a healthy, adaptive response to racism (cultural paranoia) as pathology (functional paranoia).

2. Intervention Guidelines: When working with African-Americans, a therapist should be aware of the following (Paniagua, 1994):

- The African-American worldview emphasizes the interconnectedness of all things, and African Americans emphasize group welfare over individual needs.

- The family is often an extended kinship network that includes both nuclear and extended family members as well as individuals outside the biological family. For many African Americans, the church is an important part of the extended family.

- Roles within African American families are flexible, and relationships between men and women tend to be egalitarian.

- Due to their history in the United States, African Americans may exhibit signs of "healthy cultural paranoia."

According to Boyd-Franklin (1989), African American families respond best to a **multisystems approach** that addresses multiple systems, intervenes at multiple levels, and empowers the family by directly incorporating its strengths into the intervention. Systems that may be included in treatment include the extended family and nonblood kin, the church, and community resources. Family therapy, especially extended family systems therapy, is often the treatment-of-choice. Other experts also recommend using a time-limited, problem-solving approach and directive techniques and fostering empowerment by adopting an egalitarian approach (e.g., Aponte, 1994; Paniagua, 1994). Finally, Robinson (1989) recommends using the clients' last names (e.g., Mr. Wilson) until you are invited by them to do otherwise. (The use of last names is also appropriate in the introductory stage of helping with Asian-American clients and Mexican-American clients.)

American Indians/Alaskan Natives

In contrast to members of the "mainstream" culture, American Indians and Alaskan Natives are more likely to:

- exhibit a spiritual and holistic orientation to life that emphasizes harmony with nature and regards illness as the result of disharmony;

- place greater emphasis on the extended family and the tribe than on the individual and adhere to a consensual collateral form of social organization and decision-making;

- perceive time in terms of personal and seasonal rhythms rather than in terms of the clock or calendar and be more present- than future-oriented;

- exhibit a strong sense of cooperation and generosity; and

- consider listening more important than talking.

Walker and LaDue (1986) advise mental health practitioners working with American Indians to become familiar with the historical events that have affected their lives and relationships with white Americans. One consequence of their history is that American Indian clients may be distrustful of a therapist's attempts to provide therapy in a "value-free" environment and prefer a therapist who helps them reaffirm the values of their own culture.

Therapy guidelines include focusing on building trust and credibility during initial sessions by demonstrating familiarity with and respect for the client's culture and admitting any lack of knowledge; adopting a collaborative, problem-solving, client-centered approach that avoids highly directive techniques; and incorporating elders, medicine people, and other traditional healers into the treatment process. LaFromboise et al. (1990) recommend the use of **network therapy**, which incorporates the family and community members into the treatment process. Finally, traditional American Indians who are oriented to the present may prefer interventions that work in the here-and-now and expect the therapist to address their concrete needs first (e.g., inadequate food, shelter, child care, or employment) (Sue & Sue, 1999).

Asian Americans

Asian Americans include people of Chinese and Japanese heritage, Pacific Islanders, and Southeast Asians. When working with an Asian American client, it is important to be aware of his country of origin and acculturation status since these factors will influence the client's language and customs, social relationships, attitudes toward mental illness and psychotherapy, etc.

In general, Asian Americans:

- place greater emphasis on the group (family, community) than on the individual;

- adhere to a hierarchical family structure and traditional gender roles;

- emphasize harmony, interdependence, and mutual loyalty and obligation in interpersonal relationships; and

- value restraint of strong emotions that might otherwise disrupt peace and harmony and/or bring shame to the family.

In therapy, a directive, structured, goal-oriented, problem-solving approach that focuses on alleviating specific symptoms is often preferred. Asian clients expect therapists to give concrete advice and view the therapist as a knowledgeable expert and authority figure.

Therapy guidelines including emphasizing formalism in therapy (e.g., address family members in a way that reflects their status, respect conversational distances); being aware of the role of shame and obligation in Asian cultures (i.e., to reinforce adherence to prescribed roles and responsibilities) and that modesty and self-deprecation are not necessarily signs of low self-esteem; establishing credibility and competence early in therapy by, for example, disclosing information about your educational background and experience; preventing premature termination by providing the client with an immediate and meaningful benefit; and being aware that Asian clients may express their mental health problems as somatic complaints.

Sue and Sue (2003) recommend that therapists treat an Asian client's somatic complaints as real problems: Physical complaints should be legitimized and psychosocial factors should be assessed in a less direct way. For example, the therapist could say something like, "It can be difficult to deal with aches, pains, and insomnia. How are these affecting your mood?"

Finally, Sue and Zane (1987) note that gift giving is a common ritual in Asian cultures and propose that it has beneficial effects on the involvement and motivation of Asian clients, especially when it occurs during initial therapy sessions. Examples of "**giving**" in the context of therapy include anxiety reduction, normalization of the client's problems, skill acquisition, and goal setting.

Hispanic/Latino Americans

Hispanic/Latino Americans include Mexican Americans, Puerto Ricans, Cuban Americans, and people from Spain, Central and South America, and the Caribbean. Casas and Vasquez (1989) note that Hispanics and Latinos:

- emphasize family welfare over individual welfare;
- view interdependence as both healthy and necessary and highly value connectedness and sharing;
- consider discussing intimate personal details with strangers (e.g., a therapist) as highly unacceptable, and believe that problems should be handled within the family or other natural support systems;
- adopt a concrete, tangible approach to life (rather than an abstract, long-term perspective); and
- attribute the control of life events to luck, supernatural forces, acts of God, or other external factors.

When working with a Hispanic or Latino client, a therapist is usually best advised to be active and directive and to adopt a multimodal approach that focuses on the client's behavior, affect, cognitions, interpersonal relationships, biological functioning, etc. Paniagua (1994) recommends family therapy for Hispanic/Latino clients because "it reinforces their view of 'familismo' and the extended family" (p. 50). Other guidelines include emphasizing "personalismo" (except during initial contacts when "formalismo" is preferred); being aware that Hispanic/Latino families are basically patriarchal and that sex roles tend to be relatively inflexible; recognizing that differences in degree of acculturation within a family are often a source of individual and family problems; and being aware that Hispanic/Latino clients may express their mental health problems as somatic complaints.

As noted, "**formalismo**" (formal interaction) is usually appropriate during initial contacts, but, once trust has developed, Hispanic/Latino clients are likely to prefer "**personalismo**" (personal connection and warmth). In the context of personalismo, behaviors such as gift giving and inviting the therapist to share a meal or attend family functions are not signs of dependency or a lack of boundaries. Personal greetings, handshaking, use of first names, and "small talk" may also be important to the clients.

Arab Americans

Awareness of the following can facilitate your ability to work effectively with Arab-American clients, particularly those who adhere to the traditions of their native culture (Al-Krenawi & Graham, 2000; Al-Krenawi, 1999):

- Common sources of family conflict for Arab immigrants and refugees include issues such as arranged marriages and children's social activities, and this is particularly true when acculturation levels differ from one family member to another.

- Arab societies are "high context," which means that they emphasize the collective over the individual (i.e., a strong sense of obligation to the family is expected to override one's individual preferences).

- A high value is placed on respecting one's elders, and adults are considered to be the source of wisdom and authority.

- Gender differences in Arab societies tend to be strong: (a) Arab societies tend to be patriarchal. The father is the head of the family and the legitimate authority for all family matters; the father, in turn, is subordinate to his own father. (b) A woman's social status is usually dependent on being married and raising children, especially boys. In a traditional Arab family, the women are expected to devote a lot of their time to caring for family members, and even women with careers may defer to their spouses or families for major decisions.

- The family unit is paramount and family members tend to be highly involved with one another: (a) Individuals are raised to depend on their family for support. (b) Both nuclear and extended family members are consulted when one has a problem or crisis.

- Arabs are more likely to attribute mental or physical illness to an external cause (e.g., to supernatural elements such as spirits or the participation of other people with the supernatural through the evil eye or sorcery).

- Arabs tend to disregard emotional symptoms, viewing physical symptoms as more legitimate and acceptable expressions of pain. A client who experiences and interprets his psychological symptoms physically rather than emotionally may wait to be questioned by you, may not complain much about emotional distress, and may expect to be "cured" of his symptoms without having to disclose many aspects of his personal life. Experts recommend that you incorporate the client's perception of the probable cause of his problem by, for example, using his idioms of distress in the intervention process and/or integrating traditional healing into the treatment process.

- Arab communication styles tend to be formal, impersonal, and restrained, rather than candid, personal, and expressive. It may be difficult for an Arab client to disclose personal problems and feelings to someone outside of his family or community.

- Short-term, directive treatment is recommended: (a) Set clear and concrete goals and focus on providing guidance, advice, direction, explanations, and instructions. (b) Behavioral and cognitive therapies are more appropriate than psychodynamic approaches.

- The client may expect you to serve primarily as a "teacher" who explains conditions, offers information, and provides solutions with little input from him. He may view you as a figure of authority and may conform, at least outwardly, to your suggestions because he considers it rude to disagree with you.

- Because ethnic Arab people's notions of time are more fluid than they are in the West, the client may not be very time bound; thus, making and keeping appointments at fixed times or starting and ending sessions promptly may be a source of difficulty (Sue & Sue, 2003). As part of your role as an educator, you should clearly establish early on what the rules are regarding appointment times, lateness, and missed sessions.

Muslim Females and Hijab

The word hijab refers to both the head covering traditionally worn by Muslim women and modest Muslim styles of dress in general. In Arabic, the word literally means to curtain or cover. Most Islamic legal systems define this type of modest dressing as covering everything except the face and hands in public. According to Islamic scholarship, hijab is given the wider meaning of modesty, privacy, and morality. Muslims differ as to whether the hijab should be required on women in public, as it is in countries like Iran and Saudi Arabia.

You may work with a Muslim female client who wears a veil or otherwise covers her face, so that you lack access to her facial expressions. In this situation, you must respond in ways that demonstrate your respect for the client's culture and religion. For example, you may discuss facial expressions and other nonverbal messages with the client in an effort to understand her nonverbal communications. This both shows that you consider the client to be the expert on her own culture and opens up an important channel of communication between you and the client. Another appropriate action in this situation would be to seek consultation from a colleague with relevant expertise.

B. Older Adults

1. Potential Treatment Issues: The term "gerontology" refers to the study of the biological, psychological, and social aspects of aging. Many of these aspects are reviewed in the Human Development, Diversity, and Behavior chapter. Below, we review clinical issues commonly presented by older adults who seek or are referred for mental health treatment.

Quality of life/finding meaning in life: An older person's values, needs, and goals may not match his current circumstances. For example, an older adult who values independence may be distressed because he has fewer opportunities for independence; an older individual who worked long hours and had few other interests may become depressed when he retires; or an older adult's activities may be limited due to declining physical health.

Developmental issues: An older adult with unresolved issues from earlier life stages may have difficulty dealing successfully with the last developmental stage of life (Erikson's "integrity vs. despair").

Changes and loss: Aging is associated with multiple losses that can compound over time and affect all areas of an older person's life.

Dependency: Dependency due to disability or illness can restimulate unresolved negative feelings in an older adult. Acceptance of one's increased dependence can be vital to satisfactory adjustment and adaptation.

Unfinished business: Unresolved conflicts or needs can be a source of significant stress for an older adult and can diminish mental and social functioning.

Depression: Losses, isolation, and, especially, health problems that accompany old age can sometimes lead to depression.

Bereavement/prolonged mourning: Unresolved grief (e.g., over the loss of a spouse) can result in physical illness, continued depression, and an inability to form new relationships or build a new life.

Social isolation: An older adult who lives alone or lacks family ties is at high risk for social isolation.

Family issues: Generational issues can produce conflicts within families, aging can produce crises that restimulate unresolved family issues and conflicts, and an older adult's coping style may not match the styles used by family members in response to his needs. For elderly couples, preexisting marital problems may be exacerbated by disability, illness, and/or dependency.

Adult children and caregiving: Adult children (especially daughters) may be faced with meeting the needs of their elderly parents while simultaneously attempting to maintain their careers, care for their own children, etc. This can produce overwhelming feelings of guilt, anger, grief, and ambivalence. The adult children and/or their parents may have unrealistic expectations about the situation. (Caregiving to aging parents is covered in Section X of this chapter.)

Potential risks and dangers: In addition to the above issues, you must also be aware of the various risks that may be present in the lives of older adults:

Elder abuse: Be cognizant of situations that may increase the risk of elder abuse or neglect (see also Assessment, Section IX).

Activities of daily living: For some older adults, especially those living alone, it's important to evaluate the extent to which they are able to perform basic self-care activities required for living independently.

Medication: Because drugs are metabolized differently as our bodies grow old, side-effects and idiosyncratic reactions to medications are more common, and combinations of several different medications can produce serious side-effects. As needed, consult with an older client's physician (or with a psychiatrist for psychotropic drugs) in order to understand the client's medication regimen.

Driving and dementia: Although clients with dementia should be encouraged to remain as active and independent as possible, it is also very important to address their safety and the safety of others. For example, once a client with dementia is moderately impaired, he should be prevented from driving at all costs (e.g., take away his car keys, immobilize his car).

2. Intervention: Older adults tend to underutilize and resist mental health services for several reasons including discomfort with talking about psychological problems and transference reactions toward the usually younger therapist. Although some older adults with psychiatric symptoms seek help from mental health professionals, many are more comfortable going to family physicians or clergy.

a. *General Intervention Guidelines:*

- Adopt a structured approach and assume an active role.

- Clarify the cost of your services as early as possible because the client may be reluctant to raise this issue himself, particularly if his income is limited.

- Avoid being overly familiar with the client initially. Use titles (Mr., Mrs., Miss) until after you have asked and obtained permission from the client to use his first name. This is important for demonstrating that you respect the client.

- When forming the relationship, focus on the client's obvious and concrete needs (e.g., medical care, transportation). The client will probably be more comfortable discussing these matters at first with someone he does not know well. He may need some time before he is ready to talk about personal matters with you or express his feelings.

- Use a multimodal approach – address the client's psychological, physical, and social functioning, and involve his support systems (especially the family) and a multidisciplinary team.

- Be sensitive to any hearing or vision loss the client has experienced (e.g., speak very clearly, repeat yourself as much as necessary, use nonverbal communication to compensate for his hearing deficits). You may need to slow the pace of the interview and, if the client lacks energy, should limit the length of the interview.

- Be aware that older individuals often engage in a process of **life review** in which they reminisce, tell stories, and think about past events. This process serves a useful function by helping an older person integrate his life in a meaningful way. If an older adult wishes to talk about his past during sessions, you should incorporate his desire to review his life into your work with him.

- Be aware that connections to children and grandchildren may be very important to the client. Help him work on unresolved family conflicts and unfinished business and focus on facilitating intergenerational communication.

- Explore and incorporate the client's religious beliefs and spiritual needs, particularly he is hospitalized, in hospice, or in a residential long-term care facility.

b. *Modalities and Models:* For older adults, brief therapy and crisis intervention are the most frequently used clinical intervention models. Research has found, however, that many forms of therapy can be effective with older clients (e.g., cognitive-behavioral therapy, supportive therapy, psychoanalysis). You should also consider using group intervention (e.g., bereavement groups, support groups for caregivers, self-help groups, day treatment groups, social support groups).

The research has also shown that older adults benefit to about the same degree as younger adults from psychological interventions and that they also benefit from treatments developed specifically for members of this population. Depending on the client's needs, you may choose to apply an approach specifically tailored to the needs of older adults:

- *Reminiscence therapy (RT)* is based on the assumption that reminiscence (life review) is an important and age-appropriate activity that helps older people come to terms with their lives and mortality (Butler, 1963). Prompts (objects, pictures, etc.) are used to stimulate reminiscence.

- The goals of *validation therapy* are to reduce the client's distress and assist his life review. You should empathize with the client's feelings, whether or not they are based in reality.

- *Reality orientation (RO)* is useful for clients with cognitive impairments. It incorporates techniques designed to prevent, stop, or reverse cognitive impairments and maximize remaining capabilities and focuses on the client's need to be oriented and independent.

c. Community Programs: Many programs for older adults are funded through the Administration on Aging (AoA), a federal agency that allocates funds to states and communities to support local Area Agencies on Aging; these agencies then fund senior centers, meal programs, and other programs for older people in the community.

Examples of community programs available for older adults include adult day centers and adult day care. *Adult day centers* are facilities in which seniors and other adults gather to participate in recreational, social, educational, and developmental programs. They may be used by independently functioning seniors as well as by clients of adult day care. *Adult day care programs* provide personal, social, and homemaker services to adults who are unable to care for themselves when their primary caregivers (or guardians) are not available. Those most likely to require such care are frail elderly individuals and those who are physically and/or cognitively impaired and whose caregivers must be away from them every day for extended periods. Such care may be provided in private homes, nursing homes, and other facilities.

d. Long-Term Care for Older Adults: Long-term care includes medical and social interventions for people with chronic illnesses or impairments that are designed to help the person live as satisfactorily as possible in an appropriate setting. For older adults, long-term care is available in a variety of different settings, ranging from the person's home to nursing homes.

For older adults who remain at home, **home-based and community-based services** (HCBS) are available from private home-care agencies that send nursing assistants or companions to the person's home. Long-term-care services that allow an older person to remain in his home are covered by Medicare or Medicaid.

Options for senior living and residential care include the following (Ashford et al., 2006):

- Low-income-housing tax credit properties provide affordable rental housing for older adults who meet a financial-needs test. Many do not provide special services, but some provide accessibility features.

- Independent-living senior apartments offer residences for older adults who can function independently and perform activities of daily living (ADLs) but would like to be in a sheltered environment where services are offered.

- Board and care homes or adult foster homes are independently operated homes for older (or disabled) adults that house up to 10 older people in a family-like environment. Some specialize in older adults with mental disorders.

- Freestanding assisted-living facilities provide private apartments designed for older people who need some assistance with ADLs but don't need the constant supervision or medical attention provided by nursing homes. Assisted-living homes are monitored and licensed by states and the cost is usually quite high.

- Continuing care retirement communities (CCRCs) provide independent-living residences and a continuum of care on site (e.g., an assisted-living wing for residents who need more help with ADLs, a health facility for residents who require skilled nursing care). Residents usually pay a small amount to buy in to the community and then are charged a monthly fee. Residents are guaranteed access to all services and medical-care facilities on site.

- Nursing homes generally provide skilled medical care and rehabilitation services, assistance with personal care, and supervision. A nursing home may have a specialized unit for people with dementia ("major neurocognitive disorder" in DSM-5). Social workers employed at nursing homes assist residents and their families with the transition into the facility, offer emotional support, and advocate for their needs during the resident's stay.

e. Adult Protective Services: **Adult protective services** (APS) are social services provided to abused, neglected, or exploited older and/or disabled adults. APS are intended to help vulnerable adults such as those with disabilities due to aging, health-related issues, or dementia. APS are typically administered by local or state health, aging, or regulatory departments and emphasize a multidisciplinary approach to helping victims of elder abuse. Services include social, medical, residential, and custodial care, the investigation of abuse and other maltreatment, and legal intervention in the form of court orders or surrogate decision-makers such as court-appointed guardians (see below). Many states provide adult protective services to older adults only; other states provide adult protective services to anyone over the age of 18.

f. Guardianship/Conservatorship: When an older adult can no longer adequately take care of his personal needs or finances, a **guardianship** (or "conservatorship" in some jurisdictions) may need to be established in which a judge appoints an individual, or, sometimes, an organization, to take care of the older person's personal needs and/or financial matters. The individual appointed by a judge to take care of the older person's needs and property is usually called the legal guardian or court-appointed guardian. This person may also be called the conservator, but in many jurisdictions, the term conservator applies to someone who looks after a person's assets rather than the person and his property. Establishing a guardianship (or conservatorship) requires a court proceeding.

It can be difficult to apply the principle of self-determination when working with an incompetent older adult, such as one whose judgment has been impaired severely by dementia. This concern has led to the concept of "**least restriction**" in which the "appropriate" intervention is the one that will meet the older adult's needs with the least possible restriction of his rights and capacities. As such, the goal when making decisions regarding an older adult's need for conservatorship is to properly balance his needs, particularly his need for safety, with respect for his right to self-determination.

C. Clients Who Are Gay

In this section, the term "gay" is used to refer to both men and women whose sexual orientation is toward members of the same sex.

1. Potential Treatment Issues: Gay people may seek therapy for reasons that have nothing to do with their sexual orientation or that are related to it only indirectly. Being sensitive to the needs of a gay client, however, includes recognizing how membership in a stigmatized and oppressed group may play a role in causing or maintaining his or her problem. Some of the issues that affect gay people are described below.

a. Identity Formation and Coming Out: These refer to the ways in which gay individuals acknowledge their sexuality to themselves and to others.

- For each person, the outcome of identity formation is influenced by the presence (or absence) of social supports, positive role models, and satisfying relationships and by societal attitudes and policies.
- Coming out to parents, other family, friends, coworkers, etc., may result in rejection, anger, and grief. Significant others may experience grief over the loss of the person they thought they knew; parents may feel grief over the loss of the kind of future they had always imagined for their child.

b. Relationships With Others Who Don't Know the Person is Gay: Many gay people experience difficulties in their relationships with family members and others from whom they conceal their sexual orientation (Moses, 1986). Concealing a part of one's life from loved ones, especially for an extended period of time, can produce emotional distress, interpersonal distance, misunderstanding, and conflict.

c. Fewer Role Models and Low Social Recognition: Other than the gay community, there are few places where homosexuality and the gay lifestyle are validated. Compared to straight people, gay people have fewer positive reflections of themselves in family, friends, media images, and society. This can be especially problematic for gay teens.

d. Discrimination and Homophobia: Although homosexuality is no longer classified as a mental disorder, some people still believe that being gay or lesbian is abnormal or "sick." Dealing with others who dislike or fear them is particularly difficult (and even threatening) for gay people when these attitudes produce overt negative reactions toward them (e.g., humiliating jokes, hate-filled rhetoric, the threat of violence or actual violence).

2. Intervention: Be aware of your own feelings, attitudes, beliefs, and responses toward gay people. If you lack objectivity or have discomfort that is likely to compromise your therapeutic effectiveness, you should refer the client to a different therapist.

a. Helping Gay Clients Deal With Homophobia: Gay clients may present with issues related to oppression, discrimination, or rejection by loved ones following coming out. If so, you should recognize and affirm the client's experiences while, at the same time, providing him or her with information and skills so that he or she is empowered to deal successfully with other people's responses. **Empowerment** is a key goal of intervention:

- Identify and support the client's strengths and avoid emphasizing areas of pathology or dysfunction. You don't want to make the client feel blamed and/or contribute to his or her already negative self-concept.

- Base the therapeutic relationship on collaboration, trust, and the sharing of power.

Because internalized homophobia can result in beliefs and feelings that comprise an authentic identity and develops in a relational context, a critical aspect of your work with the client may be the establishment of a supportive therapeutic alliance. Selective and timely therapist self-disclosure, for example, can be beneficial for a gay client who suffers feelings of shame, alienation, and isolation and/or fears being misunderstood, judged, or victimized by a therapist. These clients need clear evidence that the therapist respects, appreciates, and/or can relate to their lifestyle.

b. Facilitating Identity Formation and Coming Out: If a gay client's presenting problem is related to "homosexual identity formation" (see Section VII in Human Development, Diversity, and Behavior) or coming out, you should first identify the client's stage of identity formation or coming out and, then, if the client agrees, help him or her progress toward establishing a more stable and comfortable identity as a gay person. The following guidelines for intervention are useful:

- Be aware that a client who reports ambivalence about acting on his or her attraction to the same sex may be displaying features characteristic of the early stages of coming out. You should help the client explore and affirm the validity of his or her feelings. Do not automatically interpret ambivalence as a sign that a client may not actually be gay.

- Foster the client's self-determination by taking an active role in educating him or her about options and resources, instilling hope, providing a vision for how things can be in the future and how to get there, and encouraging the client to take constructive actions consistent with his or her needs and attitudes. Be careful to avoid suggestions or solutions that may be too frightening, guilt-producing, or alienating for the client (e.g., ones that are inconsistent with the client's stage of coming out, life situation, or cultural/ethnic background).

- Even after coming out to him or herself, a client may be struggling with a decision about whether and how to disclose to parents, other family, friends, and/or coworkers that he or she is gay. Your role in this situation is to help the client consider the consequences of continuing to hide his or her homosexuality. Be sure to avoid colluding with the client's secrecy, imposing your own values, or taking a position that is comfortable for you but inconsistent with the client's needs (e.g., stage of coming out or identity formation) or life situation.

- If a client is ready to come out to others, you can help him or her consider and rehearse the process and prepare for possible outcomes. This work may include providing communication, assertiveness, and social skills training as well as training in behavioral problem-solving techniques. When relevant, addressing coming out should also include (but not be limited to) a discussion about how members of the client's cultural group view homosexuality and how this may affect the client's decision to come out and the way the members of his or her support system may react.

- Consider referring the client to a support or self-help group. This can be useful for reducing isolation, strengthening group identification, increasing feelings of acceptance and self-esteem, providing validation and support, clarifying issues of common concern, and developing problem-solving skills.

Finally, for a variety of reasons (e.g., fear of the consequences of exposure, internalized homophobia, lack of knowledge about gay support networks), a client in the process of coming out may lack ties to the larger gay community. You should provide the client with information about how to get involved in gay organizations and the gay community, where to meet other gay people, how to access appropriate medical or counseling services, etc. This is especially important with gay clients who are adolescents, are older (have lived a relatively "closeted" existence for a long time), still live with disapproving family members, and/or live in rural areas.

3. "Reparative" Therapies: Reparative therapies (a.k.a. **conversion therapies**) attempt to use psychotherapy or other interventions to eliminate a person's sexual desire for a member of his or her own gender. The NASW's National Committee on Lesbian, Gay, and Bisexual Issues (NCLGB) has stated that reparative therapies violate some of the guiding principles of social work, an assertion that has been supported by NASW's policy statement on Lesbian, Gay, and Bisexual Issues (1996). Some of the major concerns about reparative therapies include the following:

- Reparative therapies assume that homosexuality is a mental disorder and that a client needs to change his or her homosexual orientation. Homosexuality was declassified as a mental disorder many years ago, and social workers should not condone portrayals of gay people as mentally ill and needing treatment because of their sexual orientation. In addition, social workers should not knowingly participate in or condone discriminatory practices with any client, including gay or bisexual clients.

- Social workers should always provide clients with accurate information, including about homosexual orientation. Reparative therapies do not inform clients that they can achieve happiness and satisfying interpersonal relationships as gay or bisexual men or women or offer alternative approaches to dealing with the effects of societal prejudice and stigmatization.

- Social workers must respect the rights of all clients – including lesbian, gay, bisexual, and transgendered (LGBT) clients – to self-determination and autonomy. Reparative therapies take for granted that the goal of treatment is always to change the client's same-sex attraction.

Finally, there is no published scientific evidence to support the effectiveness of reparative therapies, and some data has indicated that they may, in fact, be harmful (Davison, 1991; Haldeman, 1994).

D. Clients Who are Physically Disabled

1. Potential Treatment Issues: Some individuals with physical disabilities present for therapy with concerns that relate in a direct way to their disability, while others do not. In terms of the former, a client with a physical disability may have one or more of the following concerns:

- He may be depressed as a result of isolation and loss (e.g., loss of functioning of a part of the body, change in appearance and/or lifestyle).

- He may be anxious. To a degree, anxiety is considered to be a normal response when a person becomes disabled.

- He may be dealing with issues related to feelings of helplessness, violations of his privacy, or fear of death or chronic pain (Stewart, 1985).

- He may be facing discrimination at the institutional level (e.g., he may be having difficulty accessing and using needed services).

2. Intervention:

a. General Intervention Guidelines:

- Work cooperatively with medical professionals, vocational counselors, and others involved with the client's rehabilitation.

- Educate yourself about the client's physical condition, become familiar with local medical facilities and support groups that serve the disabled, and know when it is necessary to make a referral.

- Examine your own perceptions of individuals with physical disabilities and identify and question all prejudicial assumptions.

- Display accurate empathy and explore the unique concerns of the particular disabled individual you are working with: (a) Listen carefully to all of the client's concerns and explore all relevant aspects of his life. (b) Don't assume that the client's physical disability will be a focus of treatment or that the problems the client reports are the result of his disability. (c) Don't assume that certain issues (e.g., sexuality, relationships) are not important because the client has a physical disability.

- To facilitate communication with a client who is hearing-impaired, consider bringing in a professional **sign language interpreter**. Get the client's permission before doing so. The interpreter will play an important role in facilitating interviews with the client, but you must make sure that your focus remains on the client throughout. Do not use an interpreter who has a dual role with the client – for example, one who is a member of the client's family – because this could jeopardize the effectiveness of the intervention.

- Encourage the client to be active in designing and implementing the treatment plan.

- Avoid encouraging dependency or the "sick role." Emphasize empowering the client. Self-observe for countertransference feelings involving a desire to "rescue" or "do for" the client.

- When possible, counsel family members in their efforts to support the client and provide them with information and access to the resources they need in order to help themselves and the client. Emotional issues, such as guilt, self-punishment, and anger, on the part of significant others may need to be addressed. Referrals to support groups are often beneficial for family members.

- Explore environmental contributors to the client's problems (e.g., architectural barriers, negative stereotypes, experiences with discrimination and prejudice). When needed, offer the client education about his rights under the **Americans with Disabilities Act**. Consider whether you need to serve as an advocate for the client.

- Determine whether the client is receiving needed assistance from federal and local programs. Make referrals as needed and serve as the client's advocate if appropriate. Significant federal programs available to assist individuals with physical disabilities include Workers' Compensation, Supplemental Security Income (SSI), and Disability Insurance (DI or SSDI). These programs are defined in the Glossary that accompanies these materials. In addition, local programs that focus on specific disabling conditions (e.g., cerebral palsy, multiple sclerosis, blindness) can be found in most communities.

Finally, a client with an obvious physical disability may not mention his disability during the initial meeting with you. You should not ignore a client's disability. The best approach is to acknowledge it openly and ask the client if he thinks it contributes to his presenting problem.

b. Working With a Client Who Has Recently Become Physically Disabled: Adaptation following sudden physical disability usually includes the following phases of recovery (Horowitz, 1983): shock, denial, intrusive recollections, working through, and completion (see Human Development, Diversity, and Behavior, Section VII). A client in the "working through" phase is confronted with the task of grieving his losses and may develop major depression. Important guidelines for assisting clients through this phase include the following:

- To identify and effectively treat the client's depression, you must attend to his prognosis for physical improvement or decline, experience of physical pain or discomfort, premorbid affective and cognitive style, social resources, perception and interpretation of the meaning of the disability and its impact, and ability to sustain hope and find some sense of purpose or meaning in the experience. Regarding the latter, a person may come to experience disability as a challenge or, instead, perceive and experience it as one more chronic stressor that overwhelms his coping resources.

- You should also explore the effects of the client's disability on other aspects of his life, such as his ability to work, his social networks, the environmental barriers he may now face, etc.

- Physical disability of a family member usually has a significant impact on the family system. Like the client, his family members also experience many losses and subsequent grief and may have feelings of anxiety, fear, depression, despair, anger, guilt, resentment, etc. Often, there are changes in family roles, finances, leisure activities, and social contacts to which family members are forced to adapt. Addressing the needs of his family is critical for promoting the client's psychological recovery and ongoing adaptation to his disability.

- Social support is critical for effective processing and acceptance of physical disability, but the level of social support offered by friends may gradually decline over time. Individuals in the client's social network may need help in dealing with their fears of vulnerability and discomfort in the face of the disability, and they and the client himself may need to let go of socially prescribed standards of physical perfection in order to come to terms with the client's condition.

Finally, in this population, untreated depression can underlie or lead to prolonged physical pain, alcohol or drug abuse, anxiety disorders, and/or extended hospital stays. The person may also come to feel helpless or begin using his disability as an excuse to avoid activities and interactions that he is physically capable of experiencing (i.e., "secondary gain").

c. Rehabilitation: Many people with physical disabilities who enter therapy are involved in **rehabilitation**. An important focus of rehabilitation programs is on helping persons with physical disabilities to develop **independent living skills**. Services tend to be most effective when they promote independence, self-determination, and productive participation in society. For instance, the person may need to learn skills that have become necessary as a result of his disability; these skills may be associated with a job, a hobby, or any activity that will improve the quality of the client's life.

Rehabilitation for clients with physical disabilities may include occupational therapy or physical therapy. Occupational therapy helps people with certain physical, mental, or behavioral conditions develop the skills they need in order to lead maximally independent and fulfilling lives. Services include individualized treatment programs to improve the person's ability to perform daily activities, home and workplace evaluations and adaptation recommendations, performance skills assessments and treatment, adaptive equipment recommendations and training, and guidance to family members and other caregivers.

Physical therapists provide services that help restore function, improve mobility, relieve pain, and limit or prevent permanent physical disabilities in people who have been injured or have serious medical conditions (e.g., accident victims, people with disabling conditions such as low-back pain, arthritis, heart disease, head injuries, or cerebral palsy).

E. Adult Female Clients

Recently, the notion of "modern racism" has been applied to sexism. According to Swim and colleagues (1995), modern sexism is characterized by denial of continuing discrimination against women and resentment about women's demands for equality and the preferential treatment of women.

1. Feminist Therapy: The various approaches to feminist therapy share several characteristics that distinguish them from more traditional forms of psychotherapy. An essential characteristic is an emphasis on the "power differences between women and men and how that differential impacts on both men's and women's behavior" (Dutton-Douglas & Walker, 1988, p. 3). For feminist therapists, intrapsychic events always occur – and must be interpreted – within an oppressive social context.

a. View of Maladaptive Behavior: Feminist therapy is built on the premise that "the personal is political" – i.e., that a woman's circumstances always reflect the position of women in society. Consequently, symptoms are considered to be (a) related to the nature of traditional feminine roles or conflicts that are inherent to those roles, (b) "survival tactics" or a means of exercising personal power, and/or (c) arbitrary labels that society has assigned to certain behaviors in order to impose sanctions or exert social control (Travis, 1988).

b. Therapy Goals: Feminist therapists are less interested in changing their clients to fit the "mainstream" than in identifying and altering the oppressive forces in society that have affected their clients' lives. A primary goal of therapy is empowerment, or helping women become more self-defining and self-determining.

c. Therapy Techniques: Techniques that distinguish feminist therapy from other forms of therapy include the following (Cammaert & Larsen, 1988; Rosewater, 1988; Worrell & Remer, 1992):

Striving for an egalitarian relationship: Feminist therapists acknowledge the power differential that is inherent to the therapist-client relationship, but attempt to minimize it by promoting "power with" (rather than "power over"). Techniques used to achieve this goal include making appropriate self-disclosures during the course of therapy, demystifying the therapy process, and encouraging clients to set their own goals and evaluate the progress of therapy.

Avoiding labels: To avoid pathologizing clients' problems, feminist therapists do not use traditional labels to describe feelings and behaviors and de-emphasize traditional assessment and diagnosis.

Avoiding revictimization: Feminist therapists avoid blaming women for their current problems. Rather than viewing battered women as inadequate or masochistic, for example, they place the responsibility for the abuse on the abuser and emphasize the woman's strengths.

Involvement in social action: Feminist therapists believe that, to be effective, they must be social and political activists.

Issues commonly addressed by feminist therapists in their work with females include the following (Rosewater, 1988).

Depression: Depression is conceptualized as a coping strategy – i.e., as a healthy reaction to an unjust situation. With the client, you would examine role expectations underlying the symptoms and help the client direct her anger outward, rather than inward. Traditional interventions (e.g., antidepressants) may be used with some clients.

Relationships: You would encourage the client to stop evaluating her self-worth on the basis of her relationships (especially those with men).

Anger/power issues: The traditional female role prohibits the expression of anger. You would help the client express her anger appropriately and deal with the negative reactions that this may elicit from others.

Rape, incest, and battering: You must avoid revictimization. You should provide a safe environment and the conditions required for healing and resolve the client's anger, self-blame, and guilt. If a client still lives with a violent partner, you should evaluate the level of danger and help the client develop and rehearse an escape plan.

Although feminist therapy and nonsexist therapy share some characteristics, they differ in important ways. Feminist and nonsexist therapists both recognize the impact of sexism and avoid the use of gender-biased techniques. However, while feminist therapists prioritize the role of sociopolitical factors on a woman's psychological functioning and the need for social change, nonsexist therapists focus more on individual factors and modifying personal behavior.

2. Assisting Clients With Abortion Decisions:

a. Helping Adult Clients: Counseling before and after an abortion can help a woman deal with her feelings about her choice. Key counseling guidelines include the following:

- The goal is to help the woman make a decision that she ultimately believes is the correct one.

- Your role is mainly supportive. This role may include, for example, helping the woman explore how she feels about abortion, helping her weigh alternatives to abortion, and helping her consider what each available choice means for her now and in the future.

- Be careful to separate your personal values from your professional ones: No matter how you personally feel about abortion, you must recognize that the woman needs to make the abortion decision herself.

Some women experience sadness, grief, and feelings of loss following the termination of a pregnancy, and others experience clinically significant disorders, including depression and anxiety. There is no clear evidence, however, that such mental health problems are caused by the abortion itself, rather than by other factors. The research has identified several factors that are predictive of more negative psychological responses following first-trimester abortion among women in the U.S. These factors include the following: (a) perceptions of stigma, need for secrecy, and low actual or anticipated social support for the abortion decision; (b) a prior history of mental health problems; (c) other risk factors for mental health problems, such as poverty, substance abuse, or exposure to domestic violence; (d) personality factors such as low self-esteem and the use of denial and avoidance coping strategies; and (e) characteristics of the pregnancy, including the extent to which the woman wanted and felt committed to it (retrieved from apa.org in February 2011).

b. Abortion Decisions and Minors: In some states, a minor can get an abortion without telling her parents. Other states have parental consent or parental notification laws. "Parental consent" means that the minor must get permission from a parent to have an abortion if she is under a certain age, usually 18. With "parental notification," a minor doesn't need her parent's permission to have an abortion but, if the minor is under a certain age, her parents must be told about the abortion. (Remember that ASWB exams won't ask about state-specific laws.)

Key counseling guidelines include the following:

- You are not legally required to tell the minor's parents about her pregnancy. The minor is entitled to a confidential relationship with her therapist.

- You should help the minor get the information she needs in order to make the best possible decision for her own well-being. Most minors need help to thoroughly consider their alternatives and the pros and cons of each choice. In providing this help, you must avoid imposing your own values about abortion, teenage pregnancy, and teenage motherhood. You must let the minor make her own abortion decision.

- Unless secrecy is required to protect the minor from harm (e.g., physical abuse), you will usually encourage the minor to bring her parent/parents in for a family session to disclose her pregnancy and discuss her alternatives.

F. Adolescent Clients

1. Intervention Guidelines:

a. Be Directive and Active: Treatment with adolescents usually is more directive and active than it is with adults. Generally, you should be less open-ended than with an adult client and provide greater direction.

b. Involve the Parents: Mental health treatment of adolescents usually requires parental involvement:

- The degree of parental involvement varies from case to case, but most therapists providing individual therapy to an adolescent attempt, at least, to maintain an informative alliance with the parents.

- In some cases, you may determine that an adolescent's problems actually represent an opening for needed work with his parents on marital, parenting, or individual problems.

c. Be Aware of Potential Obstacles to Treatment: Adolescents are characterized by a lower tolerance for frustration, a preference for action over verbalization of feelings, ego structure immaturities, unclear communications, and a tendency to be uncommunicative and resistance prone. Some adolescents are rebellious, as well. In addition, because adolescence is a period in which individuals are attempting to separate from their parents, teenage clients often resist forming dependent relationships with other adult authority figures including therapists. An adolescent who has the capacity for self-observation and an awareness that his problems require attention is more likely to agree that therapy will be useful. Most adolescents, however, do not experience their symptoms as distressing (i.e., they experience the symptoms as **ego-syntonic**) and some may project blame for their problems onto their parents or school.

d. Be Prepared to Handle Resistance: Adolescents may exhibit resistance because they feel stigmatized about needing help, believe they are being punished for their misbehavior, and/or have displaced their problems onto their parents or teachers. Others do so because they are involuntary clients. Generally, an adolescent's resistance can be lowered if you are willing to openly and nondefensively explore the reasons behind it.

- An adolescent who is forced into therapy by his parents, school officials, or a juvenile court judge may be resistant because he resents not having a choice about being in therapy. He may have negative feelings and fears associated with coming in, including the fear that you will try to control or punish him. He may resist your interference in his life by remaining silent or actively challenge you by being uncooperative or rude. To build a constructive working relationship with an involuntary adolescent client, you often need to neutralize his negative feelings (see Section II of this chapter). Once these feelings have subsided, you can identify incentives that may encourage the client to work on changing relevant aspects of his behavior or situation. In addition, when possible, you should allow the adolescent some input into the decision to seek help.

- Many adolescents are the **identified patient** in their family, but know that they are part of a generally dysfunctional family system. When the complaint brought to treatment is one symptom of a larger problem involving the family, and family issues need immediate attention, you should usually encourage family therapy as the treatment of choice.

- The parents of an adolescent may resent questions about their family life and marriage and/or the expectation that they will remain actively involved in their child's treatment. Others have projected their teenager's problems onto teachers and the school. When parents' resistances are strong, this often indicates that your treatment interventions should begin with them. For extreme resistance or when there are parenting deficits, you must remain patient and firm and continue clarifying the situation for the family, refrain from aligning with the parents or teenager, and avoid identifying with any helplessness or covert rejection on the part of the parents. Often your outreach and persistence can offer a teenager a kind of attention his parents have not been able to provide because they are overwhelmed.

e. Self-Observe for Countertransference Reactions: Working with a teenager who is resistant, unmotivated, aggressive, impulsive, or suicidal can trigger feelings of fear, frustration, and/or anxiety. Adolescent clients also may provoke feelings of anger, rejection, and demands for compliance; other teenage clients may cause you to feel overwhelmed, helpless, or as though you want to "rescue" them.

2. Modalities and Settings:

a. Individual Therapy: Individual therapy is indicated for adolescents whose emotional disorders seem enduring enough to interfere with maturational and developmental progress. It usually takes place in conjunction with family therapy and/or group therapy and emphasizes improving the teenager's adaptive skills in the family and elsewhere. If psychodynamic approaches are used, they are usually combined with supportive elements and behavioral management techniques.

b. Group Treatment: For an adolescent, a group modality can be particularly useful because of the developmental importance placed on peers during adolescence. Parent groups can be a valuable adjunct; such groups can help parents understand the nature of their child's problems, cope with feelings of guilt, formulate guidelines for action, and develop more adaptive parenting and communication skills.

c. Treatment of Adolescents With Serious Mental Disorders: Intensive, multidimensional, and flexible treatments are indicated for adolescents who have serious mental disorders. An effort should be made to maintain and treat these adolescents in the community whenever possible. Sample modalities include the following:

Day treatment programs: These are indicated for teens who need more support and supervision than are available in their community, but who are able to live at home if they get the proper level of intervention.

Residential treatment centers: These are indicated for teens with serious mental disorders (especially those involving difficulties with impulse control) who require a highly structured and supervised setting for an extended period of time and cannot live successfully at home.

Psychiatric hospitalization: This is indicated for teens who engage in dangerous behavior, exhibit suicidality, or are experiencing exacerbation of a psychotic or other serious mental disorder.

3. Runaway Youth: Social workers meeting with runaway youth (under age 18) are generally encouraged to adhere to the following guidelines: (a) Do not automatically recommend the return of a runaway youth to his home. (b) Get as much information as you can about the family's functioning (including about possible maltreatment and parental substance use). (c) Evaluate the youth for substance abuse and other risk. (d) When indicated, arrange for the youth to attain placement in a secure setting, such as a runaway shelter. Although most teenagers cannot live for more than about two weeks in a federally funded shelter, these shelters are required to offer aftercare services.

G. Clients of Lower Socioeconomic Status

For information on assessment of clients living in poverty, see Section II of Assessment.

Sue and Sue (2003) discuss several generic characteristics of therapy that can pose barriers to effective treatment when working with clients of lower socioeconomic status. Among these "class-bound values" are the following: (a) a rigid adherence to time schedules (once-a-week meeting, 50-minute session, etc.); (b) an unstructured, ambiguous approach to problems; and (c) an emphasis on identifying long-term goals and solutions.

The use of a **strengths perspective** is a key component of effective professional efforts with clients of lower socioeconomic status. You should attend to the client's strengths (internal and external), including the positive things he has done or can do to cope with his situation and the skills or resources he may have that could help him work his way out of poverty.

Other important considerations when working with clients of lower socioeconomic status include the following:

- Among people living in poverty, feelings of frustration or hopelessness, an unpredictable lifestyle, and a preoccupation with immediate needs can pose barriers to the effective use of services that expect cooperation, adherence to schedules, and follow through on plans. Due to their life experiences (e.g., waiting for extended periods at medical clinics and government agencies), low-income clients often place less emphasis on punctuality than other clients do.

- A client who is poor may be unfamiliar with the therapy process and, therefore, may have expectations of therapy that differ from yours and/or are negative. You must avoid misinterpreting this as resistance or hostility, as doing so can impede the success of the intervention and lead the client to leave treatment prematurely.

- A client living in poverty may prefer immediate, concrete solutions to his problems over abstract, future-oriented goals, such as becoming more self-aware. He is likely to expect advice and concrete, tangible assistance from you that meets his immediate needs. He may feel frustrated, confused, or alienated if you encourage in-depth discussion of a problem or greater initiative and responsibility for decision making.

- You should work actively to reduce the social distance and power differential that may exist between you and the client. For example, try to meet with the client at times and places that are convenient for him and find opportunities to talk with him about ordinary aspects of his life. These interventions can be important for increasing the client's sense of comfort.

- Many clients living in poverty need case management services; you should connect the client (and his family) to needed services and other resources and be prepared to serve as the client's advocate, as well.

H. Immigrant and Refugee Groups

The amount of current U.S. residents born in other countries surpassed 40 million in 2011. These residents may be refugees, on an immigrant, student, or business visa, or live here undocumented. In 2011, it was reported there were an estimated 12 million undocumented immigrants living in the United States(Berg-Weger, 2016).

Social workers play a vital role in working with immigrants and refugees, documented or otherwise. Practitioners in all fields of social work should have the knowledge and skills to work with this diverse population. In direct practice, you may work with individuals and families that have immigrated to this country. You may specifically provide direct services for newly arrived refugees, human trafficking survivors, and other immigrants. In policy work, you may work as an advocate with this population, working with entire communities. Services must accommodate the cultural needs of the client(s) and the norms they adhere to. Relocation can be very traumatic on immigrant or refugee groups. They lack social support and organizational resources. Some may not even be aware of the resources they may be entitled too. Others are fearful to call attention to themselves and don't seek services needed. Undocumented individuals are ineligible for governmental programs and often underserved within community groups as well (churches or civic groups).

Many individuals and families flee their country due to persecution and violence. They come to the United States and continue to live in unstable environments. They are at risk for experiencing continued poverty, violence, and physical and mental health problems. They may also face discrimination, racial and ethnic disputes, assimilation difficulties, and in more extreme cases, human trafficking.

When working with such families, it's pertinent to obtain information about the family's relocation process, and continued stressors placed on the family in accommodating more than one culture. Family identity and values may maintain through multiple generations and will continue to influence the family's outlook, ideas and values. These aspects may be a of greater importance to place focus in service delivery than those of developmental tasks. You should also consider the lack of social supports from those within the same cultural group. Many are left behind or split up in the relocation process. Other sources of stress include struggles in obtaining employment, language becomes a huge barrier, and connecting with the native cultural group places additional tension on the family.

In your assessment, you need to be observant of the strengths within the family. Hopefulness may be diminished due to their circumstances. Hepworth et. al (2010) recommend exploring the following topics to help assess strengths and resources:

- Family traditions, rituals
- Communications
- Patterns of help-seeking behavior
- Shared goals
- Information about how a problem would be handled by the family or its community
- Individuals or institutions the family may turn to in times of difficulty
- Family capabilities, adaptation, hopes, aspirations

XV. Intervention for Specific Problems and Disorders

A. Decision-Making Difficulties

Many of the problems that clients face involve the need to make decisions. Decision making can be especially difficult for clients who are feeling overwhelmed and avoid making decisions or make decisions impulsively without adequately considering the pros and cons of every option.

A **decision-making matrix** is a useful tool for helping a client consider the pros and cons of his options and arrive at a decision. The matrix has three columns: alternative, cost, and benefit. In the "alternative" column, the client lists all of the options he is considering (for example "take the new job," "stay at my current job"). Across from each option, in the other columns, he lists the drawbacks (costs) and advantages (benefits) associated with each option. After he has listed all of the costs and benefits for each option, the client compares the options and makes a decision.

Another useful tool is a **decision-making worksheet**. If you are familiar with the significant issues and typical thoughts and feelings associated with the type of decision your client is facing, you can help the client create a decision-making worksheet to facilitate his decision-making. The worksheet focuses the client's attention on important questions, factors, and possible consequences to be considered when making the decision. Although discussing the decision can accomplish the same thing, creating a worksheet provides structure and can be assigned as homework for the client to complete between sessions.

B. Mediation and Interpersonal Conflict

Mediation is a method of conflict resolution in which a compromise between opposing parties is sought. A mediator uses various tactics to get the parties to agree on a resolution of the conflict and encourages the parties to speak freely and be more flexible about their goals in order to facilitate voluntary agreement between them. The mediator can make recommendations or suggestions, but she remains neutral, has no formal power, and cannot impose a solution or decision. If the parties cannot come to an agreement, then the mediator's work is finished. When an impasse is reached and a more formal evaluation or recommendation is needed (e.g., a court is seeking a recommendation), this role must be filled by someone other than the mediator.

The following process is useful for mediating interpersonal conflicts and disagreements experienced by couples, parents and adolescents, divorcing spouses, etc. (Sheafor & Horejsi, 2003):

> *Define the nature and source of the conflict:* Begin by helping the clients define the nature and source of the conflict. Key to this is distinguishing between a misunderstanding and a disagreement. Conflict that is caused by misunderstanding can

often be resolved through improved communication. By contrast, clients who genuinely disagree with each other may communicate effectively but be unable to find common ground or compromise.

Establish ground rules for discussing the issue: (a) Have the client agree to demonstrate respect for each other and a willingness to listen to each other and to refrain from making demands or taking a firm stand on what kind of solution they will accept. (b) Ask the clients to designate you as the person who will enforce basic rules of fairness and make sure that each party is given time to speak without being interrupted.

Facilitate discussion of the issue: (a) Do not take sides in the conflict. (b) Give each client a sufficient and similar amount of time to tell his or her side of the conflict. (c) Encourage the clients to behave differently from how they usually do when engaged in conflict (e.g., a client who usually wants to withdraw should try to confront the issue directly). (d) Encourage the clients to "think before they speak" (e.g., have them consider whether they have an ulterior motive for what they're about to say and whether what they're about to say is true, relevant, and constructive). (e) Use helping skills (clarification, paraphrase, summarization, etc.) to assist the clients to clearly express and explain their thoughts. Ask "what," "when," "where," and "how" questions to help each client be as factual as possible. Avoid asking "why" questions. (f) Acknowledge and reinforce the clients' efforts to work together productively (e.g., efforts to control their feelings of anger or to understand why the other person sees things differently). (g) Ask each client to repeat what he or she heard the other one say. The objective is to help each client acquire a basic understanding of, and some level of empathy for, the other's perspective and feelings. (h) Throughout the discussion, look for opportunities to remind the clients of what they agree on (e.g., certain values, a desire to avoid further pain).

Brainstorm potential solutions: After significant issues have been aired and the clients have demonstrated a sufficient level of mutual understanding, use brainstorming to identify potential solutions to the conflict. Seek solutions or compromises that provide some benefit to each client.

C. Difficulties Understanding or Expressing Feelings

Many clients need help with understanding and appropriately expressing their feelings, and some clients are confused, frightened, or overwhelmed by their emotions.

An *emotion* is a physiological and psychological response, while a *feeling* is the subjective awareness of that response. Emotions arise in response to perceptions of an event or situation but these perceptions may not be an accurate interpretation of what is happening. Generally, the following process takes place: (a) an event or situation occurs, (b) the person interprets and thinks about the event or situation, (c) the person experiences an emotion that is based on his interpretation and thoughts, and (d) that emotion motivates the person to engage in a certain behavior.

Sometimes learning tied to painful experiences from the past causes a person to misinterpret an event or situation, which then elicits emotions and behaviors that other people view as inappropriate. In addition, as people experience an emotion, they often think about whether it is right or wrong to be feeling the way they do, and these thoughts then elicit other emotions.

1. Helping Clients Understand and Change Emotions and Feelings: Because of the interaction between cognition and emotion, helping a client change the way he habitually interprets and thinks about events and situations can help him change and better control his emotions and feelings. The steps involved in this process are as follows (Sheafor & Horejsi, 2003):

- *Help the client learn to notice the physical sensations that accompany his emotions.* The sensations that a client feels during specific events or situations (e.g., tension, rapid heart rate) can shed light on his underlying assumptions about himself and others and his habitual ways of interpreting events and situations.

- *Help the client give names to his feelings.* This can help the client accept his feelings as real and provide him with an increased sense of control. If the client lacks a vocabulary for his feelings, use a feelings list to help him in this naming process.

- *Help the client "own his feelings."* The client has to claim a feeling as his own before he can examine it. "Owning feelings" can be difficult for a client who is accustomed to denying or ignoring how he feels. Such a client may find it helpful to name a feeling out loud (e.g., "I feel sad").

- *Help the client examine his habitual ways of interpreting and thinking about events and situations.* For most people, these patterns are learned in childhood and carried into adulthood. Work with the client to re-evaluate what he was taught as a child and decide if it is still valid.

- *Help the client look at events and situations in a different way and come up with other interpretations for his emotions.* For instance, if the client feels threatened in a situation, he can ask himself: "Is this situation actually threatening or am I interpreting it this way because of something I experienced in the past? Is there another way I could interpret this situation?" This can give the client more control over the direction and intensity of his emotions and feelings.

- *Help the client learn to choose how he will behave in response to his emotions.* A client may not be able to change his emotional reaction to an event or situation but he can make different choices about how he will behave.

2. Using a Feelings List: A "feelings list" is a written list of words that give names to feelings that people may have (e.g., abandoned, excited, guilty, detached, fearful, protected) and is a useful tool for helping certain clients identify, label, and express their feelings. This tool is particularly helpful for clients who have a tendency to suppress or misinterpret their feelings, are unsure of their true feelings, have trouble distinguishing one feeling from another, and/or have difficulty describing their feelings (e.g., they use only broad terms such as "upset"). Often these clients learned in childhood to suppress their feelings, were punished for expressing emotion, and/or had parents who invalidated or discounted their feelings. When preparing a feelings list for a particular client, be sure to consider his age, life experience, culture, and educational level.

3. Emotional Release: Social workers providing therapy often encourage their clients to ventilate their emotions and feelings as a way of building trust, reducing the client's anxiety, and initiating exploration of the problem. For many clients, the opportunity to express repressed emotion (i.e., ventilation or catharsis) in a safe environment relieves tension. Ventilation by itself, however, is rarely sufficient to bring about lasting change. Moreover, before encouraging catharsis, you must determine whether a client will be able to tolerate a great deal of emotional expression (e.g., has sufficient ego strength) without becoming overwhelmed or experiencing an increase in feelings of anxiety or depression.

D. Stress Management

The effective management of stress requires the client to understand what he needs and wants emotionally, express himself honestly, take responsibility for his own thoughts and behaviors, let go of efforts to control other people's behavior, develop realistic expectations for himself and others, have appropriate boundaries in his relationships, learn how to set realistic life goals and priorities, acquire time management skills, and take care of himself by eating well, exercising regularly, getting enough sleep, and using relaxation techniques (Johnson, 1997). Improved self-care may also include the use or development of a support system, the use of community resources, and pursuing personal and spiritual growth.

1. Cognitive Restructuring: Because cognitions influence physical and emotional responses to stress, cognitive restructuring that focuses on a client's belief system and attitudes is an important stress management intervention (Johnson, 1997):

Expectations: Negative expectations increase anxiety and can create a self-fulfilling prophecy because what a person believes will happen may influence his behavior in ways that make the feared outcome more likely to happen. Therefore, helping a client face demanding situations with a more positive attitude can facilitate improved coping and stress management.

Mental and visual imagery: The negative mental and visual images that accompany a client's negative expectations can serve to further increase his anxiety and stress. Helping the client replace negative mental imagery with positive mental imagery can further reduce the effects of life stressors and promote more effective coping.

Self-talk: The client's negative self-talk has a similar effect to that of negative mental imagery. Helping a client modify negative self-talk involves, first, facilitating his awareness of his self-talk and, then, helping him develop realistic substitute self-statements that are more positive and more favorable to effective coping.

Perfectionism and controlling behavior: Perfectionism is usually associated with unrealistic expectations for oneself and others, and placing unrealistic expectations on others is a form of controlling behavior. Often, engaging in perfectionistic and controlling behavior is a way of avoiding conflict or the discomfort or sense of inadequacy associated with perfectionism. You can help the client recognize how trying to control others' behavior produces stress, anxiety, frustration, and anger and assist him to develop more realistic expectations for himself and others and accept the fact that he has no control over how other people behave.

Anger: When anger is not expressed in appropriate ways, it causes internal stress and tension and can lead to volatile interactions with others which, in turn, can lower a person's self-esteem and damage his relationships. Chronic anger and hostility are also related to the development of physical symptoms, illnesses, and diseases. The appropriate management of anger reduces stress. You can help the client become aware that he has a choice about how he evaluates situations and teach him anger management skills.

2. Self-Control and Situational Control: With "self-control," a client who is dealing with excessive stress is helped to take responsibility for his own reactions to situations. "Situational control" then focuses on teaching the client problem-solving, assertiveness, conflict-resolution, and time-management skills. Effective time management, for example, includes (a) outlining a plan of action or the tasks to be completed, (b) clarifying priorities, (c) dividing the plan into manageable goals and tasks, and (d) allotting a reasonable amount of time to complete all the tasks. The client can also be encouraged to eliminate procrastination, combine or delegate tasks, be realistic about what he can accomplish, and be assertive in saying "no" when taking on additional responsibilities would interfere with his personal/leisure time or result in poor task performance.

3. Relaxation Techniques: The regular use of relaxation techniques is effective for preventing the development of cumulative stress. Cumulative stress is associated with high levels of anxiety that make it more difficult to deal with everyday stressors. Releasing stress and tension by using relaxation techniques gives the body a chance to recover from the consequences of stress and, thereby, facilitates a client's ability to manage everyday stressors in his life. Available relaxation exercises include the following: (a) deep breathing; (b) mental imagery, in which the client closes his eyes, uses all of his senses to create a peaceful place in his mind, and imagines himself in that place while relaxing; (c) progressive muscle relaxation, which involves tensing and then releasing all the muscle groups in the body, first as a unit and then one by one; and (d) meditation. Note that mental imagery is effective for deepening relaxation when it is used with other techniques, such as deep breathing, and it may also be used by itself. In addition, biofeedback, performed by a trained professional, can be used to help a client learn to achieve relaxation, control his stress responses, and modify his body's reactions (see also the review of behavioral therapies in Section XI of this chapter).

E. Anger Management

Anger management focuses on helping clients understand anger, recognize when they are getting angry, and take action to calm down and deal with triggering events in positive and constructive ways. It does *not* attempt to prevent clients from feeling angry or expressing anger.

1. Anger Management Strategies:

a. Helping Clients Understand Their Perceptions and Experience of Anger: Clients struggling with anger management often need assistance with understanding how they perceive anger and expressions of anger and identifying their own patterns of anger expression. The following interventions are commonly used:

- *Explore the client's beliefs about anger.* Among the beliefs that may underlie clients' difficulties with expressing anger appropriately are the following: They were socialized to believe that anger is wrong, they fear the disapproval of others, they fear the power of their own anger, they fear the anger of others, and/or they believe they are unable to control their own anger. In addition, some clients use anger to control or intimidate other people. You should help a client understand how beliefs like these influence his emotions and behaviors and replace unhealthy or irrational cognitions with more adaptive and realistic ones.

- *Help the client understand the difference between inappropriate and appropriate expressions of anger.* Inappropriate expressions of anger are associated with blame and aggression, often harm other people, and prevent others from understanding or accepting the angry person's feelings. In contrast, the appropriate expression of anger allows for the release of stress and frustration and helps others to understand and accept the person's feelings.

- *Help the client become aware of his own anger expression patterns.* Strategies you may use include the following: (a) Reflect or confront angry behaviors in sessions. Using I-statements can also be effective when responding to a client's angry behaviors. (b) Have the client list life situations that have hurt him and led to anger. Empathize with and clarify feelings of hurt from the past. Discuss forgiveness of others as a process of letting go of anger. Some clients benefit from reading books about forgiveness and/or writing letters to those who have hurt them. (c) Have the client identify all of the current causes and triggers of anger in his life. (d) Help the client become aware of how his inappropriate expressions of anger have had a negative impact on him and others.

b. *Providing Anger Management Strategies:* Clients with anger management problems need to learn specific, socially acceptable, and non-self-defeating ways to handle their angry feelings. They need to learn how to recognize anger when they are feeling it, how to express it appropriately when it occurs, and what to do if they are intensely angry.

Interventions and strategies for learning to manage anger include the following:

Cognitive restructuring: Help the client become aware of self-talk that influences his feelings of anger and replace it with more realistic, rational, and adaptive self-statements. In addition, a client with anger management problems may demand things (e.g., fairness, appreciation, agreement); if so, you can help the client become aware of this tendency and assist him to translate his expectations into desires.

Teach communication skills: Teach the client to use I-statements to express his feelings to others; encourage him to slow down when he's angry and think before he speaks (sometimes, it helps to encourage the client to "count to 10" before he responds); and remind him to listen carefully to what the other person is saying and take his time before answering. You may use role-playing in sessions to help the client learn and practice these skills.

Teach relaxation techniques: Simple relaxation techniques (e.g., deep breathing, mental imagery) can be effective for both calming angry feelings and managing the physiological arousal that anger causes.

Teach problem-solving skills: Teaching problem-solving skills is useful when the client's anger and frustration stem from or escalate when he faces problems that he can't easily overcome or resolve.

Teach strategies for "cooling off" from intense anger: Encourage the client to acknowledge and take responsibility for dealing with his feelings in an appropriate way and provide him with alternative behaviors that he can use when he feels intensely angry. Examples of these behaviors include taking a "time-out" from the situation or person causing the anger, engaging in physical exercise, talking with an empathetic support person, and journal writing.

2. Helping Couples With Anger Problems: Often, when couples present with anger management problems, one partner engages in uncontrolled expressions of anger that are perceived by the other partner as hurtful or threatening. On occasion, however, both partners have difficulties with expressing their anger in appropriate ways.

a. Goals of Treatment: When working with couples who present with either of these anger management problems, the goals of treatment for the couple are usually the following: (a) learn the purpose of anger management (i.e., to express anger in more appropriate ways); (b) become aware of the negative consequences of their current style of expressing and managing anger; (c) recognize gradations of anger and when to intervene with the partner for optimal results; (d) understand the purposes of anger and learn to satisfy their needs in more functional ways; (e) modify behaviors and self-talk that contribute to anger; (f) learn to support and care for each other when feeling hurt or vulnerable; and (g) learn to recognize and verbally express feelings of hurt in appropriate ways that don't involve outbursts of anger (O'Leary et al., 1998).

b. Interventions: Interventions that may be used with a couple include the following:

- Have each client describe how his or her anger harms the relationship.
- Have each client describe what he or she gains from anger.
- Explore how each client has tried to manage or de-escalate his or her anger in the past and identify what has worked and not worked. Help each client identify how he or she perceives the other's efforts to manage his or her anger (e.g., one partner may feel provoked by the other's withdrawal from heated situations).
- Have each client contract to accept responsibility for managing his or her own anger and to let go of efforts to control the other person's anger.
- Teach the clients communication skills to use when sharing feelings and discussing anger-related topics. Examples include I-statements and "measured truthfulness" (the latter is useful for increasing emotional safety). Have the clients practice these in sessions, provide feedback, and assign them as homework.
- Help the clients identify the behavioral, affective, and cognitive cues that signal that their anger is escalating to inappropriate levels.
- Teach the clients the elements of the "time-out" technique. These elements include self-monitor for escalating feelings of anger and hurt, signal to the partner that the conversation should stop, acknowledge the need of the partner to disengage, separate, cool down to regain control of anger, and return to a controlled discussion. Have the clients practice this technique in sessions, provide feedback, and assign it as homework.
- Teach the clients the different functions of anger (to get something, assert independence, or protect oneself) and have them identify times when their anger has been used for each of these purposes.
- Teach assertiveness and reinforce assertive behaviors in sessions.
- Use role-playing to help the clients learn and practice communication, conflict resolution, and assertiveness skills. Use role-reversal to increase each client's awareness of the other's feelings and perceptions about topics that trigger anger.

F. Powerlessness and the Empowerment Approach

Many people who want to change their lives feel powerless to do so. This sense of powerlessness is especially common in individuals who live in poverty or have experienced discrimination, oppression, abuse, or similar experiences. The **empowerment approach** is a way of working with clients to help them acquire the personal, interpersonal, and political power they need to take control of their lives and bring about changes in policies, organizations, and public attitudes that are impacting their lives and the lives of their families in negative ways (Sheafor & Horejsi, 2003).

1. Choosing an Empowerment Approach: Before choosing an empowerment strategy, you must make sure that your client has, or is able to learn, the competencies needed to bring about changes in his environment and that his difficulties are caused primarily by social or political barriers and a lack of resources. If one or both of these conditions are not met, an empowerment approach, by itself, is unlikely to be sufficient for helping the client.

2. Using an Empowerment Approach:

a. General Guidelines: Because the empowerment approach relies heavily on the principle of self-determination, it requires you to work in partnership with the client and find ways of sharing power and responsibility with him.

Overall goal: The overall goal is to help the client modify his self-limiting perceptions and negative feelings so that he can develop or regain a sense of power and control in his life. A client will usually begin re-evaluating his view of himself as powerless when he experiences success as a result of his own efforts. Therefore, it's critical to engage the client in activities that prepare him to experience success.

Your view of the client: You should view the client as a unique and worthwhile individual who is a potential resource to others and the expert on his own life and situation. For example, it's important to emphasize the client's definition of the problem and ideas about what should be done about it.

Your view of your helping role: You should view your helping role as primarily that of teacher-trainer or consultant.

b. Empowerment Approach Objectives and Strategies:

- Encourage the client view the relationship with you as a partnership in problem-solving. You want him to use your knowledge, skills, and experience to advance his own ideas for resolving the problem.

- Help the client view his past experiences of injustice and mistreatment in a new way (i.e., use reframing). For instance, you might help the client view these experiences as sources of wisdom.

- Help the client build his self-confidence and self-respect. Encourage him to take the risks necessary to learn new skills and modify self-limiting beliefs and behaviors.

- Help the client experience personal power. Allow and encourage him to make decisions and follow through on those decisions. Respect his decisions and allow him to experience the positive and negative consequences of his choices.

- Help the client understand factors that contribute to his sense of powerlessness. Ideally, the client will express and come to understand his feelings of anger, frustration, etc., and then move beyond them to take positive action.

- Encourage the client to look for learning opportunities that will help him understand the people, organizations, and systems he'd like to influence. As necessary, help him make arrangements to participate in these events.

- Help the client identify sources of power he can use (individually or with others) to improve his situation. Examples of potential sources of power include knowledge based on his life experience, motivation, time, energy, familiarity with his community, the capacity to influence others, and an understanding of particular problems.

- Once the client understands that he has some power, help him use his power in a planned way to bring about the sought-after change. In doing so, make sure he understands that bringing about change can be slow and that many factors beyond his control may affect how quickly others respond to his efforts and requests.

A lot of this work takes place in a small group, where the client can learn and practice skills such as communicating, problem-solving, leadership, persuasion, assertiveness, negotiation, and mutual support. The small group experience is also effective for helping the client overcome the sense of being different and alone (i.e., it helps him learn that others have many of the same struggles in life).

G. Child Abuse and Neglect

The information in this section focuses on psychotherapy and counseling for maltreated children and their families. For information on child welfare work, see Section XVII of this chapter. Other information on child abuse and neglect (indicators, assessment, etc.) appears in Section IX of Assessment.

Treatment of Abused and Neglected Children

1. Areas of Treatment: Treatments and services offered directly to abused and neglected children may be described in terms of four areas of need: safety, medical, developmental, and psychological (Martin, 1979).

Safety needs (need for protection): Protecting the child from further maltreatment is the first priority in cases of child abuse and neglect. Decisions related to the child's safety are ordinarily made by or in conjunction with child protective service (CPS) agency staff. Depending on the specific circumstances of the case, the decision may be to remove the child from his home or to allow the child to remain at home with supervision, part-time alternative care, or other protective services.

Medical needs: Some medical consequences of child abuse and neglect are obvious and, therefore, receive immediate medical attention. Other problems, however, are less apparent and require a thorough medical evaluation in order to be identified. Common medical problems of abused and neglected children include physical injuries, neurological damage, anemia and other nutritional disorders, hearing deficits, infections, inadequate immunizations, and neglected dental and visual needs. The assessment of these problems requires referral to appropriate medical professionals.

Developmental needs: Many abused and neglected children exhibit delays in motor, perceptual, language, cognitive, social, and/or emotional development. Mental health professionals are often involved in the assessment of developmental delays, but their treatment usually requires referral to other professionals or agencies. These treatments are provided by specialists such as physical therapists, occupational therapists, and speech therapists.

Psychological needs: Psychological consequences of child abuse and neglect are varied and include impaired impulse control, low self-esteem, low frustration tolerance, self-destructive behaviors, behavioral extremes, pathological object relations, lack of trust, depression, and anxiety. Social workers may be involved in the assessment and treatment of maltreated children's psychological problems. Psychological treatment goals, strategies, and modalities are discussed below.

2. Treatment Goals: Although the targets of treatment depend on the particular child's symptoms, there are certain goals that are common to the treatment of most children who have been physically or sexually abused or neglected, including the following: (a) help and encourage the child to think about and talk about the abuse/neglect without embarrassment or significant anxiety; (b) help the child express his feelings about the abuse; (c) reduce the intensity and frequency of emotional and behavioral symptoms; (d) clarify and modify inaccurate, distorted, or unhealthy thinking patterns that might negatively affect the child's view of himself and others; (e) help the child develop healthier attachments; and (f) educate the child about self-protective strategies.

3. Treatment Strategies: Treatment strategies for abused or neglected children often include the following:

- Cognitive-behavioral strategies to address the child's thinking patterns and emotional and behavioral responses to the abuse. Of particular importance is addressing the child's attributions of blame and responsibility for the abuse (e.g., the child should be helped to recognize that he is not to blame).

- Gradual exposure, or discussion of abuse experiences, to reduce the child's anxiety and embarrassment and give him opportunities to modify inaccurate or self-defeating thinking patterns.

- Relaxation training to address the child's fears and anxiety reactions to abuse-related cues and improve his emotional regulation.

- Educational approaches to clarify misperceptions that have developed in response to the abuse.

- Skills training to teach the child strategies for managing his negative emotions and improve his interpersonal functioning.

- Supportive techniques to help the child cope with unsupportive family members, upcoming court hearings, negative reactions from peers, etc.

- Education in the use of self-protective strategies to minimize the likelihood that the child will be abused or neglected again.

For young children, drawings, puppets, and other play techniques can be useful for helping them communicate about their abuse experiences and learn strategies for coping with negative emotions and behaving in a more organized manner. Older children and adolescents, by contrast, are usually more able to directly express their thoughts and feelings about their abuse experiences. Therapists should be flexible in their approach, however, since drawings and therapeutic games can be helpful for some older children, as well.

4. Available Treatment Modalities:

a. Individual Therapy: Individual therapy gives children the individual attention and support they often need so that they can identify and work through the psychological issues related to abuse or neglect. In addition, for many children, the first stage of individual therapy needs to focus on helping them acknowledge (directly or indirectly) that maltreatment did happen to them.

b. Individual Play Therapy: Individual play therapy provides children with a safe environment and allows them to use familiar play materials to express feelings. Play therapy is primarily beneficial for preschool and school-aged children who are unable to verbalize their feelings or who have severe psychological or behavioral problems (e.g., depression, high aggressiveness).

c. Group Therapy: Therapy groups provide children with opportunities for improving their social skills, developing satisfactory interpersonal relationships, and increasing their self-awareness and empathy. Group therapy is most effective with preadolescents and adolescents. Group therapy can be particularly important for children who have been sexually abused. One reason why is that the group exposes them to other individuals who have also been sexually abused which lets them know they are not alone in their experience.

Mental Health Treatment for Maltreating Families

Treatments for abusive and neglectful families reflect contemporary attitudes toward perpetrators of child maltreatment – the view that they are usually amenable to rehabilitation. Accordingly, the primary goal of treatment is to provide the child and parents with a broad, comprehensive, and relevant spectrum of services in order to strengthen and maintain the family constellation whenever possible.

Psychological services are often provided to various family "systems" including the perpetrator of abuse, the couple relationship, the parent-child relationship, and the entire family. Note, however, that for family treatment to proceed effectively, those who participate must acknowledge on some level that the abuse has occurred. Thus, the initial focus of intervention may be on encouraging the parents (offending and non-offending) to acknowledge and assume responsibility for what has happened in the family.

1. Treatment Modalities: Experts generally agree that treatment of abusive and neglectful families is most effective when it includes a combination of medical, educational, psychological, and other supportive services. Traditional psychological services may include individual, couple (marital), family, and/or group therapy. Group therapy is frequently used in conjunction with other treatments and services as a method for addressing such issues as the development of interpersonal and problem-solving skills.

The use of family therapy as a method for treating abusive and neglectful families is based on the premise that maltreatment is the result of family dysfunction, rather than the problems of a single identified patient. Family therapy provides a direct method for modifying the dysfunctional interactional patterns that underlie abuse or neglect. Family therapy is contraindicated, however, when the perpetrator is unwilling to cease or take responsibility for his abusive behaviors. Family therapy is also contraindicated when a parent's or child's anger or other negative feelings would be better dealt with in individual therapy. Finally, although young children can benefit from family therapy, it is most effective for children who are old enough to verbally express their feelings and needs.

2. The "Abuse Clarification" Process: Treatment for all forms of child abuse and neglect should address attributions of blame. Most perpetrators deny or minimize their responsibility for the maltreatment and project blame on other family members, usually the child who has been abused. The abuse clarification process targets attributions of blame and is addressed over time in an offender's individual or group treatment. The goal is for the offender to reach a point where he is able to clarify the nature of the abuse, assume responsibility for the abuse, demonstrate empathy for the child's responses to the abuse, and begin to participate in the development or implementation of the family safety plan. The process ideally culminates in an abuse clarification session in which the offender reads a letter written to the child victim that focuses on the offender's assumption of responsibility, empathy for the child, and commitment to the family safety plan.

A non-offending parent may be involved in an "abuse protection clarification process." This process is similar to the abuse clarification process conducted with the offender. The non-offending parent is encouraged to clarify the abuse, commit to protection of the child, and participate in the development of a family safety plan.

H. Spousal/Partner Abuse

Because, in heterosexual relationships, the male is more often the perpetrator in cases of spousal/partner abuse (intimate partner violence), the research has traditionally focused on the "battering husband/boyfriend" and the "battered wife/girlfriend," and our review reflects this emphasis.

You can find additional information on spousal/partner abuse (dynamics, indicators, etc.) in Section IX of Assessment.

1. Barriers to Seeking Help: Because each woman is unique, the barriers described in this section are by no means common to every woman who is abused by her spouse or partner. Instead, they describe reactions that are commonly found in females exposed to intimate partner violence (IPV).

a. Minimization and Denial: Some women minimize the abuse they experience – they recognize the abusive events, but don't acknowledge or understand that the abuse is harmful or wrong, sometimes because of denial, and other times because they lack information about what constitutes "abuse." Sometimes, denying or "forgetting" abusive events is what allows a woman to continue functioning, at least in a limited way, until she is ready to come to terms with the abuse. These reactions can prevent or postpone a woman's willingness and capacity to seek psychological, medical, and other forms of assistance.

Minimization and denial may cease under a number of different circumstances, including when the cost of the abusive relationship begins to exceed the positive gain or when the environment begins to provide sufficient support for the woman's decision to leave the relationship and otherwise recover from the abuse.

When you have reason to suspect that a client is in denial about abusive events (but she is not in immediate danger), you should first emphasize building a trusting relationship with her. It's important to allow the client to move past the denial at her own pace – efforts to break through her denial using assertive techniques such as direct confrontation are not recommended because pressuring the woman to acknowledge her situation can replicate the abuse she has suffered at home.

b. Self-Blame: A woman exposed to IPV may hold herself responsible for the abuse. Self-blame may stem, in part, from a cultural tendency in the U.S. to "blame the victim" and is likely to be reinforced by the batterer, who usually encourages his partner to assume responsibility for the abuse. You should emphasize, from the beginning of treatment, that there was *nothing* the woman could have done to deserve being abused.

c. Guilt and Shame: Feelings of guilt and shame about being abused are common reactions, as well. Women who have these feelings experience intense psychological pain, find it difficult to acknowledge or talk about their experiences of abuse, and may believe they don't deserve help. It's important to be aware of the manner in which you react to the woman's descriptions of abusive events so that you avoid reinforcing her feelings of guilt and shame.

d. Fear of "Punishment" from the Batterer: Many women in abusive relationships have deep, pervasive – and often justified – fears of being punished by their partners if they seek help for their abuse problems. Often a batterer will actively and forcefully attempt to prevent his partner from getting help. Thus, a battered woman who has come to therapy by herself may fear that her partner will abuse her severely if he finds out that she has sought someone's help. You may want to review the cycle of violence with the abused victim as well.

2. Assessment Procedures: The following assessment procedures are usually necessary when beginning your work with women who've been battered by their male partners:

- *Assess danger.* Some women come to therapy while still in an abusive relationship, others come in just after leaving their partner, and others seek treatment months or even years after moving out on their own. Assessing danger to the client is important in all three cases. Forms of danger that need to be evaluated include (a) the risk of further abuse, (b) suicide risk, and (c) homicide risk (i.e., a client who has just left the batterer and is in danger of being murdered by him may kill her abuser in self-defense). If relevant, danger to children in the client's household should be assessed, as well.

- *Obtain the client's own story.* Be aware that, when telling her story, the client may re-experience the emotional pain and fear associated with abusive incidents (this is true even if the abuse happened years ago). Be sure to balance your efforts to collect information with careful attention to and support of the client's emotional needs – i.e., give the client ample time to talk about what has happened, be nonjudgmental and supportive, avoid giving advice or making interpretations, and clarify any vague terms the client uses. Usually an open-ended question-and-answer session is the best way to begin this part of the assessment.

- *Assess social support.* Explore family relationships and friendship patterns, including the amount and quality of support currently available to the client.

- *Assess for signs of learned helplessness.* The client may have lost the ability to anticipate that her actions will have positive outcomes. When present, learned helplessness can severely narrow the client's alternatives.

- *Assess psychiatric symptoms* (e.g., posttraumatic stress disorder, depression, anxiety, dissociative states, eating disorders, substance use disorders). **Battered woman syndrome** refers to a constellation of abuse-related anxiety, arousal, and avoidance symptoms, including isolation and withdrawal, similar to those caused by other traumatic events (Walker, 1994). The characteristics of battered woman syndrome meet diagnostic criteria for posttraumatic stress disorder (PTSD). If the woman is experiencing intense symptoms of anxiety or depression, you may refer her for a medication evaluation so that she can experience symptomatic relief at the start of treatment.

- *Obtain a medical history and refer for medical evaluations.* The latter is important if the client has not seen a physician in a while or if she has, or may have, physical injuries. A medical professional can also check for stress-related illnesses and chronic health problems associated with having been abused. Moreover, this referral encourages the woman to focus on self-care, which may be neglected, and may further reduce her tendency to minimize the seriousness of her situation. Note that a woman exhibiting prominent cognitive symptoms should be evaluated by a neurologist (i.e., she may have experienced repeated head injuries).

- *Examine relevant legal documents.* Reading police reports can clarify the nature and extent of the abuse when a client is reluctant to provide details or minimizes her abuse experiences.

- *Interview members of her support system, if possible.* Family members can sometimes provide supplemental information about the client's current functioning and pre-abuse functioning.

Finally, it's also important to remind the client that her partner may be monitoring her computer use, including her Internet history, e-mails, social media pages, and instant messaging. Advise her to use a computer outside of her home if she seeks additional help online, and, if she leaves the relationship, to change her user names and passwords for her e-mail, online banking, and other sensitive accounts (including accounts that may reveal her location to her ex).

3. Intervention Approaches:

a. Immediate Intervention Procedures: The following interventions are important if the client is still living with her abusive partner:

- Use the "four incident technique" in which you explore four types of battering incidents (first incident, a typical incident, worst incident, and most recent incident). This helps the client identify the cues that her partner provides as tension increases, thereby allowing her to make preparations to leave before an acute battering incident occurs.

- Develop an **escape plan** with the client: This entails creating a detailed floor plan of the client's home indicating where the battering typically occurs and what exits are available to her to get away before violence erupts; and helping her plan what she'll need to have with her in order to escape (car keys, house keys, money, a change of clothes, medications, etc.) and where she will go. If there are children, the client needs to make provisions for them as well. To leave home without them puts her at risk for a custody action.

- If appropriate, encourage the client to explain to her partner that one of them may feel the need for a "time-out." She can explain that she may want to leave when she feels his anger rising and is afraid. The time-out arrangement should include a discussion of the conditions of return.

- Provide the client with detailed information for contacting a local shelter and phone numbers for hotlines (for victims of battering, for suicide) and inform her about her legal alternatives (e.g., police protection, restraining orders).

- Provide referrals for resources and services relevant to the client's needs (e.g., social service agencies) and readiness to acknowledge and address the abuse (e.g., a peer support group).

b. *Survivor Therapy:* **Survivor therapy** has emerged as one of the most effective methods for helping women recover from spousal/partner abuse and other man-made traumas (Walker, 1994). This model is based on trauma theory and feminist therapy. Among its fundamental principles is an emphasis on the woman's strengths in spite of her injuries: The "survivor therapist" explores the coping strategies a client has adopted and helps her build on these so that she can become a "survivor" instead of a "victim" and, thereby, move on with her life. An effort is also made to integrate the client's current response to abusive events into her full-life context (e.g., historical, psychological, biological, sociopolitical cultural, situational) by directly addressing changes in her cognition, affect, and behavior.

The primary goals of survivor therapy include establishing safety, re-empowering the client, validating the client and her experiences, expanding the client's options, restoring the client's cognitive clarity, encouraging the client to make her own decisions, and healing effects of the abuse. Of these goals, the first two – establishing safety and restoring the client's sense of control over her life – are considered the most important. Other survivor therapy goals may include meeting the client's concrete needs, helping the client understand oppression, identifying intrapsychic factors (such as those stemming from a client's childhood abuse), and developing the client's self-confidence.

c. *Group Therapy for Battered Women:* Group therapy can be used alone or in conjunction with individual therapy, and has several advantages over individual therapy for this population. In particular, most women abused by their partners are socially isolated and have had few, if any, opportunities to talk about their experiences. In a group, the woman has a chance to safely tell her story to others who've been through a similar experience. She may also derive strength and a sense of community from hearing others' stories and learning how they have coped. Support groups offer similar advantages.

d. *Couples Therapy:* Couples therapy may be considered when the woman is staying in a relationship with her abusive partner. Most experts believe, however, that the partners in an abusive relationship should be treated *separately* in the first stages of intervention. This is especially true when the batterer denies the abuse and/or the incidents of abuse are highly unpredictable.

The Abusive Men Exploring New Direction (AMEND) policy on couples therapy in cases of IPV recommends that it should not be offered until the following conditions have been met: there have been no reports of violence for over five months, the perpetrator has accepted responsibility for his violent behaviors, and both partners have been participating actively in treatment groups (Mikesell, 1995). In addition, couples therapy requires *both* partners to acknowledge the abuse and demonstrate a clear willingness to work toward the goal of eliminating it.

Conjoint therapy for the partners in an abusive relationship often has the following goals: teach the clients (particularly the batterer) to control their anger and resolve conflicts without resorting to verbal or physical aggression; improve verbal and nonverbal communication skills; challenge each client's inaccurate assumptions about his or her partner (including gender-based assumptions); strengthen each individual so that the relationship becomes free of all coercion; and eliminate unhealthy dependence in the relationship (Jongsma et al., 1998).

4. Batterer Intervention Programs (BIPs): The results of research on batterer intervention programs (a.k.a. spouse abuse abatement programs, or SAAPs) have been inconsistent, largely because of differences in evaluation methods. According to a report published by the U.S. Department of Justice (Jackson et al., 2003), some available data suggest that court-ordered treatment for batterers correlates with a reduction in physical violence, but does not usually end the violence or reduce more subtle forms of abuse. Whether it is the treatment itself or the motivation brought on by legal intervention that produces the reduction of violence is unclear, however.

Other studies have found that men arrested and treated resume their violent behaviors as often as do men arrested and not referred to treatment, and that there is no significant difference between men who complete batterer's treatment and men who drop out of the program.

I. Social Skills Training for Children and Adolescents

1. Social Skills Training for Children: Therapeutic approaches to helping children develop social skills and correct social-skills problems include reinforcement, modeling, and cognitive strategies. Reinforcement and modeling strategies may be used first to provide immediate gains and help motivate children to learn more complicated cognitive strategies, which are associated with longer-term gains.

a. Positive-Reinforcement Strategies: Positive reinforcement (e.g., verbal praise, attention, tangible rewards) can be used to shape socially appropriate responses. Because unsociable children benefit from seeing others rewarded for positive behavior, this approach is particularly effective when it is used as part of a group reinforcement plan in which every child is consistently rewarded with praise when he exhibits desirable social behavior (Landy et al., 2002). At the same time, children's less desirable social behaviors (e.g., aggressive behaviors, solitary play) should be ignored as much as possible.

b. Modeling: Modeling may be used to help shy or withdrawn children enter a social situation with less fear. Ideally, the models should be people who, like the children, appear initially hesitant to interact with others socially. When the models' positive social behaviors and the benefits of those behaviors are pointed out to the children, the children are likely to imitate the behaviors.

Modeling has also been shown to be effective with chronically aggressive children who have poor problem-solving skills. In this approach, adults and other children serve as models and teach the child nonaggressive conflict-resolution strategies. Children are more likely to use these new strategies if they see someone else benefit by using them.

c. Teaching Cognitive Strategies: When cognitive strategies such as coaching, problem-solving, or role-playing are used, the child actively participates in thinking about and practicing social situations to develop tools for problem-solving. Coaching, for example, has been found effective for increasing isolated children's acceptance by their peers. When using coaching, you demonstrate and provide a rationale for a socially desirable behavior, and the child then practices the behavior, first with you, and then in live settings where interaction and cooperation are encouraged. For aggressive or impulsive children, treatment may incorporate self-instructional training.

2. Social Skills Training for Adolescents: Social skills training with adolescents focuses on helping them find more effective responses for resolving the challenges of difficult social situations – that is, adolescents are taught to rely on new behaviors that lead to positive consequences, rather than prior behaviors that elicited negative consequences.

Different social skills may be taught, depending on the type of situation being addressed, but all programs divide the skills into parts so that they are easier to learn and use hypothetical social situations that require the types of social skills being taught. LeCroy (2001) outlines the following seven steps for teaching social skills to adolescents in a group setting. Those leading the training group should involve all of the participants actively during each step. This both improves the effectiveness of the intervention and keeps the process interesting and fun for the group members.

Step 1. Present the social skill being taught: (a) Solicit an explanation of the skill. (b) Ask group members to provide rationales for the skill.

Step 2. Discuss the social skill: (a) List the skill steps. (b) Ask group members to give examples of using the skill.

Step 3. Present a problem situation and model the skill: Following this presentation, evaluate the performance and ask group members to discuss it.

Step 4. Set the stage for role-playing the skill: Explain role-playing and select group members for the role-play.

Step 5. Have group members rehearse the skill: (a) Provide coaching if necessary. (b) Have group members provide feedback on verbal and nonverbal elements of the skill.

Step 6. Practice using complex skill situations: (a) Teach accessory skills (e.g., problem solving). (b) Have group members discuss situations and provide feedback.

Step 7. Train for generalization and maintenance: (a) Encourage the practice of skills outside the group. (b) Have group members discuss their own problem situations.

3. Social Skills Training in Response to Bullying: Because bullying involves powerful children harassing less powerful children, it differs from conflicts occurring between children of relatively equal status. For this reason, conflict resolution strategies such as mediation often are not effective (Dupper, 2003). Instead, one effective way to intervene when a child or adolescent is being bullied is to teach him social skills to defuse situations that might otherwise lead to his being bullied (e.g., assertiveness skills, problem-solving skills). Another useful intervention can be to teach the child to have more tolerance for the situation by understanding that he's not responsible for a bully's behavior and shouldn't get upset when a bully provokes him.

J. Parenting and Parent-Training Programs

1. The Birth of a Disabled Child: When a child is born with a disability, the parents often go through an initial phase of shock, grief, and denial. As the parents become more aware of their child's problem, they may experience a deep sense of guilt and failure. They may believe they are being punished or worry about what they might have done to cause the disability.

Resources that can enhance the parents' adjustment, as well as the child's development, include personal coping skills (e.g., problem-solving abilities) and adequate social support, including physical assistance, information, and emotional support. Additionally, parents should be given information about services and programs available as a result of the Education of the Handicapped Act (EHA) which was enacted, in part, to provide special services to children born with disabilities. Many communities provide infant-stimulation or early intervention programs for infants with disabilities and their families. The parents are encouraged to participate as their infant's teachers and are taught activities to perform with their baby at home to enhance his development.

2. Parent-Training Programs: Parent education emphasizes promoting a strong parent-child relationship. Although many parent-training programs rely on behavior management techniques, in doing so, they emphasize teaching parents how to have positive, nurturing, and skillful interactions with their children (Ashford et al., 2006). Four common approaches to parent training are described below.

a. Behavior Modification: In this form of parent education, the training involves teaching parents how to apply principles of behavior modification (e.g., reinforcement, punishment, extinction, differential reinforcement of other behaviors, stimulus control) to their children. First, parents are taught these principles and how to precisely define the behavior they would like to see changed. Then, they are helped to select a home project in which they will use the principles to modify the target behavior. Parents are also taught how to develop a method of tracking or charting changes in the target behavior.

Punishments (e.g., time-out, withdrawal of privileges) may be used when the goal is to decrease or eliminate a target behavior, but behavior modification programs usually emphasize teaching parents the value of using praise and reinforcement with their children. Parents are encouraged to write rules using positive language, "catch their child being good," and display charts illustrating their child's progress.

b. Parent-Effectiveness Training (PET): Users of Parent-Effectiveness Training (PET) assume that there is no such thing as "misbehavior" (instead, children "behave" in ways designed to get their needs met), emphasize the need for respect between a parent and child, and encourage parents to give up the use of power. The assumption is that power not only harms people and relationships, but also undermines PET's "no-lose" method of problem solving.

Strategies taught to parents include the following: (a) environmental modification (e.g., putting things where children can't reach them); (b) defining "who owns the problem," or finds the behavior unacceptable (e.g., the child, the parent, a teacher?); (c) active listening and helping the child understand, accept, and deal with his feelings (used when the child owns the problem); (d) using I-messages (used when the parent owns the problem); and (e) the "no-lose" method of problem-solving (used when active listening or I-messages don't work).

The "no-lose" method of problem-solving engages the child's cooperation and includes these steps: (a) define the conflict; (b) use brainstorming with the child to generate solutions; (c) evaluate solutions on the list; (d) see if there is a solution that satisfies both parties; (e) if so, decide how to implement the solution; and (f) evaluate the solution later to see if it worked.

c. Parent-Involvement Training (PIT): The focus of Parent-Involvement Training (PIT) is on getting parents more involved with their children. Practitioners assume that, before any behavior change can take place, the parents must believe in their child and have a relationship with him that is based on warmth, respect, and trust. The PIT program includes the following steps:

- Step 1 – the parents establish and maintain involvement with the child (e.g., they have conversations about topics of mutual interest and make it a priority to attend to their child's needs especially when he's upset).

- Step 2 – the parents help the child see what his current behavior is and understand that he has chosen the behavior.

- Step 3 – the parents encourage the child to evaluate his behavior ("Is what you are doing helping you?").

- Step 4 – the parents help the child plan increasingly responsible behavior and set realistic goals so that he will experience success. The child must make a commitment to the plan.

- Step 5 – if the child doesn't fulfill the commitment from step 4, the parents and child start again with step 3. The parents are taught to accept no excuses.

Additionally, the parents are told to never use punishment (which can cause physical and emotional pain and lead to hostility, loneliness, etc.) and to rely on praise for successes instead.

d. Systematic Training for Effective Parenting (STEP): Users of Systematic Training for Effective Parenting (STEP) view a misbehaving child as a "discouraged child" and teach parents that their child's misbehavior is motivated by one or more of the following goals: attention, power, revenge, and/or inadequacy. Parents are then trained to use techniques of encouragement and discipline: "Encouragement strategies" focus on giving the child a lot of responsibility, avoiding overprotection (allowing the child to learn from his own behavior), and avoiding doing too much for the child. "Discipline" emphasizes the use of "natural" and "logical" consequences so that the child has an opportunity to experience the effects of his choices and behavior.

The STEP program assumes that "natural" consequences and "logical" consequences are better than rewards and punishment for preventing power struggles between a parent and child. Whereas behavior modification approaches encourage parents to be responsible for their child's behavior, STEP encourages parents to allow their children to make their own decisions, and to benefit if their choices are good and suffer the consequences if their choices are bad. The idea is that children will become more responsible when their behavior is guided by "natural" consequences (real-life consequences), rather than by parental interference. When natural consequences are unavailable or would be dangerous, STEP teaches parents to use "logical" consequences instead (i.e., consequences that have direct relationship to the child's behavior).

K. Budgeting and Personal Debt

1. Envelope Budgeting: Envelope budgeting can be taught to clients who need a simple method for keeping track of their money and expenses, particularly clients who are having difficultly stretching a limited income to cover necessities and whose money transactions are conducted using cash. The first step is to help the client identify all key categories of expenditure and how many dollars must be spent on each category during each spending cycle (e.g., two weeks, one month). Then, you have the client prepare and label an envelope for each category and fill it with the amount of money required to cover the expenditure. Removing money from a designated envelope and using it as planned helps the client keep better track of his spending and what money he has left. Each time the client is paid or otherwise receives income, cash is again placed in the envelopes for the new spending cycle.

2. Managing Personal Debt: Financial problems often stem from values, attitudes, and/or shopping behaviors that result in overspending. Low-esteem may also lead people to buy more than they can afford. No matter the cause, however, clients with considerable debt tend to be under a great deal of stress, and, to get out of debt, they may need to make significant behavioral changes. As a social worker, you can assist clients in debt by providing suggestions that may help them regain some control over their financial situation, but should make known your role as social worker and not a financial advisor. You may:

- Encourage the client to reduce his spending immediately and, if possible, to stop buying items on credit.

- Help the client perform a careful analysis of what he owes and have him organize this information in a visual way (e.g., on a table) that helps him keep track of when each bill is due, what he will owe each time, what he can actually pay, and the total amount that he owes. Encourage him to flag items for which he is charged interest and to make these high-priority targets for payment.

- If the client is unable to pay a bill, encourage him to contact his creditor to explain why (discourage the client from ignoring the bill). The creditor may be willing to make a payment plan or adjustment to what is owed.

- Discourage the client from avoiding bill collectors or collection agencies who contact him. Encourage him to have candid discussions with these people about acceptable solutions to his debt.

- Consider referring the client to a consumer credit counseling program. Look for a program offered by a nonprofit agency. Before referring the client, find out who sponsors the program, what (if any) charges are involved, and how the program operates.

- If the above strategies fail to manage the client's debt, encourage him to consider a consolidation loan, in which he would take out a new loan sufficient to pay off all of his other loans and overdue accounts. The single payment on the new loan would be smaller than the combined total for the client's prior monthly payments.

- If all other strategies fail, you may need to encourage the client to consider filing for bankruptcy. In discussing this option, let him know that bankruptcy has negative consequences (e.g., bankruptcy will remain on his credit report for years). If the client decides to consider bankruptcy, advise him to seek advice from an attorney and/or a credit counseling agency.

L. Clients Who Are HIV Positive

Areas of Assessment

The following areas may turn out to need attention during intervention with a client who has HIV disease:

Emotional distress: Depression, anxiety, anger, somatization, confusion, and other symptoms of emotional distress may be precipitated by a variety of HIV-related events including social losses, disease progression, stigmatization, and diminished self-esteem. When combined with a sense of hopelessness or helplessness, frequent changes in emotional status may interfere with a client's coping efforts and adaptive functioning.

Suicide risk: Suicide risk is an ongoing concern for the reasons cited above in the description of emotional distress. In addition, clients with late stage AIDS may consider suicide as a way of allowing themselves to die with dignity or preventing loved ones from suffering. In this situation, you may face a difficult personal dilemma if you believe that people have the right to choose **rational suicide**. Whatever your personal views, however, you can be found negligent if you don't take steps to attempt to prevent a client's threatened suicide. Whenever you believe that a client is at risk for suicide, you are ethically obligated to take appropriate steps to protect the client's safety that are consistent with the level of risk.

Mental status/neurocognitive disorders: HIV infects the brain and certain opportunistic infections may affect cognitive and motor functioning.

Social support: The client may be experiencing relationship problems and/or social isolation due to anticipated or actual rejection by loved ones.

Coping patterns and strategies: Determine what coping strategies the client has used in the past, what coping strategies he uses now, and what coping strategies he needs to develop in order to handle the current situation more adaptively.

Quality of life: Quality of life will change over the course of HIV infection in association with changes in physical health, energy level, cognitive functioning, and social relationships.

Need for HIV-related information to facilitate decision-making: As a social worker, you cannot provide detailed medical information or any medical advice to a client. However, you can be a useful source of information about matters such as modes of HIV transmission and safer-sex practices, reframing HIV-related cognitions, and training in communication skills that can, among other things, help the client participate actively in his medical care.

Self-disclosure of serostatus: Find out who the client has told about his infection, whether the client has experienced rejection or discrimination as a result of disclosing, and whether the client has cut off social contacts because he fears rejection, discrimination, or stigmatization.

Need for services and resources: Find out whether the client has access to adequate and appropriate medical care and social support. Find out whether he needs assistance from federal or local programs in his community. Make referrals as needed. Serve as the client's advocate if appropriate.

Intervention

1. General Intervention Guidelines: The following guidelines are useful when working with clients who are HIV positive:

- Adopt a multidisciplinary approach (e.g., you, the physician, a neurologist, a psychiatrist for psychotropic medication).

- Focus on the client's coping skills, training in active problem-solving, support of the client's self-esteem, and provision of emotional support. Be aware that interventions emphasizing the here-and-now tend to be more effective than insight-oriented treatments.

- Empower the client to play an active role in fulfilling his own emotional needs and physical/medical needs (e.g., taking medications, eating properly, exercising, eliminating unhealthy habits and behaviors).

- Be aware that some clients need help with medical-related issues such their attitudes toward medical treatments, HIV medication compliance, and preferences related to terminal care.

- If the client has a substance use disorder that requires attention, encourage him to work toward establishing abstinence before beginning counseling on other issues.

2. Modalities and Approaches:

a. Individual Therapy:

Crisis intervention: Identifying the client's disease stage will help establish the need for crisis intervention.

Cognitive-behavioral interventions: (a) Cognitive restructuring techniques can be used to reduce distress and increase a client's sense of control. For example, you can help a client reappraise his health status, reframe the meaning of his symptoms, or maintain a more positive or realistic outlook. (b) Stress reduction techniques such as relaxation training or guided imagery relaxation techniques can be used to reduce day-to-day stress. (c) Assertiveness, problem-solving, and social skills training can be used to help eliminate barriers that are preventing a client from disclosing his infection to others and facilitate his active participation in decision-making related to his medical care. (d) As needed, help the client develop a plan for modifying health-related behaviors. Facilitate his ability to set realistic goals when planning these changes.

b. Group Therapy: Groups are most effective when they focus on changing behavior and beliefs about the disease, offering education about HIV/AIDS, and providing support in handling difficult emotions (including those of the client and his support people).

c. Peer Interventions: Some communities have AIDS buddy programs which are used to help increase the overall quality of life for people living with HIV/AIDS through mental, emotional, and spiritual support. Linking a client to a volunteer buddy program can provide an additional source of emotional support and, when needed, assistance with activities of daily living.

3. Intervention Goals and Strategies: A range of goals other than those listed below may be relevant because of a client's particular situation, but individual therapy with HIV-positive clients commonly has the following goals.

a. Help the Client Handle the Diagnosis: If a newly diagnosed client is in crisis, use traditional crisis intervention techniques (encouraging ventilation, accessing support systems, reinforcing coping strategies, etc.) to help the client gain control of his fear and anxiety.

b. Help the Client Improve His Quality of Life: Once a client's affect is stable, provide him with a framework for adapting successfully to the disease:

- Help the client develop new ways of coping and encourage him to use coping strategies that have worked in the past.

- Explore the client's fears and attitudes about the disease, his goals and priorities, and how he believes his life will change as a result of having HIV. Use direct questioning to help the client better express himself.

- As needed, provide grief counseling, cognitive-behavioral therapy, and other interventions to help the client cope with distressing emotions and regain a sense of control.

- If a client is in the later stages of the disease, encourage him to review his life and take care of unfinished business (e.g., resolve problems with loved ones).

- If a client's physical or mental abilities are impaired, help him identify new activities that are consistent with his remaining abilities and reframe his quality of life based on those activities. Validate the client's sense of loss, while also communicating a sense of hope.

- When needed, provide referral to a rehabilitation or vocational agency and offer education about the client's rights under the Americans with Disabilities Act.

c. Empower the Client:

- Help the client recognize his capacity to play an active role in his medical and mental health treatment and other activities. Use strategies that focus on building self-esteem to combat the sense of helplessness and help the client evaluate his options and their consequences.

- Mobilize friends, family, and community support services. Communication is important in this process in terms of both offering information and encouraging the client to express his feelings and needs to others.

- Encourage the client to become involved in activities that prevent rumination about the disease.

d. Help the Client Deal With Impending Death: The following interventions are useful for a client in the late stages of AIDS:

- Help the client deal with his fear of the dying process (e.g., experiencing pain) and death itself.

- Involve the entire support system because the client's loved ones will also need help coping with the dying process and their impending loss.

- Provide advocacy and linkage to help the client and support people locate and use community resources such as hospice care.

M. Working With People Near Death

1. The Needs of People Near Death: The basic needs of individuals near death include the following: (a) adequate pain management; (b) adequate medical management of other symptoms; (c) competent physical care (i.e., comfort, hygiene, personal dignity); (d) information about options for care and help with decision making; (e) reassurance and support to address anxiety and other emotional distress; and (f) an opportunity to receive spiritual support and participate in the rituals of their religion or culture.

Social workers can help meet the basic needs of people near death through direct care and by advocating on their behalf (Ashford et al., 2006). Specific interventions may include the following: (a) facilitate communication between the client (and his family) and medical professionals; (b) if a client is mentally alert, provide opportunities to talk about fears, unfinished business, and concerns for the future of loved ones; and (c) if a client is strong enough, use life review to help him reflect back on and evaluate major events of his life. Other useful interventions include relaxation techniques and encouraging the client's loved ones to talk about meaningful issues with him and listen to him.

2. Hospice Care: Hospice care is an interdisciplinary approach to caring for individuals with terminal illness when recovery is unlikely. Care may be provided in the individual's home, a nursing home, or a hospice unit in a hospital or community agency. Medicare, private health insurance, and Medicaid cover hospice care for individuals who meet eligibility criteria.

Hospice care integrates medical, psychological, and social approaches. It emphasizes quality of life, holistic approaches to pain control (psychological and spiritual pain), palliative care (specialized care when curative treatments are no longer available), and the involvement of family and others in caring for the patient. Hospice programs also support caregivers by offering convalescent and respite care. Many hospices also provide continuing contact and support for caregivers for at least a year following the death of the patient.

Social workers may discuss the option of hospice care with clients who are terminally ill. By law, the decision to enter hospice care must be left to the terminally ill person. Most hospices accept patients who have a life expectancy of six months or less and who are referred by their personal physician. In fact, one of the first things a hospice program will do is contact the patient's physician to make sure the physician agrees that hospice care is appropriate for the patient at this time. Most hospices have medical staff available to help patients who have no physician.

As soon as a patient has been accepted into the program, a hospice team prepares an individualized care plan that will, among other things, address the amount of caregiving the patient needs. The patient's family and friends deliver most of the care, but hospice staff visit regularly and are always available to answer medical questions. In addition, a hospice may have volunteers to assist with errands and provide breaks for the primary caregivers. As death approaches, it is recommended that someone be with the patient at all times, since one of the most common fears of patients is the fear of dying alone.

The members of a patient's hospice team include the patient and his caregiver(s), a doctor, nurses, home health aides, clergy or other spiritual counselors, and, often, a social worker. As needed, the team may also include volunteers who are trained to perform specific tasks and occupational, physical, and/or speech therapists.

3. Advance Directives for Health Care: Advance directives for health care are legal documents that clarify a person's health-care wishes. Clients who want to establish advanced directives should be referred to a qualified attorney for assistance.

The **Patient Self-Determination Act** (1991) requires inpatient health-care facilities that receive Medicare or Medicaid funding to notify adult patients of their right to have advance directives (a living will or durable power of attorney) if they want them. Notification must take place when a patient is admitted to a facility and, if a patient has a directive, this fact must be noted on his medical chart.

Living wills allow patients to document in advance the kind of care they want to receive or not receive at the end stage of their lives in the event that they are no longer able to communicate their preferences at that time. A common directive in living wills is a "do not resuscitate" (DNR) statement (called a "no code" in many hospitals and nursing homes). A DNR means the person does not want to receive cardiopulmonary resuscitation if he stops breathing or his heart stops beating.

Because a living will cannot address every eventuality, the patient may also want to designate a family member or friend to be his advocate and have decision-making power if he becomes too ill or impaired (physically or cognitively) to make his own decisions or communicate his medical preferences. A **durable power of attorney for health care** is used to legally designate another person to have the authority to make one's health-care decisions under such circumstances.

N. Substance Use Disorders

Unless otherwise indicated, the terms "substance" or "drug" in this section are meant to refer collectively to alcohol and other drugs of abuse (including illicit drugs and prescription medications that clients may be addicted to). For information on assessment of substance use disorders, see Section VIII of Assessment.

Levels of Care

An important part of intervention with clients who have substance use disorders is identifying the appropriate level of care to facilitate their recovery and, when necessary, protect them from medical complications that may occur when they stop using alcohol or other drugs. Available levels of care include the following:

Outpatient care: Outpatient care, the least intensive level, provides services such as addiction counseling, individual psychotherapy, group intervention (12-Step self-help, support, or psychotherapy groups), family therapy, education, relapse prevention, and continuing care. This usually consists of one to eight hours of treatment per week.

Intensive outpatient care: Intensive outpatient care is more highly structured than regular outpatient care and is recommended for individuals who require daily, rather than weekly or biweekly, support. Because individuals receive from about nine to 60-plus hours of services per week, treatment providers can monitor them closely and intervene quickly to prevent minor problems from interrupting the recovery process. An example of intensive outpatient care is partial hospitalization (day treatment) which usually provides services eight hours a day on five or more days per week.

Non-hospital residential care: Examples of non-hospital residential care include short-term halfway houses and long-term therapeutic communities. Non-hospital residential care is often recommended for individuals who have failed to make progress in less intensive levels of care. Patients are required to live in a treatment setting with other individuals in recovery. In addition, most of these programs have in-house 12-Step groups to help patients develop the habit of regularly attending meetings.

Inpatient care: Inpatient care is generally recommended only for individuals who have not made progress in less intensive levels of care and/or those who have serious problems or impairment. Patients are given 24-hour medical and nursing attention. Treatment usually includes a combination of detoxification and rehabilitation. **Indicators for inpatient care** for clients with substance use disorders include the following: (a) imminent danger to self; (b) significant psychopathology (e.g., depression); (c) serious medical complications; (d) high-risk chemical withdrawal (seizures, delirium tremens); (e) high tolerance to one or more substances; (f) previous attempts at outpatient treatment have failed; (g) an absence of social support; and/or (h) severely impaired social, familial, or occupational functioning. Note that involuntary hospitalization should be avoided, if possible, as it reduces the chances of ongoing treatment compliance.

Stages of Treatment

Most treatments for clients addicted to alcohol or other drugs occur in three stages:

Stage 1 – Treatment for medical complications and comorbid psychiatric disorders: This may consist of supervised chemical detoxification, medical treatment of a medical crisis, and specialized psychological care which may include medication to manage a psychiatric crisis.

Stage 2 – Psychosocial rehabilitation: This may occur on an outpatient basis or in a residential care setting or hospital. Services may include individual psychotherapy, addiction counseling, group therapy, family therapy, education through lectures and classes, participation in 12-Step groups, stress management training, recreational training, vocational rehabilitation counseling, and relapse prevention training.

Stage 3 – Continuing care (aftercare): This is a less intensive form of treatment and is offered when most of the goals of psychosocial rehabilitation have been met.

Goals of Treatment

In most treatment programs, the first goal is to help the client establish a drug-free lifestyle. In an outpatient setting, this may include getting a contract for abstinence from the client. By itself, however, abstinence does not guarantee that a client will go on to function well in his life. Therefore, most treatment programs focus on more than just establishing abstinence, and the following three goals are usually emphasized (Schuckit, 1994): (a) establishing a substance-free lifestyle, (b) maximizing multiple areas of functioning, and (c) relapse prevention.

1. Goal 1 – Establish a Substance-Free Lifestyle: To assist a client in establishing a substance-free lifestyle, you first increase his motivation for abstinence; then, when his activities are no longer focused on using alcohol or other drugs, you help him reconstruct his life (Schuckit, 1989).

a. Increase Motivation for Abstinence: Most research has found that an empathic, nondirective style of interviewing is more effective than a confrontational approach for increasing a client's motivation for change and reducing his resistance (Miller & Rollnick, 1991). The following strategies may be used to increase a client's motivation for abstinence:

Use motivational interviewing: Motivational interviewing (Miller & Rollnick, 2002) is often effective for increasing a client's intrinsic motivation to quit using. Its goal is to help a client develop his own commitment to change his behavior and reach a decision to do so himself.

Set smaller goals and tasks: If a client is feeling hopeless (but not facing a medical or psychiatric emergency), his motivation can be enhanced by initially focusing treatment on smaller goals and tasks.

Engage the client in goal setting: To the greatest extent possible, allow the client to participate in formulating treatment goals and selecting treatment strategies and resources. This tends to elicit greater cooperation and commitment to recovery.

Contract for abstinence: If the client is in an outpatient setting, it may be beneficial to get a contract for abstinence.

b. Reconstruct the Client's Life Without Substances: A number of different strategies can be used to help a client begin building a substance-free lifestyle. They include the following:

Repairing life: Encourage the client to discover new ways of spending his free time, help him restore damaged relationships with family members, urge him to develop relationships with friends who don't use substances, and prepare him to cope with "ordinary" daily life.

Family support: As early as possible, actively enlist the support and cooperation of the client's family members and others who are close to the client.

12-Step meetings: Encourage the client to begin attending 12-Step meetings. Many clients are urged to attend on a daily, or almost daily, basis.

Teach new coping skills: Help the client learn and develop a new set of behaviors for coping.

In addition, you should strongly discourage a client from coming to see you while intoxicated. If a client comes to your office, clinic, or agency under the influence of alcohol or other drugs or withdrawing from alcohol or other drugs, you should respond to the situation using your best judgment. This may entail rescheduling your meeting if the client's condition will prevent meaningful assessment or treatment from occurring. In the case of withdrawal from a substance, you may determine that the client needs medical attention in order to withdraw safely (for example, a client withdrawing from alcohol may be experiencing delirium tremens, or the DTs); if so, you should be as active as you need to be in arranging for the client to receive this care.

Finally, if a client can't comply with a request to come to interviews sober, his substance use disorder may be severe, and he may need hospitalization or some other controlled treatment setting that provides him with structure and safety.

2. Goal 2 – Maximize Multiple Areas of Functioning: The second major goal of addiction treatment is to help clients restore and maximize their functioning in multiple areas of their lives.

a. Medical Functioning: Chronic, heavy use of alcohol or other drugs can lead to serious medical problems including, for some substances, significant levels of physical dependence.

Detoxification programs: Some clients need to participate in **detoxification programs** (in a hospital, in a community-based inpatient program, or via ambulatory or outpatient care). The primary goal of these programs is to withdraw clients safely from alcohol or other drugs. When a withdrawal syndrome, especially a prolonged one, involves problems such as insomnia, anxiety, depression, psychosis, seizure, muscle pain, stomach upset, or drug craving, medications are usually prescribed to control the client's discomfort.

Antabuse: **Antabuse** (Disulfiram) is a biological treatment for alcoholism. When ingested with alcohol, Antabuse is extremely toxic and produces unpleasant responses such as nausea, palpitations, headache, dizziness, flushing, and coma. Antabuse is most effective when it is used in conjunction with other interventions and is typically prescribed at the beginning of treatment. In all cases, a physical examination is required to provide medical clearance for the use of Antabuse.

Methadone: **Methadone** (Dolophine), a synthetic narcotic, is a biological treatment used in heroin detoxification programs. Methadone provides a heroin user with a means of satisfying his physical dependence without providing the psychologically reinforcing positive feelings. Although methadone has been criticized because it is nearly as addictive as heroin, its withdrawal symptoms are milder and the duration of its effects is longer.

Opioid antagonists: Another biological approach is the use of **opioid antagonists**, such as Naltrexone (Trexan), which block the effects of opioid drugs, thereby inhibiting the drugs from producing the desired effects. Naltrexone has also been used successfully to reduce craving for alcohol.

b. Managing Psychiatric Symptoms and Mental Disorders: Although many psychiatric symptoms associated with intoxication or withdrawal diminish quite quickly after the person stops using drugs, in some cases, mild symptoms of depression or anxiety can persist for several months as part of a prolonged abstinence syndrome.

Transient drug-related psychiatric symptoms: For clients with transient drug-related psychiatric symptoms, appropriate interventions usually include suicide risk assessments and precautions, reassurance, and education. In addition, some of these clients require supportive, cognitive, or behavioral treatments until their symptoms diminish.

Co-occurring, independent mental disorders: In other cases, a client with a substance use disorder will also have a co-occurring, independent mental disorder. It can be difficult to establish the presence of such a disorder, however, because a client's psychiatric symptoms (mood, anxiety, psychotic) may be directly caused by his chronic or recent substance use. If these symptoms persist at an intense level after a period of abstinence, this suggests that an independent mental disorder is present. Treatment alternatives for clients with co-occurring disorders (CODs) include the following: (a) If the client has a *severe co-occurring mental disorder* (e.g., a current episode of major depression), it may be necessary to treat this condition first and stabilize the client before beginning treatment for the substance use disorder. (b) If the client has a *non-severe co-occurring mental disorder* (e.g., generalized anxiety disorder), a **sequential approach** is typically used in which the client receives treatment for his substance use disorder first and then for the other mental disorder. On the other hand, if symptoms of the co-occurring mental disorder make it difficult for the client to participate successfully in treatments for his substance use disorder, then **parallel treatment** is more appropriate. In this approach, both disorders are treated simultaneously. Parallel treatment usually occurs through different providers who coordinate their services. (c) A client with *an intense, chronic dual disorder* (e.g., a client with both schizophrenia and a substance use disorder) usually needs to participate in a program that integrates elements of both psychiatric and addiction treatment. This type of program offers an intensive level of care because a qualified client usually has more treatment complications, needs greater medical care, and progresses more slowly than other clients with substance use disorders. (NOTE: The term "dual diagnosis" was traditionally used to describe cases in which clients have both a substance use disorder and a major psychiatric disorder, such as a psychotic or bipolar disorder. The term **co-occurring disorder** has largely replaced the term dual diagnosis or dual disorder. The term co-occurring disorder applies whenever a client has both a substance use disorder and another mental disorder, regardless of the severity of the other mental disorder.)

The use of medication: Some treatments for co-occurring mental disorders (e.g., depression, bipolar disorder, anxiety, schizophrenia) involve the use of medication. Because this presents a risk of treatment conflict with the goal of abstinence from all types of substances, the following considerations and precautions are usually necessary: (a) If at all possible, other treatments should be emphasized (i.e., individual psychotherapy, self-help groups, support groups). (b) Psychoactive drugs should be used only when a client's co-occurring mental disorder is so severe that it seriously threatens his ability to function. (c) The prescribing medical professional should work closely with the client and provide medications with a potential for abuse on a daily basis, rather than in larger quantities. (d) Ideally, medication should be used mainly to reduce extreme symptoms and stabilize the client. During that period, the client should begin other treatments for the mental disorder.

c. *Family Functioning:* Because addressing family problems increases the likelihood that abstinence will be maintained, the client should be helped to restore damaged relationships with family members. Family programs commonly provide the following services: (a) client education about the interplay between the family and substance use disorders; (b) family education about the interplay between the family and substance use disorders; (c) family education about addiction, drugs of abuse, treatment, and recovery; (d) family or couples therapy sessions; and (e) involvement of family members in 12-Step groups for families of individuals with substance use disorders (e.g., Al-Anon, Alateen, Nar-Anon).

d. *Occupational Functioning:* Individuals with substance use disorders often have difficulties related to work and financial planning and management. As necessary, a client in outpatient care should be referred to vocational rehabilitation services and helped to develop patterns of financial planning that will reduce the chances of a future financial crisis.

3. Goal 3 – Relapse Prevention: Relapse prevention (RP), a self-management approach, should be emphasized at all stages of addiction treatment. The most common precipitant of relapse among people recovering from substance use disorders is the experience of anxiety, frustration, depression, or other negative emotional states.

a. Marlatt and Gordon's RPT: Marlatt and Gordon (1985) refer to the typical reaction to relapse as an "**abstinence violation effect**" that involves self-blame, guilt, anxiety, and depression, which lead to an increased susceptibility to further alcohol consumption. They propose that the potential for future relapse is reduced when the person views the episode of drinking as a mistake resulting from specific, external, and controllable factors. Their **relapse prevention therapy** (RPT) involves identifying circumstances that increase the individual's risk for relapse – i.e., situations that elicit negative emotional states, expose the individual to alcohol or alcohol-related cues, or cultivate social pressure to drink – and then implementing behavioral and cognitive strategies that help the individual prevent future lapses and deal more effectively with them if they occur (e.g., coping skills training, cognitive therapy, lifestyle modification).

b. Gorski's Model of Relapse: For Gorski (1989), the major physical correlate of drinking that predisposes a person to relapse is **post-acute withdrawal syndrome** (PAW). This syndrome occurs because a chronic drinker's body adapts over time to the effects of alcohol so that drinking ends up having a normalizing effect on his body. PAW can last for up to three months after cessation of drinking and affects higher level cognitive processes resulting in impaired abstract thinking, concentration, and memory, increased emotionality, and overreaction to stress. Thus, according to Gorski, the cognitive abilities needed for adaptive decision-making are compromised at precisely the time when psychological, behavioral, and social factors are also predisposing a newly sober person to drink.

According to Gorski, evaluation of a client with an alcohol use disorder should include assessment for signs of post-acute withdrawal syndrome using neuropsychological batteries, evaluation of the client's recall of problem-solving strategies and ability to use these strategies in appropriate ways, and determining whether his lifestyle promotes abstinence. Following assessment, you should emphasize the provision of concrete counseling. You should teach the client the warning signs of relapse and explain PAW's effects on cognitive functioning and behavior so that the client will understand the need to minimize stress in his life and self-monitor for warning signs of relapse.

Treatment Modalities and Approaches

The effective treatment of clients with substance use disorders requires you to remain flexible and monitor closely because a client's needs are likely to change over the course of treatment. You should reassess the client on a regular basis, monitor risky behaviors and stressors, track his attendance at 12-Step meetings through signed meeting cards, and conduct random drug tests, if this is indicated.

Because individuals with substance use disorders are a heterogeneous group, each client will respond best to a different type of intervention depending on his specific biopsychosocial needs.

1. Individual Psychotherapy: According to research, no single approach to individual psychotherapy is most effective for addiction treatment, and psychodynamic, behavioral, and cognitive therapies have all been found to provide useful strategies depending on a client's specific needs.

a. Indications for Individual Psychotherapy: Individual psychotherapy can be an important component of treatment for the following types of clients: (a) those whose addictions are accompanied by a co-occurring mental disorder or symptoms of such a disorder (the assumption is that, if a client's psychiatric symptoms, even mild ones, are alleviated, he will have a better chance of becoming and staying substance-free); and (b) those who are resistant to treatment, feel uncomfortable in groups, and/or fear the disclosure of personal or sensitive information.

b. Conditions for Individual Psychotherapy: You typically need to provide more structure and more frequent sessions than in traditional psychotherapy and should give special attention to developing a positive and supportive relationship with the client, formulating clear goals early in treatment, and continually monitoring the client's success with abstinence and compliance with other aspects of treatment. Outcomes are improved when individual psychotherapy is used as just one component of an ongoing, multi-service treatment program that emphasizes eliminating the client's drug use along with treating his psychiatric symptoms.

c. Goals of Individual Psychotherapy: Individual psychotherapy for a client with a substance use disorder should (a) support the goal of helping him stop using alcohol or other drugs, (b) address his addictive behaviors and the thoughts and feelings that seem to promote or maintain his substance use or occur as a result of his use, and (c) address issues and conflicts related to other aspects of his life, now and in the past, under the assumption that these issues and conflicts contribute to his current drug use.

2. Addiction Counseling: Addiction counseling (a.k.a. drug counseling) is the most commonly used psychosocial intervention in substance use disorder treatment programs. Its overall goal is to provide ongoing management of the client as he recovers. Like individual psychotherapy, addiction counseling seeks to help clients deal with drug-related consequences in their lives. However, the approach taken in addiction counseling is more direct, concrete, and specific (e.g., it doesn't address intrapsychic issues or conflicts). The addiction counselor offers support, provides structure, monitors the client's behavior, encourages abstinence, identifies problems and behaviors that contribute to the client's addiction, helps the client handle current problems in his life (especially those related to drug use), and links the client to services that contribute to resolving his problems (e.g., job counseling, medical care, legal assistance). In some treatment models, clients see both an addiction counselor and a psychotherapist, and the providers coordinate their services. The main advantage of this approach is that the counselor is available to address the client's recovery needs, while the psychotherapist focuses on providing psychotherapy.

3. Behavioral Interventions: Behavioral treatments are often one component of a multimodal treatment program. The emphasis is on changing current behavior rather than understanding it. Its goals are to eliminate the behavior maintained by alcohol or drug reinforcement and prevent renewed substance use once abstinence is initiated. Examples of elements that may be included are the following: (a) covert sensitization and other forms of aversive counterconditioning (for alcoholism); (b) training in coping skills and other self-control techniques that teach alternative methods for responding to cues that may trigger a relapse; (c) contingency management in which specific goals are set and incentives and decentives are developed (i.e., consequences that make abstinence attractive and continued drug use relatively unattractive); and (d) skills training that teaches behavioral and cognitive skills such as assertiveness, resisting social pressure, relaxation, stress management, and interpersonal communication.

4. 12-Step Programs: Self-help programs such as Alcoholics Anonymous (AA), Cocaine Anonymous (CA), and Narcotics Anonymous (NA) are almost always a critical part of treatment for substance use disorders, especially when individual psychotherapy is used. For most clients, participation in a 12-step group is expected during all phases of treatment.

a. Assumptions Underlying 12-Step Programs: (a) Alcoholism (addiction) is a disease which, without intervention, will result in death; (b) the only appropriate treatment goal is total abstinence; (c) abstinence is achieved on a day-to-day basis rather than as a life-long commitment; (d) once an alcoholic, always an alcoholic (alcoholism/addiction is a disease that can't be cured, but, instead, is controlled through spiritual change and social support); and (e) an alcoholic (addict) cannot control his drinking (drug use) without support (members are encouraged to abandon their beliefs in self-sufficiency).

b. Program Components: To help members recover and remain abstinent, 12-Step groups use the "12 steps" (which summarize the program's basic assumptions), frequent meetings, a relationship with a sponsor, and the concept of a surrender to a Higher Power.

c. Outcomes: Although some research has suggested that AA is associated with higher dropout rates than other forms of treatments, other studies have found that AA is, at the very least, more effective than no treatment. In addition, although AA is usually effective only for individuals who are motivated to recover, this is consistent with AA's goal to help only those with drinking problems who want to stop drinking.

d. Alternatives to 12-Step Programs (Other Available Support Groups): Self-Management and Recovery Training (SMART) and Secular Organizations for Sobriety (SOS) both adopt a science-based, self-empowerment approach to abstinence and recovery, and either one can be a useful alternative to a 12-Step program, especially for a client who is uncomfortable with the spiritual content 12-Step meetings (e.g., reliance on a Higher Power). SMART, for example, teaches cognitive-behavioral tools and techniques to facilitate four areas of self-directed change: building and maintaining motivation to abstain; coping with urges; problem-solving (managing thoughts, feelings, and behaviors); and lifestyle balance (balancing momentary and enduring satisfactions).

5. Group Therapy: The use of group therapy is recommended when a client lacks a positive social support system and is beyond the initial stages of detoxification. Group therapy offers clients an opportunity to resolve problems in a social context and, therefore, can address goals that can't be addressed in individual psychotherapy or addiction counseling.

6. Family Therapy: Family therapy by itself is inadequate for clients with serious substance use disorders but frequently is an important adjunct to other treatments. Family treatment is particularly indicated when the client lives with his family.

a. Key Concepts: Most approaches to family therapy rely on general systems and cybernetics concepts, which, over time, have been applied to the treatment of chemically dependent family systems:

Family as a system: The family is regarded as a system, with each member representing a component of the larger system. Addiction is understood as a functional or structural imbalance in the system rather than as a problem belonging to the addicted family member only, and treatment emphasizes resolving the imbalance.

Homeostasis: Families have a built-in mechanism (a feedback loop) that serves to restore their homeostasis, or balance, when it has been disrupted. The result is that the family is returned to its previous level of functioning. Homeostasis doesn't necessarily reflect a healthy underlying structure: When a problem like a chronic substance use disorder is successfully treated, homeostasis is disrupted and family members may use dysfunctional means to restore it (e.g., they may bring alcohol into the house when a recovering member is trying to stay sober). When chemical addiction is serving a homeostatic function for the family, treatment will emphasize restructuring the family's sense of balance after abstinence disrupts that balance.

Identified patient: Whatever the symptom, a family therapist will work to shift the family's focus of attention from the identified patient to the distress or dysfunction of the family as a whole. When the presenting problem is a family member with a substance use disorder, the therapist emphasizes and works with the "alcoholic or addicted family" rather than "the alcoholic or addict and his family."

b. *Phases of Family Therapy:* Regardless of the model selected, therapy with the family (or couple) usually begins with a thorough assessment of how and how much the client's substance use disorder has affected the family. Family treatment then generally involves three phases: (a) Developing a system for establishing a substance-free state for the client; (b) selecting a workable method of family treatment; and (c) addressing the family's readjustment after drug use has stopped. In particular, after the client has stopped using drugs, the family may pass through a "honeymoon" phase when they deny all major conflicts. Alternatively, when the client becomes abstinent, previously ignored family problems may come into focus. Consistent with the concept of homeostasis, if these problems are not addressed, the family will deal with them by encouraging the client to return to his drug use. In these cases, long-term family therapy may be indicated to ensure that true, second-order change occurs within the family.

7. Harm Reduction: Harm reduction refers to a set of interventions and policies intended to reduce the negative consequences of high-risk behaviors. For alcohol and other drug use, harm reduction is an alternative treatment approach that views the reduction of harm as a legitimate goal for substance users. Rather than requiring abstinence, harm reduction attempts to meet clients "where they are" and, therefore, incorporates a range of strategies, from safer use, to controlled or managed use, to abstinence.

a. *Principles of Harm Reduction Practice:* The key principles of harm reduction (HR) practice include the following:

- HR accepts that alcohol and other drug use exists and focuses on minimizing its harmful effects, rather than on judging or condemning drug use or drug users. A basic tenet of HR is that there has never been and never will be a drug-free society.

- HR does not attempt to minimize or ignore the harm associated with drug use. It understands drug use as a complex issue that encompasses a range of behaviors from severe abuse to total abstinence and acknowledges that some ways of using drugs are safer than others.

- HR considers the quality of individual and community life and well-being (e.g., reductions in rates of suffering, disease, death, and crime) as the criteria for successful drug-related interventions and policies. In other words, "success" doesn't require the elimination of drug use.

- HR advocates using education, prevention, and treatment to reduce harm from drugs and drug use. HR recognizes that many different interventions may work, but asserts that interventions must always be based on science, compassion, and human rights.

- HR advocates for the nonjudgmental, noncoercive provision of services and resources to people who use drugs and the communities where they live in order to assist them in reducing harm.

- HR identifies drugs users themselves as the primary change agents for reducing the harms of their drug use and seeks to empower drug users to share information and support one another in strategies that meet their own conditions of use.

- HR recognizes that poverty, racism, social isolation, trauma, gender-based discrimination, and other social inequalities affect people's vulnerability to and capacity for effectively dealing with drug-related harm.

- HR seeks to reduce the harms of drug policies that rely on interdiction. These harms include the arrest and incarceration of users and the proliferation, sale, and use of adulterated "black-market" drugs.

b. Harm Reduction Therapy for Alcohol and Other Drug Use: Harm reduction therapy (HRT) is a nonjudgmental approach to helping people with alcohol and other drug problems reduce the negative impact of drug use in their lives. It addresses the psychological, emotional, social, and occupational implications and impacts of drug use:

- HRT is based on the principles of collaboration, respect, and self-determination.

- HRT is based on the belief that drug problems develop in individuals through an interaction of biophysical, psychological, and social factors. HRT practitioners assume that people use drugs for a variety of different reasons.

- The goals of a client seeking HRT can range from abstinence to controlled (safer) use. That is, in HRT any treatment goal that helps reduce harm to the client is valid, and abstinence is just one of several available goals. In this way, treatment is tailored to fit the client rather than requiring the client to fit a treatment approach.

- HRT assumes that both the client's drug use and his chosen treatment goals are based on an evolution of his desire to improve his health, relationships, and overall functioning.

HRT models are used in a variety of service delivery settings, including outpatient settings, residential treatment, homeless programs, traditional drug treatment programs, medical settings, and community outreach programs.

c. Other Harm Reduction Strategies: Within communities, harm reduction strategies and programs include heroin maintenance programs (e.g., providing users with medical prescriptions for pharmaceutical heroin, or diamorphine); needle and syringe exchange programs; DanceSafe (a nonprofit group in which volunteers at raves and similar events perform free tests on pills that participants bought on the assumption that they contained MDMA); and HAMS. HAMS is a free, peer-led support and informational group for people who want to reduce harms associated with their drinking habits. HAMS information and support are available via the Internet and in live meetings. The acronym HAMS stands for Harm Reduction, Abstinence, and Moderation Support.

Other applications of harm reduction include safer-sex education programs for adolescents and pre-teens and programs for people who are at risk of harming themselves through behaviors such as cutting. The latter programs focus on education and the provision of medical services for wounds and other negative consequences with the goal of moderating the harmful behavior and keeping people safe as they learn new methods of coping.

8. Employee Assistance Programs: An employee assistance program (EAP) is a voluntary, work-based program that offers free and confidential assessments, short-term counseling, referrals, and follow-up services to employees who have personal or work-related problems. EAPs address a broad range of issues affecting mental and emotional well-being and job performance, including not only substance use disorders but also other psychological disorders, stress, grief, and family problems. EAPs may also help organizations prevent and cope with workplace violence, trauma, and other emergency response situations.

Treatments for Tobacco Use Disorder

There is evidence that a smoking cessation intervention increases the likelihood of long-term abstinence when it includes three elements: (a) nicotine replacement therapy; (b) multicomponent behavioral therapy that includes, for example, skills training, relapse prevention, stimulus control, and/or rapid smoking; and (c) support and assistance from a clinician (APA, 1996). Options for medication include nicotine replacement with gum, patches, or electronic cigarettes, the antidepressant bupropion (Zyban), and the prescription medication varenicline (Chantix). Clients taking Chantix must be warned that it may lower their ability to tolerate alcohol and is linked to a rare risk of seizures.

O. Treatment for Various DSM-5 Disorders

1. Intellectual Disability: Interventions for persons with intellectual disability emphasize providing education and training that enhance the skills needed to live productively and independently. Education is often supplemented by behavioral techniques targeting communication skills, self-control, adaptive functioning, and aggressiveness, self-stimulating and self-injurious behaviors; supported employment; and interventions that provide parents and other family members with support in accepting and adapting to the client's disability (often including help with identifying and using community resources). Medication is sometimes used to manage some of the behaviors associated with intellectual disability (e.g., aggressiveness, self-injurious behaviors).

2. Childhood-Onset Fluency Disorder (Stuttering): Childhood-onset fluency disorder may be alleviated, especially in young children, by reducing psychological stress at home: Parents can be instructed to stop reprimanding their child when he stutters, to generally reduce their demands, and to help their child learn to cope with frustration.

For older children and adults, **habit reversal training** has been found to be effective. It was originally designed as a treatment for nervous habits and motor tics and incorporates awareness, relaxation, motivation, competing response, and generalization training. For stuttering, the competing response is regulated breathing which requires the individual to stop speaking when stuttering is anticipated, to take a deep diaphragmatic breath by exhaling the remaining air in his lungs, to inhale slowly while consciously relaxing the muscles in his throat and chest and mentally formulating the words to be spoken, to start speaking as he begins to exhale, and to exhale smoothly and slowly (Ryckman, 2008). May also require a referral for speech therapy.

3. Autism Spectrum Disorder: Interventions incorporate a variety of strategies including parent management training, special education, training in self-care and social interaction skills, and vocational training and placement using sheltered workshops and supported employment. Shaping and discrimination training are behavioral techniques that were originally used by Lovaas in the 1960s, and they continue to be used to improve communication skills. Applied behavior analysis (ABA) is used in many schools and treatment clinics; it encourages positive behaviors and discourages negative ones in order to improve a variety of skills and includes carefully tracking the child's progress. Medication is sometimes used to manage certain behaviors associated with autism (hyperactivity, stereotypical behaviors, withdrawal, aggression). Parents must be supported and assisted to develop coping strategies needed to live with and parent a child who has autism spectrum disorder. They should also be encouraged toward active participation in their child's classroom program.

4. ADHD: Methylphenidate (Ritalin) and other central nervous stimulants have beneficial effects on the core symptoms of ADHD in about 75 percent of cases (Swanson et al., 1993), and these drugs appear to be effective not only for children but also for adults with this disorder.

There is also evidence that behavioral interventions are effective for reducing the symptoms of ADHD. Parent training in child behavior management and teacher training in classroom management are two commonly used interventions and involve training parents or teachers in the use of positive reinforcement, time-out, and other behavioral strategies (Barkley, 2002b). In addition, **self-directed strategies** (self-instruction, self-monitoring, self-reinforcement) have been found effective for helping children with ADHD gain more control over their own behavior and academic performance while relying less on support from parents, teachers, and peers: (a) *Self-instruction* is used to train children to complete tasks: First, a practitioner models a task approach by stating thoughts aloud before each action; second, the child duplicates this approach; third, the child gradually reduces the volume of each thought statement; and finally, the child makes each thought statement covertly while completing the task. (b) *Self-monitoring* involves having children observe and record the occurrence of their own behaviors. (c) *Self-reinforcement* involves teaching children to track and assess their own performance and provide appropriate feedback to themselves.

5. Specific Learning Disorder: Educational therapies are the treatment of choice for specific learning disorders. These interventions appear to be most beneficial when they adopt an individualized approach that begins with a careful assessment of the child's strengths and weaknesses.

6. Tourette's Disorder: The treatment of Tourette's disorder usually includes pharmacotherapy, and the antipsychotic drugs haloperidol and pimozide have been studied most extensively and have been found to be effective in about 80 percent of cases. A drawback of their use is the potential for negative side-effects, which many patients find intolerable (Shapiro & Shapiro, 1993). In addition, an SSRI is usually useful for alleviating the obsessive-compulsive symptoms that often accompany this disorder. Note that, because psychostimulant drugs have been found to increase tics in some individuals, the hyperactivity and inattention that often accompany Tourette's disorder are often treated, instead, with clonidine (which is usually used to treat hypertension) or desipramine (an antidepressant). Finally, comprehensive behavioral treatment for tics (CBIT) is an evidence-based treatment for children and adults with Tourette's disorder and incorporates habit reversal training, relaxation training, and psychoeducation (e.g., Piacentini et al., 2010; Wilhelm et al., 2012).

7. Schizophrenia: The introduction of the antipsychotic drugs in the 1950s is considered the most important development in the treatment of schizophrenia, and their use is credited with reducing both hospitalization and relapse rates (see Appendix II in Assessment for information on these drugs). The effectiveness of an antipsychotic drug is enhanced when pharmacotherapy is combined with individual cognitive-behavioral therapy, psychoeducation, social skills training, supported employment, and other interventions for the person with schizophrenia and psychosocial interventions for the family. Family-based interventions are particularly beneficial when they target high levels of **expressed emotion** (EE) among family members, which have been linked to high relapse and rehospitalization rates for people with schizophrenia (e.g., Kavanagh, 1992). High-EE is characterized by open criticism and hostility toward the client or, alternatively, overprotectiveness and emotional overinvolvement.

Specific interventions for the acute, stabilization, and stable phases of schizophrenia include the following (American Psychiatric Association, 2004):

Acute phase: The primary goals of treatment during the acute phase of schizophrenia are to reduce stressful or overstimulating relationships, events, and environments and promote relaxation. Achieving these goals requires providing the client with a structured and predictable environment, simple and clear communications and expectations, low performance requirements, and a nondemanding, supportive relationship with the therapist; and giving the client and his family information on the nature and management of schizophrenia as appropriate to the client's capacity to understand information. The family should also be provided with information about community resources and organizations.

Stabilization phase: In the stabilization phase (which follows right after an acute illness episode), the goals are to reduce stress on the client, provide support to minimize the likelihood of relapse, enhance the client's adaptation to life in the community, and facilitate the process of recovery and ongoing reduction of symptoms. Interventions include offering the client psychoeducation about the course and outcome of schizophrenia and factors that influence its course and outcome (including treatment adherence); and promoting his adjustment to life in the community through setting realistic goals. The therapist should encourage the client to be involved in community-based activities and rehabilitation services, but must not exert undue pressure on him to perform at high levels either socially or vocationally because this may produce stress that increases the risk of relapse. If the medication regimen initiated during the acute phase has proved effective, the regimen and monitoring are usually continued for at least six months.

Stable phase: For a client in the stable phase, the goals are to sustain symptom remission or control, maintain or improve his level of functioning and quality of life, and ensure that any increases in symptoms, relapses, or adverse medication side-effects are properly treated. The selection of psychosocial interventions is based on the individual client's needs and social context. Among the psychosocial interventions that have demonstrated effectiveness in this phase are **social skills training** to address functional impairments in social skills or activities of daily living and supported employment to improve vocational functioning.

8. Bipolar I Disorder: Treatment for bipolar disorder usually includes the mood stabilizer **lithium**. For people who don't respond to lithium, an anti-seizure drug such as carbamazepine may be effective; and, for those experiencing acute mania, an antipsychotic drug may be used. An antidepressant may also be prescribed to treat depressive symptoms. However, there is some risk that an antidepressant will trigger a manic episode when combined with a mood stabilizer, with the risk being greater for the TCAs than the SSRIs (Gijsman et al., 2004).

Unfortunately, lithium compliance is a frequent problem, with studies showing that patients who discontinue taking lithium often do so because they feel better and think medication is unnecessary, are unwilling to give up the "highs" of mania, or do not like the drug's side-effects. There is evidence that compliance with drug treatment and overall treatment effectiveness are enhanced when pharmacotherapy is combined with a psychosocial intervention (e.g., Craighead, Miklowitz, Frank, & Vajk, 2002). Interventions that have been found effective for bipolar disorder include cognitive-behavioral therapy (CBT), family-focused treatment (FFT), and interpersonal and social rhythm therapy (IPSRT) (Miklowitz et al., 2007).

9. Major Depressive Disorder: Treatment for depression often consists of a combination of an antidepressant and psychotherapy. Antidepressant treatments are normally continued for several months following resolution of a major depressive episode to prevent relapse.

Beck's cognitive therapy is based on the assumption that depressive symptoms can be eliminated by altering the cognitions that underlie them. Considerable research has supported the effectiveness of cognitive therapy, especially for mild to moderate episodes of depression. Generally, in the earlier phases of treatment and in the treatment of the more severely depressed patients, the behavioral techniques of Beck's cognitive therapy are likely to be more useful than the strictly cognitive interventions. Because it is often necessary to concentrate initially on restoring the client's functioning to the premorbid level, techniques such as scheduling activities, assigning graded tasks, and behavioral rehearsal are given more attention than identifying and modifying dysfunctional cognitions.

From the perspective of **interpersonal therapy** (IPT), depression is caused and maintained by interpersonal problems that are the result of disturbances during early development, especially during the attachment stage (Klerman et al., 1984). The focus of IPT is on current relationships, and specific problems addressed during therapy include grief reactions, interpersonal disputes, difficult role transitions, and interpersonal deficits.

Finally, electroconvulsive therapy (ECT) is not often used but has been found effective for very severe endogenous forms of depression that involve delusions or suicidal ideation or that have not responded to antidepressants. The primary undesirable effects of ECT are temporary anterograde and retrograde amnesia, confusion, and disorientation, but these effects may be reduced by administering ECT unilaterally to the right (nondominant) hemisphere (McCall et al., 2000).

10. Separation Anxiety Disorder: Treatment for separation anxiety disorder ordinarily includes systematic desensitization or other behavioral intervention and, for older children and adolescents, cognitive approaches (e.g., identifying and replacing negative self-statements). When the disorder includes school refusal, a primary goal of treatment is an immediate return to school to avoid academic failure, social isolation, and other secondary impairments (First & Tasman, 2010).

11. Specific Phobia: The treatment-of-choice for specific phobia is exposure with response prevention (especially in vivo exposure) that exposes the individual to the feared object or situation while preventing him from engaging in cognitive or behavioral avoidance (Wolitzky-Taylor, Horowitz, Powers, & Telch, 2008). Refer to Section XI in this chapter for more information on in vivo exposure with response prevention (**flooding and systematic desensitization**).

12. Social Anxiety Disorder: Exposure with response prevention has been found to be effective for social anxiety disorder, and its benefits may be enhanced when it is combined with social skills training or cognitive restructuring and other cognitive techniques. Treatment may also include an SSRI or SNRI or the beta-blocker propranolol, which reduces the physical symptoms of anxiety and is particularly effective for treating performance anxiety (Blasey, Belanoff, DeBattista, & Schatzberg, 2013).

13. Panic Disorder: Cognitive behavioral interventions that incorporate exposure are the treatment-of-choice for panic disorder. For example, **panic control therapy** (PCT) is a brief treatment that incorporates psychoeducation, relaxation training, cognitive restructuring, and interoceptive exposure (exposure to the physical sensations associated with panic attacks). Panic disorder is also responsive to imipramine and other TCAs, SSRIs, SNRIs, and benzodiazepines. However, the risk for relapse is high when drug treatment is used alone, with 30 to 70 percent of patients experiencing a return of symptoms within months of discontinuing the drug (Mavissakalian, Perel, & DeGroot, 1993).

14. Agoraphobia: Treatments for agoraphobia are most effective when they incorporate in vivo exposure with response prevention (**flooding**). The research is not entirely consistent with regard to whether graded exposure that begins with the least feared situations or intensive (ungraded) exposure that begins with the most feared situations is most effective, but there is some evidence that the two types have similar short-term effects but that intensive exposure has better long-term effects (Feigenbaum, 1988).

15. Generalized Anxiety Disorder (GAD): Treatment for GAD normally involves cognitive-behavioral therapy; and, for many individuals, a combination of cognitive-behavioral therapy and pharmacotherapy is most beneficial. Drugs that have been found useful for GAD include the SSRIs and SNRIs or, when the individual is nonresponsive to an antidepressant, a benzodiazepine or the anxiolytic buspirone (Buspar).

16. Obsessive-Compulsive Disorder (OCD): A combination of exposure with response prevention (e.g., a client delays washing his hands for a period of time to allow his anxiety to decrease on its own without his ritual) and the tricyclic clomipramine or an SSRI is usually the treatment-of-choice for OCD. Exposure is often supplemented with thought stopping or other interventions that directly target obsessions. Because antidepressants are associated with a high risk for relapse once the drug is discontinued, they are rarely used alone.

When systematically applied, exposure with response prevention results in habituation of anxiety associated with obsessions so that rituals are no longer needed to reduce anxiety. Treatment eventually serves to reduce anxiety and dysfunction, but clients should be told that their anxiety level is likely to *increase* during initial exposure sessions (i.e., the reduction of ritualistic behaviors that takes place early in treatment is often accompanied by short-term increases in anxiety and obsessions).

17. PTSD: The treatment-of-choice for PTSD is a comprehensive cognitive-behavioral intervention that incorporates exposure, cognitive restructuring, and anxiety management or similar techniques. An SSRI is often prescribed to reduce comorbid depression or anxiety; and, for some patients it may reduce the symptoms of PTSD, although the risk for relapse is high when the drug is discontinued (e.g., Davidson et al., 2001).

Cognitive incident stress debriefing (CISD) and eye movement desensitization and reprocessing (EMDR) have been used to treat PTSD but are controversial: CISD involves providing treatment to the victims of a trauma within 72 hours of the event whether or not they have exhibited symptoms and is usually administered during a single lengthy session. Research on its effects has found that it may actually worsen symptoms (Litz et al., 2002; Rose, Bisson, & Wessely, 2001). EMDR has been found to have beneficial effects but there is evidence that they are due to exposure and other nonspecific factors rather than eye movements (Foa & Meadows, 1997; Seidler & Wagner, 2006).

18. Anorexia Nervosa: The first priority is to assess risk and refer to a physican for medical clearance. Treatment of anorexia should focus on gettingt the individual to gain weight in order to avoid or curtail medical complications. This may require hospitalization and often entails the use of contingency management that makes rewards contingent on maintaining weight at a minimal level. Individual, group, and/or family therapies are then used to ensure that initial weight gains are maintained.

In terms of individual therapy, cognitive-behavioral therapy is generally considered the treatment-of-choice. The cognitive-behavioral approach of Garner and his colleagues (Garner & Bemis, 1985; Garner, Vitousek, & Pike, 1997) emphasizes modifying the individual's dysfunctional beliefs about weight and food, including the value of being thin and the consequences of eating, and involves the following stages: (a) establishing a positive therapeutic alliance and enhancing the client's motivation; (b) normalizing the client's eating patterns and body weight (e.g., by having the client self-monitor his daily caloric intake and eating behaviors and thoughts and feelings elicited by those behaviors and using techniques to modify the client's eating pattern); (c) identifying, evaluating, and modifying the client's beliefs about weight and food using Socratic questioning, decatastrophizing, and other cognitive techniques; and (d) preparing the client for termination of therapy and identifying ways for preventing relapse (e.g., by developing a plan for dealing with the reemergence of symptoms).

Finally, family-based treatments have also been found to be effective for anorexia. However, there is evidence that a high level of expressed emotion (negative and critical attitudes and comments) among family members is associated with an increased risk for relapse (Butzlaff & Hooley, 1998) and that family therapy is more effective when families with high expressed emotion receive separated family therapy (in which parents are seen separately from the patient with anorexia) rather than conjoint family therapy (Eisler et al., 2000).

19. Bulimia Nervosa: The key objectives of treatment include helping the individual gain control over symptomatic eating behaviors and modifying dysfunctional beliefs about eating, shape, and weight. Treatments usually incorporate nutritional counseling and cognitive-behavioral techniques such as self-monitoring, stimulus control, cognitive restructuring, problem-solving, and self-distraction during periods of high-risk for binge eating. Imipramine and fluoxetine have been found effective for reducing binge eating and purging and improving dysphoria. However, comparisons of cognitive-behavioral therapy and antidepressants have generally found the former to be associated with lower relapse and treatment dropout rates (e.g., Agras et al., 1992).

20. Enuresis: The most common treatment for enuresis is the **bell-and-pad** (also known as the night, moisture, urine, or enuresis alarm), which causes a bell to ring when the sleeping child begins to urinate. The night alarm has been found effective in up to 80 percent of cases, although about one-third of children exhibit some degree of relapse within six months of the initial treatment (Forsythe & Butler, 1989). The effectiveness of the night alarm may be increased when it is combined with other behavioral techniques such behavioral rehearsal or overcorrection. Although imipramine reduces wetting frequency in 85 percent of cases and suppresses wetting entirely in 30 percent of cases, most children relapse within three months after discontinuing the drug. Research investigating the usefulness of desmopressin, a synthetic version of an antidiuretic hormone, has shown that it also has good short-term, but poor long-term, effects (Mellon & Houts, 2006).

21. Encopresis: Common treatments for encopresis include behavioral-educational interventions including teaching the child and parents about the disorder, establishing a program of consistent toilet use, and providing the child with positive reinforcement for appropriate toilet use. The use of mild punishment, such as requiring the child to clean his clothing after a soiling event, is also advocated by some experts. There is some evidence that behavioral techniques are more effective when they are combined with medical management of the disorder.

22. Insomnia Disorder: The primary non-pharmacological treatment for insomnia disorder is a cognitive-behavioral approach that incorporates several strategies including the following: (a) **Sleep-hygiene education** provides guidelines for improving sleep-related behaviors (e.g., avoiding napping during the day, avoiding caffeine and alcohol in the evenings, avoiding strenuous physical and mental activity just before bedtime). (b) Stimulus control is used to strengthen the bed and bedroom as cues for sleep and weaken them as cues for other activities and includes instructing the client to go to bed only when tired, to use the bed only for sleep and sexual activity, to get out of bed and go to another room if still awake 20 minutes after going to bed, and to get up at about the same time each morning. (c) Relaxation training (e.g., progressive muscle relaxation or guided imagery) is used to reduce anxiety and stress and promote mental and physical relaxation. (d) Cognitive therapy is used to correct faulty attitudes and beliefs about sleep and counterproductive sleep strategies.

23. Sexual Dysfunction: The first step in the treatment of a suspected sexual dysfunction should always be referral for a medical evaluation. For erectile disorder, a complete absence of erections during REM sleep suggests an organic etiology. If it is determined that the disorder is due to psychogenic (emotional or mental) factors, treatment ordinarily includes the use of cognitive-behavioral techniques that have, for the most part, been derived from the work of Masters and Johnson (1970). The targets of these techniques are the dysfunctional behaviors themselves, related anxiety (e.g., performance anxiety), faulty attitudes and beliefs, and deficient knowledge and skills. The drug sildenafil citrate (Viagra) is often prescribed for this disorder. Although it does not affect a man's sexual desire, it increases his ability to maintain an erection.

Overall, sex therapy has been found to be most successful for premature ejaculation and genito-pelvic pain/penetration disorder (previously vaginismus). Commonly used techniques include **sensate focus**, which is used to treat various sexual dysfunctions and helps reduce performance anxiety, and the start-stop and squeeze techniques, which are used to treat premature ejaculation and are designed to increase the man's control over the ejaculatory reflex. Premature ejaculation has been linked to low serotonin levels, and the SSRIs have been found to be effective for some individuals (Althof et al., 2010).

24. Conduct Disorder: Interventions for conduct-disordered (or delinquent) youth are most effective when they target preadolescents (rather than adolescents); emphasize behavioral change, skills acquisition, social learning and modeling, and taking responsibility for one's behaviors; and include family intervention. With regard to the latter, Patterson and his colleagues (1992) have developed **parent management training** (PMT), which teaches parents to reward the positive behaviors of their children and replace using physical punishment for undesirable behaviors with time-out, response cost, and similar techniques. **Multisystemic treatment** (MST) is an alternative approach that targets the individual, family, school, and community and combines behavioral, cognitive, family systems, and case-management strategies (Borduin et al., 1995).

Outpatient psychotherapies that promote insight and emotional expression should be avoided because they tend to increase aggressiveness in this population. In addition, using medication to manage behavioral symptoms is not recommended because clients with conduct disorder need to take responsibility for their behavior and, if possible, develop internal controls. Medication may be used, however, to manage symptoms of a co-existing disorder such as major depression or ADHD.

25. Neurocognitive Disorders: Interventions for delirium have two primary goals: treatment of the underlying cause of the disorder and reduction of agitated behaviors. The second goal is addressed by a combination of environmental manipulation (providing an environment that minimizes disorientation) and psychosocial interventions (e.g., having a calm, friendly family or staff member stay with the patient). In addition, haloperidol or other antipsychotic drug may help reduce agitation, delusions, and hallucinations.

Interventions for **Alzheimer's disease** often include a combination of group therapy (especially therapy that emphasizes reality orientation and reminiscence); behavioral techniques and antipsychotic drugs to reduce agitation; antidepressant drugs to alleviate depression; and environmental manipulation and pharmacotherapy to enhance memory and cognitive functioning. With regard to the latter, drugs such as tacrine (Cognex) and donepezil (Aricept) are useful for reversing cognitive impairment and improving some behavioral symptoms in individuals with mild to moderate Alzheimer's disease, but they do not cure the disorder and improvements are only temporary. Finally, outcomes are best for patients when they remain at home with their families, and families are less likely to institutionalize a family member with Alzheimer's disease when families are provided with adequate support, psychoeducation, skills training, and other individual and family interventions (e.g., Mittelman, Epstein, & Pierzchala, 2003; Mittelman, Haley, Clay, & Roth, 2006).

26. Antisocial Personality Disorder: When feasible, residential treatment should be the primary modality for clients with antisocial personality disorder since controlled and structured settings are associated with more favorable treatment outcomes.

Individual psychotherapeutic relationships are almost never effective for changing antisocial behavior, and this is true even when external controls such as a court order are in place. Generally, approaches that reinforce appropriate behaviors and attempt to make connections between the client's actions and feelings have the highest likelihood of being effective. Usually the content of therapy focuses on the client's emotions (or lack thereof) including the discovery and labeling of appropriate emotional states (e.g., ones other than anger or frustration). As the client learns to experience various emotional states, one of the first may be depression. The client will probably be unfamiliar with feelings of depression, and the therapist working with him should be supportive and empathetic when these feelings come up. Reinforcing the client's appropriate emotions is often beneficial, as well, and, usually, the client's experiencing intense affect is a sign of progress in therapy.

Suggestions for managing **resistance** in clients with a history of antisocial behavior include the following: (a) Explore the client's fear of change or concerns about the consequences of changing. The client is likely to view his symptomatic behavior as adaptive (ego syntonic); therefore, to increase motivation for change, you often need to make his antisocial behavior ego dystonic. One effective way of doing this is to help the client see how his behavior is self-destructive (this approach is also effective for actually changing the client's behaviors). (b) Explore and confront or interpret active resistance. (c) Consider the use of appropriate incentives and rewards. (d) When resistance is severe and/or accompanied by dangerous behavior, consider admission to an inpatient treatment facility. Experts recommended terminating treatment only if the client's resistance continues after the therapist has tried all other available solutions such as those listed above.

Participating in group therapy can be effective for increasing motivation to change in some clients with a history of antisocial behavior. These groups should consist of individuals with the same or similar symptoms. Finally, no research has suggested that any medication is effective in the treatment of antisocial personality disorder itself. Medications should only be used to treat clear, acute, and serious co-occurring mental disorders.

27. Borderline Personality Disorder: Individuals with borderline personality disorder are very demanding to work with and tend to form very intense relationships with their therapists. One approach to the treatment of borderline personality disorder is Linehan's (1987) **dialectical behavior therapy** (DBT), which is reviewed in Section XI of this chapter. Research on DBT has confirmed that it reduces premature termination from therapy, psychiatric hospitalizations, and parasuicidal behaviors (e.g., Linehan et al., 2006). In addition, medication is sometimes used as part of the treatment plan for borderline personality disorder (e.g., neuroleptics for disturbances in cognition, lithium for mood swings, MAOIs or other antidepressants for depression, or anxiolytics for anxiety).

XVI. Case Recording and Managed Care, and E-Therapy

Social work records demonstrate and encourage the quality of client services. A case record is written by the social worker and comprised of information about a client, his situation, and the services provided during intervention.

A. Case Recording

1. Guidelines Concerning Case Records: Case records can be subpoenaed, and clients and other personnel have access to them. Therefore, it's important for social workers (and agencies that employ them) to develop and apply policies and practices that provide as much confidentiality as possible.

As a social worker, you should adhere to the following guidelines concerning case records (Hepworth et al., 2006):

- Maintain and update case records to ensure they are accurate, relevant, timely, and complete.
- Record only what it essential to the functions of the agency.
- Identify observed facts and distinguish them from opinions.
- Use descriptive terms, not professional jargon.
- Do not record unverified medical or psychiatric diagnoses.
- Do not record details of clients' intimate lives. Instead, describe intimate problems in general terms. Do not include verbatim process recordings in case files.
- Do not remove case files from your agency except under extraordinary circumstances and with special authorization.
- Keep case files in locked filing cabinets and give keys only to personnel who need frequent access to the files. Take similar precautions to protect data stored electronically (e.g., require passwords).
- Do not leave case files on desks or in other public areas within the agency where others may be able to access to them. Do not keep case information on computer screens where others may see it.
- Take precautions to ensure that information transmitted through the use of computers, e-mail, fax, voice mail, answering machines, and other technology is secure. Do not convey identifying information.

2. Recording Procedures: A number of recording procedures used by social workers are described below.

a. Diagnostic Summary Recording: Diagnostic summary recording (Hamilton, 1946) was designed to individualize the client and the intervention process. According to Hamilton, a social worker's record-keeping skills resulted from her ever-increasing understanding of clients and improved professional competence, and, thus, record-keeping skills had to be learned through social work practice. For Hamilton, intervention entailed ongoing psychosocial assessment of the client in search of information significant to successful treatment and effective record-keeping. In this way, record keeping was a developmental process of recording, rather than a final product, and the record itself could only be as good as the intervention it documented. Although diagnostic summary recording had a significant influence on early social casework recording, diagnostic summaries tend to vary widely in their content and organization, and many contemporary social workers find diagnostic summary recording to be ineffective in today's complex social agencies.

b. Process Recording: **Process recording** is a detailed method of recording that is often used to help new social workers and social work students learn practice skills. More experienced workers may use process recording when they are having unusual problems with a client and want to maintain a detailed record that can be examined by a supervisor, consultant, or peers. In this way, the record can serve as a basis for assisting a social worker with suggestions on how she might overcome these problems. Experienced social workers may also use process recording for one or two cases in their caseload as a way of further developing their practice skills and self-awareness. Otherwise, however, most practitioners consider process recording to be too time consuming to use in daily intervention.

Early process recording (1920s) entailed documenting word-for-word what the social worker and client said in each meeting. Today, process recording is a system for recording information about social worker-client interactions during treatment. It does not require verbatim documentation of client-worker interactions. Rather, the case record begins with face-sheet information about the client and relevant social, physical, and economic data. A description of the presenting problem follows and includes all data the social worker has gathered about the client's problem. The record then contains the worker's description of treatment objectives, obstacles to achieving the objectives, means to reaching them, and, when relevant, a contract signed by the worker and client. Next, the record contains entries for each contact the client makes with the worker and agency, including not only face-to-face contacts but also telephone contacts and contacts with family members. The entries include the date and time of the contact and a summary of information obtained, including the worker's subjective impressions.

For teaching and training purposes, a social work student's process recording for a session may include the following elements: the date, location, and length of the session; the names of those who attended the session; the purpose of the session; her plan for the session; a description of interaction and content (e.g., topics discussed, information obtained, significant exchanges, mood and feeling tone of the session); her role and activities (e.g., techniques and skills used); her assessment of the client's problem, concern, or situation; her assessment of the client's response to her and the helping process; her assessment of her own performance during the session (including strengths and limitations and problems encountered); and her plan for the next interview or meeting with the client.

c. Person-Oriented Recording: Some social workers and agencies use person-oriented recording to maintain accountable and goal-oriented documentations of their interventions with a client. The record is a variation of the problem-oriented record (see below) and contains a database, treatment plan, assessment, progress notes, and a progress review. The latter entry allows a social worker to evaluate a client's progress over specified periods of time (e.g., every two weeks).

d. Problem-Oriented Recording: **Problem-oriented recording** (POR) is used in many medical and mental-health settings, including social agencies. It is an efficient method of record-keeping that is highly focused on specific client problems, their progress, and resolution – irrelevant information is kept out of the record. Advantages associated with POR include the following: It shows the interrelatedness of a client's problems; it promotes case coordination and teamwork by facilitating interprofessional communication; it facilitates continuity of service, monitoring of progress, and follow-up; it offers others (supervisors, consultants, etc.) an efficient way of reviewing how a particular problem was addressed; and it makes social workers more easily accountable than other less focused, chronological records. On the other hand, POR tends to oversimplify problem definition and intervention and may overlook important client needs and assets.

When using this method, a client's record is comprised of four elements:

Database: The database contains face-sheet information (e.g., age, gender, income, family members); the presenting problem(s); relevant demographic, cultural, and medical information; the client's address, etc. This information is collected at intake.

Problem list: The problem list (with each problem assigned a unique number) is developed on the basis of database information and is a record of a client's problems from which problems are checked off as they are resolved. Problems are described in behavioral language, and the use of diagnostic labels is discouraged. The problem list is maintained on a separate page of the case record.

Initial action plan: The action plan is a list of all steps that may be taken to resolve the client's problems and is formulated from the database information.

Progress notes (implementation of the plan): The progress notes include regular entries that correspond to the problem list. The social worker's actions are recorded in the main body of the record and she uses the problem numbers to reference each action to a specific problem. The action plan and progress notes often follow a SOAP charting format.

e. SOAP Charting: **SOAP** is a charting system used in many medical and mental-health professions. It assists social workers in organizing information about clients and entails classifying information according to the acronym "SOAP." This arranges client records according to four components:

Subjective information (S): Subjective information is derived from a client's self-report (e.g., the symptoms he reports, how he says he feels about his situation).

Objective information (O): Objective information (sociodemographic data, medical information, etc.) is derived from direct observation of a client and systematic data collection.

Assessments (A): This includes the social worker's assessments and conclusions based on subjective and objective information about the client.

Plan (P): This describes what the social worker and agency plan to do to resolve the client's problems.

f. Standardized Forms: Many agencies use standardized forms to gather specific data about clients, social workers, and services. Some agencies use these forms as only face-sheets and worker activity reports, others use them for all record-keeping, and others fall somewhere between these two extremes. Because they typically require short answers or checkmarks and are highly systematized, standardized forms simplify the recording process, ensure that required information is collected, and permit easy access to information about services that were provided to clients. The information on these forms is useful for planning, monitoring, and evaluating services.

g. Narrative Recording and Casenotes: Narrative recording is a flexible recording format that allows a social worker to decide for herself what is important to include in a client's record. To prepare a narrative record, the social worker first creates handwritten notes describing her day-to-day actions and activities related to a case; then, at a later date, she reviews her casenotes and prepares a summary of her work with the client. In order to create a useful summary, the worker must develop a system of note-taking that maintains a chronological record of her activities, facilitates summarization, and keeps her casenotes in one place. One effective system is to use a loose-leaf notebook containing sheets designed for brief handwritten notes and chronological entries (Sheafor & Horejsi, 2003).

Narrative recording is associated with several disadvantages – it tends to be time consuming and produces lengthy records in which specific information is difficult to locate.

h. Computerized Recordkeeping: Various forms of information technology, or IT (a.k.a. information and communication technology, or ICT) are available to improve practice effectiveness, workload management, and administrative accountability in social work. Among these are database programs that provide an efficient way to maintain and access information about clients and work-related activities (e.g., appointments, do-to lists).

Regarding a client's case record, you may record on a database such information as demographic data, intake information, social history, treatment plans, and progress notes. You can then easily retrieve this data to track the client's progress. You may also merge this data with data concerning other clients to prepare reports. You should be aware, however, that the role of IT in social work has been a source of debate, particularly in regard to case records. When a database requires you to enter client information into predefined fields, the case record will capture only selected, objective data about the client. It will not allow you to record subjective impressions or unique data about a client's personal or situational characteristics.

B. Managed Care and Service Provision

The growth of managed care in the United States was driven by the enactment of the Health Maintenance Organization Act of 1973.

The goals of managed care are to control the overuse of health-care services and overcharging by professionals and ensure that proposed health care is consistent with accepted standards. In practical terms, managed care involves (a) procedures for monitoring the delivery of health care and health-care benefit plans and (b) the participation of third-parties (parties other than the patient and physician) in the delivery of health-care services.

1. How Managed Care Monitors Delivery of Health Care and Benefit Plans: Monitoring is primarily done through peer review, utilization review, and case management:

Peer review: In managed care, peer review is a mechanism used by medical staff to evaluate the quality of total health care provided by the managed care organization (MCO). Peer review is used in all managed care settings and is the most common method used for monitoring utilization by physicians ("utilization" refers to the use of services and supplies).

Utilization review: Utilization review (UR) is one of the primary tools utilized by MCOs and health plans to control overutilization, reduce costs, and manage care. A UR evaluates the appropriateness of health-care services delivered to a plan member on a prospective, concurrent, or retrospective basis and can be performed by a peer review group or public agency. A typical UR involves the use of protocols, benchmarks, or data with which to compare specific cases to an aggregate set of cases. Those cases falling outside the protocols or range of data are reviewed individually. MCOs will sometimes refuse to reimburse or pay for services that do not meet their own sets of UR standards.

Case Managers (Gatekeepers): The use of case managers as "gatekeepers" is another way that managed care attempts to contain health care costs. In managed care, case management refers to the monitoring and coordination of treatment given to patients with specific diagnoses or requiring high-cost or extensive services. The goal is to accommodate the services needed by the patient through a coordinated effort to achieve the desired health outcome in a cost-effective way. A case manager works with the patient, providers, and the patient's insurer to coordinate the services. The case manager may be a doctor, nurse, or social worker. In an HMO, for example, the "gatekeeper" is the patient's **primary care physician** (PCP) who controls how the patient uses other services in the plan. Patients enrolled in an HMO choose a PCP who provides, arranges, coordinates, and authorizes all aspects of their health care (i.e., the PCP evaluates a patient to determine if additional care is needed and makes referrals to specialists).

Related terms include preadmission review, pre-admission certification, pre-authorization, and pre-certification (pre-cert), which all mean essentially the same thing. In managed care, pre-cert is a method of controlling and monitoring utilization by evaluating the need for a service (i.e., elective inpatient admission and identified outpatient services) before the service is provided: A decision is made concerning the "need" for the service and whether or not the payer, MCO, or insurance company will pay for the service.

Another related term, prior approval, refers to a formal process for obtaining approval from a health insurer before a specific treatment, procedure, service, or supply is provided. Completing this process ensures that the patient receives full benefits for the specified services. Health insurers may require prior approval for specific services or products including home-health assistance, durable medical equipment, surgery, or skilled nursing facility stays. Generally, prior approval (a.k.a. prior authorization) is required for non-emergency services that are expensive or likely to be overused.

2. Fee for Service and Capitation: Fee-for-service (FFS) is the traditional method of payment for health care services in which specific payment is made for specific services rendered. Payment may be made by an insurance company, the patient, or a government program such as Medicare or Medicaid. With respect to the physician or other provider of service, FFS refers to payment in specific amounts for specific services rendered. In relation to the patient, FFS refers to payment in specific amounts for specific services received. This is in contrast to the advance payment of an insurance premium or membership fee for coverage through which services or payment to the supplier are provided.

The term **capitation** is defined as "a set amount of money per person" (Barker, 2003, p. 56). Managed care companies typically define capitation in terms of cost per plan member per month (a fixed amount of money per person). That is, physicians are paid a specific dollar amount during an established period of time to cover the medical needs of a specific number of patients. For instance, a primary care physician in a capitated plan may be paid $30 per month per member enrolled with her, and this amount will remain the same whether a particular plan member sees the physician five times during one month or not at all (i.e., the physician is paid "by the head" not by the visit or procedure). Physicians who exceed their capitated payment may not be able to cover their costs and, as a result, may limit their medical services.

3. Managed Care Organizations and Managed Care Plans: A "managed care organization" (MCO) is a body that combines the functions of health insurance, delivery of care, and administration. Some MCOs include only physicians, while others include combinations of physicians, hospitals, and other providers (such as mental health professionals).

Managed care programs, such as HMOs, are sometimes referred to as managed care organizations; other times, they're called managed care plans. Examples of network-based managed care programs are HMOs, PPOs, and POS plans.

a. Health Maintenance Organizations (HMOs): An **HMO** is a type of insurance plan in which contracted health-care providers (e.g., physicians, hospitals, and other health professionals) are paid in advance for their services. An HMO is paid monthly premiums or capitated rates by "payers," which include employers, insurance companies, government agencies, and other groups representing covered individuals.

HMOs are the most restrictive form of managed care benefit plans because they limit the procedures, providers, and benefits available to enrollees. The members of an HMO (i.e., the individuals enrolled in and covered by the HMO and their dependents) are required to use participating or approved providers for all health services, and, generally, all services have to meet approval by the HMO through its utilization program. As noted earlier, an HMO member must choose a primary care physician, who then directs the member's medical care and determines whether he should be referred for specialty care. Provided that a member stays within his network of doctors, an HMO typically covers all or most of the member's doctor visits and hospitalizations, except for a minor co-pay.

An HMO may "subcapitate" to other groups. For example, it may "carve-out" certain benefit categories such as mental health, and subcapitate these to a mental health HMO. ("Carve-out" refers to the separation of a medical service, or group of services, from the basic set of benefits; in other words, certain services that are covered benefits – e.g., behavioral health care – are administered and funded separately from general health care services. Common carve-outs include psychiatric, rehab, and chemical dependency services.)

There are several different HMO models. An independent practice association (IPA), for example, is a type of HMO that contracts with a group of physicians to provide service to the HMO's members. Typically the physicians are paid on the basis of capitation, which, in this context means, a set amount of money for each enrolled person assigned to that physician or group of physicians whether or not the enrolled person seeks care. The contract is usually nonexclusive, allowing individual doctors or the group to sign contracts with multiple HMOs. Physicians who participate in IPAs usually also serve fee-for-service patients not associated with managed care. A group practice without walls (GPWW) is similar to an independent practice association. This type of physician group, however, is a legal and formal entity in which certain services (e.g., billing and collection, marketing) are provided to each physician by the entity, and the physician continues to practice in his or her own facility. A GPWW is sometimes called a "clinic without walls."

b. Preferred Provider Organizations (PPOs): **PPO**s are groups of providers contracted by insurance companies.

PPO members (i.e., individuals covered by the PPO and their dependents) are encouraged to use the insurance company's network of doctors and hospitals. These providers have been contracted to provide services to the plan's members at a discounted rate. PPO members do not need to choose a primary care physician and can see doctors and specialists within the network at their own discretion. Services provided by an *out-of-network* physician are typically covered at a lower percentage than services offered by a network physician. Additionally, if a member sees a provider outside of the plan's network, he may have to pay the charges up front and then submit his own claim for reimbursement.

PPO members usually must pay an annual deductible before the insurance company begins paying their claims. Once the deductible is met, they are required to make a co-payment for most doctors' office visits. Some plans may also require members to cover a percentage of the total charges.

c. Point-of-Service Plans or Point-of-Service Option (POS): A POS plan combines certain features offered by HMO and PPO plans. As with an HMO, members of a POS plan are required to choose a primary care physician (PCP) from the plan's network of providers, and services provided by the PCP are typically not subject to a deductible. Usually POS members receive a higher level of coverage for services provided or referred by their PCP. Services provided by non-network providers may be subject to a deductible and will likely only receive partial coverage. If services are provided outside of the network, members usually have to pay up front and submit a claim to the insurance company themselves.

4. The Effects of Managed Care on Practice: The service limitations imposed by managed care programs are usually acceptable when clients have minor disorders or problems in living. Clients with persistent mental illnesses or more serious problems, however, may need more sessions than are allowed by their managed care plans. In such cases, a social worker's ethical responsibility to her clients supplants any limitations imposed by the client's managed care plan (or other insurance coverage). Therefore, when a decision made by a managed care company impacts the quantity or quality of care you can provide for a client, you have a duty to serve as your client's advocate. This includes initiating an appeal on behalf of the client to challenge the denial and argue for provision of the treatment you have determined the client needs (i.e., treatment consistent with the standard of care you would normally provide your clients). You should document in detail every step of the appeal process, including all contacts with the managed care company and provide the company with support and documentation for your position (e.g., therapy and progress notes, test results, confirming opinions of colleagues).

In addition, when relevant, you should discuss known or anticipated limitations imposed on your services by a client's managed care plan in the first meeting with the client. The first session should also include a discussion of what steps will be taken if the managed care plan denies the client services he needs.

C. Online Therapy (E-, Internet, Cyber Therapy, Internet Counseling)

Methods of providing online therapy include structured e-mail exchanges, "chat" sessions in which real-time information is exchanged via the computer keyboard, and group "chat" sessions that are moderated by a social worker. Online therapy may be used to provide psychoeducation and supportive services to relatively high functioning individuals. Online therapy is never appropriate for high-risk individuals and should not be used to diagnose or provide psychotherapy for mental disorders. One reason for these restrictions is that an e-therapist lacks adequate access to the client's nonverbal behaviors. Another reason is that electronic counseling has not been subjected to appropriate scientific research to determine its efficacy as a primary or sole modality for individuals experiencing mental disorders.

Social workers who offer services online must meet certain accepted practice standards, including the following (Gingerich, 2002):

- Describe clearly and completely what your services consist of and do not consist of.
- Fully and accurately disclose your professional credentials and experience.
- Fully inform clients about how online services work, the skills they will need in order to use your online services, and what the possible risks are, including breaches of confidentiality.
- Request the client to provide his name and contact information in case of an emergency. (This is the recommended best practice, but a person receiving e-therapy can, from a legal standpoint, remain anonymous if he wishes to. A social worker, of course, can decline to provide online services to individuals who insist on remaining anonymous.)
- State your fee structure clearly (see also below).
- Deliver services exactly as you advertise.
- Make sure you have made provisions to ensure the confidentiality and privacy of your online communications.
- Maintain records of the services you provide according to professional and state-mandated standards.

In addition, NASW's Code of Ethics (Standard 1.03e) states, "Social workers who provide services via electronic media (such as computer, telephone, radio, and television) should inform recipients of the limitations and risks associated with such services."

With regard to fees, e-therapists should clearly state the amount of their fee on their Web page and also communicate with clients about the fee before providing their services. In terms of the fee charged, many e-therapists charge their basic hourly fee and charge for the time they spend reading and responding to each e-mail. If an e-therapist accepts credit cards, she must allow payment through a secure server or provide a telephone or fax number for the client to call with his credit card information (the therapist should *never* ask a client to send credit card information by e-mail, or in any nonsecure Web form). An e-therapist may alternatively ask client to pay by mail, via a check or money order.

Finally, the National Association of Social Workers and Association of Social Work Boards Standards for Technology and Social Work Practice ("Technology Standards") provide guidance for the use of technology in social work practice. The following are among the issues addressed by this document: (a) advocating for technology access by clients with special needs or limited access; (b) appropriate matching of online methods, skills, and techniques to the cultural and ethnic characteristics of clients; (c) development of security policies and procedures; (d) accurate marketing practices and verification of client identity; and (e) compliance with relevant laws and regulations in all states where services are provided (i.e., online practice may be subject to regulation in both the jurisdiction in which the client receives services and the jurisdiction in which the social worker provides services).

XVII. Child Welfare Work, School Social Work, and Health Social Work

A. Child Welfare Work

Child welfare is a specialized area of social work concerned with the maintenance of adaptive social conditions for children and the improvement and prevention of maladaptive ones. Child welfare workers intervene when a family has failed or is at risk of failing to meet a child's basic needs or when the parent-child roles are dysfunctional in some way.

Components of Child Welfare Systems

1. Child Protective Services (CPS): In most jurisdictions, child protective services (CPS) is the agency mandated by law to conduct the initial investigation of a report of child abuse or neglect. CPS also offers services to abused and neglected children and their families. Usually CPS is a unit within a state's or county's Department of Social Services (some states use different names for this agency such as Department of Human Resources or Department of Public Welfare). In addition, some states use other names for the CPS agency, such as Department of Children and Family Services. More information on CPS appears below.

2. Foster Care: Foster care is full-time substitute care of a minor outside his own home by people other than his biological or adoptive parents or legal guardian. For more information on foster care, see Section III of Human Development, Diversity, and Behavior.

3. Juvenile and Family Courts: These are courts that have jurisdiction over child maltreatment cases and child protection cases, including those involving foster care or adoption. In jurisdictions without a designated family court, general trial courts hear child welfare cases along with other civil and criminal matters.

4. Other Child Welfare Services: Other child welfare services include family preservation services (see below), family reunification services, adoption, guardianship, and independent living programs. These services, in combination with the other components of child welfare systems, address family problems associated with child abuse and neglect.

Family preservation services are services for children and families designed to help families at risk or in crisis. They include the following: (a) pre-placement prevention services (e.g., intensive family preservation programs) designed to help children at risk of foster care placement remain with their families; (b) services designed to help children return to families from which they have been removed or be placed for adoption, with a legal guardian, or in another permanent living arrangement; (c) programs designed to provide follow-up care to families to whom a child has been returned after foster care placement; (d) respite care of children to provide temporary relief for parents and other caregivers (including foster parents); and (e) services designed to improve parenting skills in such areas as child development, family budgeting, coping with stress, health, and nutrition.

Child welfare services have often been classified as either supportive care, supplementary care, or substitute care: (a) *Supportive services* are usually provided in the family's home and are designed to enhance the existing strengths of the family. Examples include education, counseling, and family therapy. (b) *Supplementary services* provide parenting functions (such as day-care) while the child remains in the home. (c) *Substitute care services* replace the biological parents or guardians either permanently or temporarily. They include respite care, foster care, and adoption.

Child Protective Services

The foremost goal of **child protective services** is the protection of abused and neglected children. Interventions for child abuse and neglect have become less punitive over time and more therapeutic, with a related emphasis on general social welfare. Two primary goals of intervention are to treat and rehabilitate the parents and, where possible, keep families intact. Family treatment is often a multidisciplinary undertaking that may include professionals such as social workers, teachers, doctors, members of the legal profession, child care providers, and other mental health workers. Some communities have set up multidisciplinary teams to identify maltreatment, intervene with families, develop policies and programs, and provide community education and consultation services to child protective service workers.

1. The Role of Social Workers: Social workers play important roles in child protection as both policy planners and providers of direct services to families. Social workers are often found in public social agencies as caseworkers providing therapy to maltreating families and supervising and managing supportive child welfare services on behalf of those families. Social workers also work in child protective service agencies assisting legal authorities with investigations to determine if children need protective services, helping families and children acquire services, and, at times, providing services themselves.

2. Child Protective Services Tasks and Functions:

a. Reports and Intake: CPS agencies receive reports of child abuse and neglect. Social workers employed at these agencies answer the phones and gather information from individuals in the community who call when they believe that a child has been abused or neglected. The social worker taking the call assesses whether the referral information meets her state's definition of an appropriate referral, usually with the aid of a screening checklist commonly known as a risk assessment intake instrument. If the information fits the state's definition, then an investigation is initiated.

b. Investigation/Assessment: First, an **initial assessment** is conducted to investigate the report, determine whether a safety plan is needed, and decide whether continuing services should be offered to the family. The initial assessment may be conducted by a CPS worker alone or in conjunction with others such as law enforcement or another service provider, and includes interviews and gathering of other relevant information. The first step usually involves a visit to the family's home and a discussion between the CPS worker and the parent(s) (or legal guardian) of the allegation of abuse or neglect. During the visit, the worker observes and evaluates the family and its living situation. The investigation may also include psychological and medical evaluations of the alleged victim(s) and consultation with other professionals involved with the family (with due consideration for the family's right to confidentiality). During the initial assessment, the CPS worker is concerned with two primary questions: First, is the allegation of abuse or neglect true, and, second, is the child in danger? When an allegation is substantiated, a child protection case is opened. When the child is at high risk for additional abuse or neglect, he is immediately removed from the home. All phases of the investigation may be enforced, if necessary, through a court order (e.g., a court order may be needed if the parents refuse to allow the investigation).

If the report is substantiated, a **family assessment** follows. The purpose of this assessment is to understand which of the risk factors and protective factors identified in the initial assessment should be the focus of continuing services provided to the family. The family assessment should be strengths based and include as much participation by the family as possible.

c. Planning and Intervention: The main purpose of planning is to collaborate with the family in selecting the goals and services that will help reduce the risk of further maltreatment. Available plans include the safety plan, case plan, and concurrent permanency plan:

- The purpose of the *safety plan* is to control safety threats as they are uniquely occurring within the particular family. The plan may be an "in-home ongoing safety plan" or an "out-of-home ongoing safety plan." The latter is required when separation of the child from the safety threats (e.g., from his parents) is necessary to ensure the child's safety.

- The *case plan* (also called the treatment plan, service plan, or service agreement) is designed to help the family achieve safety, permanency, and well-being and is based on the strengths and needs identified by the family and social worker. The case plan matches the intensity of service with the intensity of need. It describes the services to be provided to the family and how the services will be provided, identifies community partners, defines the service goals and their objectives and tasks, and specifies anticipated outcomes.

- When one is needed, a *concurrent permanency plan* is developed to address both how family reunification can be achieved and how permanency with a new caregiver can be achieved for the child if efforts to reunify the family fail. (For more information on this plan, see The Decision Process in Child Protective Services, below.)

Following planning, the family's caseworker arranges and coordinates the identified services for the family, encourages the family to use the services, and ensures that the services are meeting all of the family's needs (i.e., she may serve their case manager). She also keeps track of treatment progress and effectiveness, typically through regular visits to the family's home. The worker may also provide certain services herself. A typical intervention may include the following kinds of services:

Concrete services: These may include housing, transportation, economic assistance (e.g., TANF, SSI), and Food Stamps, among others. Because such services often improve a family's overall welfare, they frequently play a significant role in reducing the risk of further abuse or neglect.

Supportive and supplementary services: These services are used to enhance the family's existing strengths and provide parenting functions. Specific examples include day-care, medical care, parenting classes, and vocational and educational assistance. Many families also receive **respite care services**, which are usually classified as a form of substitute care. Supportive services also include therapy. Families often receive conventional forms of therapy (e.g., individual, family, or group therapy), but most child welfare workers agree that nontraditional forms of therapy are more effective with maltreating parents.

Examples include self-help groups like Parents Anonymous and outreach programs that allow the mental health worker to work with a family in its home on issues such as empowerment, parenting skills, and stress reduction.

d. Evaluation of Family Progress and Case Closure: Evaluation is concerned with assessing achievement of the outcomes, goals, and tasks defined during planning and determining the extent to which risk factors have decreased and protective factors have increased. The purpose of case closure is to identify whether risk has been sufficiently reduced so that the family no longer needs services.

3. The Decision Process in Child Protective Services: Below we describe the typical steps and decisions taken after a CPS agency receives a child abuse or neglect report, with a particular focus on what happens if a child is removed from his home (adapted from Badeau & Gesiriech, pewfostercare.org).

First, the abuse or neglect report is received and the CPS agency responds. If the agency finds, during an initial assessment, that the report is unfounded, then the case is closed. If the agency finds evidence that the child is at risk for further abuse or neglect, then the initial assessment continues to determine whether the child can remain safely at home with supervision or support services for the family. If the initial assessment indicates that the child is at high risk for further abuse or neglect, the CPS worker petitions the court recommending removal of the child from his home under the supervision of the child welfare agency. In an emergency situation, the agency will usually remove the child before receiving a court order and place him in emergency or temporary foster care.

The petition to remove the child from his home then results in a series of **judicial hearings**: (a) First, an emergency custody hearing, or protective hearing, is held. At this hearing, the judge determines whether the child has been abused or neglected. (b) If the judge determines that the child has been abused or neglected, the case proceeds to an adjudicatory and dispositional hearing. At this hearing, the judge decides, based in part on the CPS agency's recommendation, to do one of the following: send the child home without services, send the child home with supervision and support services, or remove the child from his home. This same set of options is considered at each subsequent case review hearing.

A child who is removed from his home is then considered to be in state custody and becomes a "ward" of the court" or "dependent" of the court (some states use the term "ward" in this context, while others use the term "dependent"). He and his family are assigned a caseworker from the child welfare agency.

After the child is removed from his home, the court needs to approve an initial placement and reunification plan. This **case plan**, developed primarily by the family's caseworker (ideally with participation by the family), details the following: (a) the types of services that the child and family will receive; (b) reunification goals, including visitation schedules and a target date for the child's return home; and (c) concurrent plans for alternative permanent placement options should reunification goals not be met. This is the "concurrent permanency plan" mentioned earlier.

Additionally, federal law requires that the case plan describe how the state will achieve a safe placement for the child in the least restrictive, most family-like setting in close proximity to his biological parents and how the placement is consistent with the child's best interests and special needs. There are several kinds of **foster care placement** available for a child who is removed from his parents' or legal guardian's home:

- The child may be placed in the home of a relative (kin placement). Federal law recognizes a preference for kin placement, but the primary considerations when placement decisions are made are the child's health and safety.

- The child may be placed in a non-relative foster family home. Foster parents receive stipends to pay for room and board, child care, and clothing and may also receive Medicaid coverage for the children in their care.

- The child may be placed in a residential facility or a group home. Generally, a child will be placed in therapeutic foster care, residential child care, or residential psychiatric care if he has emotional, behavioral, physical, or medical needs and requires a higher level of supervision and treatment.

The court reviews and may modify the recommended case plan.

Following the child's placement, a **case review** must be held every six months, during which the court evaluates progress. The review examines whether the placement is still necessary and appropriate, whether the case plan is being properly and adequately followed, and whether progress has been made toward reunifying the family. The case review must also set a target date for the child's return home, adoption, or other permanent placement. In addition, within 12 months of a child's initial placement or following a determination that reasonable efforts to reunite the family are not required or have been unsuccessful, a **permanency planning hearing** (or permanency hearing) must be held for the child. If the court determines, upon reviewing the case, that the biological parents have been successful with the court-ordered reunification plan, then the child is reunited with his parents, and the case is closed.

Alternatively, if the biological parents have not completed the court-ordered reunification plan, the child welfare agency will petition the court for the **termination of parental rights** (TPR). Federal law requires states to initiate TPR proceedings for children who have been in foster care for 15 of the most recent 22 months; for infants determined to be abandoned; in cases in which a parent has killed another of his or her children; and in certain other situations involving severe abuse or neglect. States may elect not to initiate TPR proceedings if the child is in a relative's care, the child welfare agency has documented a compelling reason that TPR would not be in the child's best interest, or the state has not provided necessary services to the family. In addition, at any point during the court process, a parent may voluntarily relinquish his or her parental rights.

If the parents' rights are terminated, a **permanency plan** for the child is created. According to federal law, a permanency plan must document the steps taken to place the child and finalize an adoption or legal guardianship, as well as child-specific recruitment efforts undertaken to find an adoptive family or legal guardian for a child. Federal law also requires states to concurrently begin seeking and approving a qualified adoptive family for the child whenever a state initiates TPR proceedings.

A child who does not return to his parents' home following foster care placement may leave foster care (and the child welfare system) under the following circumstances: (a) The child may be placed with an adoptive family. A court holds an adoption hearing to finalize the adoption. (b) The child may be placed in the custody of a legal guardian (e.g., a relative, a foster parent, another adult who has a relationship with the child). Guardianship is less legally secure than adoption, but it offers the child a degree of permanency and stability without requiring the termination of his parents' rights. In terms of parents' rights with respect to the child, the following rights are transferred to the legal guardian: protection, education, care and control, custody, and decision-making. (c) A child may "age-out" of foster care at age 18 or 21 (depending on the state) without being reunited with his family, adopted, or placed in another permanent home. Through federally funded independent living programs established under the Foster Care Independence Act (1999), state child welfare agencies provide services (basic living skills training, housing assistance, educational opportunities, etc.) to help adolescents in foster care prepare for the transition from living within the child welfare system to living on their own as adults.

B. School Social Work

The main goal of school social workers is to enable students to learn and function in the school environment. In working to achieve this goal, school social workers draw on ecological concepts and rely on an **ecosystems perspective** in which they focus on the reciprocal interactions of students with environmental factors. School social workers assume the following (Dupper, 2003):

- Each student is an inseparable part of the social systems in which he must function (i.e., home, school, peer group, neighborhood).

- A student's problems are due to a lack of "goodness of fit" between the student and his environment (problems are not located "within" the child). In other words, behavior and learning problems at school are the result of a discrepancy between the student's academic and behavioral competencies and the academic and social tasks of the school environment. Correcting this discrepancy requires addressing both the student's coping skills and specific environmental stressors.

A key factor that differentiates school social work from other professional roles in schools is a focus on issues of parent involvement and school-family-community partnerships. A school social worker mobilizes all facets of a student's life situation in an effort to foster a supportive learning environment for the student and serves as a vital link between a student's school, home, and community.

School social workers adopt a strengths-based and empowerment approach to their practice. They seek to identify and build on existing strengths within students and the social systems in which students must function.

1. Role, Tasks, and Activities of School Professionals: School social workers are members of an interdisciplinary team of school professionals.

a. *School Social Workers:*

Roles and tasks: The roles and tasks of school social workers include maintaining open communication between the home and school; advocating for at-risk students and their families; empowering families to share their concerns with school officials; helping families understand their children's educational needs; consulting with teachers about students' living situations and neighborhood conditions; making referrals to community agencies; tracking students involved with multiple agencies; and working with the community to identify and develop resources to better serve the needs of at-risk students and their families. In some school settings, a school social worker may also provide short-term therapy to children and families.

Activities: School social workers participate in conferences concerning students' behavior and academic progress; collaborate with teachers and other school professionals in assessing students' needs and developing strategies to meet those needs; prepare developmental assessments and social histories required for multidisciplinary evaluations of students (see Social Development Studies, below); provide individual and group counseling to students; conduct classroom activities; and design, implement, and evaluate school-based prevention programs.

b. *Other School Professionals:*

School psychologists: School psychologists administer and interpret the results of academic and psychological tests for students with learning and/or behavioral problems; provide individual and group counseling for students; provide consultation to classroom teachers; work with students' parents; and, as members of multidisciplinary teams, determine students' eligibility for special education services.

School counselors: In elementary schools, school counselors provide individual and small group counseling to students, conduct activities in classrooms, sometimes serve as disciplinarians, and sometimes serve as a linkage between school and home. In secondary schools, school counselors focus primarily on helping students with class schedules, monitoring students' academic progress, and assisting students with college and career choices.

School nurses: School nurses provide vision and hearing tests to determine possible obstacles to learning and monitor students who have health problems.

2. Interventions Made By School Social Workers: The interventions made by school social workers both assist students directly (student-focused interventions) and target harmful conditions in the school, students' families, the neighborhood, and the community, particularly conditions that negatively impact at-risk students (system-focused interventions).

a. *Student-Focused Interventions:* Student-focused interventions may target the following: (a) internalizing behavior problems (withdrawn, anxious, and depressed behaviors); (b) externalizing behavior problems (aggressive, disruptive, and acting out behaviors); (c) serious social problems affecting students' learning and functioning at school (such as abuse or homelessness); and (d) disabilities such as specific learning disorders, autism spectrum disorders, ADHD, and emotional disturbance. Some students with disabilities qualify for special education services under the Individuals With Disabilities Education Act (IDEA). Many student-focused interventions attempt to enhance the social competencies of at-risk students by teaching specific skills and increasing environmental supports (Dupper, 2003).

Before implementing student-focused interventions (with the exception of crises), school social workers conduct thorough assessments with students using both formal and informal procedures. Assessments are often completed by an interdisciplinary team of school professionals. In their assessments, school social workers seek to prevent the inappropriate labeling of students by evaluating adaptive behavior and cultural and environmental factors that may be impacting a student's learning or behavior at school.

b. *System-Focused Interventions:* System-focused interventions attempt to (a) make the school, family, neighborhood, and community more responsive to students' needs, and (b) minimize the harmful impact of risk factors that may result in or intensify problematic student behavior.

A school's "culture" and "climate" influence students' behavior and may interfere with their progress and success. Therefore, school social workers often intervene to change their school's culture and climate. "Culture" refers to the beliefs and expectations that are apparent in the school's daily routine (i.e., the norms and beliefs shared by students, teachers, administrators, and others at the school). "Climate" has been described as the "heart and soul" of the school, or what makes the students, teachers, and others love the school and look forward to being there (Freiberg & Stein, 1999, p. 28).

The culture and climate of a given school are determined by the presence of various risk factors and protective factors. Examples of risk factors include large school size; the absence of a stimulating and innovative curriculum; low academic expectations; crime and violence; differential grading procedures; punitive or inadequate attendance policies; and hostile or suspicious relationships between administrators and school staff or between school staff and students. Protective factors, when they are present, can lessen the impact of risk factors affecting a school and result in a more positive school culture and climate.

3. Programs and Services for Students With Disabilities:

a. The Individuals With Disabilities Education Act (IDEA): The Education for All Handicapped Children Act (P.L. 94-142) was passed in 1975, mandating that public school education must accommodate the needs of all children. The law guarantees an appropriate free public education to all children ages 3 to 21 who need special education services including those with a physical disability, specific learning disorder, intellectual disability, or autism spectrum disorder. Over time, P.L. 94-142 has been amended, and, in 1990, it was renamed the **Individuals with Disabilities Education Act**, or IDEA, (P.L. 101-476). In the IDEA, the term "handicap" was replaced throughout with the term "disability."

Thus, for every eligible student, each state guarantees special education and related services (e.g., by a school social worker, speech therapist, occupational therapist, etc.). Usually, the students are placed in public schools, and the school district pays for all necessary services using the funds disbursed to it under the IDEA.

Underlying goal of the law: An underlying goal of P.L. 94-142 and the IDEA is to eliminate the categorical labeling and placement of children with disabilities into special classrooms. The underlying philosophy is that of **normalization**, in which children with disabilities can have maximum involvement with nondisabled peers and experience a minimum of isolation or separation, which contributes to the learning and sensitivity of both groups of children.

Key features of the law: An **individualized educational program** (IEP) must be developed for each student with a qualifying disability. The IEP must be written by a team of school personnel (which may include the school social worker) in collaboration with the student's parents and must provide the **least restrictive environment** for each student – this environment must be as similar as possible to the regular classroom setting, taking into account the nature of the student's disability. The IEP guides the development and delivery of special education supports and services to the student. It serves as an agreement between the school and the family on the educational goals of the student and outlines the specific skills the student needs to develop and appropriate learning activities that build on the student's strengths. Note that the IDEA applies to students attending public schools only: A court concluded in 1996 that the IDEA and its regulations do not require a public school to make comparable provisions for a disabled student who is voluntarily attending private school.

Other provisions of the law include a guarantee of due process to parents and students (i.e., the parents' right to appeal the identification, evaluation, placement, and education of their child) and the assurance that testing and evaluation materials will not be racially or culturally biased and that no single procedure will be used as the sole criterion for placing a student in a special class. Both a student's parents and his teachers are permitted to appeal decisions made about the best classroom placement for him, but the final decision about a student's placement is made by the local school district.

Amendments to the original law: The Education of the Handicapped Amendments of 1986 (P.L. 99-457) included, in particular, a section that requires early intervention (until age 3) for children who are developmentally delayed or at risk of significant developmental delays.

Another set of amendments, the Education of the Handicapped Amendments of 1990 (P.L. 101-476), sought to improve access to needed services for students and their families. For example, an ombudsperson program was created to help students and their families receive the services they need.

The original law was also amended to address transition services, which are defined as a coordinated set of services that promote students' movement from the school environment to post-school activities such as postsecondary education, vocational training, supported employment, and independent living. In addition, "social work services" were added to the definition of "related services" and "early intervention services" included in the law.

b. Assessment of Students With Disabilities: A school social worker should be familiar with the requirements and mandates of the IDEA and may need to inform the parents of a student with a known or suspected disability of their legal rights under the IDEA.

Three conditions must be met before services under the IDEA will be put into place for a student: (a) a student must be experiencing educational performance problems at school, and these problems must be documented; (b) a student must be referred for an evaluation by the local school district (the evaluation can be requested either by a parent or teacher); and (c) an evaluation must be completed.

If the evaluation determines that the student has a disability that is adversely impacting his educational performance at school, an individualized educational program will be developed. The IEP is normally developed with input from the child's parents and teacher(s), the school psychologist, a representative of the public schools who is knowledgeable about special education programs, and, sometimes, the school social worker and/or school guidance counselor. The student's unique needs relating to education, behavior, and social issues are discussed in meetings, and strategies for meeting those needs are developed. If the student is to receive any specific services, these are also listed in the plan. Once the IEP is developed, a meeting with the parents occurs once a year to review the student's progress and make any alterations to reflect his changing needs. School social workers play an important role in the attainment of IEP goals by mobilizing needed services both within and outside of the school.

If a child is found to be ineligible for services under the IDEA, his parents may do one or more of the following, sometimes with appropriate assistance, such as information giving and advocacy services, from the school social worker:

- *File an appeal.* A school social worker (or the local school district) can inform parents of the specific procedures that they must follow to appeal the decision. State and local laws differ regarding appeals; however, many appeals include arbitration, mediation, and due process hearings. As noted earlier, the child's parents as well as his teachers are permitted to appeal the decision, and the final decision is made by the local school district.

- *Request that their child be re-evaluated for services under Section 504 of the Rehabilitation Act of 1973.* This federal civil rights law is designed to protect the rights of individuals with disabilities in programs and activities that receive federal financial assistance from the U.S. Department of Education. Children not eligible under the IDEA for special education may be found eligible for services under this law.

- *Seek support from other resources.* Parents may also be advised to contact a Protection and Advocacy Agency or Parent Training and Information Center in their state. The former assist parents in resolving educational issues and provide information to parents on special education laws; and the latter offer information on laws relating to education and assist in resolving problems between parents and their child's school.

c. *Available Classroom Placements for Students With Disabilities:* Regarding classroom placement for students with disabilities, the following terms and concepts are relevant:

Mainstreaming: **Mainstreaming** refers to the participation of students with disabilities in general ("regular") education classrooms to the extent appropriate for meeting their needs. Often a student is placed in a general education class during specific time periods of the school day based on his skills, and, during other times, receives instruction in a special education classroom. The concept of mainstreaming is based on the premise that students with disabilities may benefit both academically and socially from being in general education classrooms. A mainstreamed student may be assessed in the classroom in a slightly different way, but he learns mostly the same material as his nondisabled peers and must demonstrate that he is benefiting from his classroom placement.

Inclusion: With **inclusion**, students with disabilities are educated with their nondisabled peers, with special education supports and services provided as needed. The concept of inclusion is based on the belief that students with disabilities deserve to have the same education as their nondisabled peers. Inclusion involves more of a moral position, and a student in an inclusion classroom usually needs only to show that he is not being harmed by being included in the classroom even if he is not necessarily making any significant gains. Advocates of inclusion tend to place more emphasis on life preparation and social skills than on the acquisition of grade-appropriate academic skills.

Special education classroom: In special education classrooms (a.k.a. self-contained classrooms or resource rooms), students with disabilities are given the chance to work one-on-one with special education teachers who address the students' needs for remediation during parts of the school day.

Compared to full-time placement in special education classrooms or special schools, both part-time and full-time placement in regular classrooms have been shown to improve academic achievement in students with mild academic disabilities.

Under the IDEA, mainstreaming or inclusion in regular education classrooms, with supplementary supports and services as needed, is the preferred placement for all children with disabilities. Children with disabilities may be placed in a more restricted environment only if the nature or severity of their disability makes it impossible to provide an appropriate education in the regular classroom.

4. The Role of School Social Workers in Assessing Students' Needs: A key activity of school social workers is collaborating with other school professionals in assessing students' needs and developing strategies to meet those needs. Under the current version of the IDEA, "related personnel" must be included on the team that develops a student's IEP; "related personnel" include school social workers, and, therefore, a school social worker is likely to be a part of the team assembled to develop a student's IEP.

Important ways that school social workers contribute to the evaluation of students' needs and the development of strategies to meet those needs is by preparing social developmental studies (SDS), conducting functional behavioral assessments (FBA), and helping to implement behavior intervention plans that include positive behavioral interventions and support (PBIS).

a. Social Developmental Studies (SDS): A social developmental study (SDS) is used to assist in identifying what educational environment will be most favorable to learning and development for a student. The SDS is a comprehensive assessment of the student's functioning that includes his prenatal and birth history, family functioning, personal strengths, cultural and environmental factors that may be contributing to his behavior and learning at school, and current social functioning. Assessment data is collected using direct observations, interviews with parents or guardians, interviews with teachers, and sometimes, interviews with the student.

b. Functional Behavioral Assessments (FBA) and Positive Behavioral Interventions and Support (PBIS): School teams developing an IEP for a student are required to conduct a functional behavioral assessment (FBA) and to implement a behavior intervention plan that includes positive behavioral interventions and support (PBIS) designed to help the student acquire more effective ways of interacting with his environment. Conducting an FBA involves gathering information about the purpose of the target behavior (a behavior problem) and the environmental and instructional factors associated with it (factors that predict and maintain the behavior). FBA results then facilitate the development of an individualized behavior support plan. This plan usually includes procedures for teaching the student alternatives to the problem behavior(s) and making changes to environmental and instructional factors associated with the problem behavior(s).

5. Other Issues Addressed by School Social Workers:

a. Harassment at School: School social workers must be familiar with existing policies on harassment in their schools and, if there are none, should be active in developing such policies. All school personnel should receive training on sexual harassment and the school's policies; schools should encourage parents to participate in ensuring that the school's policies and practices are consistently implemented; schools should have a plan for what will be done when an incident of harassment is reported to a school official; students should know how to file a complaint; and incidents of harassment should be addressed immediately (Ashford et al., 2006).

Students who are harassed at school are at increased risk for school failure. School social workers should pay particular attention to the needs of students who are vulnerable to being victimized because of their known or presumed sexual orientation or gender identity or their race or culture. Other vulnerable students include those who are being reintegrated into the school from residential or juvenile justice settings (Dupper, 2003). In the latter case, a lack of coordination between the educational and justice systems can make it difficult to meet the educational needs of a student on probation or in aftercare status. Adequately meeting the needs of vulnerable students often requires a school social worker to not only work with these students individually to make them feel welcome, but to also direct efforts toward changing the attitudes and beliefs of school administrators, teachers, other students, parents, and the community and school policies that adversely affect these students.

b. Bullying at School: Because bullying involves powerful students harassing less powerful students, it differs from conflicts occurring between students of relatively equal status. For this reason, conflict resolution strategies such as mediation often are not effective (Dupper, 2003). The school social worker should make every effort, and encourage other school personnel to make similar efforts, to protect bullied students from harassment. In dealing with a bully and his parents, the primary intervention is to speak with the bully individually and tell him in absolute terms that bullying will not be tolerated and will end. In helping the student who has been bullied, it is important to remember that the student may have been threatened with more bullying if he reports the harassment to anyone. The student may be too afraid to ask for help and may ask his parents not to contact the school. Many schools use SEL (**Social Emotional Learning**), a program which focuses on developing awareness of emotions/empathy in situations involving bullying and harassment.

c. Potentially Violent Students: Indicators suggesting the potential that a student may be violent include violent drawings or writings, threats of violence toward others, past violence or aggressive history, the recent ending of a relationship (boy/girlfriend, best friend), self-isolation or feelings of being isolated from others, being teased or perceptions of being teased or harassed, animal torturing, substance abuse, stressors at home, low school interest, social withdrawal from peers and/or family, inappropriate use of or access to firearms, and being viewed by peers as "different" (Juhnke et al., 1999).

School social workers should make sure that school officials know that assessment tools designed to identify students who may be at risk of violence can be misused. No single risk factor can identify every violent student, and any single risk factor taken on its own is very likely to misidentify a student as potentially violent. Generally, school social workers and other school personnel should focus on students exhibiting multiple risk factors. Some individual risk factors call for immediate attention, however: A student making violent threats toward others should be required to undergo a comprehensive assessment and parental conferencing, and a student experiencing symptoms resulting from substance abuse should be provided with appropriate interventions immediately (Dupper, 2003).

d. School Leavers (Dropping Out): Students who leave school before graduating may do so for a variety of personal and/or school-related reasons. Examples of personal reasons include needing to work to help support the family, becoming a parent, family conflict, having friends who dropped out, or having an alcohol or other drug problem. School-related factors contributing to dropout include, among others, impersonal schools, large class size, inadequate preparation for high school, poor grades, conflict with teachers or peers, humiliation about repeating a grade, disciplinary problems, suspensions or expulsion, feeling alienated, and feeling unsafe. For most school leavers, dropping out has little or nothing to do with a lack of ability; instead, school leavers tend to be students who are disengaged from school for one or more of the reasons listed above.

Dupper (2003) reminds school social workers to look beyond the personal reasons that may cause students to "dropout" of school and also consider school factors that contribute to "pushing" students out of school. In developing interventions to address the needs of students at risk for leaving school early, school social workers must give adequate attention to identified school-related factors.

C. Health Social Work: Interventions in Health Care Settings

Health social workers are found in a range of settings including hospitals, outpatient clinics (such as urgent care centers), HMOs, dialysis centers, hospices, palliative care, and skilled nursing facilities, and take on many roles in the planning, delivery, and evaluation of patient care. NASW's Standards for Social Work in Health-Care Settings require that health social workers work to foster and maintain patients' physical and psychosocial well-being and promote conditions that ensure patients get the greatest possible benefit from the services they receive.

Hospital social workers (also known as medical social workers) are typically employed by hospitals, skilled nursing facilities, or hospices. They work with patients and their families in need of psychosocial help. Among the services provided by hospital social workers are (a) assessment of patient and family needs; (b) counseling and support for emotional needs, crisis situations, coping and adjusting to illness and treatment, grief and bereavement, and financial needs, etc.; (c) advocacy for patients and families; (d) case management and referrals to community services and agencies; and (e) assessment of discharge needs.

While doctors and other health professionals in direct patient-care settings must usually attend first to patients' medical issues, hospital and other health social workers are trained to focus on the full range of physical, emotional, and environmental factors that impact patients' well-being and that of their families. They provide services to meet the patient's/family's medically related emotional and social needs, with an emphasis on how these affect the patient's medical condition, treatment, and recovery, and, as relevant, safe transition from one care environment to another. ("Direct patient care," which was mentioned above, is care that involves face-to-face contact and interaction with the patient.)

1. The Tasks of Health Social Workers:

a. Direct Service Tasks: In direct patient-care settings, health social workers perform assessments of patients' situations and develop and implement interventions to address patients' needs and those of their families. As in other social work settings, intervention is directed at helping patients problem-solve and cope with stressors and linking patients with resources, services, and opportunities. To achieve these goals, health social workers (a) work with patients and the members of patients' social support networks (often the family), (b) collaborate with members of interdisciplinary teams, and (c) coordinate services for patients from the community and entitlement agencies. They also advocate for patients' needs.

At the primary care level (which we define below), health social workers serve as consultants, educators, and collaborators with health-care providers to help them integrate the person-in-environment perspective into their medical practice.

b. Indirect Service Tasks: At the macro level, health social workers provide supervision or administration in health facilities, promote effective and humane service systems, and develop and improve social policy (Gehlert & Browne, 2006).

2. Biopsychosocial Approach to Health Care:
In the past, health-care service delivery relied on a medical model, an approach that focused primarily on the biological aspects of disease. Now health-care providers are increasingly adopting a biopsychosocial approach in which the biological, psychological, behavioral, social, and environmental aspects of physical illness and injury are all evaluated and, as necessary, treated. One factor that has contributed to the

growing acceptance of the biopsychosocial model in medicine is research showing that the cost of providing brief psychosocial interventions to patients is offset by savings in the overall use of medical services.

Providing interventions that address all aspects of a patient's physical illness or injury requires the use of an **interdisciplinary team** of direct patient-care professionals. As members of these teams, health social workers play a vital role by using their specialized knowledge and skill to clarify for the other team members the psychosocial dimensions of a patient's physical illness or injury.

3. Levels of Health Care:

a. Inpatient vs. Ambulatory Care: With inpatient care, a patient is admitted to a hospital for major diagnostic, surgical, or therapeutic services. Ambulatory care, by contrast, is medical care delivered on an outpatient basis (i.e., it is given to patients who are able to "ambulate," or walk about). Sites where ambulatory care can be delivered include physician offices, hospital emergency departments, and urgent care centers.

Some visits to emergency departments result in hospital admission and would be considered emergency medicine visits rather than ambulatory care. Most visits to hospital emergency departments, however, do not require hospital admission. In fact, many of these visits are not true emergencies and would be better addressed in an urgent care center. Urgent care centers are designed to evaluate and treat conditions that are not severe enough to require treatment in a hospital emergency department but do require treatment beyond normal physician office hours or before a physician appointment is available. Urgent care facilities are also called minor emergency facilities.

b. Primary, Secondary, and Tertiary Medical Care: Primary medical care is provided to patients who are pre-symptomatic or in the early symptomatic stages of an illness. The primary care physician, or PCP, is a physician/medical doctor who provides the first contact for a patient with an undiagnosed health concern; the PCP may also provide continuing care of a variety of medical conditions.

Secondary medical care is care provided by medical specialists, such as cardiologists, urologists, and dermatologists, who generally do not have first contact with patients; instead, they provide care at the request of a patient's PCP. Acute care is a branch of secondary medical care. Acute care provides treatment for a disease for a short period of time (i.e., the patient is treated for a brief but severe episode of illness). Many hospitals are acute care facilities that seek to discharge a patient with appropriate discharge instructions as soon as he is considered healthy and stable. Uninsured or underinsured patients who are unable to pay for medical services often turn to acute care settings, such as hospital emergency departments, for their medical care needs.

Tertiary health care is consultative care by specialists working in a setting that has personnel and facilities for specialized evaluation and treatment. This care is usually provided upon referral from a primary or secondary medical care provider. Examples of tertiary care services include specialist cancer care, neurosurgery, and burn care.

4. Psychosocial Assessment in Health-Care Settings:
Some patients seen by health social workers have been referred to them by other professionals. Often, these patients are referred as a result of psychosocial issues that may interfere with effective medical treatment. A hospital social worker, for example, may not see all patients who come to the emergency

department but will be asked to assess and provide services (either directly or through referral) to patients who have been raped or abused by a partner or spouse. In other settings, a health social worker does see every patient. A health social worker at a dialysis clinic or transplant center, for instance, sees every patient so that she can evaluate the psychosocial issues that may affect the patient as he undergoes a difficult medical procedure and address any issues that could interfere with a successful medical outcome.

a. Evaluation of Strengths and Needs: In health-care settings, psychosocial assessments emphasize evaluation of the strengths and needs of patients and the members of their social support network (particularly family members) in order to identify factors that may contribute to or interfere with successful medical care and outcomes. In meeting with patients and their families, health social workers usually collect information about the following areas (Germain, 1984):

- The patient's illness, injury, or disability (hereafter referred to in this list as simply "illness").

- The patient's and family's beliefs about the nature of the illness and its causes, the personal meaning they attach to it, and their ideas about effective treatments.

- The patient's and family's coping resources; pre-existing problems that may interfere with coping with the illness; and actual, potential, or feared effects of the illness on personal, interpersonal, or environmental issues for the patient and family.

- The patient's and family's quality of affect (e.g., anxiety, depression, guilt); level of cognitive-perceptual functioning; self-concept; and initial coping efforts (including defenses such as denial); and interpersonal and communication patterns in the family.

- Social and cultural factors (e.g., race, ethnicity, religion, social class, occupation) that may influence the patient's and family's coping patterns and perceptions and expectations regarding the illness experience, the "patient" role, and treatment.

- Gender and age factors (including individual and family developmental stages and tasks) and their implications for successful coping.

- The availability of concrete resources, information, and social network support and the responsiveness of the health-care facility to the particular needs of the patient and his family (including whether adjustments or changes to the patient's physical setting are needed).

Familiarity with issues commonly faced by medical patients and their families is important for facilitating accurate assessment. Pollin (1995) has identified eight issues that patients and families typically deal with when faced with illness or long-term disability: loss of control; loss of self-image; dependency; stigma; abandonment; fear of expressing anger; isolation; and death.

An assessment tool called the Family Crisis Oriented Personal Evaluation Scales may be used to facilitate identification of a family's problem-solving and coping strategies. These scales assess the family's ways of acquiring social support, capacity to reframe stressful events to make them more manageable, capacity to seek and accept help, use of spiritual support, and ability to tolerate painful situations or situations that cannot be changed.

b. Evaluation of Mental Health Issues: Patients with acute or chronic physical conditions (illness, injury, disability, etc.) and those who undergo a medical crisis often experience psychological distress as a result, which can range from mild to significant. A health social worker may use a mental status exam and/or screening instrument designed to identify specific mental health symptoms to facilitate detection of mental health issues that require further assessment and/or special attention (e.g., mood, anxiety, or trauma-related symptoms or disorders).

To more fully understand the nature of a patient's mental health issues and what may underlie or influence them, a health social worker will generally evaluate the following interacting domains: (a) the mental health symptoms themselves; (b) physical conditions; (c) medications being taking; (d) substance use; and (e) social and cultural factors such as race, ethnicity, cultural background, spiritual background, age, gender, sexual orientation, socioeconomic status, employment status, and family and social support.

Examples of factors that may influence a medical patient's mental health issues (including his response to physical symptoms and illness) include the following:

- How the members of his culture define and perceive illness, express pain, or experience and describe symptoms. For example, somatization – the expression of feelings of distress through physical symptoms – is more common in some cultural groups than in others.
- Experiences with racial discrimination or homophobia.
- Living in poverty, which is associated with an increased risk of acute and chronic stressors.
- Limited access to health care, lack of insurance, or lack of access to linguistically and/or culturally appropriate services.
- Difficulties within his social support network (e.g., isolation, unsupportive family or friends).
- Pre-existing mental health problems (e.g., mood disorder, anxiety disorder, substance use disorder).
- Prior exposure to trauma, which can affect how a person experiences physical illness.

A patient experiencing mild psychological distress will usually benefit from psychoeducation regarding his physical illness or injury and supportive counseling to enhance his coping and stress management. A patient experiencing significant psychological distress, by contrast, will often require more intensive psychosocial intervention such as psychotherapy and/or psychopharmacology (e.g., antidepressant medication).

5. Psychosocial Intervention in Health-Care Settings: Psychosocial intervention must always be based on a careful assessment (see above) and should emphasize providing assistance to address the identified needs. Following assessment, a health social worker (with the patient's consent, whenever possible) shares her findings with the members of his treatment team.

Psychosocial interventions in health care settings often include one or more of the following:

- Providing **psychoeducation**, or explaining the disease and its treatment to patients and, often, their families. All information must be provided in a manner that is sensitive to the patient's developmental level, literacy level, and other characteristics. This activity is an important way of fulfilling the key role in health social work of facilitating communication between patients and health-care providers.

- Helping patients and their families learn about and access services and resources in their community that can assist them, including local and federal entitlement programs. This requires health social workers to be familiar with the eligibility requirements of these programs. In some settings, health social workers provide case management services to patients.

- Using clinical skills to help patients and their families cope with the illness/injury itself and treatments recommended for it. This may involve providing **supportive counseling** to help a patient cope with his diagnosis, providing grief counseling for the losses the patient will experience as a result of his illness or injury, and encouraging the patient to follow through with the recommended medical treatments in order to maximize his quality of life.

- Providing supportive counseling to patients struggling with difficult and/or intrusive treatment regimens.

- Providing couples and family counseling or leading groups to assist family members with issues of adjustment following a patient's diagnosis or medical crisis or issues of grief following the death of a patient.

- Meeting with family members to discuss end-of-life care for the patient.

6. Assisting with End-of-Life Decisions: Some health-care providers do what they believe is appropriate in terms of medical treatments regardless of what is included in a patient's living will or other advanced directive, and this practice is especially common when the patient's family is divided over what the medical treatments for the patient should be. When the members of patient's family are divided in this way, the hospital social worker can meet with them to help family members understand one another's feelings and preferences, and encourage family members to make, or accept, decisions that reflect not their own preferences but those of the patient.

A hospital social worker may also assist patients and families who are undecided about medical treatments: She may, for example, help the patient and family understand the implications of their own and each other's preferences and, ultimately, help the family accept the patient's preferences and decisions.

7. Discharge Planning: Health social workers in hospitals provide discharge planning for some patients. Discharge planning involves coordinating further care for patients with complex or chronic health problems who will need additional, often long-term, comprehensive care after they leave the health-care facility. Often, these patients need not just traditional medical follow-up care but also community-based non-medical services, such as psychoeducation.

Appropriate discharge planning requires a multidimensional assessment of the patient, and this can be difficult to achieve in the current health-care environment in which the time-frame for hospital stays is usually short. To counter this problem, hospital social workers may do preadmission screenings of patients to identify areas of risk and need and start the process of locating and linking patients and families to community resources before discharge.

8. Other Health Social Work Interventions and Roles:

a. Crisis Intervention: Social workers in some health-care settings, such as hospital emergency departments, provide crisis intervention services for patients experiencing medical crises and/or psychosocial emergencies. This work requires expertise in such areas as domestic abuse, homelessness, and substance abuse, as well as skills for intervening effectively in crisis situations (e.g., assisting battered women, helping family members deal with the death of a patient).

b. Single-Session Therapy (SST): Single-session therapy (SST) is an intervention used in hospital emergency departments and acute ambulatory care settings to address crisis situations. SST may be used in non-crisis situations as well, when patients or their families choose to have only a single contact with the social worker or when short hospital stays allow for only one session. Good candidates for SST include patients with circumscribed problems, good coping skills, and a functional support system. SST is not recommended for patients with severe and persistent mental disorders, substance use disorders, eating disorders, or symptoms stemming from early or prolonged trauma or abuse.

SST does not attempt to resolve all of a patient's presenting problems in one session or provide him with all of the help he needs or wants. Instead, its goal is to provide the patient with a positive experience that will enable him and his family to make good use of other medical services, follow through with recommended treatment, discharge, and referral plans, and be open in the future to additional treatment if he needs it (Hoyt et al., 1992).

c. Consultation: In ambulatory care settings, a health social worker may serve in a consultant role in which she clarifies for other members of a medical team the psychosocial issues that could affect the course or outcome of a patient's physical illness or injury. The social worker may, for example, help physicians identify patients whose somatic complaints are manifestations of depression or anxiety and then assist in rendering health services to these patients, providing such services as crisis intervention, psychoeducation, brief therapy, or case management.

Intervention Processes and Techniques for Use with Larger Client Systems

The remaining sections of this chapter review intervention processes and techniques for use with larger systems. Interventions with larger systems are undertaken to improve the effectiveness and efficiency of service delivery and bring about changes in policies, programs, or budgets. They don't involve personal contact with clients and are usually performed with a committee, coalition, or other group. Examples of activities associated with these interventions include policy management, administration, program evaluation, and intervention with communities.

As noted in the Assessment chapter, macro practice, is associated with intervention processes and techniques. At the macro level, interventions are intended to benefit relatively large groups (i.e., a specific client population, residents of a community, or personnel at an agency).

Introduction to Macro Level Intervention

Macro-level interventions are designed to improve either the quality of life for clients or communities served or the quality of work life for employees at an organization so that they can provide optimal services to clients or communities (Netting et al., 2004). Usually the focus of macro change is on just a segment of a community or organization – entire towns, cities, or counties or total organizations are rarely the focus of change efforts led by social workers.

Because a macro orientation focuses on sociopolitical, economic, environmental, and historical factors that impact people's lives, macro practice is an important way of fulfilling social work's commitment to achieving greater social and economic justice on behalf of underserved, vulnerable, or oppressed populations. If *social justice* were achieved, all citizens would have the same basic rights, protections, opportunities, obligations, and social benefits; if *economic justice* were achieved, resources would be distributed in a fair and equitable manner.

1. Systems Involved in the Macro Change Process: The following systems are critical to the macro change process (Netting et al., 2004; Kirst-Ashman & Hull, 2006).

a. Initiator System: The initiator system consists of the person or group who first recognizes the existence of a community or organizational problem and calls attention to it. Sometimes this individual is a social worker. Other initiators are people indigenous to the community or organization who have experienced the problem and/or tried to resolve it but feel powerless to affect the system. These initiators should be empowered and encouraged to participate in the intervention. Sometimes they can serve in leadership positions and bring in other supporters.

b. Change Agent System: A change agent is the individual (the social worker) who initiates the change process. The **change agent system** includes the change agent and a core planning committee or task force that initially analyzes the problem, the population, and the community or organization where the change will take place (the "arena"). If the change effort will draw on resources from an organization, then that organization will need to sanction the change and should be made part of the change agent system. This may require getting formal approval from the organization's executive board (board of directors). Ideally, the change agent system will also include members of the initiator system. The function of the change agent system is to act as an initial coordinating, or steering, committee until a broader range of participants can be incorporated into the effort; after the initial stages, coordinating functions are shifted to the action system (see below).

c. Client System: The **client system** is made up of the individuals who will become direct or indirect beneficiaries of the change. This will be either (a) a group of clients with similar characteristics or qualifications for receiving services or resources or (b) an organizational or community segment that will benefit from the macro-level intervention. A "target population" gives focus to an initial population analysis and represents a broad spectrum of people experiencing the problem, while the "client system" refers to those people who actually are intended to benefit from the proposed change. Sometimes they are the same, sometimes they are not.

d. Support System: The support system includes other individuals and groups who may be willing to support a change effort if they are needed. This encompasses everyone in a community or organization who has an interest in the success of a proposed change, including those who may receive secondary benefits. Initiator, change agent, and client systems can be seen as part of the support system in that they all have an interest in supporting the change.

e. Controlling System: The controlling system is comprised of the individual or group with the power and formally delegated authority to approve a proposed change and require its implementation. If the change involves a public agency or publicly funded or regulated services, those in control may be elected officials; if the change involves a private agency, those in control may be a board of directors. The controlling system is not necessarily the individual or group at the highest level of authority, however, and change agents, therefore, need to identify the highest level to which they must appeal in order to receive approval for the proposed change.

f. Host and Implementing Systems: A *host system* is the organization or unit with formally assigned responsibility for the area to be addressed by a proposed change. Typically, the host system is located below the controlling system on an organizational chart, and, in most macro changes, the host system will be a subunit of an organization that will be expected to implement the policy change, new program, or project. The *implementing system* includes employees and/or volunteers within the host system who will have day-to-day responsibility for implementing the change. Because the perspectives of the controlling system, host system, and implementing system regarding the proposed change may differ, each system should be examined separately.

g. Target System: The **target system** is the individual, group, structure, policy, or practice that needs to be changed so that the primary beneficiaries of the change effort can receive its intended benefits (i.e., it is the system that is the target of intervention efforts). The target system sometimes is difficult to define. In many cases, values, attitudes, practices, and policies, as well as the provision of services, all need to change, and change efforts often have to address multiple targets. The target system may or may not be part of the controlling, host, and/or implementing systems. The decision about who comprises the target system is made based on what change needs to take place and who needs to be persuaded or convinced to support it.

h. Action System: The **action system** is comprised of individuals from any or all of the other systems who have an active role in planning and implementing the intervention and seeing it through to completion. Although the change agent system forms the core of the action system, other participants also should have important roles in decision-making and be added as the change effort proceeds. For example, these individuals can serve on an expanded steering committee or in a decision-making group that participates in implementing and monitoring the change. The action system should include representatives from as many other systems as possible, including the target system if the relationship is not overly adversarial.

2. Application of Systems Theory to Macro Practice: Assumptions associated with general systems theory guide the models used in macro practice to bring about planned change in communities and organizations.

a. Implications of Systems Theory for Macro Practice: The implications of systems theory for macro practice include the following (Hardina, 2002): (a) Changes in one part of a system (e.g., a community or organization) bring about changes in other parts of the system. (b) Actions in subunits (subsystems) of the system influence what happens both within the subunit and within the larger system. (c) The effort to return to a steady state (equilibrium) is a driving force in most systems.

b. Analogies Used to View Social Systems: Martin and O'Connor (1989) identify five analogies used to view social systems. Social workers may use these analogies when approaching social systems, particularly communities and organizations.

- The *mechanical* analogy views social systems as machines. All parts of the system work closely together. They are integrated and well coordinated. Practice models that derive from this analogy aim to organize the community or organization to make conditions more pleasant and restore order.

- The *organismic* analogy compares social systems to living organisms. Each part of the system has a special function, and, if each part performs its function as intended, the parts work together for the common good. This analogy may apply if key people in a community or organization can agree on how to resolve the problem.

- A *morphogenic* analogy applies when change is ongoing and the structure of the system is continually emerging. Under these circumstances, fundamental change can occur because there's no chance of returning to how things were before (i.e., to "status quo"). Change is likely to be unpredictable, and social workers should be open to a wide variety of solutions and interventions.

- The *factional* analogy assumes that conflict is fundamental and instability and change are ongoing (i.e., a social system is comprised of competing subunits that are disposed to conflict). Conflict is so basic that change is likely to be disorderly and unstable. Rather than assuming that order can be restored, social workers using this analogy face conflict head-on.

- Finally, the *catastrophic* analogy assumes that social systems change so much and so often that they appear chaotic. There is extreme conflict and contentiousness in the system and a lack of order and predictability, and it can be difficult to determine the system's future direction.

As the above descriptions imply, some social systems are more open to change than others, and a social worker's interventions need to vary depending on her assessment of the social system and amount of conflict (Netting et al., 2004):

- Mechanical and organismic analogies are focused on preservation of the status quo, incremental change, and efforts to restore consensus. In other words, they focus on order rather than conflict and assume that social systems seek to maintain the status quo and re-establish equilibrium in the event of change. For example, when an agency is machine-like and closed, personnel may see the external environment as a threat, may focus more on internal operations, and may resist change. Critics of systems theory contend that these analogies fail to take into account unexplained change, conflict, and situations in which community or organizational members not only disagree but are deeply divided.

- Morphogenic, factional, and catastrophic analogies, by contrast, recognize conflict and change. They assume that conflict and change are inevitable and to be expected. Unlike mechanical and organismic analogies, they account for situations in which there is unexpected change or conflict and the members of a social system are very divided. Therefore, these analogies apply when there is deep division in a social system, when harmony can't be restored, or when there are dynamics that require significant change. For example, when a community is very divided, the social worker needs to establish linkages between groups before attempting to effect significant change.

3. Approaches to Macro-Level Change: Available approaches to change in macro practice include the following:

Policy approach: "Policy" is a formally adopted statement that reflects goals and strategies or agreements on a course of action. Policies may be established by elected representatives, boards, or administrators, or by a vote of the people affected. Change agents may determine that a new policy is needed in order to change a situation or that an existing policy that is unnecessarily restrictive needs to be altered.

Program approach: Programs are prearranged sets of activities designed to achieve a set of goals and objectives. In macro practice, most programs are intended to provide services directly to clients or communities; others, such as fund-raising or public relations programs, are of a supportive nature. Change agents may determine that a new program needs to be established to serve a special population group or that an existing program needs to be changed so that it will be more responsive to client or community needs.

Project approach: Projects are similar to programs but exist for only a limited time and are more flexible. Projects deemed successful are often permanently established as programs. Change agents may determine that creating a project to demonstrate a new intervention is more appealing to decision-makers than making a long-term program commitment. If so, they may select a *demonstration* or *pilot project* as a first approach and then attempt a more comprehensive program change if the project is successful.

Personnel approach: This approach may be appropriate when people (personnel) are experiencing unresolvable differences and ongoing conflict. Change agents proceed carefully before involving themselves in personnel issues, however. For example, they consider whether the proposed personnel-related intervention is being considered for appropriate reasons – i.e., is it being considered as a way of improving the quality of life for clients or the community or improving the quality of work life for agency personnel so that clients or the community can be better served? Netting and colleagues (2004) recommend using personnel and practice approaches only when policy, program, or project approaches are determined to be ineffective or not feasible.

Practice approach: This approach addresses the way organizations or their personnel go about doing their work. Practices are less formal and more elusive than policies. Practice issues sometimes can be resolved by consensus among staff; other times, they need to be addressed at higher levels in the organization. Taking a policy (rather than practice) approach usually results in a more effective and more permanent solution for ineffective or inappropriate practices.

XVIII. Policy Practice

Policy practice in social work involves "efforts to influence the development, enactment, implementation, modification, or assessment of social policies, primarily to ensure social justice and equal access to basic social goods" (Barker, 2003, p. 330). Social workers involved in social policy planning are frequently concerned with the following policy questions (NASW, 1995): What kind of society, community, or organization is sought and what kind of relationships are sought? How should resources be used? How should goods and services be allocated? How should power and services be divided? What constitutes distributive justice? (The concept of *distributive justice* suggests that public policy should allocate resources in a participatory and democratic way.)

All social workers, not just those directly involved in policy practice, should be committed to maximizing the quality of social policy decisions: They should make sure that social policies follow certain values such as promoting justice, equality, and self-determination.

1. Needs Assessment: A common way of assessing human service needs is through needs assessment. Needs assessment is used to identify the incidence, prevalence, and nature of a problem within a community. Its overall purpose is to assess the adequacy of existing services and resources for addressing a target condition or problem, and, thereby, identify the need for different services or resources. Ultimately, the results should provide information about unmet service needs including an understanding of the following: the quantity of existing services (does the level of service meet the need?); the quality of existing services (are the services effective?); and the direction of existing services (e.g., are service delivery approaches appropriate to the real needs of clients?).

The most useful approach for needs assessment is **survey research**. Sometimes this involves reviewing existing surveys of target population members, providers, and others. Other available approaches for needs assessment include gathering opinions from key informants through community forums, public hearings, interviews, and focus groups; collecting service statistics (utilization, waiting lists, caseload data, etc.); locating epidemiological studies (studies on the origins of problems) or studies of the incidence and prevalence of problems; or using social indicators (e.g., unemployment rates) (Meenaghan & Gibbons, 2000).

2. Policy Management:

a. Policy Management Steps: The steps involved in policy management have been defined in different ways by different authors. A summary of these steps appears below (NASW, 1995):

> *Step 1. Formulate the policy problem and make policy recommendations:* Formulating a policy problem or issue includes examining the socioeconomic, political, and organizational conditions in which the target problem exists. Tasks, in sequence, include the following: (a) determine the existence of a policy problem or issue (i.e., a "problem" exists when parties disagree over a policy or the social conditions it affects); (b) define the nature of the policy problem and its socioeconomic context; (c) identify factors contributing to the problem; (d) identify key policy issues and their implications; (e) evaluate current policies and programs; (f) examine the history of efforts to resolve the

problem; (g) identify key individuals and decision-making entities; (h) define, assess, rank, and recommend policy alternatives and calculate costs and benefits; (i) estimate the effects of the recommended policies; and (j) make policy recommendations.

Step 2. Implement the policy: Legislative, administrative, and judicial policies are converted into legislation, organizational directives, programs, projects, etc. In other words, approved policy is translated into practice — a social worker engaged in policy management organizes, oversees, and evaluates how the new policy will be implemented, or put into action, in an agency or community. Tasks, in sequence, include the following: (a) operationally describe the policy and the resources needed to carry it out; (b) define the levels at which the policy will be implemented (local, state, federal, etc.); (c) list and analyze legislative, administrative, and judicial considerations; (d) develop political strategies; (e) select monitoring methods and criteria for evaluating the implementation process; and (f) monitor and evaluate the outcome or results achieved and make recommendations about the continuation or closing of the program or project or its modification.

b. *Policy Management Approaches* (Feldman & Khademian, 2004):

Inclusive management: The **inclusive management model** is concerned with direct public (community) participation – it emphasizes the relationship between public managers and the public and encourages managers to focus on building the capacity of the public to participate in the policy process. One way that this capacity is built is through a focus on the structure and maintenance of relationships with the public, and this has implications for how managers carry out their responsibilities: (a) First, inclusive managers are concerned with facilitating problem-solving within the community, rather than making decisions on behalf of the community. (b) Second, the model shifts the focus of management control efforts from a more traditional centralized system to one of localized control.

Additionally, in building relationships with the public, managers are encouraged to focus on specific characteristics of these relationships, particularly trust and connection. Trust is believed to emerge around a common identity of people working to address public problems – managers use methods that facilitate direct connections with the public and the development of identity-based trust. Inclusive managers similarly encourage their employees to focus on relationship building; they facilitate the development of relationships between their employees and others who are concerned with the issues their employees work on.

Principal-agent model: The **principal-agent model** emphasizes direct accountability to elected officials. It has the following characteristics: (a) Managers are related to the public through a chain of command, with elected officials at the top. In other words, in the principal-agent model, elected officials mediate connections with the public through a hierarchy and oversight of public programs. (b) Managers focus on the technical implementation of public policies defined by elected officials. Rather than relying on a substantive "policy" expertise, public managers use their managerial expertise to facilitate the effective and efficient implementation of policies.

Expertise model: The **expertise model** emphasizes the application of professional judgment on behalf of the public. This model has the following characteristics: (a) The relationship between the public and public managers is mediated by the use of professional expertise on behalf of the public. Managers assume that public interests are represented through elected officials but also use their professional expertise to increase the knowledge of politicians about public interests and the best ways to serve them. (b) Managers focus on the application of managerial skill and substantive policy expertise to improve public policy outcomes. Rather than accountability directly to politicians, accountability is to the proper use of professional expertise.

c. Analysis of Proposed Policies: A procedure known as **policy analysis** is used to evaluate both proposed and existing social policies. Chambers (2000) offers the following basic guide for analyzing policy proposals (which may include proposed programs).

Step 1 – Social problem analysis: This step is similar to step 1 of the policy management process, when the policy problem is formulated. The social worker seeks to obtain a clear understanding of the problem that created the situation necessitating a new policy (or program) or policy change. The social worker (a) identifies how the problem is defined and locates estimates of its magnitude; (b) determines the causes and consequences of the problem; (c) identifies ideological beliefs or principles underlying descriptions of the problem (e.g., beliefs about how things "should be," opinions about the cause of the problem); and (d) identifies who gains and who loses from the existence of the problem and how serious the negative consequences are for the "losers."

Step 2 – Social policy analysis: The social worker then assesses the social policy or program that has been proposed. She (a) examines the policy and program history (is the target problem a new problem, have conditions, values, or perceptions changed over time, how does the proposed policy or program differ from past efforts to deal with the problem?); and (b) identifies how the proposed policy or program would operate (what are its goals and objectives, who would be eligible to benefit from it, what benefits or services would be delivered, what administrative structure would be required and how would it work, how would the program be financed and how much money would be required?).

Step 3 – Draw conclusions: After collecting this information, the social worker makes a judgment as to the merits of the policy (or program) so that she can decide whether to support it, oppose it, or suggest a compromise. The following questions can be considered: (a) Is the policy or program proposal appropriate for addressing the problem identified; (b) does the solution adequately deal with both the causes and consequences of the problem; (c) will it yield an outcome different from approaches used in the past; (d) would the costs associated with the proposed solution be justified by the potential outcomes; and (e) are there better solutions that might be proposed?

d. Analysis of Existing Policy: For an *existing* policy, policy analysis involves a systematic evaluation of the process by which the policy was formulated and the policy itself. The evaluation focuses on whether the process and policy are rational, clear, explicit, equitable, legal, politically feasible, consistent with social values, cost-effective, and better than all available alternatives in both the short-term and long-term. Approaches used to analyze existing policy include the following: (a) evaluation of *process* (i.e., the sociopolitical factors involved in policy formulation); (b) evaluation of *product* (i.e., the values and assumptions that influence policy choices and decisions); and (c) evaluation of *performance* (i.e., the cost-benefit outcome of implementing the policy).

XIX. Planning, Implementing, and Evaluating Macro Change

The major steps involved in an episode of macro change include the following:

Step 1: Analyze the problem, population, and arena.

Step 2: Develop a working hypothesis of etiology about the problem.

Step 3: Develop a working hypothesis of intervention based on relevant findings from the earlier steps and the working hypothesis of etiology.

Step 4: Select an approach to change: policy, program, project, practice, or personnel.

Step 5: Build support for the change.

Step 6: Estimate the probability of success.

Step 7: Decide whether to pursue the change effort.

Step 8: Select strategies and related tactics to get the change approved by relevant decision makers and others.

Step 9: Plan the intervention.

Step 10: Prepare to implement the intervention.

Step 11: Monitor the intervention.

Step 12: Evaluate the effectiveness of the intervention.

In this section, we review Steps 3 through 12, in which the intervention is planned, implemented, monitored, and evaluated. Steps 1 and 2 are discussed in Section XII of your chapter on Assessment.

The assessment activities performed when initiating an episode of community or organizational change allow change agents to develop a working hypothesis of etiology. Once those activities are completed, change agents can begin working toward effecting the desired change in the community or organization. The tasks involved in changing a macro system include (a) developing a hypothesis of intervention, (b) selecting an approach to change, (c) building support for the change, and (d) and planning, implementing, monitoring, and evaluating the intervention (Netting et al., 2004). All of these tasks are reviewed in this section.

A. Build Support and Plan the Intervention

Develop a Working Hypothesis of Intervention

The steps for developing a working hypothesis of intervention are as follows: (a) re-examine all relevant findings from analyses of the problem, population, and arena; (b) distill relevant quantitative data and other information into a clear working hypothesis of etiology; (c) use the working hypothesis of etiology to generate ideas about interventions that appear relevant to the problem; and (d) use the proposed interventions to develop the working hypothesis of intervention.

The resulting working hypothesis of intervention should be a testable statement (or series of statements) that identifies a target population (or specific subgroup) and problem, the change or intervention proposed, and the results expected from the intervention.

A combined hypothesis of etiology and working hypothesis of intervention would generally contain a statement similar to this one: "Because of the following factors drawn from analyses of the problem, population, and arena [a list of the most important causal factors] ... the results have been [a list of the effects or the identified problems] ... and, if the following interventions are implemented [a list of proposed interventions] ... the following results can be expected [a list of intended outcomes from intervention]."

Select an Approach to Change

Change agents determine what approach (or combination of approaches) is most likely to produce the desired change. Important questions in selecting the change approach are who or what needs to be changed in order for the problem to be resolved, what is the appropriate point of entry, and what approaches (or combinations of approaches) are most likely to yield the desired results? As noted earlier, available approaches to change include the policy approach, program approach, project approach, personnel approach, and practice approach.

Build Support for the Change

Change agents develop a plan, including strategies and tactics, designed to convince decision-makers, funders, and others to accept and support the change.

Schneider and Lester (2001) identify three groups who may oppose a change effort and, therefore, should be recognized by change agents: (a) individuals or groups who need more knowledge about relevant issues and who might support the change if they have adequate information; (b) individuals or groups who are indifferent or neutral and need to be convinced; and (c) individuals or groups who are certain about their opposition and may be hostile.

1. Define and Assess the Participants:

a. Build Coalitions (Coalition Building): While the initial phase of macro change can be performed by a small group of people who recognize the problem (i.e., the change agent system), for the effort to proceed successfully, a broad base of support is usually required, and, therefore, a key part of strategy development usually involves the building of **coalitions**. Building support for the change begins with identifying major participants, or "stakeholders," relevant to the proposed change. In order to identify these individuals and ensure that participation will end up being representative of a wide variety of relevant groups and interests, change agents consider all of the key systems involved in macro practice – initiator, change agent, client, support, controlling, host, implementing, target, and action. All of these systems could be within one organization, and, usually, many of them will overlap.
(**Stakeholders** are any people in a community with a particular interest in what happens with an agency or program; they may be for or against a service or program.)

b. Assess Each System's Readiness to Support the Proposed Change: Understanding a system's readiness to support the change requires assessment of the following:

- The system's openness to change.

- The system's commitment to the change effort, including level of enthusiasm and degree of consensus within the system about the design of the proposed change.

- Resources the system has available to promote the change and to implement the change.

- Individuals or groups outside the systems who are likely to actively oppose the change effort. (Most proposed changes that require spending public funds face external resistance from groups who are competing for the funds.)

In addition, systems supporting the change should identify their own vulnerabilities (e.g., problems with their supporting data, a system member who can be pressured to change his or her mind).

2. Examine Elements Affecting Whether the Change Will Be Accepted:

a. Consider Which Social System Analogy Applies: In attempting to understand the climate in which the proposed change will take place, change agents consider which of several analogies used to view social systems might apply: mechanical, organismic, morphogenic, factional, or catastrophic. Regardless of how the problem is defined or how conflict is viewed, however, change agents must be prepared to face opposition or resistance to the proposed change. For example, even when the target system agrees to collaborate, there may be disagreements about specifics of the proposed change.

b. Consider Political and Interpersonal Factors: In this context, "politics" refers to the different ways individuals important to a change effort may respond when asked to support the change. When taking into account political and interpersonal factors, change agents typically do the following:

- They assess the political and interpersonal strengths and liabilities of each participant in each system so that they can make the best use of each person involved in the change effort.

- They consider whether anyone key to the success of the change effort has been left out, how much conflict they can expect to encounter, and how opponents will frame their opposition. They carefully analyze the political appeal, merit, and intensity of support for each perspective, including their opponents'.

- They recognize that problems which have existed for a long time can be difficult to change because people become desensitized and community and organizational leaders may not be easily persuaded that a problem actually exists. For emerging problems, change agents examine the issue of **urgency**: In communities, problems that threaten survival needs (such as food, clothing, shelter, safety, and medical care) are more likely to be recognized by those in a position to approve changes. In organizations, problems that affect the budget or funding tend to receive a higher priority than other problems.

c. Consider Resources: Because decision-makers often claim that a proposed change will cost too much or that resources are not available, change agents prepare preliminary calculations of cost for staff, salaries, facilities, etc. (Although decision-makers usually want to perform their own analysis of costs, a change agent's estimates can serve as a basis for comparison.) Change agents also consider what the problem will cost the community or organization if nothing is done and frame this cost in a manner that might persuade decision-makers to support the proposed change.

3. Estimate the Probability of Success: At this point, change agents and other participants weigh the relative strength of supporting and opposing forces and decide whether the change effort should proceed or not. **Force field analysis** may be used to identify and assess significant factors that promote or inhibit change in a community or organization and is one way of facilitating an informed decision about the likelihood of success. Five steps are involved in a force field analysis (Lewin, 1951):

Step 1 – Clearly and succinctly specify the objective (the change one hopes to achieve).

Step 2 – Identify the social forces that will determine if the objective will be achieved. On the left side of a sheet of paper, list "driving forces" (those who are expected to support the objective); and, on the right side, list "restraining forces" (those who are expected to oppose the objective). Examples of "forces" include powerful individuals, groups, organizations, coalitions, or elected officials who have a stake in the issue; individuals who will be served by the program; and professionals familiar with the approach to be used in the proposed program.

Step 3 – Determine the relative strength of each driving and each restraining force. Each force is assessed on three factors: power; the consistency with which it has taken its position; and amenability, or the extent to which it is open to outside influence. For each factor, a high or low rating is given and noted on the lists from Step 2.

Step 4 – Identify individuals or groups who might influence the outcome by successfully opposing a driving or a restraining force, thereby changing its strength. Once a potential individual or group has been identified for each force, record its rating of high or low strength.

Step 5 – Select strategies and tactics based on the above assessments. For example, the assessments may show that one goal should be to weaken restraining forces by enlisting help from influential individuals or groups.

4. Decide Whether to Pursue the Change Effort: Change agents and other participants then decide whether to pursue the change effort or abandon it. Changes that have a good chance of succeeding should be pursued, while those that are likely to be defeated should be postponed until they are more fully developed or the timing is better.

5. Select Strategies and Tactics to Get the Change Accepted: In this context, "strategy" refers to efforts designed to make sure that a proposed change is accepted, while "tactics" are specific techniques used to maximize the chances that a strategy will be successful and the proposed change will be accepted.

Brager and colleagues (1987) identify four properties of tactics used by change agents: (a) they are planned; (b) they are used to evoke specific responses; (c) they involve interaction with others; and (d) they are goal-oriented. Netting and colleagues (2004) add one other property: A tactic does no harm to members of the client system, and, when possible, client system members are involved in tactical decision-making.

Strategies for getting a change accepted fall into three categories – collaboration, campaign, and contest (Schneider & Lester, 2001). As explained below, Netting and colleagues (2004) use these three categories to describe the relationship between the action and target systems. Change agents may begin with one strategy (category) and move on to others, depending on the evolving relationship between the action and target systems.

Collaboration: **Collaboration** is used when there is a working relationship in which the action and target systems agree that change must occur (i.e., the target system agrees, or is readily convinced, that change is needed and supports the allocation of resources). Collaboration implies a joint venture in which parties agree to work together toward a change that neither could accomplish alone and requires communication, cooperation, and coordination. Collaboration tactics include the following:

Implementation: Activities associated with implementation include conducting research and studying the issue, developing fact sheets and alternative proposals, creating task forces, conducting workshops, and communicating regularly with the opposition (Schneider & Lester, 2001).

Capacity building: Approaches associated with **capacity building** include participation and empowerment. Participation refers to activities that involve members of the client system in the change effort. Empowerment focuses on building a capacity for greater self-direction among members of the client system and teaching them how to participate in decision-making processes and take more control over decisions that affect their lives.

Campaign: **Campaign** is used when the target system needs to be convinced of the importance of the change or persuaded to allocate resources, but communication is still possible between the action and target systems. The effectiveness of a campaign determines whether collaboration or contest is used next. Campaign tactics include the following:

Education: Educational tactics are used to inform. Action system members present perceptions, opinions, data, and information about the proposed change in an effort to convince target system members to think or behave differently. Education may not work because opponents of the change often undertake their own educational efforts to influence decision-makers and there are few absolute "truths" in dealing with most problems. When education fails, change agents often turn to persuasion.

Persuasion: Persuasion involves efforts to convince others to accept and support one's perspective on an issue – in this case, to convince decision-makers that the change is worth pursuing. To use persuasion effectively, action system members must understand the motives and reasoning of the target system so that they can identify incentives and information that are likely to have the desired effect. Those selected for leadership positions in the action system should have the ability to persuade and be viewed as credible by members of the target system. Sometimes clients can be powerful spokespersons.

Co-optation: **Co-optation** addresses opposition by absorbing target system members and other opponents into the action system. Once people become part of the action system, they are likely to assume some "ownership" of the change effort. An effective way of co-opting opponents (as well as neutral parties) is to help them recognize some sort of self-interest in the proposed change. It can be particularly useful to co-opt people who are viewed as powerful by the target system – these people may be neutral and have no interest in blocking the change effort, but, if they can be convinced to support it, their participation may influence target system members who respect their opinions.

Co-opting individuals is called **informal co-optation**, and co-opting organized groups is called **formal co-optation** (i.e., an entire group agrees to support the change). Formal co-optation of a number of groups leads to **coalition building**.

Lobbying: The action system may determine that it is necessary to change agency policy, amend legislation, or develop new legislation in order to achieve their goal. This form of persuasion addresses policy change under the domain of the controlling system. Haynes and Mickelson (2000) define the following guidelines for lobbying: always be factual and honest; support presentations with available data; and include in discussions the two main concerns of decision-makers – cost and the social impact of what is proposed. If cost is high, change agents should estimate the costs of allowing the problem to remain unresolved.

Mass media appeal: This tactic involves the development and release of stories to the media in an effort to influence public opinion and, thereby, pressure decision-makers to support the change and/or allocate resources. If the proposed change is presented to the public in a positive way, then the refusal of a decision-maker (e.g., an elected representative who is concerned about public opinion) to support it can be presented as negative. Use of mass media requires assurance that the cause will be presented accurately and consideration of clients' rights to privacy. Electronic advocacy (e.g., via online discussion groups designed to educate people about an issue) can be an effective way of rapidly reaching large numbers of people.

Contest: **Contest** is used when neither collaboration nor campaign is possible because of disagreement or conflict between the action and target systems (i.e., the target system can't be persuaded to accept the change or allocate resources and/or the target system refuses to communicate with the action system). Because contest tactics are confrontational, when using them, action system members should be prepared for open and public confrontation. Contest tactics include the following:

Bargaining and negotiation: Here, action and target systems confront each other with the reasons why they support or oppose the change. These tactics occur when there is a power differential between parties and a compromise needs to be made. They are more formalized than persuasion and sometimes involve a third-party mediator (e.g., when communication has ceased between the action and target systems). For **negotiation** to occur, the action and target systems must both perceive that they have something to gain (i.e., that the other system has something they want). And for target system members to agree to negotiate, they must understand something about the action system's intentions and perceive the action system as having some legitimacy. Bargaining and negotiation can result in a win/win situation, a win/lose situation, or a lose/lose situation.

Large group or community action: This tactic involves training and organizing numerous people who are willing to form a pressure group and advocate for change through forms of **collective action** involving pressure tactics (e.g., picketing, disruption of meetings, sit-ins, boycotting). While peaceful demonstrations are legal activities, civil disobedience tactics intentionally break the law. Action system members must be ready to face the consequences of their actions, and change agents should make all participants aware of the risks.

Class action lawsuit: This involves suing an entity for a perceived violation of the law and an expectation that the court's ruling will apply to an entire class of people. This tactic is often used on behalf of vulnerable populations who are unlikely to have the capacity or resources to protect their own rights. Action systems who use this tactic may use public interest law organizations as resources.

Plan the Intervention

Before planning the intervention, action system members may prepare a written document that clearly explains the problem, describes the proposed change and its expected results, and lists the strategies and tactics selected to get the change accepted. This document may be distributed to participants for comment as a way of achieving consensus; any disagreements should be addressed before planning the details of the intervention.

Planning the intervention – whether using a policy, program, project, personnel, or practice approach – involves establishing the goal, developing objectives, listing activities, and establishing timeframes, due dates, and responsibilities. The resulting "action plan" should be in writing, and copies should be distributed to those who will be involved in its implementation. The plan will be used to orient and train implementers and serve as the basis for monitoring and evaluating the effectiveness of the intervention.

1. Establish the Goal: Setting a goal and objectives involves translating the concepts and ideas generated during analysis into concrete terms. The **goal** for the intervention defines the overall outcome expected if the intervention is successful. It reminds participants of the real purpose of the change effort and can be used to facilitate consensus among people with differing views. The goal is stated in outcome terms and should include a target population, a boundary, and an expected result or outcome. The processes or methods that will be used to achieve the goal should not be included in the goal statement.

2. Develop Objectives: Objectives move the change effort toward its goal; they are highly specific and spell out the details of the intervention in measurable terms, including expected outcomes and the processes that will be used to achieve them.

a. Outcome Objectives and Process Objectives: Developing objectives begins with looking over the working hypothesis of intervention and translating the proposed interventions into objectives. Objectives may be developed around each proposed intervention. There are two types of objectives – outcome and process – and, typically, a macro-level intervention will include one goal, a number of outcome objectives, and several process objectives for each outcome objective.

Outcome objectives: One outcome objective is generally written for each intervention and it specifies the result or outcome to be achieved with and for the target population (or client system). An outcome should be stated as a quality-of-life change for the client or consumer of services.

Process objectives: One or more process objectives are written for each outcome objective. A process objective specifies the process to be followed in order to achieve the result. When an outcome objective and its related process objectives have been established, it should be evident that the process objectives, when completed, will lead to achievement of the outcome objective; and that the outcome objective, when accomplished, will move the effort toward the goal.

b. Components of Objectives: A complete objective, whether outcome or process, has four parts (Kettner et al., 1985):

Timeframe: The timeframe ideally is stated in terms of the month, day, and year by which the result will be achieved (outcome objective) or the activity will be completed (process objective). This information will be needed later for monitoring purposes.

Target: (a) For an outcome objective, the target is those individuals who are expected to be the primary beneficiaries of the intervention. (b) For a process objective, the target is those who will participate in the process named in the objective. The more precise the target, the greater the likelihood of a successful intervention.

Result: An objective includes a phrase that specifies the expected result or outcome that will be achieved when all activities have been completed. (a) For an outcome objective, the result is the expected quality-of-life change(s) for the target population (or client system) as a result of the intervention (e.g., reduction of alcohol abuse, more control over community decision-making). (b) For a process objective, the focus is on what result will provide evidence that the objective has been achieved (e.g., the client completes 10 counseling sessions). The result is stated in a way that is concrete and observable.

Criterion for measuring or documenting the result: An objective specifies the criterion that will be used to determine whether the objective has been achieved. (a) The criterion for an outcome objective usually begins with, "as measured by ...." Specifying a criterion in this way ensures that only one standard will be used to measure results. For example, if improving self-esteem is the desired result, then the result should be measured by a standardized test of self-esteem. (b) Process objectives may be directed toward completion of part of the process by clients or other participants or toward production of products or achievement of milestones. A variety of criteria can be used to measure the result of a process objective. In most cases, process objectives use the phrases, "as documented by ..." or "as demonstrated by ...." Completion of a course, for example, can be documented by receipt of a certificate. The focus is on record-keeping and other documentation that will clearly demonstrate that the result has been achieved.

3. List Activities for Process Objectives: The final step in developing the intervention plan is to itemize activities. Each activity represents a step that, when accomplished, will move the change effort closer to achievement of a process objective. Activities should specify the work to be done, the person responsible, and a timeframe.

The **Gantt chart** (Gantt, 1919) is a useful format for setting up activities. The chart is made up of columns and rows. Each row represents an activity, and columns are used to identify an activity number, the person responsible, and the beginning and ending dates. In this way, Gantt charts illustrate how various tasks should be listed under major activities, clarify the beginning and ending points projected for each task, and show, at a glance, what efforts must be made within a specific time period.

Finally, **PERT** (program evaluation review technique) can be useful for systematically connecting goals to means of achieving them. It involves determining and listing program objectives, activities, resources; the time needed to achieve the objectives; and the order in which activities should be performed.

B. Implement, Monitor, and Evaluate the Intervention

1. Prepare to Implement the Intervention: During assessment and planning, the change effort is carried out by, as well as on, many interacting and overlapping individuals and systems. In preparation for implementation and before involving clients, consumers, or participants, the intervention must become more formalized. This usually requires completing a number of tasks.

An important initial task is to select a **lead person** or **coordinator**. This person will encourage others to get the job done, maintain morale, and motivate participants; she will be critical to the success of the intervention and, therefore, should be selected carefully.

Another significant task is to address logistical considerations such as facilities, equipment, personnel (including volunteers), and other **resources**, including determining what resources need to be made available before the intervention plan is implemented. If the intervention is a new program or project with its own funding and other resources, then formal job descriptions and job announcements need to be developed and additional personnel need to be selected. In a large-scale change, it's best to first recruit, select, and hire the lead person and then have that person assume a leading role in selecting other staff. Additional staff and volunteers may be new or may be drawn from current organizational employees or community groups, but, either way, there should be a job description for each position and a selection process that includes interviews. Earlier participants in the change process may become part of a policy-making or advisory board to provide consultation and guidance for the intervention. Coordination and communication among old and new participants is important for facilitating successful implementation.

Selected personnel should go through an orientation. Early participants may also participate in the orientation as a means of maintaining the continuity of the change effort. Plans for ongoing training are then addressed based on what is learned from early implementation experiences and the training needs expressed by staff and volunteers.

2. Monitor the Intervention: The specifics of monitoring and evaluation depend on the size and scope of the intervention, but, in all cases, these processes require data collection and the building of a management information system to keep track of efforts and accomplishments. The lead person is typically the only participant who has an overview of all the activities, and, therefore, she is responsible for integrating different parts of the intervention.

a. Monitor Technical Activities: The intervention's objectives move the change effort toward its goal; they spell out the details of the intervention in measurable terms, including expected outcomes and the processes that will be used to achieve them. There are two types of objectives – outcome and process – and, typically, a macro-level intervention will include one goal, a number of outcome objectives, and several process objectives for each outcome objective.

Achieving one process objective involves completing a series of activities, and, often, one activity is a prerequisite for the next and later activities. If activities have been itemized, preferably in Gantt chart form, then monitoring technical activities simply requires confirming with the person responsible that the activity has been started/completed on the date specified. When activities don't meet deadlines or other problems arise, the lead person must engage in problem-solving and decision-making to get the intervention back on track.

b. Monitor Interpersonal Activities: Monitoring interpersonal activities requires establishing and communicating to all participants a process for addressing interpersonal tensions, poor performance, apathy, resistance, etc. In larger, more permanent programs, formal appraisals are conducted and maintained in personnel files. In less formally structured efforts (particularly in community change), frequent conferences, staff meetings, or peer review sessions are used to allow participants to express their concerns before they affect performance or morale.

3. Evaluate the Effectiveness of the Intervention: In this context, evaluation focuses on the outcomes or results specified in outcome objectives. Thus, after all activities and processes are completed, one refers back to the outcome objectives to determine whether the intervention has been successful. The use of sound techniques for collecting and aggregating data and information and preparing clear displays of outcomes and succinct reports help to solidify support for the change from key stakeholders. Continual feedback and communication with supporters and participants also increase the chance that the change (such as a new program) will become a permanent part of the organization or community.

a. Compile Periodic Evaluation Reports: Evaluation requires collecting and organizing data and information. Tracking the performance of each client or participant should include establishment of a baseline at the beginning of the intervention and periodic measurement of progress. This may involve a pre- and posttest or the tracking of a single indicator (e.g., a client gets a job). If the intervention involves a large-scale program with many clients or participants, data should be entered into a computerized system. (Additional information on program evaluation appears in Section XXI of this chapter.)

b. Prepare a Report for Stakeholders: Once data for all outcome objectives are collected, aggregated, and compiled, an end-of-the-year report is prepared for funding sources and other stakeholders. (Most funding and sponsoring sources expect at least annual reporting on progress and results.) This report usually includes the following sections: overview of rationale for the change effort; description of interventions; goals and objectives; first-year findings (tables, graphs, and charts with explanations); and recommendations for what should be changed in the next and succeeding years.

Rapp and Poertner (1992) offer the following suggestions for report writing: (a) establish a standard (numbers are meaningless without standards for comparison); (b) limit the presentation to major findings; (c) use simple, attractive graphs, charts, and tables wherever possible; (d) explain graphs, charts, and tables in simple, jargon-free language; and (e) make aggregation meaningful – make sure that those who use the report can identify data and information that are meaningful to them at their level in the organization or community.

XX. Organizations and Organizational Theory

Organizations are composed of people, tools, and resources structured to accomplish specific objectives. Defining features of organizations include the following (Daft, 2004):

- *Organizations are goal directed.* Organizations exist for a specified purpose.

- *Organizations are social entities.* Because organizations are made up of people with both strengths and weaknesses, they too exhibit both positive and negative attributes; and, just as patterns of behavior develop in people, they also develop in organizations.

- *Organizations are deliberately structured and coordinated "activity systems."* Every organization has a structure that includes policies for how it should be run, hierarchies, and different units (or departments) working in various ways to help the organization function. Each unit within an organization has distinct responsibilities, but all units work toward the same goal. "Activity systems" are actions carried out by designated units and are guided by the practical application of knowledge to achieve specified goals. An organization coordinates the functioning of its various activity systems to improve its efficiency and effectiveness.

- *Organizations are linked to the external environment.* Organizations are in constant interaction with other systems in their social environment (their "task environment") including individuals, groups, other organizations, and communities. Agencies providing social services interact with clients, funding sources, legislative and regulatory agencies, politicians, community leaders, and other social services agencies.

One implication of the latter feature is that organizations can be seen as **open systems** that maintain themselves through constant interaction with the external environment (i.e., ongoing inflow and outflow of energy through permeable boundaries):

Inputs, throughputs, and outputs: All systems, including organizations, are comprised of parts (e.g., the people in an organization) that receive inputs, operate on those inputs via throughput, and produce outputs:

Inputs: In social agencies, inputs include resources (funding, staff, facilities), clients, the types and severity of clients' problems, and the values, expectations, and opinions about the agency held by community members, funding sources, regulatory bodies, and other parts of the environment.

Throughput: These are the services provided by the agency (i.e., its technology) and the way the agency is structured to apply its technology to the inputs it receives.

Outputs: In social agencies, output is the completion of a service to a client. The key aspect of service output is outcome, which is a measure of quality-of-life change for the client.

Feedback: A feedback mechanism is a feature of any cybernetic system (a cybernetic system is a self-regulating system that can get information from its surroundings, interpret that information, and adjust its functioning based on the information). Like biological organisms, organizations are cybernetic systems – to survive, they have to get information from their environment and make adaptations to fit external conditions. These efforts lead an organization to behave and organize itself in particular ways.

A. Organizational (Agency) Structure

Ways of structuring roles and responsibilities within social agencies and other organizations range from fully bureaucratized operations to ones that allow substantial worker autonomy. **Public agencies** tend to be bureaucratized, meaning that policymakers and program administrators retain significant control over agency functioning. **Private nonprofit agencies** are more likely to have decentralized authority and fewer rules and regulations – staff members usually have more control over their work activities and flexibility in how they perform their jobs.

1. Bureaucratic Model: A **bureaucracy** is a highly rational, stable, and predictable system that has the following characteristics:

- Clearly defined rules (usually written) that determine organizational functions. This ensures uniformity and consistency.

- A vertical hierarchy of responsibility and authority, with power centralized at the top.

- Authority that is distributed in a stable way and whose powers are strictly defined.

- Formalized channels of communication.

- Task-specific division of labor based on individual skill and competence – jurisdictions are fixed and official, routine activities are delegated as fixed and official duties, and duties are performed by individuals with specific predefined qualifications.

- Selection, promotion, compensation, and retention based on technical competence (personal considerations are not relevant). A person who holds a bureaucratic office (a "bureaucrat") receives a fixed salary and is motivated by the possibility of being promoted.

- Impersonal relationships among staff.

- Maintenance of a central system of records to summarize activities of the organization.

Max Weber, who coined the term bureaucracy, used the term "authority" to describe power that is exercised with the consent of those being led. Bureaucracies reflect "rational/legal authority," or power that is assigned based the ability to achieve instrumental goals.

Although the bureaucratic model is widely used, it may not be the best design for social agencies. Various terms have been used to describe the problems that arise in bureaucracies: (a) Merton (1952) used the term *learned incompetence* to describe employees in bureaucracies who rely so much on a policy manual to make their decisions that they are unable to think logically or creatively about clients' problems. (b) Lipsky (1984) used the term *bureaucratic disentitlement* to describe situations in which clients fail to receive benefits or services to which they are entitled because of worker decisions that are based on internal organizational considerations rather than service needs. (c) Hasenfeld (1983) discussed *goal displacement*, which he described as the tendency of organizations to lose sight of their mission and focus, instead, on the concerns of units within the organization (i.e., with goal displacement, preservation of the bureaucracy becomes an end in itself).

2. Alternatives to a Bureaucratic Structure: In an **adhocracy**, an organization creates internal structures on an issue-by-issue basis, with ad hoc groups of employees addressing each issue. The ad hoc groups have substantial authority and are required to follow only a few agency-wide rules and regulations. Ad hoc agencies have a "flat" administrative structure, meaning that all staff positions are about equal. Although they are relatively unstructured and tend to be less stable, agencies adopting this approach can respond to problems in a timely way and are able to undergo change quickly. They are particularly effective when the nature of the work is fluid.

In the *matrix structure*, supervision is assigned to a function rather than a person. Staff often have more than one supervisor. Finally, in the *collegial structure*, workers engage in joint activities when tasks require overlap, but, otherwise, operate more or less independently. An example is a private counseling clinic in which several mental health professionals form a partnership to buy a building and equipment and share support staff. Each partner has the same amount of authority and generates his or her own income.

3. The Structure of Social Agencies: Most social agencies fall somewhere along a continuum between pure bureaucracies and fully ad hoc structures. Larger agencies typically need to divide the work: They often use a *functional structure*, in which second-level administrators run units within the agency and/or supervise groups of workers and report to the agency's executive director. The executive director coordinates the units and oversees the work of unit managers. Smaller agencies can have more or less *flat administrative structures*, in which an executive director heads the agency (e.g., represents staff with the board and community) and other staff members report directly to that executive.

In addition, an agency may temporarily supplement its usual structure with a *project-team approach*, in which a group of workers is organized around a specific task for a limited period of time. Although assigned to a specific unit or supervisor for their main job, these workers are temporarily assigned to a team that cuts across units to address a specific problem.

4. Formal Organization vs. Informal Organization: Both formal and informal structures within an organization influence its effectiveness. The **formal organization** refers to social groupings that are expressly formed and re-formed by the organization to achieve specific goals (e.g., task groups, committees). The concept of the formal organization is associated with Weber, who introduced the term bureaucracy and defined its characteristics (see above.)

The **informal organization** refers to voluntary relationships that form among agency personnel. The informal organization is thought to have a significant impact on the way employees actually behave and perform their job tasks. For example, informal groups norms, as opposed to formally prescribed standards, are believed to determine the productivity of individual members of staff (see the Human Relations Model, below).

B. Management Theories

1. Scientific Management: Scientific management can be traced to Frederick Taylor (1911) who applied the scientific method to the study of job productivity. He used time-and-motion studies to identify how workers could complete their tasks in less time and with greater efficiency. For Taylor, scientific management involves the following:

- Scientifically analyzing jobs into their component parts and then standardizing those parts.

- Scientifically selecting, training, and placing workers in jobs for which they are mentally and physically suited.

- Fostering cooperation between supervisors and workers to minimize deviation from scientific methods of work. This is achieved by promoting recognition of mutual goals.

- Having managers and workers assume responsibility for their own share of their work.

One of the first steps in scientific management is to complete a careful study of the work, usually by identifying the best worker and studying that person. This study is done to find the "one best" way of doing the job, to develop the best possible tools for achieving it, to fit workers' interests and abilities to particular assignments, and to find the level of production the average worker can sustain. Following this, managers provide incentives to workers to increase productivity. Taylor believed that employees are motivated primarily by economic self-interest and argued that money is the most effective motivator.

2. Universalistic Management: Universalistic management theorists focused on Taylor's concern with maximizing productivity and sought broader principles to explain the ideals of rational management. Henri Fayol identified structural characteristics that managers should promote and developed the following six principles (Scott, 1981):

- Scalar principle – there should be a hierarchical structure with a pyramid-shaped chain of command.

- Unity of command principle – each person should have only one immediate supervisor.

- Span of control principle – a supervisor should have a manageable number of subordinates (usually six to eight).

- Exception principle – subordinates should be responsible for routine matters covered by rules so that supervisors can take care of unusual circumstances not covered by rules.

- Departmentalization principle – emphasis should be placed on division of labor, and similar functions should be grouped together.

- Line-staff principle – there should be a distinction between line functions (those central to completing basic organizational activities) and staff functions (those that are supportive or advisory).

A manager adopting these six principles would create an organization that reflects many characteristics of a bureaucracy; and applying these principles would result in outcomes similar to those of scientific management – predictability, efficiency, and maximum individual productivity.

Although the approaches of Taylor and Fayol don't always apply well to social agencies, social work has begun to adopt more "scientific" approaches to practice, including procedures and protocols to guide professional activity in certain situations. In addition, the accountability movement has resulted in more rigorous demands concerning the design of interventions and measurement of outcomes (Netting et al., 2004).

3. Human Relations Model: Rather than focusing on organizational structure, the human relations model is concerned with the needs, motives, and relationships of workers within an organization.

Underlying the development of the human relations model was the research conducted by Elton Mayo and colleagues at the Hawthorne Plant of the Western Electric Company between 1927 and 1932. Although Mayo's original intention was to investigate the effects of physical conditions on job performance, results of his studies ended up demonstrating the importance of psychological and social factors. In the "relay room" experiments, Mayo found that productivity increased regardless of what changes were made in the level of illumination. Subsequent interviews with workers revealed that improved productivity was due to such factors as the novelty of the experimental situation, the workers' interest in the experiment, the special attention they were receiving as research subjects, and the fact that those chosen to participate in the study worked together as a smaller group. In other words, social, not environmental, factors produced the increase in productivity. (The fact that performance can be altered by the way people are treated as participants in an experiment is now called the **Hawthorne effect**.)

These experiments also found that **informal work group norms** have a significant impact on worker productivity. Mayo found, for instance, that production above or below the informal norm resulted in social pressure to conform: Workers who produced too much were called "rate busters" by their coworkers, while workers who produced too little were called "chiselers."

Etzioni (1964) summarizes the basic principles of the human relations approach as follows:

- The level of production is set by social norms rather than by physiological capacities.

- Workers are more likely to derive satisfaction from social relationships than from instrumental activities, and managers are more likely to increase workers' productivity if they are responsive to the workers' social needs.

- Noneconomic rewards and sanctions have a significant effect on workers' behavior and limit the impact of economic incentive plans. Workers may be unwilling to exceed what the group as a whole can do, even if this means that they will earn less money.

- Workers behave as members of a group rather than as individuals. Therefore, a manager's attempts to influence how workers behave are more likely to succeed when they are directed toward the group (i.e., an individual may be unwilling to change if he is not accompanied by the other members of his group).

- Informal leadership is important because it influences worker behavior in ways that can either strengthen or weaken formal leadership (i.e., leadership acting through formal organizational structures).

- Democratic leadership is more effective than authoritarian leadership for promoting cooperation and the willingness to change.

A pure human relations management model is rarely used today, but its tenets influenced other approaches that focus on true empowerment for workers and brought attention to factors that remain relevant today, such as teamwork and positive attention from management (Netting et al., 2004).

4. Theory X and Theory Y: The differences between scientific management and the human relations approach are reflected in McGregor's (1960) distinction between Theory X and Theory Y managers. McGregor used Maslow's hierarchy of needs as a basis for understanding the behavior of workers in an organization: He maintained that workers are more than just social creatures – they are also self-actualizing beings whose ultimate goal at work is to meet their higher-order needs. To illustrate this, McGregor identified two opposite approaches to management – Theory X and Theory Y – and suggested that a manager's view of her role depends on her assumptions about employee characteristics.

- McGregor conceptualized **Theory X** as a relatively domineering style of management. Theory X managers believe that employees dislike work and avoid it whenever possible, and, as a result, they must be directed and controlled.

- **Theory Y** transfers decision-making power to lower-level workers and assumes that management's task is to recognize workers' higher-order needs and to design organizations that allow them to achieve these needs. Theory Y managers view work as being "as natural as play" and assume that employees are capable of self-control and self-direction.

McGregor believed that the level of motivation demonstrated by workers is directly related to their manager's beliefs, and that a Theory Y approach is more likely to produce an effective organization. In other words, according to McGregor, loosely structured organizations are better at promoting productivity because they allow workers to meet their higher-order needs through their work. Studies have shown, however, that Theory Y does not apply well in all organizations: A Theory Y management style appears to work well in organizations in which tasks are loosely defined and variable. In organizations where tasks are predictable and repetitive and require precision, a Theory X management style appears to be more effective (Morse & Lorsch, 1970). Although, in social work, tasks often are loosely defined and appear well suited to a Theory Y management style, many social agencies still operate using a Theory X management approach.

Note that Frederick Herzberg's (1966) studies on worker motivation provided support for McGregor's contentions. Herzberg divided motivational factors into two categories: extrinsic factors (e.g., wages, hours, working conditions, benefits) and intrinsic factors. Intrinsic motivators lie within the work itself and include such factors as the sense of satisfaction one derives from completing a task successfully. Herzberg discovered that, in the long run, extrinsic factors tend to minimize levels of dissatisfaction with the job, but do not motivate workers to be more productive. Only *intrinsic factors* motivate workers to become more productive.

5. Management by Objectives (MBO): In contrast to other management approaches, management by objectives (MBO) begins with a desired outcome and then structures the organization to achieve that outcome. An emphasis is placed on producing clear statements about expectations for the coming year, making these statements available to employees, breaking goals and objectives into tasks, and monitoring progress throughout the year. Success is measured by the extent to which objectives were achieved.

In a social agency, MBO emphasizes establishing objectives that are consistent with the agency's mission and linking them to measurable outcomes, and staff participate in defining the objectives they will achieve within an established period of time. "Objectives," in this context, are results that the agency has to achieve in order to remain viable in terms of its mission. Objectives are defined during the "inputs" stage of MBO; efforts to achieve the objectives are part of the "activities" stage; and results are measured during the "outputs" stage. Certain obstacles can interfere with the achievement of objectives. "Input traps," for example, include initial actions or conditions that limit the agency's operations or services (e.g., unclear goals, overdirection or underdirection of staff); and "activity traps" are obstacles that can arise during the activities stage, such as an overemphasis on busy work or personality conflicts (Skidmore, 1995).

While MBO tends to improve collaboration and cooperative activity, on a day-to-day basis the organization focuses heavily on steps that need to be taken to reach intermediate objectives, and this may cause it to lose sight of its ultimate goals. In addition, MBO relies on a "rational system analogy," which assumes that organizations are directed by rational actions designed to achieve certain goals – structuring organizational operations around goals and objectives can be problematic, however, because organizational goals often change (Netting et al., 2004).

Finally, consistent with MBO, many social agencies require the development of an annual plan that defines explicit goals and objectives for each program. MBO is also consistent with the increased attention paid to outcomes (vs. process) in the development of social work practice approaches. MBO, along with the accountability movement, establishes program outcomes as major criteria affecting decisions about funding and program continuation.

6. Participatory Management: Participatory management is a decision-making strategy in which administrators involve all those who are likely to be affected by a proposed organizational decision or change. It includes building voluntary consensus and commitment among personnel, clientele, sponsors, and other interested parties to achieve organizational goals. Pine, Warsh, and Maluccio (1998) and others report that worker satisfaction and productivity generally increase when participatory management techniques are used.

7. Managing Diversity: Thomas (1991) identified diversity as the key variable affecting productivity and considered effective management of diverse populations to be a critical leadership skill. To help organizations deal effectively with a diverse workforce, Thomas proposes the following framework for understanding organizational culture, which divides diversity into three phases. Although many social agencies have had diverse workforces for many years, only some have moved beyond the affirmative action phase.

Affirmative action: This includes programs and efforts designed to bring ethnic minorities and women into an organization. Thomas views affirmative action as a temporary step toward managing diversity.

Valuing differences: This phase consists of staff training and personnel development that (a) promote acceptance and mutual respect across racial and gender lines, (b) enhance understanding of differences, (c) help workers understand their own feelings and attitudes toward differences, and (d) enhance working relationships among people who are different.

Managing diversity: If an organization is unprepared to deal with a diverse workforce, it may need to engage in a long-term strategy to change its fundamental culture. This requires a complete understanding of its existing culture and a planned transition to a new culture that supports full utilization of a diverse workforce.

C. Organizational Behavior and Decision-Making

1. Natural Systems Model: Selznick (1949) and others believe that organizational behavior is best understood by using a natural system analogy. "Natural systems" are entities that behave in ways that are similar to biological organisms: They are aware of their own self-interest and seek to protect themselves. The natural system model predicts that an organization will make decisions that, above all, allow it to survive, even if this means that it must change its original mission. Etzioni (1964) describes this as a distinction between real goals and stated goals: If an organization cannot serve both sets of goals at the same time, then its real goals (e.g., self-preservation) will almost always determine its actions. Organizations that focus too much on their own survival may become much less effective at providing services.

2. Political Model: A "political model" views organizational behavior in terms of a complex interaction of forces that are similar to those found in any typical political environment (Pfeffer, 1981). In particular, individuals with power make their decisions based not only on what is best for the organization, but also on (a) what is best for themselves, (b) the competing self-interest of all those with power within the organization, and (c) the interests of powerful organizations in the environment. This combination of interests is called the "political context" and it means that organizational behavior may be "instrumental" (serving the presumed goals of the organization as a whole) or "parochial" (serving the perceived self-interest of an individual or unit).

3. Political Economy Model: Wamsley and Zald (1976) propose that process in organizations is best understood by examining the interaction of political and economic interests internal and external to the organization. "Political," in this context, refers to the processes used by the organization to attain power and legitimacy. "Economic" refers to the processes used by the organization to get resources (clients, staff, funding, etc.). The political economy model suggests that individual interests and goals, the power used by those who hold these interests, environmental resources, and the relative influence of those who control the resources all interact in a way that creates the character of an organization. This character changes as the political economy of the organization changes.

4. Organizational Culture: According to Schein (1990, p. 9), organizational culture is a pattern of basic assumptions "developed by a group as it learns to cope with its problems of external adaptation and internal integration" and passed on to new members as the right way to think and feel about problems. Schein argues that culture and leadership are closely related in organizations and that, to examine how change occurs in an organization, one has to understand its leader's assumptions. He also contends that organizational culture is a palpable sense of group identity that has a powerful influence on both communication and decision-making within the organization. Even without being explicitly promoted, patterns affecting the organization's functioning may develop, and organizational members may react emotionally if one of those patterns is violated.

5. Decision-Making Theories: Simon (1957) described organizations as aggregations of individual decisions and proposed that organizational decision-making is behavior that occurs in response to certain stimuli. He distinguished between two models of individual decision-making:

Rational-economic model: The **rational-economic model** proposes that decision-makers maximize benefits by systematically searching for and weighing all possible alternatives before selecting the optimal one. This model assumes that decision-makers have complete information about all possible alternatives and are able to process the information in an accurate, unbiased way.

Bounded rationality (administrative) model: The **bounded rationality model** proposes that various constraints (capability, time, resources, etc.) force decision-makers to be less than totally rational. As a result, decision-makers often **satisfice** rather than optimize – they consider solutions as they become available and then select the first solution that meets the minimum criteria of acceptability.

March and Simon (1958) identified three categories of constraints: (a) personal characteristics (habits, abilities) that people bring to the decision-making process and that influence their actions in certain ways regardless of the circumstances surrounding a specific decision; (b) motivations, values, and loyalties (e.g., identification with a group whose values differ from those of the organization might limit a person's rational behavior); and (c) the fact that decision-makers can't know all of the variables that could influence a decision or all of the possible consequences of the decision.

Although decisions made by individuals in an organization (especially administrators) have a major impact on the organization, decision-makers rarely, if ever, have all of the information they need to make informed decisions. Additionally, all decisions carry some risk. As implied above, the process of **satisficing** (March & Simon, 1958) suggests that a decision-maker's goal is not necessarily to produce a "perfect" outcome by her decision (this may never be possible). Rather, a decision-maker tries her best to reduce uncertainty so that she is able to make a decision that provides a reasonable chance of producing an "acceptable" outcome. In the context of bounded rationality, satisficing is an effort to achieve "satisfactory outcomes" through decision-making.

A criticism of decision-making models is that they overlook (a) the influence that informal structures often have on decisions; (b) situations in which an individual may seek personal or unit gain (rather than rationality); and (c) influences external to the organization that may affect decision-making.

XXI. Administration in Social Work

Many social workers work in social agencies, and one of the roles that social workers may take as macro practitioners is that of administrator of a social agency.

A. Social Agencies

A **social agency** is, "An organization or facility that delivers social services under the auspices of a board of directors and is usually staffed by human services personnel ... . [It] provides a range of social services for members of a population group that has or is vulnerable to a specific social problem" (Barker, 2003, p. 401). "Social services" are activities carried out to help people solve problems and improve personal well-being (e.g., health, quality of life, self-sufficiency, family relationships, functioning in the social environment). Some social services are "institutional" and others are "personal." *Institutional social services* are provided by major public service systems (e.g., public agencies) that administer benefits such as financial assistance, housing programs, health care, or education; while *personal social services* address more individualized needs involving interpersonal relationships and the ability to function within one's immediate environment. A social agency has a **catchment area** – this is the geographic region in which all potential clients are served by a given agency. An agency also has a **mission statement**, which is a relatively permanent description of the reasons for the agency's existence.

Social agencies are either public or private:

- **Public agencies** are run by a unit of government and generally regulated by laws that directly affect policy. Whether at the federal, state, county, or city level, public agencies are established by legislation adopted by elected officials and funded by tax dollars. The services provided by public agencies include institutional social services (e.g., economic assistance, housing programs, health care, education).

- **Private agencies** (a.k.a. voluntary agencies) are privately owned and are operated by people who are not employed by a government. The services provided by private agencies include personal social services. A **board of directors** presides over a private agency and has ultimate responsibility for its programmatic and financial operations. In a public agency, by contrast, a board of directors has less power and takes on more of an advisory or administrative role.

Private social agencies can be either nonprofit or for-profit (proprietary). Most are nonprofit corporations that are funded by voluntary donations, government grants, contracts, and fees. Nonprofit agencies are operated to achieve a service provision goal, not to make a financial profit for their owners. For-profit, or proprietary, agencies provide social services that often are similar to those provided by nonprofit private agencies, but one of their major purposes is to make a financial profit for their owners.

Some private agencies enter into **purchase of service (POS) contracts** with public agencies and are paid to provide specific services. These private agencies are funded, in part, by tax money – under the POS model, the government remains in charge of financing and decision-making functions, but the delivery of services is moved to the private sector.

(Note: The term "proprietary practice" refers to the delivery of social services for profit, typically by self-employed professionals in nonclinical settings. The term "private practice" means more or less the same thing as proprietary practice, but private practice usually refers to clinical practice. Social workers in private practice assume responsibility for the nature and quality of the services provided to their clients in exchange for direct payment or third-party reimbursement [Barker, 2003].)

B. Overview of Administration in Social Agencies

1. Definition of Administration: Barker (2003) defines administration in social work as, "... methods used by those who have administrative responsibility to determine organizational goals for a social agency or other unit; acquire resources and allocate them to carry out a program; coordinate activities toward achieving selected goals; and monitor, assess, and make necessary changes in processes and structure to improve effectiveness and efficiency ... The term also applies to the activities performed in a social agency that contribute to transforming social policy into social services" (p. 8). Barker adds that, in social work, the term "administration" is often used synonymously with "management."

According to Lewis (1978), the emphasis on fiscal accountability that emerged in the late 1960s meant that social agency administrators had to shift their primary focus from concerns about how best to address social problems (client needs) to issues of operational efficiency, budgetary compliance, and, now, information management.

2. Administrative Objectives, Tasks, and Activities: Social agency administrators have three basic objectives: (a) meet specified organizational goals, (b) protect the agency so that it survives, and (c) promote the growth of the organization. To achieve these objectives, administrators perform the following tasks:

- Turn social mandates (e.g., policies) into organizational goals, policies, and procedures.
- Develop organizational structures and processes and communicate these to staff, usually in written form.
- Acquire and allocate resources (human, financial, and technical).
- Select and develop the technologies (e.g., type of service/treatment) needed to meet specified organizational goals.
- Improve organizational effectiveness.
- Evaluate organizational and staff performance to determine when change is required in order to achieve organizational goals.

To accomplish these tasks, administrators perform two basic kinds of activities: **Maintenance activities** are concerned with efficiency. They include those administrative functions that enable the agency to survive, such as problem-solving, maintaining resources, standardizing procedures, and controlling and coordinating the agency's functions. **Service activities** are concerned with quality. They include such administrative functions as setting goals, developing staff, evaluating programs and staff, and representing the agency to the community (public relations).

3. Administrative Functions: Administration in social work encompasses the following eight functions, which will be reviewed in detail in the remaining pages of this section.

Manage agency policies and programs: An agency's policies and programs define its mission, goals, and objectives. Administrators (a) partialize and rank conflicting goals and objectives; (b) create and maintain the organization's formal structure (an organization's "structure" defines how it will carry out its activities); and (c) resolve problems that arise between members of the system or between subsystems (e.g., units or departments) in regard to implementing the agency's programs and services.

Develop resources: Administrators obtain funding for the agency's programs. This may involve private fundraising, political advocacy to raise funds, developing grant proposals, and/or combining funds with other organizations for shared projects.

Budgeting: Administrators allocate the agency's resources. They project demands on the agency's funds, project the agency's revenues, evaluate the relative costs and benefits associated with various spending alternatives, and allocate the agency's finite resources. An agency's budget is considered to represent a summary of its policies, goals, values, priorities, and programs.

Evaluate programs: After the agency's goals and objectives have been established and pursued, program evaluation is done to see how well they were achieved.

Personnel and staff development: This includes recruitment, selection, and orientation of new staff; supervision; training; consultation; and peer review.

Develop and maintain relations with other organizations in the environment: This function is performed in order to obtain and maintain funding and authorization (e.g., credentialing, licensing) and coordinate the agency's services with those of other organizations in the environment.

Public relations: Administrators represent the agency to the community. This includes educating the public about the agency's services and the problems they target, finding support for the agency and its mission, and standing up for the agency if the agency or its staff is accused of wrongdoing.

Management: The management function involves enforcing rules and roles within the organization. This is accomplished via leadership, forming task groups (e.g., committees, project teams), resolving conflicts within the agency, and collecting and using information about the agency to aid in decision-making.

4. The Role of the Agency's Board of Directors: Administrators are responsible for managing the daily operations of an organization and handling the majority of personnel matters. In a *private* or *voluntary social agency*, however, the board of directors has ultimate responsibility for the agency's programmatic and financial operations. In *public* agencies, a board of directors has less power and takes on more of an advisory or administrative role.

a. Board Functions: A board of directors is authorized to establish an agency's policies and objectives and monitor and manage the activities of personnel responsible for the day-to-day application of the policies. The board also serves as the primary linkage between the agency and the community and is responsible for any liabilities resulting from the agency's actions.

In a *private* or *voluntary* social agency, a board of directors performs the following functions:

- *Policy development* (i.e., the board maintains the general direction and overall control of the agency). The board develops the policies that guide the agency; administrators communicate these policies to staff; and staff implement them. Staff may carry out policies in a number of appropriate ways, but, because the board is ultimately responsible for the performance of the agency, it holds staff (including executives) accountable to specific performance standards.

- *Program development* (i.e., the board directs short-term and long-term planning of the agency's activities). A complete program includes a problem analysis; goals and objectives; program and service design; a data-collection and management-information system; a plan for monitoring for efficiency, quality, and client outcomes; and a plan for evaluation.

- *Personnel* (i.e., the board employs the organization's administrators or executive directors). The board has the authority to hire and fire administrators, and the executive director reports to the board of directors. In addition, productive relations between the board and nonadministrative staff rely on a clear delineation and communication of both the board's and the staff's roles and responsibilities.

- *Finance* (i.e., the board facilitates the agency's ability to acquire the resources it needs).

- *Public relations.* The board interprets the agency to the community and develops and maintains relationships with key agency stakeholders.

- *Accountability* (i.e., the board evaluates administrators and operations of the agency). Although nonadministrative-staff evaluations are conducted by supervisors (or administrators), the board is ultimately responsible for the quality of the services delivered by staff, and, therefore, staff are given an opportunity to discuss with board members their concerns about policies so that policies may be modified when the organization's goals and objectives are not being met.

b. Board Members: The board of a social agency usually consists of volunteers who are influential in the community. For example, they may be individuals with high status, technical competence, or power (such as money). These individuals are presumed to lend credibility to the agency and, often, they are able to influence the decisions of others. Other people who serve on a board have influence because of characteristics such as good communication skills, which are important for linking the agency to the community, or a willingness to work hard to achieve the agency's goals and to motivate others to do the same. Additionally, board members ideally represent views that are prevalent in the community. This demonstrates that the agency's values are consistent with those of the community. In private agencies, board members are usually elected.

C. Management of Policies and Programs

1. Social Policy: Social policy includes government decisions that affect the quality of life and welfare of people. Most policies instituted at the federal level address political, financial, legal, and human needs factors, but give little regard to the organizations that will deliver the new program or service or the relationship of the new program or service to programs and services already being provided. As a result, after new social policies are initiated, problems with their implementation often arise in social agencies. Typical obstacles to successful implementation include unclear communication, negative attitudes toward the policy on the part of agency staff, a lack of resources to carry out the policy, and existing organizational procedures that prevent the new policy from being implemented effectively.

2. Agency Policies: Agency policies are standards adopted by organizations and programs that provide services. A given agency's policies and programs, as determined by its directors, define the agency's mission and goals. Agency policies usually specify how the agency is structured, formalize job descriptions, identify what qualifications supervisors and workers must have, define rules that govern what a worker may or may not do, define proper procedures for carrying out work-related activities, establish wage and salary standards and how much vacation employees may have, etc.

An agency's **personnel policies**, in particular, define the privileges, rights, and responsibilities that the employer (agency) grants to and expects from a worker, as well as what a worker can expect from the agency. A typical social service agency manual of personnel policies and procedures ("personnel manual") will cover the following topics: a description of the agency's philosophy, mission, goals and objectives, and programs or services; employment (e.g., nondiscrimination and affirmative action policies, types of employment); working hours and conditions; salaries and wages; employee benefits (e.g., insurance, vacations); employee rights and responsibilities and grievance procedures; performance and salary reviews; staff development; general policies and procedures (e.g., outside employment); general office practices and procedures; and termination (e.g., grounds for termination, resignation, retirement).

3. Communicating Policy Changes: A key function of administrators is monitoring the implementation of all of the agency's policies, including those imposed by laws, outside funders, and other influences outside the organization. When policy changes occur at an agency, they should be communicated to staff clearly and in a timely manner, ideally both in written form and in staff meetings where staff can ask questions and voice their concerns, such as concerns about how the new policy will affect their work. Presenting information both in written form and verbally is important because repetition promotes effective communication among those working at an agency. New agency policy should also be incorporated into the agency's manual of personnel policies and procedures.

Finally, a key principle of effective administration is democratic involvement in the formulation of agency policies and procedures: When staff are part of **participatory administration**, they perform better, which, in turn, improves the performance of the agency (Skidmore, 1995).

D. Create and Maintain the Agency's Formal Structure

The term "organizing" is used to describe the process of creating and maintaining an agency's formal structure. In turn, an agency's structure determines how it will carry out its activities. Topics related to organizational structure and key administrative (management) theories (e.g., bureaucracy, Theory Y, scientific management) were reviewed earlier in this chapter. Recall from that section that both formal and informal structures within an organization influence its effectiveness: The formal organization refers to social groupings that are expressly formed and re-formed by the agency to achieve specific goals (e.g., committees), while the informal organization refers to voluntary relationships that develop among agency personnel.

E. Resource Development and Budgeting

The concept of **resource dependence** refers to the fact that organizations, as open systems, must rely on elements in the surrounding environment to obtain the resources they need to operate and survive over time. They must continually adapt to changing environmental contingencies, and their survival may depend on the extent to which they formalize exchange agreements with other organizations in their task environment. In general, the greater the variety of funding an agency has, the better its fiscal health and service flexibility will be, in part, because the loss of one funding source is unlikely to threaten the agency's overall viability. On the other hand, having many funding sources usually means that the agency's operations are more complex (e.g., there are more regulatory constraints and accountability expectations). While an agency with only one funding source risks becoming rigid and overly specialized, an agency with many funding sources may have trouble defining or sustaining its mission.

1. Revenue Sources: Major sources of cash revenue for social agencies include government funds, donated funds, fees for services (direct payments from clients, payments from third parties such as private or public insurers), fund-raising campaigns, and miscellaneous sources such as investments. Mechanisms for disbursement of funds from the federal government include **block grants** (i.e., lump-sum appropriations in which specific allocations are left to local governments); **matching funds** (which, for example, provide a certain amount of federal funds for each dollar expended by state-level agencies); and **grant programs** (in which funds are targeted for a specific use and restricted to that program). Government contract funds are those in which a nonprofit or for-profit agency contracts with a public agency to provide specific services to specific clients.

Full-pay clients pay the agency (personally or via third-party reimbursement) an amount equal to or higher than the cost of their services; these clients are resources that agencies try to attract and are most likely to serve. Non-full-pay clients pay less than the cost of their services or pay nothing at all. Because revenues for serving these clients must be generated from other sources (donations, profits earned from serving full-pay clients, etc.), agencies may not seek these clients and/or may create eligibility barriers to limit their numbers. The act of selecting only the best-fitting, full-pay clients (and rejecting or referring the others) is known as "cherry picking" or "creaming" and is unethical.

An issue related to cherry picking is **boundary control**, which refers to the ability of an agency to reject clients it does not want to serve, usually ones who are poor or have complex, long-standing problems. Boundary control is generally highest in for-profit organizations, where the main goal is making money, and lowest in governmental organizations, which are supposed to provide a safety net for clients who can't get services elsewhere.

2. Resource Mobilization and Coordination:

a. Resource Mobilization: Resource mobilization involves organizing and making available an agency's resources, including its existing funds; the funds it will raise; its information base, personnel, and volunteers; and the knowledge and talents of its board members and others who can provide assistance. This process is critical when social resources fail to meet current needs or are scarce, inadequate, or fragmented. To successfully mobilize resources, the agency must be clear about its needs and mission, identify its target population, and effectively communicate this information to the public. Mobilizers then devise strategies to build support for the program (including funding) and then maintain that support by, for example, informing supporters of the program's results. Resource mobilizers must be skilled at "dramatizing" the problem addressed by a program so that those who control social resources will become committed to helping resolve it.

b. Resource Coordination: After acquiring support for a program, social agency administrators must ensure that the support is channeled effectively. Resource coordination is a managerial process in which the goals and activities of individuals are coordinated so that they can achieve the objectives they have agreed to pursue. Resource coordination techniques include the following:

Bargaining: Two parties each attempt to gain the other's cooperation by either offering to provide or threatening to withhold a desired resource.

Persuasion: An appeal is made to the other party in an effort to get them to change their minds and support your position.

Coalition building: Two or more parties coordinate their activities — they promote joint efforts and share responsibilities, goals, and resources. Coalition building is particularly important when resources are limited.

Authority: Many consider authority to be a method of last resort. It is typically used when resource holders are reluctant to provide a needed resource.

3. Strategies for Obtaining Funds:
Private agencies provide social services outside government auspices and their funding comes from private contributions. To obtain funds, administrators of private agencies must advocate on behalf of the agency and be skilled at fund-raising activities such as arranging fund-raising campaigns, developing grant proposals, managing third-party billings, and determining appropriate client fees and training staff to implement those fees. Administrators in public, or government, agencies must be skilled at dealing with the government; in particular, they must be skilled at negotiation.

4. Budgeting and Budgeting Systems:
When budgetary administration is effective, it results in the productive allocation of human, financial, and technical resources. Resource allocation is considered productive when it allows the agency to achieve its objectives. In other words, the major question in the budgetary process is how resources can be allocated efficiently so that the agency's service capability will be maximized. Examples of **budgeting systems** include the following:

Line-item budgeting: Line-item budgeting is a simple budgeting technique that involves identifying expenditure categories and estimating the number of dollars that would be needed to cover all expenses in each category for one year. Categories typically include personnel and operating expenses such as rent, utilities, supplies, and travel.

Functional budgeting and program budgeting: Functional budgeting and program budgeting are more sophisticated budgeting techniques that have been developed for application to social agencies. They are based on program planning and budgeting systems (PPBS). Both approaches produce cost and expenditure data in relation to programs rather than for the entire agency. They produce data such as total program costs, cost per unit of service, cost per output (client completion of program or service), and cost per outcome (the cost of producing measurable change in a client's quality of life). Martin (2000) calls this last item "outcome budgeting." Outcome budgeting can be useful for facilitating cost-benefit and cost-effectiveness evaluations and helping agencies maintain a focus on the measurement of outcomes.

Zero-based budgeting: With zero-based budgeting (ZBB), an agency starts from scratch, or with a "clean slate," at the beginning of each year (i.e., it starts with no money) and must describe and justify every financial request it makes for the coming year. This type of budgeting encourages close scrutiny of how money is spent and why. Many consider ZBB to be an impractical approach to budgeting in a social agency, however, as it requires agency decision-makers to re-examine every expenditure on an annual basis.

Management by objectives: When using MBO, all organizational activities are directed toward accomplishing certain designated objectives. These objectives form the basis for budgeting, and the relative contributions of various activities to these objectives determine spending priorities.

F. Program Evaluation

In social work, **program evaluations** are conducted to obtain information that can be used to improve social programs, organizational effectiveness, potential grant solicitation, and social service accountability. The evaluation of social programs emphasizes the assessment of specific intervention approaches rather than broad questions such as how effective casework is in general. As a type of applied (in natural environments) research, evaluation research differs from more theoretical or academic research in several ways. Most important, perhaps, is that evaluation research is conducted to assess the utility of social programs in order to facilitate decisions about them (e.g., whether a program needs modification, should be extended to other sites, is cost-effective). Most social agencies maintain reporting systems to collect program data – these systems account for program effort, client characteristics, etc., but, unlike program evaluation, they reveal little about whether the agency is meeting its objectives or reducing social problems.

1. Benefits of and Obstacles to Program Evaluation: Program evaluation is both a key to optimizing an agency's effectiveness and a tool for satisfying social and professional demands for accountability. Social agencies must account for their funding to outside sources such as political bodies, private funding sources, and/or government offices, all of whom demand information about the effectiveness and efficiency of the agency's programs.

Obstacles to program evaluation may include a fear of external political consequences that could result if there is a negative evaluation, resistance by staff in the agency, and a lack of resources (e.g., funds), interest, or support for the evaluation. To help overcome these obstacles, an evaluation should be presented to staff in light of goal achievement rather than simply imposed on them by administrators and should involve participation by those whose program components are to be included in the evaluation.

2. Criteria for Program Evaluation: Common criteria for program evaluation include the following:

- Effort – evaluates the resources needed to reach program objectives.
- Impact – examines the program's effect on social change.
- Effectiveness – determines how well the objectives of the program were met in terms of client change.
- Efficiency – assesses the economics of program operation in relation to its accomplishments (the ideal outcome is maximum performance using minimal resources).
- Quality – examines professional competence and standards of service.

In addition, government initiatives have established performance standards for agencies that use government funding. These standards cover the following:

- *Efficiency accountability* is concerned with the ratio of outputs to inputs (i.e., volume of service provided to dollars expended). Agencies that seek donated funds often attempt to demonstrate efficiency by attending to such measures as the ratio of administrative costs to total expenditures.
- *Quality accountability* is concerned with the provision of services and identifies agencies that meet a quality standard and those that do not. Some of the indicators used by agencies to evaluate quality include accessibility, communication, competence, conformity, durability, humaneness, performance, reliability, and responsiveness (Martin, 1993).
- *Effectiveness accountability* emphasizes the results, effects, and accomplishments of social programs: Are clients better off after coming to this agency? Do the programs and services offered resolve the client problems they are funded to address?

3. Approaches to Program Evaluation: Commonly used approaches to program evaluation include the following:

- An *outcome model* emphasizes the evaluation of expected results. If productivity is being evaluated, a **quantitative outcome model** is used to measure, in numbers, program factors such as activity, revenue, and so forth. If clients' perceptions of a program are being evaluated, a **qualitative outcome model** is used.
- Rather than evaluating expected results, the *goal attainment model* focuses on evaluating only those outcomes specified in a program's objectives.
- A *systems analysis* studies the impact of other organizations and the environment on a program and investigates variables that might be related to program changes.
- The *cost-analytic model* uses costs as independent variables to determine their effects on variables that are thought to indicate change resulting from the program (e.g., in the form of benefits translated into cost savings). (Independent variables, dependent

variables, and other terms and concepts associated with research design and statistics are defined in the appendix at the end of this chapter.)

- *Descriptive* and *quality assurance models* monitor whether and how well administrators and staff have adhered to relevant standards in the implementation of the program.

4. Program Evaluation Process: All steps of program evaluation should include discussions involving all individuals participating in or affected by the evaluation (i.e., administrators, program sponsors, evaluators, staff) and focusing, in part, on how the evaluation will benefit the program.

The steps involved in program evaluation include: (a) specify the program's goal and objectives; (b) define relevant parameters (e.g., specify the target population, the criteria that will be used to define a target behavior [outcome], and the criteria that will be used to determine whether the program's goal and objectives have been met); (c) specify the techniques and procedures to be used to achieve the program's goal and objectives; and (d) collect relevant data.

The methods used to collect data about a program depend, in part, on the purpose of the research. Shaughnessy and Zechmeister (1985) distinguish four types of evaluation research, which each rely on particular research techniques:

- When the purpose of the research is to assess the needs of the target population (i.e., **needs assessment**), survey research is most useful.

- When the purpose of the research is to facilitate program planning (e.g., determining where and when the program should be conducted and which activities should be included), surveys, archival research, and participant observation are most useful.

- When a program is in the process of being developed or implemented, the goal of the research is **formative evaluation** – i.e., obtaining information to determine what modifications are needed so that the program achieves its goal and objectives. In this situation, observational methods are most helpful. Formative evaluation tends to be less threatening to program personnel because its results are used to modify a program rather than to make decisions about whether it should continue. Results of formative evaluation are not usually generalizable to other programs.

- Once a program has been developed and implemented, the research goal is **summative evaluation**, or evaluation of the program's effects. Summative evaluation is most useful when it involves a true or quasi-experimental research approach (these approaches to research are defined in the appendix at the end of this chapter). Summative evaluation results may be generalized to other programs, situations, and populations and used to make decisions about closing programs or opening other programs similar to the one that was evaluated.

5. Program Evaluation Stages: An overview of the steps taken by administrators (and others) in conducting social program evaluation is provided below.

a. Stage 1. Initial Planning: (a) Determine whether sufficient staff, time, and resources exist to conduct the evaluation. (b) Identify and involve consumer(s) of the evaluation (those who will ultimately make decisions about the program, based on evaluation results). (c) Attempt to obtain support from the program's staff and encourage them to participate fully in the evaluation process. (d) State the program's goal for client service, or outcome, and its objectives. Defining the program's activities and their anticipated effects is essential for ensuring that the evaluation will be meaningful. Selected variables should be chosen for their relevance to the evaluation and the program's goal.

b. Stage 2. Select and Implement a Research Design: Select an appropriate research design and then accumulate, classify, measure, examine, and interpret the data. Approaches used in evaluation research include experimental or quasi-experimental designs, single-subject (single-case) designs (e.g., AB or ABAB designs), case studies and qualitative designs, correlational designs, and descriptive survey designs. The last two are the most commonly used in social program evaluation and are described below:

- **Correlational studies** are used to examine connections between program variables and intended program outcomes. Two major types of correlational design are group comparison and one-group before-and-after designs: (a) A group comparison design involves treating one group using the selected program and then comparing that group in terms of the dependent variables to another group whose members either did not participate in the program or participated in only selected parts of the program. (b) The one-group before-and-after design involves measuring one group on the dependent variables before and after its participation in the program.

- The **descriptive survey design** relies on representative sampling and is used to obtain explicit, quantitative data that can be generalized to certain other populations. Subjects participate in an interview or fill out a questionnaire and then data from these are analyzed using descriptive and correlational statistics. Descriptive survey designs are used not only to obtain measures on dependent variables at different points in time but also to estimate client satisfaction with programs and to conduct needs assessments.

A **Client Satisfaction Questionnaire** (CSQ), for example, may be used to solicit client opinions about the services they received. It asks clients to rate aspects such as the success of the intervention, the competence of the staff, general delivery services, etc. When responses are placed in rank order, one can compute an average score from multiple clients to derive an indicator of client satisfaction regarding the services. Typically, the questionnaire is administered at the point of termination or shortly thereafter. CSQs do not request much detailed information – if more information is desired, the CSQ might be supplemented by a phone or face-to-face interview on specific variables related to satisfaction or dissatisfaction. Several variables influence the outcome of such surveys including when they are conducted (e.g., during or after treatment), client response rates, how the sample was selected, and how the instrument is presented to clients.

c. Stage 3. Report and Implement Evaluation Results: After data are collected and interpreted, the results are reported and applied. Depending on the type of evaluation conducted (formative or summative), the application of results may involve changing programs, continuing or discontinuing them, and/or starting similar programs. Results must be reported in language that consumers (e.g., funders) will understand, and conclusions should carefully separate facts from hypotheses that require further testing.

G. Staff Development

The goals of staff development are to enhance an agency's human resources and improve its services by improving technology and staff skill. For staff development to achieve its goals, it must be systematic and cannot be simply an internal agency procedure but, rather, must be linked to the community.

1. Human Resources Plans: Strategic planning at an agency focuses on establishing goals, processes, and actions that determine future directions. Once these are established, they form the basis for human resource planning – i.e., for predicting personnel needs to implement the mission. The elements that make up a human resource plan are described below (Schmidt et al., 1992).

a. Job Analysis and Job Description: Basic to a human resources plan is a **job analysis** that identifies what tasks a job entails, determines the relationships between and among positions, and specifies qualifications for positions. The process of job analysis involves gathering, evaluating, and recording accurate, objective, and complete information about a given position from several sources (e.g., information about the knowledge and skills required to carry out job tasks). The end product provides a complete review of the requirements and expectations associated with a particular job. From this information, a more concise **job description** is developed. A job description, in turn, is the basis for organizing the various components of a human resource plan – recruitment, selection, orientation, supervision, training and development, performance appraisal, and termination procedures.

b. Recruitment and Selection Plan: Recruitment requires a careful strategy (e.g., choosing the recruitment territory and audience) because staff will need to be selected from the pool of applicants generated by the strategy. Agencies also assess the diversity of their staff and attempt to recruit people from diverse groups to ensure a representative staff. Selection involves reviewing applications to eliminate applicants who are not qualified or don't fit the agency's needs and identify the three to five applicants with the best qualifications. The latter individuals are then interviewed. Screening criteria and interview questions should be developed in advance and match the qualifications and expectations established in the job analysis.

c. Orientation, Supervision, Training, and Development: New employees are provided a complete orientation to the job, the workplace, and the community. After this, a plan for supervision, training, and development is initiated. These processes are used to help a new worker enter the job smoothly and provide information, knowledge, and resources that will help her be productive and successful.

d. Performance Appraisal: A well-designed human resource plan must have a performance-appraisal system based on the job analysis. Tasks identified in the job analysis should be used as a basis for designing the performance-appraisal instrument. Criteria and procedures for performance evaluation should be specified in writing and given to employees at the time of hiring.

e. Policies and Procedures for Termination: These policies should be distributed in writing at the time of hiring. They must include a description of grounds for termination; clear, objective, and measurable criteria for identifying what constitutes unsatisfactory performance or unacceptable behavior; and procedures and time-frames for notifying workers of poor performance well before reaching the stage of termination.

2. Staff Development Methods: The primary methods of developing existing staff include continuing education, consultation, peer review, performance appraisal, and supervision. Continuing education and consultation are described below. Peer review is described in Section I of Professional Relationships, Values, and Ethics; performance appraisal and supervision are reviewed in Section IV of Professional Relationships, Values, and Ethics.

a. Continuing Education: Continuing education enables social workers to remain aware of and use new technological developments in the field. Continuing education can be accomplished through in-house trainings, lectures, conferences, seminars, effective interorganizational relationships, and supervision. Membership in local, state, and federal boards also contributes to this function.

The NASW Code of Ethics includes a specific standard related to competence and continued enhancement of social work skills. The NASW Standards for Continuing Professional Education require administrators to implement agency policies in support of continuing professional education and to provide leadership for continuing professional education, and require social workers to assume personal responsibility for their continuing professional education and to complete 48 hours of continuing professional education every two years.

b. Consultation: **Consultation** is "a process in which a human services professional assists a consultee with a work-related (or caretaking-related) problem within a client system. It has the goal of helping both the consultee and the client system in some specified way" (Dougherty, 1990, p. 8).

Several principles guide consultation: (a) Consultation always has a problem-solving, or educational, function. (b) A consultant has no administrative authority over staff members, so that a consultee may turn down the consultant's suggestions. The determining factor is the value of the consultant's idea not her status as a consultant. (c) Consultation relies on the quality of the relationship between the consultant and consultee. Thus, a consultant must be skilled at developing and maintaining relationships with consultees.

In social work, two types of consultation are commonly used. In program and organizational consultation, administrators hire a consultant to increase the effectiveness of direct services provided by the agency. In **case consultation**, a consultant with expertise in a particular area is hired or asked to work with a social worker to help her provide direct services to a particular client or client population. Case consultation focuses on the client and how to best help him, but the consultant only interacts with the social worker and others who are working with the client – she has no direct contact with the client. Either a social worker or her supervisor may determine the need for consultation on a case. Consultation is used by most social workers on an as-needed basis.

H. Interorganizational Relations

Most social agencies are part of an interorganizational network of agencies that provide similar services to similar population groups. When relations among these organizations are managed effectively, this situation can be the basis for growth and professional and social development. Without effective management, however, this situation can result in competition and conflict among organizations over task and domain.

1. Agency Domain: "Domain" refers to what an organization does and who it serves. Social agencies use a process called **domain setting** to establish themselves and their roles among other organizations within their environment. A part of this process is **domain legitimation**, in which an agency gains acknowledgment of the claims it makes about its sphere of expertise and activities. There is sometimes a difference between what an agency says its boundaries are (the claimed domain) and what these boundaries actually are (the de facto domain) (Greenley & Kirk, 1973). In addition, agencies wanting to take advantage of available resources sometimes adjust their domains as a means of securing the resources.

2. Objectives of Linking With Other Organizations: Linkage involves bringing together the resources of different agencies and coordinating efforts on behalf of a client or social objective. When linking their efforts with those of other agencies, administrators have two objectives: to enhance service resources (agencies depend on one another for the exchange of resources) and to improve organizational effectiveness.

3. Informal Linkages vs. Formal Linkages: The approach an agency takes to establishing linkages with other organizations influences the resulting level of cooperation in their interactions. Because informal linkages tend to be undependable, formal linkages are typically more effective. Formal linkages, for example, allow clients to be served better by making it easier for them to access the service capabilities of more than one agency. Although formal linkages may reduce autonomy and flexibility, they improve service delivery, clarify expectations, and facilitate the exchange of resources.

4. Factors That May Keep Organizations From Working Together: Factors that may prevent organizations from working together include the following: (a) competition for scarce resources, especially when organizational or program survival depends on securing money that could be allocated to other agencies; (b) categorical funding and other restrictions affecting how funds can be spent (this makes it difficult to share resources or assign them to a new purpose); (c) a desire for agency or professional status and power that create "turf" problems and interfere with planning, cooperation, and conflict resolution; and (d) differences in agency philosophies, values, and practice frameworks that pose barriers to agreement on a common purpose and approach (Sheafor & Horejsi, 2003).

5. Ways of Linking With Other Organizations: Constructive ways for an agency to link with other organizations include the following (Netting et al, 2004):

Communication: Communication between agencies may be formal or informal. Formal communication may include information and referral. Informal communication may include groups that meet to discuss community issues or staff who talk about their programs at conferences. Interagency information and understanding can also be facilitated through the use of brochures, pamphlets, and media. Communication may involve an *affiliation* process, which involves an ongoing, explicit relationship between agencies.

Cooperation (linkage): With cooperation (or linkage) agencies agree to work toward similar goals. For example, two agencies that work with the same target population but provide different resources may arrange to meet regularly to discuss common concerns and maintain a sense of continuity for clients of both agencies.

Coordination: Coordination implies a concerted effort to work together – separate agencies draft agreements outlining ways in which coordination will occur. Federations, associations, and coalitions may be formed. Case management programs attempt to provide a coordination function so that service delivery flows across informal and formal providers of care.

Collaboration: Collaboration implies a joint venture. Joint ventures are agreements in which two or more agencies agree to set up a new program or service. Consortia and networks are typically established for collaborative purposes. Agencies that serve the needs of a special population may collaborate to assess need, examine the fit between needs and services, and work together in pursuing funding for programs. Federal and state contracts may require active collaboration, and RFPs from private foundations usually require those seeking grants to explain clearly how they will collaborate with others.

Consolidation: Here, agencies merge, often because one or both agencies have become unable to function autonomously. A horizontal merger occurs when, for example, two mental health centers consolidate into a single organization. An example of a vertical merger is when a hospital absorbs a home health-care provider. A conglomerate merger occurs when agencies or other units within a community form a confederation of numerous smaller units under a large umbrella agency. These actions are generally limited to nongovernmental agencies.

6. Administrative Strategies Used to Maintain Social Service Viability: Certain administrative strategies may be used to maintain the viability of social services that are provided by multiple agencies. Yankey (1995) and others recommend that administrators undertake **strategic planning**, a process used to develop and maintain a strategic fit among the mission of the organization, the strengths and weaknesses of the organization, and opportunities and challenges in the organization's external environment. Strategic planning requires examining all aspects of the agency's operations (including its goals, priorities, and purpose, the needs of its clients, and the allocation of its resources) and also examining other agencies involved in meeting similar social needs. In undertaking this analysis, administrators should be prepared to consider a variety of alternative ways of delivering services, including mergers and relationships between nonprofit and for-profit agencies. A frequently used tool in strategic planning is the **SWOT analysis** which is useful for positioning the agency to maximize its strengths and capitalize on its opportunities and helps it respond effectively to its environment before a crisis develops (Yankey, 1995). The SWOT analysis entails examining the internal Strengths and Weaknesses of the organization in relation to the Opportunities and Threats presented in its external environment.

After strategic planning, administrators may need to consider **cutback strategies**. That is, depending on the results of their examinations, administrators may do one of the following: (a) cut back on administrative and staff expenditures (e.g., increase workloads, contract out services) or reduce services (e.g., eliminate programs, limit the availability of programs); (b) share costs among organizations and initiate mergers; or (c) form coalitions to create a broader base of action to achieve goals. The latter entails involving other interested groups (particularly in the political arena) in the development of cooperative strategies among two or more agencies. Administrators must weigh carefully the costs and benefits of all these approaches.

7. Examples of Areas in Which Agencies Can Collaborate: Areas in which agencies may collaborate include the following (Sheafor & Horejsi, 2003):

- Purchase of services – one agency contracts with another to provide services (e.g., a public agency purchases services from a private agency).

- Joint budgeting – multiple agencies commit a part of their budget to a specific activity (this is often done to create the match needed to obtain a grant).

- Joint funding – multiple agencies pool their funds to achieve an objective that no single agency can achieve on its own.

- Joint studies – multiple agencies fund and conduct research or needs assessments.

- Centralized information processing – multiple agencies share data processing systems used in recordkeeping, program planning, grant management, or case management.

- Public relations – multiple agencies jointly plan and disseminate information about programs and community needs.

- Centralized information and referral service – multiple agencies fund and operate a centralized service to guide clients to appropriate agencies.

- Coordination of client services – multiple agencies exchange information and share in decision-making required for case management, case coordination, handling of grievances by clients, etc.

- Sharing of special services – multiple agencies pool resources so that all have access to outside consultants, specialists, transportation for clients, or staff training.

- Loaner staff – an agency "loans" a staff person with special expertise to another agency for a special project.

- Volunteer bureaus – multiple agencies work together to recruit and train volunteers needed by each agency.

I. Public Relations

Social agencies operate in community environments that are constantly changing and that influence the quality and quantity of service delivery and the availability of resources. For an agency to survive, its personnel must develop relationships within its environment, and, therefore, an important administrative task in social agencies is connecting the agency to its environment. In relating to the community, administrators emphasize activities that improve and promote their agency's services and standing in the community. From an administrative standpoint, public relations includes three service tasks — education, outreach, and advocacy – each of which plays an important role in improving the agency's effectiveness and the welfare of the community.

1. Education: In this context, education involves educating the public and other service providers about the social problems an agency is addressing and the services it provides.

This can be done best by emphasizing the human aspects of social problems and their treatment rather than by using statistics and program details. Education also brings the agency's services to the attention of the public and, therefore, can enhance its standing in the community.

2. Outreach: Outreach involves efforts to bring the agency's services or information about their availability to people in their homes or other natural environments. This may include **case finding** efforts, in which social workers seek out and identify individuals or groups who are vulnerable to or experiencing the problems that their agency addresses. Outreach may also target the general population since individuals not experiencing a problem may provide referrals, or associates of the target population since target population members may be difficult to reach (e.g., if the target population is single parents, outreach efforts may occur in day camps or medical clinics).

A particularly effective way of approaching outreach is emphasizing how the problem affects individuals; however, outreach also addresses the overall effects of the problem, its scope and treatment, and the projected outcome of treatment (what service recipients can expect). Outreach should always provide potential clients with realistic expectations of agency services. Other avenues used to achieve outreach include public speaking, interagency collaboration, written material, and online outreach.

3. Advocacy: In social agency administration, the role of advocacy is to educate or inform the public to persuade key people that a particular change is needed. Advocacy may, for example, result in the acquisition of resources for solving a social problem. Here, the goal is to gather support from financial and decision-making powers (i.e., individuals, state, county or federal agencies, sectarian or nonsectarian groups). (In this context, "sectarian groups" are those committed to a particular interest or purpose.)

J. Management

The "management" function of administration is concerned with enforcing roles and rules in the agency and collecting, organizing, and using information about the agency.

1. Leadership:

a. Formal vs. Informal Leadership: A person is said to have a leadership role when she has the power and/or ability to influence others. There are two types of leadership: **Formal leadership** is official and assigned; **informal leadership** is unofficial but, like formal leadership, involves power and influence over others.

b. Leadership Styles: A number of studies on leadership have focused on leadership styles or behaviors. In an early study, Lewin, Lippert, and White (1939) compared the effects of three leadership styles: (a) **Autocratic** leaders make decisions alone and instruct subordinates what to do on the basis of those decisions; (b) **democratic** leaders involve subordinates in the decision-making process; and (c) **laissez-faire** leaders leave it up to their subordinates to make decisions with little guidance or help.

Lewin and colleagues found that subordinates with democratic leaders tend to be the most satisfied, motivated, and creative, are more likely to continue working when the leader is not present, and have better relationships with their leader. In terms of productivity, however, autocratic leaders are associated with greater quantity of output (at least while the leader is present).

2. Task Groups: In an organization, a task group (or task force) is temporary grouping created to achieve a specific, predefined goal or function. Task group meetings of various kinds provide a forum for staff to exchange information and give and receive feedback and support, for tasks to be distributed, and for planning, decision-making, and problem-solving. In an effective task group, the participants know why they are meeting, what tasks need to be accomplished, who is supposed to carry out the group's decisions, and when their work is done. Skillful leadership by administrators or others at the agency is necessary for ensuring that meetings are productive, task-oriented, and satisfying to staff members. Two functions comprise the effective use of task groups in an agency: task accomplishment and group maintenance.

- *Task accomplishment* emphasizes the group's productivity and requires the group to be well organized and goal-oriented. To ensure task-group productivity, leaders must plan carefully before meetings (e.g., with regard to purpose, agenda, and timing), lead meetings effectively, and follow up on decisions made during meetings. Ideally, administrators allow staff to participate in such tasks as agenda-setting for the meetings, and most social agencies use majority rule and consensus approaches during meetings to arrive at decisions.

- *Group maintenance* refers to participants' satisfaction with the group and includes both emotional and social components. An understanding of how groups develop is useful for promoting an effective task group. For example, a newly formed group is usually dependent on the leader for direction, and the leader's tasks at this time include helping the members relate to one another, establishing understanding and agreement on the group's goals and expectations, and facilitating the development of norms. As the group develops, the leader should encourage members to take more responsibility for group activities and processes. The leader also needs to be skilled at conflict resolution so that conflicts can be quickly resolved and the group can resume work toward its goals.

3. Group Decision-Making Techniques: The following are techniques that have been developed to improve the quality of group decisions:

Brainstorming (Osborn, 1957): Brainstorming involves encouraging group members to verbalize all ideas that come to mind regardless of how absurd they may seem and requiring members to refrain from evaluating each other's ideas until after the brainstorming session is over. The research on brainstorming has not been very supportive; however, its effectiveness is improved when group members are heterogeneous in terms of skills, feel comfortable with each other, and have been adequately trained in brainstorming.

RISK technique: The RISK technique is used to facilitate committee or group members in expressing their concerns about an issue or proposed action. The leader takes a nondefensive posture and communicates an interest in having all group members express their concerns, complaints, issues, and anticipated problems. This encourages members to express their views and to listen and attempt to understand one another.

Nominal group technique: The nominal group technique (NGT) encourages active involvement by all group participants and is useful for helping consensus-oriented committees or groups arrive at a decision. It is particularly suited for groups of 6 to 9 people; if used with more people, the committee or group should be divided into smaller groups. The four main elements of NGT are: (a) participants generate ideas in writing; (b) round-robin feedback is given from group members, with each idea recorded in a brief phrase on a flipchart; (c) the group discusses (clarifies and evaluates) each recorded idea; and (d) individual voting is used to establish priorities among the ideas and a group decision is mathematically derived through rank ordering or rating.

4. Managing Conflict Within the Agency:

a. Potential Causes of Conflict: Conflict within social agencies may be caused by a variety of factors including task interdependence if individuals or groups have differing priorities, goals, or performance expectations; unclear or overlapping task assignments; poor communication; differences in performance standards or reward systems; competition for resources; and interpersonal conflicts. Other significant sources of conflict in an organization include the following:

Conflict between organizational domains: **Domain theory** (Kouzes & Mico, 1979) views an organization as having three separate but interacting domains – policy, management, and service – which can come into conflict with each other. These domains are described below. Potential reasons for conflict include the following: (a) Because each domain has its own norms, members of different domains may lose the ability to work together; (b) because each domain develops its own sense of identity, each domain may have a different view of the organization's mission; and (c) because each domain has its own way of seeing and doing things, each domain may develop a different perception of events, issues, problems, and potential solutions:

Policy domain: The **policy domain** consists of individuals who have the authority to define the organization's mission, policies, and goals (e.g., the director, those who report to the director). Policy domain members have a lot of contact with community groups, government bodies, and others outside the agency who represent the public in some way and often serve as representatives of these interest groups. Individuals in the policy domain use procedures such as bargaining and negotiating to determine how to allocate resources and power and to resolve disputes among individuals who have power and resources. The goal of the policy domain is to obtain a fair share of available resources for the agency and to divide these resources fairly among the agency's units, staff, and clients.

Management domain: The **management domain** includes individuals who are charged with seeing that an organization's policies are implemented (e.g., middle managers, supervisors of direct service staff). The management domain sets goals and objectives for staff and programs and monitors staff and program performance. Its primary goals are cost efficiency and program effectiveness.

Service domain: The **service domain** includes individuals who provide services to clients. Its members are concerned with autonomy, self-regulation, and innovation, and their goals are high service quality and adherence to professional standards of practice and the agency's policies. Service staff may gather with peers (in case conferences, consultation groups) and focus on resolving specific client problems.

Conflict between professional standards and organizational policies: A social worker may come into conflict with the agency where she works, often in regard to one or both of the following: (a) Organizational rules and policies – sometimes an organization's policies and procedures don't support a social worker's professional standards and values. An organization might expect a social worker to follow its policies even when they contradict a professional value, ethic, or standard. (b) Authority – an agency might not allow a social worker to participate in making decisions about matters involving some aspect of her professional work over which she should have responsibility or control. We discuss in the Professional Relationships, Values, and Ethics chapter how social workers should go about resolving such conflicts; essentially, you should do your best to follow the profession's Code of Ethics and other professional standards.

b. Conflict Resolution Strategies: For an agency to function effectively, administrators must find ways of resolving both overt and covert interpersonal conflicts among staff members. The management of conflict in an organization entails four basic steps: (a) recognize an existing or potential conflict, (b) assess the conflict situation, (c) select an appropriate resolution strategy, and (d) intervene.

Strategies for intervening into conflicts may be "structural" and/or "interpersonal." Examples of **structural approaches** include reorganizing and clarifying work assignments, modifying or establishing procedures, and addressing the inequities in pay or status that led to the conflict. A specific example of structural method is organizational redesign. This is most useful when conflict is due to problems related to the coordination of work among different departments or units of the agency. One redesign technique involves creating self-contained work groups that have the resources to achieve their own goals. Alternatively, communication and coordination between departments can be facilitated by providing a liaison.

Interpersonal approaches are used when structural methods are inappropriate or have been ineffective. They include a variety of problem-solving methods used to arrive at a mutual definition of and solution to the conflict. Formal interpersonal methods for resolving a conflict include bargaining (opposing sides exchange offers, counteroffers, and concessions either directly or through representatives); mediation (a neutral third party uses various tactics to facilitate voluntary agreement between the disputants); and arbitration (a third party settles the dispute).

5. Collecting and Managing Information About the Agency: The benefits of collecting information in a social agency are realized only when administrators use the date to improve organizational operations; that is, data must be communicated to staff and used to identify problems and facilitate decision-making that will improve agency and staff performance.

a. Areas in Which Social Work Uses Information Systems: An **information system** (IS) is any combination of information technology and activities that use the technology to support operations, management, and decision-making. Key areas in which social work uses information systems include the following:

- Agency management – facilitate billing, budgeting, goal-setting, program evaluation, and policy and planning decisions; and track clients as they move through the service delivery system (see also MIS, below).

- Policy planning – ensure that services meet client needs, help boards and administrators deal with large amounts of data, and facilitate advocacy and fund raising.

- Service delivery – help social workers manage their work (e.g., collect client data, facilitate scheduling, track and monitor client services) and support their interactions with clients (e.g., provide access to referral sources, administer and score psychological tests and report results, assist with assessment and education of clients, as with Computer Assisted Instruction).

- Client self-help – enable clients to educate and help themselves and obtain information about their problems.

- Education – streamline the information base of practice decisions so that social work students can use trial-and-error when learning to make professional decisions.

Decision support systems (DSS) involve using computers to collect and organize information and make decisions from among specified choices – the computer program uses a predefined set of rules and facts to determine the best decision, and an administrator then accepts or rejects the computer's decision.

In addition, some agencies have Web sites that allow online completion of forms, provide links to resources, enable communications with staff, etc. Ideally, agencies also have IT staff available to maintain and upgrade their computers and software.

b. Management Information Systems: **Management information systems** (MIS) are used in social agencies to acquire, process, analyze, and disseminate data that are useful for carrying out the goals of the organization efficiently. They may be used to track staff activity and the services provided to clients. Client information is either analyzed in aggregate form (e.g., individual identities are not shown) or there are stringent requirements for protecting the privacy of clients and confidentiality of information about them. Using these systems is believed to enhance goal attainment.

c. The Productive Use of Information: For information to be used productively in an agency, the following must occur: (a) Staff at all levels of the agency must be able to accurately and quickly gather, store, and retrieve performance information. This enables all personnel to identify problems in staff or agency performance. (b) Information that will guide management decisions must be readily accessible. Administrators must have ready access to data that will enable them to problem-solve. (c) Administrators must be skilled at converting information into action (i.e., at enabling and motivating staff to change their behavior based on performance information).

XXII. Community Practice Models and Activities

A. Community Organization

Community organization uses planned **collective action** to help individuals deal with social problems and improve their social well-being. The individuals who are helped have common interests or are from the same geographic region and may consist of a group, neighborhood, or constituency (interest group). Collective action refers to an organized effort that includes many people and attempts to effect political, economic, or cultural change. Community organizers assume that, if many people work together, they can better influence those who have power.

The basic methods used in community organizing include identifying problem areas, analyzing causes of problems, formulating plans, developing strategies, mobilizing resources, identifying and recruiting community leaders, and encouraging relationships among community leaders to facilitate their efforts.

1. Community Organizers and Their Roles: Community organizers may be social workers or other professionals, local community leaders, people who hold political office, or government bureaucrats. Community organizers serve as facilitators – they oversee a planned effort to achieve goals for the development of a community. For example, they may function as consultants, help develop grants, or serve as active leaders. Alternatively, Rothman (1996) has defined the roles of social workers in community organizing as enabler, planner, and activist.

> *Enabler:* The social worker brings together individuals, groups, or organizations to develop and/or sustain community groups. The social worker usually is nondirective and emphasizes communication and the development of a shared identity among members of the group.
>
> *Planner:* This role is usually taken by a social worker employed in a state agency. Rather than focusing on developing or maintaining community groups, her objective is to develop strategies for service delivery in the community.
>
> *Activist:* The social worker advocates for or against a current service or a suggested policy. She emphasizes the interests of a particular group and helps citizens develop plans to accomplish specified goals.

2. Goals and Objectives of Community Organizing: The overall goal of community organizing is to help community members achieve social justice and economic and social development. Because it emphasizes citizen involvement, however, its primary goal can be seen as twofold: to (a) resolve social problems and improve social welfare and (b) develop the capacity of people to help themselves.

Resolve social problems and improve social welfare: Regardless of what issue the community organizes around, community organizing attempts to correct the imbalance between those who have power and those who do not. This primarily entails efforts to reallocate resources (wealth and power) so that they no longer are in the hands of only a few (i.e., so that there is a better balance between resources and needs). To achieve this, community organizers (a) obtain information about problem areas to facilitate social planning and action, (b) educate the public about social problems, (c) encourage the public to support and participate in programs and activities to improve social welfare, (d) organize and facilitate relationships among community groups, (e) develop social services, and (f) improve standards of social welfare.

Develop the capacity of community members: Community organizing emphasizes not only collective action but also helping community members help themselves. Therefore, another key purpose of community organizing is developing the skills of community members. For community members, community organizing emphasizes two related objectives:

Capacity building: Community organizers help citizens develop their capacity for self-help. Citizens who participate in community organizing activities develop their abilities to organize, analyze problems, plan, and lead.

Task accomplishment: Citizens involved in community organizing strive to accomplish a series of tasks that will improve social and economic conditions in their community. They also seek to influence those who shape the direction of their community and plan its external development.

3. Community Organizing Steps, Processes, and Techniques:

a. Step 1 – Determine the Issue: The community organizer conducts surveys, needs assessments, and other research to get a database of information about the community. She identifies problems and analyzes their causes. When selecting an issue to work on, she determines the likelihood that the public will support the effort, compares potential issues in terms of their probabilities for successful outcome, and considers how vulnerable the target system is because this will influence the likelihood that the effort will succeed.

b. Step 2 – Activate Citizens: The community organizer activates the interest of citizens in the planned activity. This may require her to help community residents develop a feeling of common identity and interest and demonstrate for them how their welfare will improve if the effort is successful. In addition, the nature and extent of citizen participation is associated with the concept of **relative deprivation**. This concept assumes that people are motivated to change their circumstances by subjective feelings of deprivation rather than by their actual circumstances. According to Matza (1964), the nature of a person's subjective feelings depends on three factors: how his experience compares to that of intimate others, what the person has been accustomed to before, and what the person anticipated his life would be like. Therefore, a person may accept genuine deprivation if those around him are equally deprived or if he never expected to do better; and people who initially participate in social action-oriented movements are likely to be those who have reached a higher economic level rather than those who are the most deprived. Considering the relative deprivation of individuals who might participate in an activity is a useful community organizing tool.

The following are techniques that may be used by community organizers to activate citizens:

- *Hold meetings.* In public meetings, citizens discuss ideas; the community organizer plans these meetings carefully so that they have a specific purpose. In private meetings, the community organizer outlines her plan for the community (while respecting residents' self-determination). Last, in committee (working group) meetings, individuals from other meetings who have demonstrated their concern about the issue gather to achieve a specific task.

- Conduct a *public education campaign.*

- Use *grass-roots organizing* to help community members develop stronger relationships, identify their common interests, and organize in a way that allows them to accomplish their goals. The emphasis is on organizing all people who will be affected by the change, not just community leaders.

- Use **conflict induction** to encourage community members to debate their differences. The community organizer introduces certain issues to force members of the group into active confrontation, debate, and new coalition building.

- Use **polarization** to emphasize the differences between community groups and intensify the conflict so that group members become motivated to increase their involvement and coalitions become stronger. This, in turn, enables the groups to eventually achieve their objectives.

c. Step 3 – Plan the Effort: The community organizer plans and organizes **coalitions** and facilitates decision-making in meetings of citizens from the community. Coalitions may be alliances among influential groups or among less powerful groups to increase their influence. Examples of groups with whom community organizers may work include the following: (a) *Institutional-relations groups* are community groups that mediate the relationships between institutions and individuals (e.g., trade unions, civil rights groups). Like organizations, these groups have rules and procedures, a stable structure, and a specialized sense of purpose. They may help a community organizer whose goal is to help service consumers meet their needs and protect their interests. (b) *Organization-development groups* are community groups with large, fluid memberships that serve to introduce individuals to others with similar interests. Their activities may include rallies or demonstrations. These groups may help a community organizer expand a constituency, broaden a base of support, and develop new coalitions.

To develop coalitions and facilitate group decision-making, community organizers often use co-optation and/or satisficing: (a) **Co-optation** is used to minimize expected opposition to the effort (i.e., the opponent is included in the planning group). (b) **Satisficing** is used to facilitate decision-making and keep groups progressing toward their goals. With satisficing, the chosen alternative is a compromise.

d. Step 4 – Carry Out the Effort: During this phase, community organizers use one or more of the following techniques:

- *Advocacy* – empower community members so that they acquire their own political and/or legal power.

- *Strengthen coalitions* among existing community groups.

- *Facilitation* – provide support to an existing community group's leadership.

- *Negotiation* – assist groups with competing interests to communicate, bargain, and compromise so that they ultimately reach mutually acceptable agreements. With negotiation, the community organizer sides with one party (e.g., the client system).

- *Mediation* – help competing groups settle their differences, find compromises, or reach mutually satisfactory agreements. With mediation, the community organizer remains neutral.

e. *Step 5 – Evaluate the Effort:* In this step, the community organizer, for instance, conducts a community survey.

4. Sample Community Organizing Models: Most community organizers use elements of different models, depending on the demands of the intervention.

a. *Social Planning:* **Social planning** emphasizes long-term goals for the community; often the goal is to provide the community with needed goods and services. Those with power ("power centers") are sought as sponsors of social programs. Community planners and social workers join interdisciplinary teams to accomplish goals. The process is technical – it emphasizes fact-gathering, rational decision-making, and regulated change by experts.

b. *Social Action:* **Social action** emphasizes changing power relationships and reallocating resources through institutional change. Power centers are targets of social action because they are "oppressors." The client system is organized so that it can influence political processes and challenge existing power arrangements and structures. Those leading the effort clarify and polarize issues, which leads to negotiation between more equal parties.

c. *Locality or Community Development:* Locality or **community development** focuses on economic and social progress for an entire community, including enhancing a community's ability to help itself. Power centers are sought as potential collaborators. The change process involves education, the development of indigenous leadership, self-help, and voluntary participation and it relies on small task-oriented groups that encourage discussion and the development of consensus. (See also Part B, below.)

d. *Community Social Work Model:* One other model that has received attention in the U.S. is community social work, or community-oriented social work. This model, used widely in the United Kingdom, doesn't consist of a specific method but, rather, emphasizes that all those involved in social work (administrators, as well as direct care providers) should consider community members as partners in the delivery of social care.

B. Community Development

Community development is concerned with **social justice** and consists of efforts by professionals and community members to improve social ties among community residents, motivate residents for self-help, develop reliable local leadership, and create or restore local institutions. Community development relies on a grass-roots, nonbureaucratic approach that emphasizes community solidarity. A community development effort is always purposeful and must involve a clear strategy and set of activities. It may address such issues as mental health, the environment, the economy, or consumer interests. Associated interventions include social action, public education, and national and local planning. In social work, community development is considered an important administrative function since social agencies are concerned with the well-being of the communities in which their services operate.

1. Goals and Objectives of Community Development: The overall goal of community development is to organize and coordinate the efforts of groups to work together toward improving their quality of life or resolving a specific problem. The specific objectives vary, but typical examples include the following: expand community resources, increase educational and economic opportunities, improve service delivery, improve social and political functioning, and/or help community residents gain self-sufficiency. To achieve the selected objectives, community developers increase social and political awareness of the causes of problems, improve the ability of local community leaders to address these problems, and change the social framework of relationships between the community's residents and its power structures.

2. Community Development Approaches: Two important approaches used in community development are "political action" and "social support":

- *Political action* emphasizes the development and use of community or organizational power to encourage change in specific institutions or programs. It emphasizes grass-roots decision-making and the involvement and influence of local citizens.

- The *social support approach* attempts to acquire resources for community services. It emphasizes promoting and maintaining support networks at all levels, including interpersonal, interorganizational, and community.

3. Community Development Processes: Community development efforts vary depending on the circumstances of the intervention, but they always rely on face-to-face groups. Group meetings focus on the needs and issues that community members and professionals want to address. During meetings, a community developer works to empower community residents, expand their knowledge and skills, and develop their leadership abilities, while also developing solutions to specific community problems. The participation of local citizens, groups, and organizations is central to community development and has an influence on the outcome of an effort. Thus, community developers emphasize self-help and voluntary cooperation among a community's residents and solicit the collaboration, or at least tolerance, of community power centers even though these structures are often the targets of the social change effort.

4. Social Worker Roles in Community Development: Community developers take on a variety of roles including consultant, planner, coordinator, catalyst who cultivates groups, and enabler who facilitates group processes.

On the whole, community developers are more directive than other human service workers, while still believing in the ability of community members to resolve their own problems. Community development theory suggests that community members can and must be organized to work together to clarify their needs and priorities and use their own skills and resources to implement programs for the welfare of their community. Therefore, the community developer's role is to educate the community and facilitate program development consistent with this philosophy.

C. Macro-Level Advocacy

Advocacy involves representing, championing, or defending the rights of others. Macro, or community, practice often involves **cause advocacy** (a.k.a. class advocacy), which is work on behalf of groups of people who lack the resources or ability to advocate for themselves. (In case advocacy, by contrast, a social worker advocates for individual cases or clients).

1. Cause Advocacy Guidelines: Cause advocacy guidelines include the following: (a) Cause advocacy may be required when an organization performs its functions poorly or hurts its clientele, but it can be difficult to change some organizations. Social workers should focus on goals that are manageable and reasonably achievable. (b) Teamwork often produces better outcomes. (c) Advocates should be prepared to be assertive. (d) Advocates should be flexible – the behavior they select should depend on the need or goal of the effort. (e) Advocates should be prepared to use a variety of strategies. Generally, collaborative strategies should be tried first; confrontational strategies should be used only when the situation requires it (Kirst-Ashman & Hull, 2006).

2. Cause Advocacy Tactics:

a. Persuasion: Persuasion can include providing the target system with additional information that may lead it to make a different decision. Hoffman and Sallee (1994) have identified three useful ways to persuade others: (a) *Inductive questioning* – ask the target system a series of questions designed to make them re-think their original decision. (b) *Provide arguments on both sides* – state not only your own opinions and facts but also those of the other side. This lets the target system know that you understand their arguments but still think your position makes more sense. (c) *Persistence* – persevere without being abrasive.

b. Fair Hearings, Grievances, and Complaints: Fair hearings, grievances, and complaints are administrative procedures designed to ensure that individuals who have been denied benefits or rights to which they are entitled get fair treatment. In **fair hearings**, clients notify the agency that they want to have a fair hearing concerning a decision-maker's actions. Usually an outside person is appointed to hear both sides of the argument. If the hearing examiner finds that the decision-maker has violated state or federal policies, she will direct him or her to comply with the rules and award the clients their benefits. This approach is appropriate when a public agency has been denying benefits to a group or violating rules that they are required to follow.

Grievances and complaints are other ways of dealing with decision-makers who have violated policy. **Grievance procedures** are usually part of an agency's own policies. Many organizations employ an **ombudsperson** to represent a person or group that has a complaint of oppression, discrimination, or mistreatment. **Complaints** are provided for in certain laws (e.g., the Americans with Disabilities Act). Sometimes, the threat of using a formal grievance or complaint process is enough to change a decision.

If an agency has no policy for a fair hearing or appeal, confrontational tactics can be used, such as seeking advice from an attorney. An attorney's letter suggesting the possibility of legal action may be sufficient to cause decision-makers to change their position.

c. Embarrassing the Target of Change: "Embarrassing the target of change" may involve, for example, sit-ins, demonstrations, or using the media to call attention to the problem.

d. Political Pressure: "Political pressure" involves the use of political power to force change that would not otherwise occur (e.g., calling a city council member or member of the state legislature). Not all organizations or situations respond to political pressure. Public organizations, however, are likely to be sensitive to the concerns of the elected officials who control them.

e. Petitioning: "Petitioning" involves collecting signatures on a petition that asks an organization to act in a specified way. A drawback of this tactic is that the target system might assume that those who signed the petition don't actually feel all that strongly about the issue. One way to increase the effectiveness of petitions is to present them in a public forum such as a city council meeting.

D. Community Mental Health Intervention

The field of "community psychology" or "community mental health" advocates a set of values consistent with political liberalism (Prilleltensky, 1990), including empowerment, promoting a sense of community involvement, a respect for cultural diversity, and an explicit commitment to social change. Community psychology's historical roots are diverse, but its modern spirit has been integrated, at least in part, through the **Community Mental Health Center Act** and its various amendments. This Act established a number of goals and programs consistent with the values described above, including short-term hospitalization for mental health patients; outpatient, residential, and aftercare services for discharged mental health patients; emergency mental health treatment that is available 24 hours a day; specialized services for children and the aged; and rehabilitation for drug and alcohol abusers.

1. Characteristics of Community Mental Health Intervention: Key characteristics of community mental health intervention include the following (Korchin, 1976):

- An emphasis on the role of social and environmental factors in the development and maintenance of behavior. The environmental factors addressed by community mental health intervention include all of the larger mediating structures that make up the context of the individual (e.g., family, interpersonal networks, social and political systems).

- A belief that system-oriented (vs. person-oriented) interventions are effective for enhancing the functioning of both systems and individuals.

- A focus on *prevention* rather than treatment of mental disorders.

- The view of the mental health worker's role as a consultant and collaborator rather than only as a direct provider of psychological services.

- A belief that, because mental health problems are often related to social factors, mental health professionals should be concerned with social reform.

- A strong reliance on naturalistic ecological research, epidemiology, and program evaluation.

2. Intervention Goals: Many of the principles and strategies of community mental health intervention were derived from the field of public health, which emphasizes the prevention of disease, and, consequently, community mental health intervention stresses prevention over treatment. Methods of prevention are classified as primary, secondary, or tertiary:

- **Primary preventions** are aimed at reducing the prevalence of mental and physical disorders by decreasing the incidence of new cases. Primary prevention is accomplished by making an intervention that promotes mental or physical health available to all members of an identified group or population. Examples include immunization programs, prenatal nutrition programs for low-SES mothers, "Meals on Wheels," and public education programs on drug and alcohol abuse.

- **Secondary preventions** attempt to decrease the prevalence of mental and physical disorders by reducing their duration through early detection and intervention. In contrast to primary preventions, secondary preventions involve identifying specific individuals and providing those individuals with appropriate treatments. Using screening tests to identify entering first graders with reading disabilities so that they can be provided with an educational intervention is an example of a secondary prevention.

- **Tertiary prevention** programs are designed to reduce the duration and consequences of mental and physical disorders. Rehabilitation programs, programs that provide alternatives to hospitalization (e.g., halfway houses), and education programs designed to improve community attitudes toward former mental patients are all forms of tertiary prevention.

Appendix: Research Design and Statistics

NOTE: The exams administered by the ASWB require only *basic knowledge* of research design and statistics. This appendix is provided to ensure that you are familiar with basic terms and concepts that you need to know in order to understand the procedures used in practice evaluation, program evaluation, and evaluations of macro change episodes. We encourage you to review this appendix to gain this level of familiarity and find definitions of terms and concepts used elsewhere in these materials. Ideally, for your exam, you will have a "recognition level" of knowledge of the material in this appendix – i.e., recognizing terms and concepts from this appendix will help you understand and answer exam questions on practice evaluation, program evaluation, and basic statistics without being thrown off by unfamiliar terminology.

A. "Research" and "Statistics" Defined

1. Research: Research can be defined as the empirical (observed), systematic investigation of the relationship between two or more variables. For research to be systematic, it must be based on a plan that specifies: the general research strategy; the population of interest; the method that will be used to select a sample from the population; the nature of the variables to be studied; and the conditions under which the study will be conducted.

2. Statistics: Statistics encompasses the methods used to organize and analyze numerical data. These methods are divided into two basic types:

- **Descriptive statistics** are used to describe and summarize data. A researcher might use a table or a graph, for example, to summarize the set of test scores she has collected in a research study.

- **Inferential statistics** are used to draw conclusions about relationships between independent and dependent variables. A researcher would use an inferential statistical test to determine whether or not the relationship between variables she has found in a research study is statistically significant.

B. Variables

1. Variables vs. Constants: A variable is any characteristic, behavior, event, or other phenomenon that is capable of varying, or existing in at least two different states, conditions, or levels. Examples are gender, anxiety (high, average, low) and therapy (cognitive, client-centered, psychoanalytic). When a characteristic is restricted to a single state or condition, it is called a constant. Gender would be a constant in a study that included only male subjects.

2. Independent and Dependent Variables: In research, variables are often categorized as independent or dependent.

- A variable is an **independent variable** (IV) when it is believed to affect or alter status on another variable (the dependent variable). The independent variable is sometimes referred to as the "treatment" or "intervention" and is symbolized with the letter "X." In a research study, subjects are assigned to different groups representing different levels of the independent variable.

- Conversely, a variable is a **dependent variable** (DV) when status on that variable seems to "depend on" status on another variable (the independent variable). The dependent variable is considered the outcome of the treatment, is measured by pretests and posttests, and is symbolized with the letter "Y."

For experimental and correlational research (which will be defined in this appendix), you can usually identify a study's independent and dependent variables by framing the research question in the following way: What effect does INDEPENDENT VARIABLE(S) have on DEPENDENT VARIABLE(S)?

Example Research Studies: To demonstrate how the above question can be used to identify a study's independent and dependent variables, the three research examples that are used in the discussions of research design and statistics will now be introduced:

Study #1 – Self-control procedure for children with ADHD: An investigator has designed a self-control procedure that incorporates several cognitive-behavioral techniques including self-monitoring, self-instruction, and self-reinforcement. The investigator believes use of the self-control procedure will improve the academic achievement of children who have received a diagnosis of attention-deficit/hyperactivity disorder (ADHD). She plans to test her hypothesis by comparing the academic achievement of children with ADHD who have and have not received training in the procedure.

Example: The research question would be completed in the following way for Study #1: What are the effects of a SELF-CONTROL PROCEDURE on the ACADEMIC ACHIEVEMENT of children who have received a diagnosis of ADHD? Completion of the question indicates that Study #1 has one independent variable (self-control procedure) and one dependent variable (academic achievement).

Study #2 – Treatments for schizophrenia: An investigator wants to assess the effects of various combinations of four therapy approaches (family therapy, individual psychotherapy, a combination of the two, and no therapy) and three levels of phenothiazines (high dose, low dose, and placebo) on the behavioral and cognitive functioning of hospitalized patients who have received a diagnosis of schizophrenia. Her study will involve assigning hospitalized patients to one of the twelve treatment groups and, after a period of time, administering the Brief Psychiatric Rating Scale (BPRS) and WAIS to all of the patients.

Example: For Study #2, the research question is: What are the effects of THERAPY and PHENOTHIAZINES on the BPRS and WAIS SCORES of hospitalized patients who have received a diagnosis of schizophrenia? This question indicates that Study #2 has two independent variables (therapy and phenothiazine level) and two dependent variables (BPRS and WAIS scores).

Study #3 – Characteristics of successful salespeople: An organizational psychologist has been hired by a computer manufacturing company to identify factors that predict success as a computer salesperson so that, eventually, job selection measures for this position can be developed. The psychologist decides to assess the product knowledge, attitude toward the company, and interpersonal assertiveness of a group of salespeople and determine each salesperson's dollar amount of sales during a three-month period.

Example: For Study #3, the research question is: What are the effects of PRODUCT KNOWLEDGE, ATTITUDE TOWARD THE COMPANY, and INTERPERSONAL ASSERTIVENESS on the DOLLAR AMOUNT OF SALES of computer salespeople? Study #3 has three independent variables (product knowledge, attitude toward the company, and interpersonal assertiveness) and one dependent variable (dollar amount of sales).

3. Manipulated and Organismic Variables: A manipulated variable is an independent variable that is controlled by the experimenter. When the experimenter can identify the levels of the variable and determine who will receive which levels, the variable is a manipulated variable. An organismic (subject) variable, by contrast, is an independent variable that is a characteristic of the subjects (e.g., IQ, self-esteem, height) and, therefore, that cannot be manipulated by the investigator.

Example: In Studies #1 and #2, the independent variables are "manipulated" variables: The investigator in each study will be able to determine which levels of the IVs will be administered to subjects. In Study #3, the three IVs are "organismic" variables, or subject characteristics that cannot be controlled by the psychologist. Although the psychologist in Study #3 will be able to determine if there is a relationship between the study's independent and dependent variables, because of the inability to manipulate the independent variables, she will not be able to determine if any observed relationships are causal in nature.

C. Samples and Sampling

A research design should specify the population of interest and the method that will be used to select a sample from that population. To maximize the generalizability of a study's results (i.e., to maximize the study's "external validity"), the sample must be representative of the population from which it was drawn so that people in the sample are similar to those in the population in terms of characteristics relevant to the research study.

The best way to make sure that a sample is representative of the population is to use one of the following sampling techniques.

Simple random sampling: When using **random sampling**, every member of the population has an equal chance of being included in the sample. Random sampling reduces the probability that a sample will be biased in some way, especially when the sample size is large.

Stratified random sampling: An investigator can use stratified random sampling to ensure that each "strata," or population characteristic, is represented in the sample. This involves dividing the population into the appropriate stratum (e.g., gender, age, education level, socioeconomic status, ethnic/cultural background) and randomly selecting subjects from each stratum.

Cluster sampling: Cluster sampling entails selecting units (clusters) of individuals and then randomly selecting individuals from those units. Cluster sampling is useful when it is not possible to identify or obtain access to the entire population of interest.

D. Control Groups

As noted previously, the effects of an independent variable can be assessed only when there are at least two levels of that variable. To determine if a treatment has an effect on a dependent variable, the treatment must be compared to something. The comparison group is often referred to as the **control group**.

In psychotherapy research, the tradition has been to compare an experimental group that receives the treatment to either a no-treatment or placebo control group. No-treatment control groups often consist of individuals who have been placed on a wait-list, while subjects in a placebo control group are exposed to nonspecific factors (e.g., therapist warmth and attention).

E. Research Strategies: Descriptive vs. Experimental Research

Researchers employ a variety of strategies to investigate variables and their interrelationships. These strategies can be divided into two basic types: descriptive and experimental.

1. Descriptive Research: Descriptive research is conducted primarily to collect data about variables rather than to test hypotheses about the relationships between variables. In other words, a descriptive study is conducted to describe "how things are." Observational studies, surveys, archival research, and case studies are ordinarily classified as descriptive research.

a. Observational Studies: Observational studies involve observing behavior in a systematic way, often in a naturalistic context. Naturalistic field studies and **participant observation** are examples of observational studies. One method of recording the behavior of interest is to obtain a narrative record of the behavior as it actually occurs. Protocols (protocol analysis) are one type of narrative record. They provide a complete record of everything a person said or did during a period of time.

An alternative to obtaining a complete record of a behavior is to record only specific aspects of the behavior. This entails employing some method of behavioral or situational sampling. Methods of behavioral sampling include interval recording and event sampling. Interval recording is a type of time sampling that involves observing a behavior for a period of time that has been divided into equal intervals and recording whether or not the behavior occurred during each interval. Event sampling involves observing a behavior each time it occurs. Finally, situational sampling is useful when a goal of the study is to observe a behavior in a number of settings.

b. Case Studies: The term **case study** is most associated with an in-depth description and analysis of a single person but can also involve an intensive investigation of a single institution, agency, community, or other social unit. Case studies differ from observational studies in that the latter are usually concerned only with current behaviors, while case studies provide descriptions of behaviors that occur over time.

Two shortcomings of case studies are that: (a) Their results usually do not allow an investigator to draw conclusions about the exact nature of the relationships among variables (e.g., to determine if variability in one variable causes variability in another variable); and (b) the information derived from a case study might not be generalizable to other cases.

2. Experimental Research: Experimental research is conducted specifically to test hypotheses about the effects of one or more independent variables on one or more dependent variables. Experimental research is classified as either true experimental or quasi-experimental.

a. True Experimental Research: All experimental research is characterized by some degree of experimental control, or the ability to control experimental conditions and variables. However, only **true experimental research** provides the amount of control necessary to conclude that observed variability in a dependent variable is actually caused by variability in an independent variable. When conducting a true experimental study, an investigator is able to randomly assign subjects to the different treatment groups (i.e., to different levels of the IV). The random assignment of subjects to groups, or randomization, helps ensure that any observed differences between groups on the dependent variable are due to the independent variable rather than to other factors.

> *Example:* Study #1 would be a true experimental study if the investigator randomly assigns subjects to either the self-control procedure (experimental) group or the no self-control procedure (control) group. Because she randomly assigned subjects to groups, the investigator would be better able to conclude that an observed difference between the experimental and control groups on the measure of academic achievement at the conclusion of the study is, in fact, due to the effects of the self-control procedure.

b. Quasi-Experimental Research: **Quasi-experimental research** also involves investigating the effects of an independent variable on a dependent variable but does not provide an investigator with the same degree of control as true experimental research. Most important, in quasi-experimental research, an investigator cannot control the assignment of subjects to treatment groups either because: (a) the independent variable is an "organismic" (subject) variable; (b) because the investigator must use intact (pre-existing) groups; or (c) because the study includes only one group.

> *Example:* Study #1 would be a quasi-experimental study if the investigator had to use children attending one school as experimental group subjects and children attending another school as control group subjects. Because the investigator did not randomly assign subjects to groups, she could not be certain whether a difference between the groups on the dependent variable was due to the self-control procedure or to initial differences between the groups or other confounding factors.

Ex-post facto research and developmental research are usually classified as quasi-experimental. **Ex-post facto** ("after the fact") studies involve assessing the effects of an independent variable after it has occurred or been applied and, consequently, do not permit an investigator to randomly assign subjects to treatment groups.

Developmental research is conducted to assess changes that occur in variables as a function of time (e.g., as the consequence of increasing age, psychological development, or physical development). Developmental research can utilize either a cross-sectional, longitudinal, or cross-sequential methodology:

- **Cross-sectional studies** evaluate changes over time by comparing groups of people of different ages or developmental levels at the same point in time. Cross-sectional studies are susceptible to cohort (intergenerational) effects. **Cohort effects** occur when observed differences between subjects of different ages are due to differences in experience or other factors rather than to the effects of increasing age or developmental level.

- **Longitudinal studies** investigate changes by assessing the same group of people over an extended period of time. While longitudinal studies overcome the problem of cohort effects, they are more difficult to conduct because of time and cost factors and high subject dropout rates. Data collection about a time period can be either retrospective, which involves asking subjects to reflect back on their experiences and/or attitudes; or contemporary, which involves collecting data at different times about the present situation. Retrospective studies often involve collecting relevant histories from the subjects.

- To overcome the problems associated with cross-sectional and longitudinal research, a **cross-sequential design** can be used. This design combines cross-sectional and longitudinal methodologies by assessing members of two or more age groups at two or more different times.

3. Evaluation Research: Evaluation research (program evaluation) is conducted to assess the value or effectiveness of psychological, educational, and other social programs. As a type of applied research, evaluation research differs from more theoretical or academic research in several ways. Most important, perhaps, evaluation research is conducted to assess the utility of social programs in order to facilitate decisions about them. Evaluation research is also reviewed in Section XXI of this chapter.

4. Qualitative and Quantitative Research: The various methods of research can also be categorized as either qualitative or quantitative.

- **Qualitative research** is conducted to obtain a holistic description of the quality of relationships, actions, situations, or other phenomena. It uses a naturalistic, contextual approach, emphasizes understanding and interpretation, and is primarily inductive in nature. The investigator's perspective is an important element of the entire research process. Participant and nonparticipant observation, interviews, and document analysis are strategies used by qualitative researchers.

- **Quantitative research** is conducted to obtain numerical data on variables. It makes use of empirical methods and statistical procedures, emphasizes prediction, generalizability, and causality, and is primarily deductive. Although the investigator's perspective may be reflected in the purpose of the study, it is minimized in the analysis and interpretation of the data. Quantitative research can be either descriptive (non-experimental) or experimental (see above).

F. Methods of Control in Experimental Research

When conducting an experimental research study, an investigator is ordinarily attempting to answer the following basic research questions:

- Is there a relationship between the independent and dependent variables?
- If so, is the relationship a causal one?

The ability of a study to provide accurate answers to these two questions depends on the extent to which the study's design allows the investigator to control the three factors that can cause variability in the dependent variable. These factors are: (a) the independent variable (experimental variance); (b) systematic error (error due to extraneous variables); and (c) random error (error due to random fluctuations in subjects, experimental conditions, methods of measurement, etc.).

Although quasi-experimental research provides some control over the three sources of variability, an investigator's control is maximized when she conducts a true experimental study. The ways in which true experimental research provide control are discussed below.

1. Maximizing Variability Due to the Independent Variable(s): True experimental research enhances a researcher's ability to maximize variability due to the independent (experimental) variable by allowing her to make the levels of the independent variable as different as possible so that its effects on the dependent variable can be detected.

2. Controlling Variability Due to Extraneous Variables: An extraneous variable is a variable that is irrelevant to the purpose of a research study but that confounds the study's results because it has a systematic effect on (correlates with) the dependent variable.

True experimental research maximizes the control an investigator has over extraneous variables by nullifying, minimizing, or isolating their effects. Specific techniques available to a researcher when using a true experimental research design include the following:

Random assignment of subjects to treatment groups (randomization): An investigator can equalize the effects of all known and unknown extraneous variables by randomly assigning subjects to the different levels of the independent variable. The random assignment of subjects to groups is considered the most "powerful" method of experimental control and is the primary characteristic that sets true experimental research apart from other types of research.

Holding the extraneous variable constant: An investigator can eliminate the effects of an extraneous variable by selecting subjects who are homogeneous with respect to that variable. The primary shortcoming of this method of control is that it limits the generalizability of the research results.

Matching subjects on the extraneous variable: Another way to ensure that groups are equivalent with regard to an extraneous variable is to match subjects in terms of their status on that variable and then randomly assign matched subjects to one of the treatment groups.

Building the extraneous variable into the study ("blocking"): An extraneous variable can be controlled by including it in the study as an additional independent variable so that its effects on the dependent variable can be statistically analyzed. When using this technique, subjects are not individually matched but are, instead, "blocked" (grouped) on the basis of their status on the extraneous variable. Subjects in each block are then randomly assigned to one of the treatment groups.

Statistical control of the extraneous variable: When an investigator has information on each subject's status (score) on an extraneous variable, she can use the analysis of covariance (ANCOVA) or other statistical techniques to remove variability in the dependent variable that is due to the extraneous variable. In essence, the ANCOVA controls an extraneous variable (the "covariate") by equalizing all subjects with regard to their status on that variable.

3. Minimizing Random Error: Experimental research (especially true experimental research) helps an investigator minimize the effects of random fluctuations in subjects, conditions, and measuring instruments by allowing her to control experimental conditions and procedures. To minimize the effects of random error, an investigator can, for example, make sure that subjects do not become fatigued during the course of the study, that the experimental setting is free from distractions and fluctuations in environmental conditions, and that all measuring devices are reliable.

G. Internal and External Validity

When an investigator conducts a research study, she ordinarily not only wants to find out if there is a relationship between independent and dependent variables but also wants to determine if that relationship is generalizable to other people and circumstances. In other words, the basic research questions that an investigator wants to answer can be expanded to include a third question:

- Is there a relationship between the independent and dependent variables?
- If so, is the relationship a causal one?
- Can the relationship between independent and dependent variables be generalized to other people, settings, times, and operations?

A research study is said to have **internal validity** to the extent that it allows an investigator to obtain accurate answers to the first two research questions and **external validity** to the degree that it enables the investigator to obtain an accurate answer to the third question.

The specific research designs are susceptible, to varying degrees, to factors that can limit a study's internal and external validity.

1. Threats to Internal Validity: Internal validity is threatened whenever an investigator cannot control the three sources of variability described in the previous section: If an investigator cannot maximize the effects of the independent variable, control the effects of extraneous variables, and/or minimize the effects of random error, she cannot be certain whether observed variability (or lack of variability) in the dependent variable is attributable to the independent variable or to some other factor.

Campbell and Stanley (1963) have identified seven "generic" extraneous variables that, if not controlled, can threaten a study's internal validity:

Maturation: Maturation refers to any biological or psychological change that occurs within subjects during the course of a study as a function of time that is not relevant to the research hypothesis but that affects the status of most or all subjects on the dependent variable in a systematic way. Fatigue, boredom, hunger, and physical and intellectual growth are all potential maturational effects that can limit a study's internal validity.

History: History threatens a study's internal validity when an event outside or within the experimental situation systematically affects the status of subjects on the dependent variable.

Testing: Because taking a test can alter a person's performance on the test when it is readministered, pretesting can threaten a study's internal validity whenever exposure to a pretest might alter subjects' performance on the posttest.

Instrumentation: Changes in the accuracy or sensitivity of measuring devices or procedures during the course of a research study can confound the study's results. For instance, if a rater's accuracy improves over time, any change in the subjects' pretest and posttest performance might be due to the rater's increased accuracy rather than to the effects of the independent variable.

Statistical regression: The tendency of extreme scores on a measure to "regress" toward the mean when the measure is readministered is called statistical regression. Statistical regression threatens a study's internal validity whenever subjects have been selected because of their extreme status on the dependent variable (or a related measure).

Selection: Selection is a threat to a study's internal validity whenever the method used to assign subjects to treatment groups results in systematic differences between the groups at the beginning of the study. Selection is often a problem when intact groups are used.

Attrition (mortality): Attrition poses a threat to a study's internal validity when subjects who drop out of one group differ in an important way from subjects who drop out of other groups.

2. Threats to External Validity: A study has external validity when its findings can be generalized to other people, settings, and conditions. Campbell and Stanley (1966) have identified four factors that can threaten the external validity of many different types of research studies:

Interaction between testing and treatment: The administration of a pretest can "sensitize" subjects to the purpose of the research study and thereby alter their reaction to the independent variable. When a study's results have been contaminated by such "pretest sensitization," they cannot be generalized to people who have not been pretested.

Interaction between selection and treatment: Subjects included in a research study can have characteristics that make them respond to the independent variable in a particular way. When this occurs, the results of the study cannot be generalized to people who do not have those characteristics. An interaction between selection and treatment is often a problem when subjects are volunteers. Volunteers tend to be more motivated than non-volunteers and, consequently, might be more responsive to the treatment.

Reactivity (reactive arrangements): Research participants can respond to an independent variable in a particular way simply because they know their behavior is being observed. When a study has been contaminated by **reactivity**, its results cannot be generalized to conditions in which reactivity does not occur. Several other phenomena are sometimes included in the category of reactivity:

Hawthorne effect and evaluation apprehension: The behavior of research subjects can reflect a Hawthorne effect, which is the tendency of subjects to perform better because of the attention they are receiving as research participants, or evaluation apprehension, which causes subjects to act in ways they believe will help them avoid negative evaluations.

Demand characteristics: The behavior of research participants can also be altered by **demand characteristics**, or cues in the experimental setting that inform subjects of the purpose of the study or suggest to subjects what behaviors are expected of them.

Experimenter expectancy: An experimenter can unintentionally provide subjects with cues (demand characteristics) that inform them of what behavior is expected of them or can act in ways that do not affect research subjects directly but that bias the results of the study. There is evidence, for example, that experimenters are more likely to recheck their calculations when they conflict with the research hypothesis than when they support it.

Reactivity can be controlled by using unobtrusive (nonreactive) measures, deception, or a single- or double-blind technique. In a **single-blind technique**, research subjects are kept uninformed about the experimental hypothesis and which level of the IV they have been assigned to. In a **double-blind technique**, both research participants and the experimenter are kept uninformed about which level of the IV that each subject is receiving.

Multiple treatment interference (order effects, carryover effects): When a study involves exposing the same subjects to two or more levels of an independent variable (i.e., when the study utilizes a "within subjects design"), the effects of one level of the independent variable can be affected by previous exposure to another level. When this occurs, the results of the study cannot be generalized to situations in which people will be exposed to only one level of the independent variable. Multiple treatment interference can be controlled by using a counterbalanced design in which different subjects (or groups of subjects) receive the levels of the independent variable in a different order.

H. Experimental Research Designs

The specific research designs available to investigators can be divided into two basic types: group designs and single-subject designs. Single-subject designs may be used in practice evaluation and are also described in Section VIII of this chapter. In this appendix, we repeat some of this instruction, this time illustrating the information by using our example research studies.

1. Group (Multi-Subject) Designs: As their name implies, the group designs include one or more groups of subjects. The specific group designs are often classified as either between groups designs, within subjects designs, or mixed designs.

a. Between Groups Designs: When a between groups design is used, the effects of different levels of an independent variable are assessed by administering each level to a different group of subjects and then comparing the status or performance of the groups on the dependent variable.

Example: The investigator in Study #1 assesses the effects of the self-control procedure by comparing the academic achievement of children who have been trained in the procedure (experimental group) with that of children who have not been trained in the procedure (control group).

The simple two-group design can be expanded in two ways. One way is to include more than two levels of a single independent variable. Another way to expand a two-group design is to include two or more independent variables (with each variable having at least two levels). Whenever a study includes two or more independent variables, it is referred to as a factorial design. The primary advantage of a factorial design is that it provides more thorough information about the relationships among variables by allowing an investigator to analyze the main effects of each independent variable as well as the interaction between variables.

b. *Within Subjects (Repeated Measures) Designs:* When using a within subjects design, all levels of the independent variable are administered, at different times, to all subjects. Consequently, comparisons of the different levels of the independent variable are made within subjects rather than between groups of subjects.

The single-group time-series design is one type of within subjects design. When using this design, the effects of a treatment are evaluated by measuring the dependent variable(s) before and after the treatment is applied. This procedure allows subjects to act as their own no-treatment "controls."

Example: The investigator in Study #2 assesses the effects of a low dose of phenothiazines on BPRS scores by administering the BPRS to a single group of patients at one week intervals for two months before and two months after patients begin receiving a low dose of the drug.

In another type of within subjects design, two or more levels of an independent variable are applied at different times to all subjects and the dependent variable is measured after each level is applied.

Example: The investigator in Study #2 compares the effects of a low and high dose of phenothiazines on BPRS scores by giving the low dose of the drug to a group of patients for two months and administering the BPRS; and then giving the same patients the high dose of phenothiazines for two months and administering the BPRS. The effects of the phenothiazines will be analyzed by comparing the BPRS scores obtained by the patients after each dose was administered to them.

c. *Mixed Designs:* As its name implies, a mixed design combines between groups and within subjects methodologies. Counterbalanced designs are usually classified as mixed designs because they permit comparisons both between groups and within subjects.

Example: In Study #2, the investigator would be using a mixed design if therapy approach is treated as a between-groups variable (patients receive only one type of therapy), while phenothiazines is treated as a within-subjects variable (the placebo, low dose, and high dose are administered sequentially to all patients).

Mixed designs are common in research studies that involve measuring the dependent variable over time or across trials. In this type of study, time or trials is an additional independent variable and is a within-subjects variable because comparisons on the dependent variable can be made within subjects across time or across trials.

Example: In Study #2, the investigator decides to compare the effects of four levels of therapy (family therapy, individual therapy, a combination of the two, and no therapy) by assigning patients to one of the levels and measuring the short- and long-term effects of therapy by administering the BPRS at two-month intervals for 24 months after therapy begins. Because the study includes a between groups variable (therapy) and a within subjects variable (time), its design is a mixed design.

2. Single-Subject Designs: While the single-subject designs are often used to investigate the effects of an independent variable on the behavior of one subject or a small number of subjects, they can also be used with groups of subjects.

Two important characteristics distinguish the single-subject designs from those classified as group designs:

- Each single-subject design includes at least one baseline (no treatment) phase and one treatment phase. As a result, when using a single-subject design, subjects act as their own **no-treatment controls**.

- The dependent variable is measured repeatedly at regular intervals throughout the baseline and treatment phases. If status on the dependent variable is stable within each phase of the study and changes only at the same time the independent variable (treatment) is applied or removed, then it is likely that any observed change in the dependent variable is due to the effects of the independent variable rather than to history, maturation, or other extraneous factor.

There are actually a large number of single-subject designs but probably the most commonly used are the AB design and its extensions and the multiple baseline design.

a. AB Design: The simplest single-subject design is the **AB design**, which includes a single baseline (A) phase and a single treatment (B) phase. As in all single-subject designs, the dependent variable is measured at regular intervals during both phases.

Example: The investigator in Study #2 decides to assess the effects of a low dose of phenothiazines on the BPRS scores of one patient. Using the AB design, she administers the BPRS to the patient at two-week intervals for three months during the baseline (A) phase of the study and for three months during the treatment (B) phase. If the patient's symptoms decreased only after he began receiving the phenothiazines, these results would suggest that a low dose of phenothiazines lowers symptom severity.

b. Extensions of the AB Design (ABA, ABAB, etc.): The AB design can be expanded to include more than one baseline and one treatment phase. Because any expansion requires the withdrawal of the treatment during the second and subsequent baseline phases, the extensions of the AB design are referred to as reversal and withdrawal designs.

For example, when an ABA design is used, if status on the dependent variable returns to the initial baseline (no treatment) level during the second baseline (A) phase, an investigator can be more certain that an observed change in the dependent variable during the treatment phase was actually due to the independent variable rather than to an historical event or other extraneous factor.

The reversal designs are considered inappropriate when withdrawal of a treatment during the course of a research study would be unethical (e.g., when the treatment has successfully eliminated a self-injurious behavior).

c. Multiple Baseline Design: If a reversal design is inappropriate for ethical or practical reasons, an investigator might use a **multiple baseline design**. The multiple baseline design does not require withdrawal of a treatment during the course of the study but, instead, involves sequentially applying the treatment either: (a) to different behaviors of the same subject (multiple baseline across behaviors); (b) to the same subject in different settings (multiple baseline across settings); or (c) to the same behavior of different subjects (multiple baseline across subjects). Once the treatment has been applied to a "baseline" (behavior, setting, or subject), it is not withdrawn from that baseline during the course of the study.

> *Example:* To test the effects of the self-instructional component of the self-control procedure on attention span, the investigator in Study #1 trains a child in self-instruction and then tells him to use the technique when working on arithmetic homework in three different settings: first when working alone in a quiet room; then when working in the library; and then when working in the classroom. The investigator measures the child's attention span in all three settings at regular intervals during the baseline and treatment phases. If the child's attention span in each setting did not increase until self-instruction was applied to it, these results would confirm that self-instruction is useful for improving attention span in three different settings.

Sequentially applying an intervention to different settings helps an investigator determine if the intervention is actually responsible for any observed changes in the target behavior: If the behavior changes in a particular setting only after the intervention has been applied in that setting, an investigator can be more certain that the change is attributable to the intervention rather than to history or other factors.

I. Scales of Measurement

As reported earlier, descriptive statistics are used to describe and summarize data, while inferential statistics are used to draw conclusions about relationships between independent and dependent variables.

The first consideration when choosing a descriptive or inferential statistical technique is usually the scale of measurement of the data that is to be described or analyzed. There are four different measurement scales: Each involves dividing a set of observations into mutually exclusive and exhaustive categories. The differences between the four scales are that each provides a different kind of information and allows different mathematical operations to be performed.

1. Nominal Scale: A nominal scale of measurement divides variables into unordered categories. Sex of salespeople in Study #3 is a nominal variable since salespeople will be classified in terms of two unordered categories (male and female). Other examples of nominal variables include political affiliation, eye color, and DSM diagnosis.

The primary limitation of this measurement scale is that the only mathematical operation that can be performed on nominal data is to count the number (frequency) of cases in each category.

2. Ordinal Scale: An ordinal scale not only divides observations into categories but also provides information on the order of those categories. With an ordinal scale, it is possible to say that one person has more or less of the characteristic being measured than another person. An example is a Likert-type scale using these ratings 1 = strongly agree, 2 = agree, 3 = disagree, or 4 = strongly disagree. Other examples of ordinal scales include high/moderate/low and win/place/show. Also, whenever data are reported in terms of ranks (e.g., 1st, 2nd, 3rd), an ordinal scale is being used.

A limitation of ordinal scores is that they do not lend themselves to determining just how much difference there is between scores. For example, we can't say that the person with a rank of 10 has twice as much of the characteristic as the person with a rank of 5, only that he is ranked higher.

3. Interval Scale: The interval scale has the property of order as well as the property of equal intervals between successive points on the measurement scale. Scores on standardized IQ tests are usually considered to represent an interval scale, and, as a result, we can say that the interval between the scores 90 and 95 is equal to the interval between the scores of 100 and 105. Examples of interval scales include temperature when measured on a Fahrenheit or Celsius scale and scores on most standardized educational and psychological tests.

Note that interval scales sometimes have a zero point but that it is arbitrary rather than absolute. A score of zero on a test that provides interval scores cannot be interpreted as an absolute lack or absence of the characteristic being measured by the test.

With an interval scale, the property of equal intervals allows you to perform the mathematical operations of addition and subtraction with the data.

4. Ratio Scale: The ratio scale has the properties of order and equal intervals as well as the property of an absolute zero point. When data are measured on a ratio scale, a score of 0 indicates a complete absence of the characteristic being measured. In Study #3, if exact dollar amount of sales is being used as the measure of sales success, it would be possible to conclude that a person selling $1,000 worth of goods is twice as successful as a person selling $500 worth of goods. Examples of ratio scales include temperature when measured on a Kelvin scale, number of correct items on a test, and reaction time in seconds or minutes.

An absolute zero point makes it possible to multiply and divide ratio scores and to determine more precisely how much more or less of a characteristic one subject has compared to another.

J. Descriptive Statistics

Descriptive statistics are used to describe or summarize a distribution (set) of data. Descriptive techniques include tables, graphs, measures of central tendency, and measures of variability.

1. Tables and Graphs: A set of data can be organized in a table known as a frequency distribution. Frequency distributions are constructed by summarizing the data in terms of the number (frequency) of observations in each category, score, or score interval. "Cumulative frequencies" indicate the total number of observations that fall at or below each category or score.

Bar graphs, histograms, and frequency polygons are three types of graphs. The choice of a graph depends on the scale of measurement: Bar graphs are used when the data represent a nominal or ordinal scale, while histograms and frequency polygons are used with interval and ratio data.

2. Shapes of Distributions:

a. Normal Curve: Distributions can assume a variety of shapes. When a sufficiently large number of observations are made, the data for many variables take the shape of a **normal curve**. The normal curve is symmetrical, bell-shaped, and defined by a specific mathematical formula. The normal curve is very important: When we know that scores on a variable are normally distributed, we can draw certain conclusions about the number of cases that fall between specific points in the distribution.

b. Kurtosis: The term kurtosis refers to the relative peakedness (height or flatness) of a distribution: When a distribution is more "peaked" than the normal distribution, it is referred to as leptokurtic. When a distribution is flatter than the normal curve, it is called platykurtic. (A normal curve is mesokurtic.)

c. Skewed Distributions: Distributions can also be asymmetrical rather than symmetrical. In one type of asymmetrical distribution known as a skewed distribution, more than half of the observations fall on one side of the distribution and a relatively few observations fall in the tail on the other side of the distribution. Skewed distributions can be either positive or negative.

- In a **positively skewed distribution**, most of the scores are in the negative (low score) side of the distribution and the positive tail is extended because of the presence of a few high scores.

- Conversely, in a **negatively skewed distribution**, most scores are located in the positive (high score) side of the distribution and the negative tail is extended due to the presence of a few low scores.

To remember the difference between a positive and negative skew, you might want to remember that it is "the tail that tells the tale."

3. Measures of Central Tendency: Although tables and graphs provide important information about a distribution of data, an investigator usually wants to describe the data she has collected with a single number. To be useful, this number should convey a maximum amount of information, summarize the entire set of observations, and be a "typical" measure of all of the observations. Measures of central tendency are the descriptive techniques that address these goals; and the mode, the median, and the mean are the most commonly used measures of central tendency:

Mode: The **mode** is the score or category that occurs most frequently in a set of data. A distribution can be multimodal; that is, it can have two or more scores or categories that occur equally often and more often than any other score or category. A distribution with two modes is called bimodal. When all scores occur equally often, the distribution does not have a unique mode. The primary advantage of the mode is that it is easy to identify. A disadvantage is that the mode is not useful for other statistical purposes and serves only as a descriptive technique.

Median: The **median** is the score that divides a distribution of data in half when the data have been ordered from low to high. When a set of data has an odd number of observations, the median is equal to the middle observation. One advantage of the median is that, if one score in a distribution is extremely high or low, the value of the median is not affected.

Arithmetic mean: The **mean** is the arithmetic average. It is calculated by summing all values in a distribution and dividing the sum by the number of values in the distribution. One advantage of the mean is that, of the three measures of central tendency, it is the least susceptible to sampling fluctuations.

The relationship between the three measures of central tendency in skewed distributions is as follows: In a positively skewed distribution, the mean is greater than the median which, in turn, is greater than the mode – i.e., mean > median > mode. In a negatively skewed distribution, the relationship between the three measures is reversed: The mode is greater than the median, which is greater than the mean – i.e., mode > median > mean.

When selecting a measure of central tendency, the first consideration is the data's scale of measurement. As indicated below, the more mathematically complex the data, the greater the choice of a measure of central tendency:

- Nominal scale – mode.
- Ordinal scale – mode or median.
- Interval or ratio scale – mode, median, or mean.

A researcher normally wants to choose the measure of central tendency that lends itself to the greatest number of mathematical operations. As noted above, however, the mean is sensitive to the value of all scores in a distribution. For this reason, even when a variable has been measured on an interval or ratio scale, the median is often used when the distribution is very skewed.

4. Measures of Variability: A measure of central tendency often provides an incomplete description of a distribution of data, and a researcher will also want to calculate a measure of variability. Measures of variability indicate the amount of heterogeneity or dispersion within a set of scores and include the range, the variance, and the standard deviation:

Range: The range is calculated simply by subtracting the lowest score in a distribution from the highest score. Because the range is based only on the two most extreme scores, it can be misleading when a distribution contains an atypically high and/or low score.

Variance (mean square): The variance provides a measure of the average amount of variability in the distribution. It is a more thorough measure of variability than the range because its calculation includes all of the scores in the distribution rather than just the highest and lowest scores. Calculation of the variance requires squaring each deviation score. For this reason, the variance is difficult to interpret and is used primarily in inferential statistics rather than as a descriptive technique.

Standard deviation: The **standard deviation** is more commonly reported as a measure of variability than the variance because it is expressed in the same unit of measurement as the original scores. The standard deviation is calculated by taking the square root of the variance. It can be interpreted directly as a measure of variability: The larger the standard deviation, the greater the dispersion of scores. This method of interpretation is particularly useful when comparing the variability of two or more distributions.

Another way to interpret the standard deviation is in terms of the normal distribution. Whenever the shape of a distribution of scores approaches normal, it is possible to draw certain conclusions about the number of cases that fall within limits that are defined by the standard deviation: For example, if a test has a mean of 50 and a standard deviation of 5 and scores on the test are normally distributed, about 68 percent of people have scores between 45 and 55 (45 = one standard deviation below the mean; and 55 = one standard deviation above the mean).

K. Introduction to Inferential Statistics

As reported before, inferential statistics are used to make inferences about the relationships between variables. In this section, the concept of "statistical inference" is discussed to provide you with background that will help you understand the inferential statistical tests described later in this appendix. It is extremely unlikely, however, that an ASWB exam will ask specific questions about the concept of statistical inference.

1. The Logic of Statistical Inference: Inferential statistics allow researchers to test hypotheses and make inferences about the relationships between independent and dependent variables in a population based on data collected from a sample drawn from that population.

Example: The investigator in Study #1, for example, will want to determine if there is a relationship between training in the self-control procedure and scores on an academic achievement test for all children who have received a diagnosis of ADHD. Since the investigator won't have access to the entire population of children with this disorder, she will evaluate the effects of the self-control procedure on a sample of children drawn from the population. The investigator will then use an inferential statistical test to analyze the data she collects from the sample. Results of the statistical test will enable her to make an inference about the effects of the self-control procedure on the academic achievement test scores for the population of children who have ADHD.

a. Population Parameters and Sample Statistics: As noted above, when conducting a research study, an investigator does not have access to the entire population of interest but, instead, estimates population values based on obtained sample values. In other words, an investigator uses a sample "statistic" to estimate a population "parameter." For example, an investigator may use a sample mean to estimate a population mean.

b. Sampling Error and Sampling Distributions: An estimate of a population parameter from a sample statistic is always subject to some inaccuracy. In other words, because of the effects of sampling error, sample statistics deviate from population parameters and from statistics obtained from other samples drawn from the same population. The smaller the sample, the greater the effects of sampling error. (**Sampling error** is a type of random error that is due to uncontrolled factors.)

The relationship between sample statistics and a population parameter can be described in terms of a "sampling distribution," which is defined as the frequency distribution of the statistics (e.g., means, standard deviations, variances) of a very large number of equal-sized samples that have been randomly selected from the same population. In other words, a sampling distribution is not a distribution of individual scores but a distribution of sample means or other sample values.

Theoretical sampling distribution: Researchers do not actually construct a sampling distribution of means by obtaining a large number of samples and calculating each sample's mean. Instead, researchers depend on probability theory to tell them what a sampling distribution would look like. The sampling distribution defined by probability theory is called a "theoretical sampling distribution," and it is based on the assumption that an infinite number of equal-sized samples have been randomly drawn from the same population.

Central limit theorem: The characteristics of a sampling distribution of means are specified by the Central Limit Theorem, which makes the following predictions: (a) Regardless of the shape of the distribution of individual scores in the population, as the sample size increases, the sampling distribution of means approaches a normal shape. (b) The mean of the sampling distribution of means is equal to the population mean. (c) The standard deviation of the sampling distribution of means is equal to the population standard deviation divided by the square root of the sample size.

Standard error of the mean: The standard deviation of a sampling distribution of means is also known as the "standard error of the mean." The standard error provides an estimate of the extent to which the mean of any one sample drawn from a population can be expected to vary from the population mean as the result of sampling error.

The sampling distribution is the foundation of inferential statistics. It is the sampling distribution that enables a researcher to make inferences about the relationships between variables in the population based on obtained sample data.

2. The Logic of Hypothesis Testing: An investigator usually conducts a research study to test the hypothesis that there is a relationship between independent and dependent variables.

Example: In Study #1, the research hypothesis might be, "If children with ADHD are taught the self-control procedure, then their academic achievement test scores will increase."

One way to test the veracity of this hypothesis would be to use an inferential statistical test to compare the mean achievement test score for a sample of children who have received training in the procedure to the appropriate sampling distribution of means. The results of the statistical test would indicate whether an observed effect of the procedure was due to sampling error or to a real relationship between the self-control procedure and academic achievement test scores.

Testing a hypothesis about the relationship between variables involves the following steps:

- translating the verbal research hypothesis about the relationship between the independent and dependent variables into two statistical hypotheses: the null hypothesis and the alternative hypothesis;

- conducting the study and analyzing the obtained data with an inferential statistical test; and

- deciding, on the basis of the results of the statistical test, whether to retain or reject the statistical hypotheses.

a. Defining the Statistical Hypotheses: An investigator tests a verbal research hypothesis about the relationship between variables by simultaneously testing two competing statistical hypotheses: the null hypothesis and the alternative hypothesis.

The **null hypothesis** is expressed in terms of a specific population parameter that implies there is no relationship between the independent and dependent variables.

Example: The investigator in Study #1 decides to assess the effects of the self-control procedure on academic achievement by comparing the mean achievement test score of a sample of children with ADHD who have been trained in the procedure to the mean score of the population of children with ADHD. Assuming that the mean test score of children in the population is 50, the null hypothesis in this case is that the mean test score of children who have received training in the procedure will also be 50.

In other words, in the above example, the null hypothesis predicts that the self-control procedure will have no effect on achievement test scores, and, consequently, children who have received the training will be indistinguishable from children who have not. From the perspective of the null hypothesis, any observed difference between the sample mean and the population mean will be due to sampling error rather than to the effects of the self-control procedure. In a research study, it is always the null hypothesis that is first rejected or retained; the decision to reject or retain the alternative hypothesis is secondary.

The **alternative hypothesis** is expressed in terms of a population parameter that implies there is a relationship between the independent and dependent variables. In most situations, it is the alternative hypothesis that most closely resembles the verbal research hypothesis.

Example: The alternative hypothesis for Study #1 is that the mean score of children who receive training in the self-control procedure will not be equal to the mean score of the population of untrained children – i.e., will not be equal to 50.

Notice that the alternative hypothesis merely states the opposite of the null hypothesis. This is because it is not possible to assign an exact value to it before the research study is conducted (this value is unknown and will, ideally, be revealed by the study's outcome).

There are actually two possible alternative hypotheses. A nondirectional ("two-tailed") alternative hypothesis merely states that the null hypothesis is false. It does not predict whether the population parameter estimated by the obtained sample statistic will be greater than or less than the parameter predicted by the null hypothesis. In contrast, a directional ("one-tailed") alternative hypothesis not only states that the null hypothesis is false, but also predicts whether the population parameter estimated by the obtained sample statistic will be greater than or less than the parameter specified in the null hypothesis.

b. Analyzing the Data Using an Inferential Statistical Test and Making a Decision: After stating the null and alternative hypotheses and collecting the sample data, an investigator analyzes the data using an appropriate inferential statistical test.

The inferential statistical test yields a t, an F, or other value that indicates where the obtained sample statistic falls in the sampling distribution for the parameter predicted by the null hypothesis. The sampling distribution is divided into two regions: a "rejection region" and a "retention region."

- The **rejection region** lies in one or both tails of the sampling distribution and contains the sample values that are unlikely to occur simply as the result of sampling error. If the results of the statistical test indicate that the sample statistic is in the rejection region of the sampling distribution, the null hypothesis is rejected and the alternative hypothesis is retained. The investigator concludes that the independent variable has actually had an effect on the dependent variable.

- The **retention region** lies in the central portion of the sampling distribution and consists of the values that are more likely to occur. If the statistical test indicates that the sample statistic lies in the retention region of the sampling distribution, the null hypothesis is retained and the alternative hypothesis is rejected. In this case, the investigator concludes that the independent variable has not had an effect.

The size of the rejection region is defined by **alpha**, or the **level of significance**. If alpha is .05, then 5 percent of the sampling distribution represents the rejection region and the remaining 95 percent represents the retention region. The value of alpha is set by an investigator prior to collecting and/or analyzing the data. In other words, the investigator specifies what proportion of the sampling distribution will represent the region of unlikely values. In behavioral research, alpha is commonly set at either .05 or .01.

When the results of an inferential statistical test indicate that the sample statistic lies in the rejection region of the sampling distribution, the study's results are said to be **statistically significant**. For example, when alpha has been set at .05 and the statistical test indicates that the sample statistic is in the rejection region, the results of the study are "significant at the .05 level."

c. Decision Outcomes: Regardless of whether an investigator decides to retain or reject the null hypothesis, there are two possible outcomes of her decision: The decision can be either correct or in error.

There are two decision *errors*, a Type I error and a Type II error.

Type I Error: A **Type I error** occurs when an investigator rejects a true null hypothesis. For example, if the investigator in Study #1 concludes that the self-control procedure does increase achievement test scores but the observed improvement in scores was actually due to sampling error, the investigator has made a Type I error.

The probability of making a Type I error is equal to **alpha**. As the value of alpha increases, the probability of rejecting a true null hypothesis also increases. Because an investigator sets the value of alpha, by setting the level of significance (usually .05 or .01), she always knows the probability of making a Type I error.

Type II Error: A **Type II error**, occurs when an investigator retains a false null hypothesis. In Study #1, if the investigator concludes that the self-control procedure does not improve achievement test scores when it actually does, the investigator has made a Type II error.

The probability of making a Type II error is equal to **beta**. Although the exact value of beta is not set by an investigator and cannot be directly calculated for a particular study, the probability of making a Type II error can be indirectly influenced: A Type II error is more likely when the value of alpha is low, when the sample size is small, and when the independent variable is not administered in sufficient intensity.

There are also two possible *correct* decisions. An investigator can make a correct decision either by: (a) retaining the null hypothesis when it is true (1 - alpha), or by (b) rejecting the null hypothesis when it is false (1 - beta). It is the second type of correct decision that an investigator ordinarily wants to make. When a statistical test enables an investigator to make this decision, the test is said to have **power**.

Obviously, investigators want to maximize their statistical power whenever they conduct a research study. Investigators can maximize their statistical power by doing several things, including the following: (a) increasing alpha; (b) increasing the sample size; (c) maximizing the effects of the independent variable; (d) minimizing error; and (e) using a "parametric test" (these are explained in the next section).

L. Inferential Statistical Tests

The selection of an inferential statistical test is based on several factors. The first consideration is the scale of measurement of the data to be analyzed. When a study has independent and dependent variables, it is the measurement scale for the dependent variable that is of interest since it is the data on the dependent variable that will be analyzed with the statistical test. The second consideration is the design of the study. Characteristics of the research design that help determine which statistical test to use include: (a) the number of independent variables or, if there is only one independent variable, the number of levels of that variable; (b) whether the groups are independent or correlated; (c) whether there are any extraneous variables that need to be controlled; and (d) the number of dependent variables.

1. Parametric vs. Nonparametric Tests: Inferential statistical tests are categorized as either parametric or nonparametric. Both types of tests share the assumption that the sample has been randomly selected from the population but they differ in several important ways.

a. Parametric Tests: The **parametric tests** are used to evaluate hypotheses about population means, variances, or other parameters. The parametric tests are appropriate only when the variable of interest has been measured on an **interval** or **ratio scale** and when certain assumptions about the population distribution(s) are met. Violation of these assumptions can increase the probability of making a Type I or Type II error.

Assumption #1: The first assumption for a parametric test is that the value of interest is normally distributed in the population. If the sample distribution departs markedly from the shape of a normal curve, the population distribution might not be normally shaped, and a parametric test should probably not be used.

Assumption #2: When a study includes more than one group (e.g., an experimental and a control group), the variances of the populations that the different groups represent are assumed to be equal. If sample variances are significantly different, a parametric test might yield inaccurate results.

The parametric tests are relatively "robust" with regard to violations of the above assumptions. This means that some deviation from a normal curve or from homoscedasticity will not necessarily invalidate the test's results. (With "homoscedasticity," there are equal variances in two or more samples or populations; with "heteroscedasticity," there are unequal variances in two or more samples or populations.)

b. Nonparametric Tests: The **nonparametric tests** are used to analyze data on variables that have been measured on a **nominal** or **ordinal scale**.

These tests do not make the same assumptions about the shape of the population distribution(s) as the parametric tests. Moreover, the nonparametric tests are used to evaluate hypotheses about the shape of an entire distribution rather than the distribution's mean, variance, or other parameter. A shortcoming of the nonparametric tests is that, because they involve using less precise (nominal or ordinal) data, they are less powerful.

2. Tests for Nominal Data: The **chi-square test** is used when a study involves nominal data or data that are reported in terms of the frequency of observations in categories. The chi-square test would be appropriate, for example, for comparing the number of people who prefer one of four political candidates.

The chi-square test is used to determine if the distribution of observed (sample) frequencies is equivalent to the distribution of expected frequencies. The expected frequencies are the frequencies predicted by the null hypothesis – i.e., that there are no difference between categories.

Single-sample chi-square test: The single-sample chi-square test is used when a descriptive study includes only one variable and the data to be analyzed are the number of observations in each category (level) of that variable.

Example: The investigator in Study #2 (treatment of schizophrenia) is interested in finding out if the 120 patients in her study differ with regard to family background in terms of psychopathology. She determines how many of the patients have either (a) one biological parent who has received a diagnosis of schizophrenia; (b) both biological parents who have received a diagnosis of schizophrenia; or (c) both biological parents who have not received a diagnosis of schizophrenia. The investigator's study is a descriptive study and includes only one nominal variable.

Multiple-sample chi-square test: The multiple-sample chi-square test is used when a descriptive or experimental study includes two or more variables and the data to be analyzed are the number of observations in each category.

Example: The investigator in Study #2 wants to determine if a patient's specific diagnosis is related to family background and determines each patient's DSM diagnosis and family history. The expanded study can be considered either a descriptive study with two variables or an experimental study with one independent and one dependent variable (family background is the IV and diagnosis is the DV).

3. Tests for Ordinal Data: A number of inferential statistical tests are available for analyzing ordinal data. Among these are the Mann-Whitney U test, the Wilcoxon matched-pairs test, and the Kruskal-Wallis test, which are used to analyze rank-ordered data. These and other tests for rank-ordered data are generally more powerful than tests for other types of ordinal data.

4. Tests for Interval and Ratio Data: The Student's t-test and the analysis of variance are the most commonly-used inferential statistical tests for variables measured on an interval or ratio scale. There are several versions of both tests that are each appropriate for a different research design.

a. Student's t-test: The Student's t-test is used to evaluate hypotheses about the differences between two population means as estimated by group (sample) means. When more than two means must be analyzed, the analysis of variance is usually preferred.

b. Analysis of Variance: The analysis of variance (ANOVA) is used to compare two or more means. It tests the hypothesis that the population means estimated by the group (sample) means are equal. Different forms of the ANOVA are used for different research designs. For example, the **one-way ANOVA** is the appropriate statistical test when a study includes one independent variable and two or more independent groups. (Note that, if a study involves comparing the means of only two groups, the t-test for independent samples and the one-way ANOVA are interchangeable. The convention, however, is to use the t-test when a study includes only two groups and the ANOVA when a study includes three or more groups.)

Like the t-test, the analysis of variance compares means but does so in a more complex way by analyzing variability around means. More specifically, the ANOVA enables a researcher to evaluate the relative contributions of different factors to the total amount of variability observed in a set of scores. This is done by partitioning the sum of squares. The mechanics of this process are beyond the scope of an ASWB exam.

> *Example:* The investigator in Study #2 compares the effects of three levels of phenothiazines on WAIS scores by obtaining a sample of 75 patients and randomly assigning them to either the high dose, low dose, or placebo group. After subjects have taken the drug or placebo for three months, she administers the WAIS to all subjects and uses the one-way ANOVA to compare the mean IQ scores of the three groups. Results of the study will allow the investigator to assess whether different levels of the phenothiazines have different effects on WAIS scores.

The **factorial ANOVA** is the appropriate statistical test when a study includes two or more independent variables. (When a study has two IVs, the factorial ANOVA is also called a two-way ANOVA; when it has three IVs, it is called a three-way ANOVA; etc.) The logic underlying the factorial ANOVA is basically the same as that underlying the one-way ANOVA. The difference is that the variability between groups is "partitioned" even further.

> *Example:* The investigator in Study #2 wants to compare the effects of various combinations of phenothiazines (high dose, low dose, placebo) and therapy (individual therapy, family therapy, combined individual and family therapy, no therapy) on cognitive ability. She obtains a sample of 120 patients and randomly assigns them to one of the treatment groups. After three months, the investigator administers the WAIS to all patients and uses a two-way ANOVA to analyze the data she has collected. Results of the study will allow the investigator to assess the main effects of phenothiazines, the main effects of therapy, and the interaction between phenothiazines and therapy.

M. Correlational Techniques

Correlational techniques are used to assess the strength of the relationship between two or more variables. Investigators are often interested in correlation because they want to use one variable as a predictor or estimator of another variable. When correlational techniques are used for this purpose, the X (independent) variable is often referred to as the predictor, while the Y (dependent) variable is called the criterion.

The various correlational techniques are divided into two basic types: bivariate and multivariate. Bivariate techniques (which are described below) are used to assess the degree of association between two variables, and multivariate techniques are used to assess the relationships among three or more variables.

1. Frequency Distributions and Scattergrams: The relationship between two variables can be described using a frequency distribution or scattergram. A bivariate frequency distribution presents the relationship between variables in a table format. If the variables have been measured on an interval or ratio scale, their relationship can also be presented in a scattergram (scatterplot).

In a scattergram, the X variable is placed on the horizontal axis, while the Y variable is located on the vertical axis. Each data point in the scattergram corresponds to the two scores obtained by a single person. When data points in a scattergram are widely scattered, this means that the variables have a weak relationship. Conversely, when there is a narrow scatter of data points (when the data points assume the shape of an ellipse), this indicates a strong relationship.

2. Correlation Coefficient: The relationship between two variables can also be summarized with a single number known as a correlation coefficient. There are a number of correlation coefficients, and the selection of a coefficient is based on the scale of measurement of the variables to be correlated.

The Pearson Product Moment Correlation Coefficient (**Pearson r**) is the coefficient most commonly used with interval and ratio data. The Pearson r represents the average degree of association between two sets of data. The Pearson r ranges in value from +1.0 to -1.0. The magnitude of the coefficient indicates the relationship's strength: The closer the coefficient is to +1.0 or -1.0, the stronger the relationship; the closer the coefficient is to 0, the weaker the relationship. The sign of the correlation coefficient indicates the relationship's direction: When there is a positive (+) or direct correlation between X and Y, the values of Y increase as the values of X increase. Conversely, when there is a negative (-) or inverse correlation, the values of Y decrease as the values of X increase.

The correlation coefficient is sometimes erroneously interpreted in terms of causality. If a true experimental method is used, a researcher can infer a cause-effect relationship between variables when a correlation coefficient is large. However, a large coefficient alone does not indicate that variability in one variable causes variability in the other variable.

A correlation coefficient can, of course, be interpreted directly in terms of its magnitude: The larger the coefficient, the stronger the relationship; the smaller the coefficient, the weaker the relationship.

When the correlation coefficient is squared (which is sometimes called the "coefficient of determination") it provides a measure of shared variability. Put another way, the squared correlation indicates the proportion of variability in Y that is explained by, or accounted for by, variability in X. For example, if the correlation coefficient for sales success and product knowledge is .60, then 36 percent (.60 squared = .36) of variability in sales success is accounted for by product knowledge. The remaining 64 percent is due to other factors such as attitude toward the company, motivation to sell, previous sales experience, and sales territory.

Finally, correlation coefficients can be tested to determine if they are statistically significant. The null hypothesis in this situation is that the correlation coefficient in the population is equal to zero. This hypothesis is tested by comparing the obtained sample coefficient to an appropriate critical value. The magnitude of the critical value is determined by two factors: the level of significance and the number of observations in the sample. The fewer the number of observations, the larger the correlation coefficient must be in order to be significant.

3. Regression Analysis: As noted previously, investigators are often interested in correlation because their goal is to use a predictor to predict, or estimate, performance on a criterion. Regression analysis is the technique that allows such predictions to be made.

An assumption underlying regression analysis is that there is a linear relationship (see below) between the two variables of interest. The relationship can be described by a regression line, or "line of best fit."

> *Example:* The investigator in Study #3 determines the degree of association between product knowledge and yearly sales by administering the product knowledge test to a sample of 35 current employees and, from employment records, determining each employee's sales for the previous year. From this data, the investigator derives a significant correlation coefficient and calculates a regression equation. She then uses the regression equation to facilitate selection decisions by administering the product knowledge test to applicants for sales jobs and using the equation to predict an applicant's future yearly sales.

The degree of predictive accuracy when using a regression equation is, of course, directly related to the magnitude of the correlation coefficient. Unless the correlation coefficient is equal to +1 or -1, there will be some error in prediction. The standard error of estimate is often used to construct a "confidence interval" around a predicted Y score. The process used to construct a confidence interval is beyond the scope of an ASWB exam.

(With a linear relationship, if you know the score of a subject on one variable then you can determine the score on the other variable exactly. With behavioral data, however, there is almost never a perfect linear relationship between two variables. The more the points tend to fall along a straight line the stronger the linear relationship.)